Draping for Apparel Design

Draping *for* Apparel Design

Helen Joseph-Armstrong

Fairchild Publications

New York

To all who find pleasure in the art of draping beautiful garments.

The author wishes to thank all the people who willingly gave of their time to help make the draping text a useful tool to the beginner and professional patternmaker. Special thanks go to Yuki Hatashita for her encouragement and helpful suggestions; Shelia Wert for sharing her knowledge as a draper in the garment industry; Michelle Lettinger for grading the basic sleeve and for the printed size measurements; Mia Carpenter, whose fashion sketches give the draping text its flare; Jovita Chow, along with Vincent James Maruzzi, who rendered the draping and technical sketches clearly; Sharon Tate for offering computer prints from her text, *Inside Fashion Design;* and to my students, who helped hone draping instructions for difficult design projects.

Other readers selected by the publisher were also very helpful. They include Susan Baker, Otis College of Art and Design; Bonnie D. Belleau, Louisiana State University; Elizabeth K. Davic, Kent State University; Penny Greene Draves, Minneapolis Community and Technical College; Janet Hethorn, University of Delaware; Jacqueline Keuler, Fashion Institute of Technology; Kathy Mullet, Radford University; Elaine Zarse, Mount Mary College.

The author appreciates the assistance given by Olga Kontzias, Mary Siener, and Joann Muscolo at Fairchild Publications.

Authors note: Where errors may occur it is hoped that they do not interfere with the completion of the drape project. Please fax (310) 322-6542 to notify the author of possible errors, and to offer suggestions that will improve the text.

Helen Joseph-Armstrong
The Fashion Center
Los Angeles Trade Technical College
Los Angeles, CA 1999
Fax: (310) 322-6542

Executive Editor: Olga Kontzias
Production Editor: Joann Muscolo
Editorial Assistant: Beth Applebome
Art Director: Mary Siener
Production Manager: Priscilla Taguer

Text Design: Rebecca Lemna
Cover Design: Marisa Gentile

Full Editorial & Production Services: Chernow Editorial Services, Inc.
Agnew's, Inc.

Library of Congress Catalog Card Number 99-71391

ISBN: 1-56367-102-6

GST R 133004424

Printed in the United States of America

Preface

Draping for Apparel Design was written to give aspiring and professional draper/designers a reliable source for creating garments through draping. Among the available patternmaking methods, draping is unique. It is the only patternmaking system that relies on fabric in creating designs. The fabric is manipulated, molded, and shaped through the skillful use of the draper/designer's hand, until the design is replicated in three-dimensional form. Draping also allows for an evaluation of the design at each of the incremental steps of the drape. Draping does not rely on the aid of a pattern to create designs, although a draper may choose to incorporate part(s) of an existing pattern in the preparation of the muslin to assist in the drape. It is also true that those using the flat patternmaking method may incorporate some aspects of draping in creating specific designs. This does not minimize the value of either patternmaking method, but it does enhance the pattern-maker's ability to create design patterns accurately and within time constraints. The basic sleeve is not draped, although it could be, but the results would be dubious. It is drafted and utilized for the development of other designs.

The strength of Draping for Apparel Design is based on its clear explanation of the three principles of pattern-making. Application of the principles with the techniques of draping allows the draper to move confidently from design to design. The instructions are easy to follow and the drape illustrations are as realistic as possible. Other strengths of this book are the draping plans that accompany each design project. The planning involves design analysis. Through analysis, the draper identifies which draping technique(s) to apply in the creation of a specific design. This will be a guide to the draper/designer through the draping steps. The book emphasizes the drape of foundation garments as a base for building more complex designs. Prototypes of popular designs are illustrated and are to be referred to for designs closely associated with the project. As knowledge and confidence is gained, the draper/designer will be able to move easily from the less complicated to more advanced projects.

Draping for Apparel Design is divided into six sections. The contents reveals the extent of the information covered. Chapters 1 through 3 provide the initial information that prepares the draper/designer for the following projects of the text. In Chapter 4 the fundamentals of draping are discussed as part of the drape of the basic dress foundation. The complete project includes instruction for muslin preparation, grainline placements, draping steps, trueing the muslin pattern, fitting analysis and correction, and making the final paper pattern, including pattern information. Chapters 5 and 6 introduce the draping principles and manipulating techniques for changing the location and creative use of the dart excess and for adding fullness. Bodice stylelines complete this group of chapters.

In Chapters 7 through 11, the knowledge gained from the previous bodice design are applied to skirt projects. Designs in Chapters 8 through 10 (collars, built-up necklines, and cowls) are based on the fundamentals of draping with additional instructions for their special features. Facings in Chapter 11 are for reference in deciding the type of facing that may be needed.

Chapters 12 through 13 introduce the torso drape for the development of the one-piece dress. The draping instructions of the Princess, panel, empire, and tent designs and foundations are based on knowledge gained from the bodice

design projects in Chapter 6. Outside contour draping is illustrated for strapless tops. Fitting problems and corrections are addressed. Instructions include the development for the support of this type of garment. Bias draping is introduced in Chapter 14. The problems that may be encountered in handling bias are discussed and suggestions are offered in the preparation for the drape.

The basic sleeve is used in the muslin preparation of the drape of the kimono, raglan, and drop shoulder designs in Chapter 15. Shirts and blouses in Chapter 16 are based on the drape of the torso foundation, with design features added. The shirt foundations include the basic yoke and the oversized shirt. The jackets and coats in Chapter 17 are also based on the drape of the torso foundation, with added instructions for enlarging the drape for jackets and coats. The draper/designer is free to choose the styleline of the jacket or coat.

Chapter 18 covers the pant drape. Muslin preparation is taken from the instructions for drafting pants. The reason is to avoid the difficulty of draping between the crotch and to be able to control the location of the straight grain (creaseline) when marked on the muslin. The advantage of draping is controlling the design of the pant throughout the drape. The characteristics of different types of knits is discussed in Chapter 19. This information will assist the draper in selecting the correct knit suitable for the design. A knit foundation is illustrated for use in expediting other knit designs. Several knit designs are based on this foundation, if desired. Bodysuits, and swimwear can be draped or can be based on the drape of the knit foundation. Again, the preparation of the fabric is based on drafting instruction.

Helen Joseph-Armstrong

Contents

Fabric Characteristics and Terms

The techniques for draping fabric correctly require an awareness of the fabric's characteristics. Knowledge of the distinctions among fabrics enables designers/drapers to select the most appropriate fabric for the flow and line of each design. In addition to reading books devoted to textiles, drapers/designers should collect swatches while shopping and catalogue them by width and content. In this way, a personal reference library can be created.

Fabrics are classified according to quality, structure (weave, knitted, fused, nonwoven-fused, or plain), texture, weight, and hand (how fabric feels to the touch). They are contrasted by being either crisp or soft, thick or thin, heavyweight or lightweight, loosely or firmly woven, flat or textured, silky or rough, transparent or opaque, and sleazy or luxurious. When evaluating a fabric, see how it drapes when raised at one end and how it responds after being crushed in the hand.

For example, woven fabrics are judged by the number of threads per inch. The closeness of the weave, or the thread count, is determined by adding the number of warp threads per inch by the number of filling (weft) threads. High-quality percales have 220 threads per inch, while inexpensive muslin has only 128 threads per inch or 80 square. Knitted fabrics are created differently and will be discussed in later chapters.

Fabric Terms

Figure 1.1

Bias A diagonal, or angle, line that is cut or sewn across the weave of the fabric.

Crossgrain (weft) Yarns woven across the fabric from selvage to selvage. It is the filling yarn of woven fabric. Crosswise grain yields to tension.

Grain The direction in which a fiber is woven or knitted.

Lengthwise grain (warp) Yarns parallel with the selvage; it is twisted more tightly than the crosswise grain.

Selvage The narrow, firmly woven finished edge on both sides of the fabric length.

True bias A diagonal line that intersects with the length and crosswise grains at a 45° angle. True bias has maximum give and stretch, easily conforming to the contour of the figure. Flares and cowls drape best when on true bias.

Muslin

Figure 1.2

Muslin is a plain woven fabric made from bleached or unbleached yarns in a variety of weights, including:

Coarse weave Best for draping and test fitting a finished garment.

Lightweight weave For softly draped garments.

Heavyweight weave Firmly woven fabric used to drape tailored garments, coats, and suits.

To release the tension clip along the selvage edge; the selvage may be cut away.

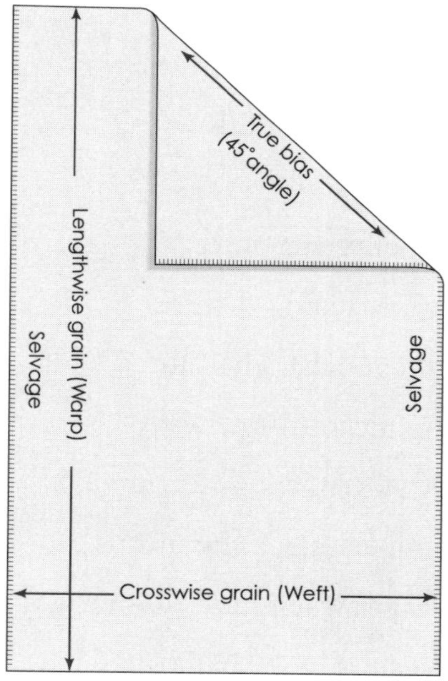

Figure 1.1

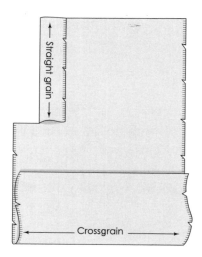

Figure 1.2

Finding the Crossgrain

Bowing and Skewing on the Grain

Figure 1.3

Bowing and skewing is characterized as being "off grain." That means the weft grain(cross-grain) is not at a right angle to the warp grain (straight grain). This occurs during the weaving and finishing process. Rip the fabric to determine if there is bowing, or skewing, or a combination of both. If too severe, skewing can cause the garment to twist after washing.

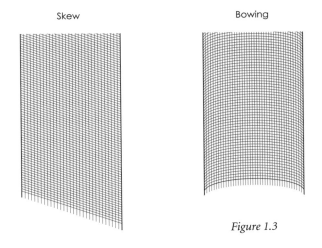

Skew Bowing

Figure 1.3

Aligning Grainlines

Figure 1.4

Pick a thread with a pin at one side of the selvage and pull it through the selvage to the other side. Then, sew a red thread to replace the pulled yarn. French drapers often use this method.

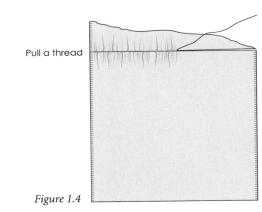

Pull a thread

Figure 1.4

Figure 1.5

Pull diagonally at opposite ends of the fabric until the crossgrain is at a right angle to the straight grain. The draper can follow this procedure to prepare the muslin for draping. However, retail garments will most likely be cut in fabrics that bow, or skew, unless corrected at the request of the manufacturer at the time the fabric is ordered.

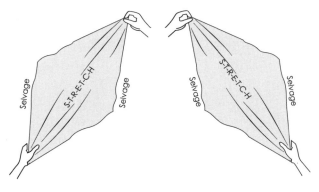

Selvage S·T·R·E·T·C·H Selvage Selvage S·T·R·E·T·C·H Selvage

Figure 1.5

Model Form: Preparation, Measurement, and Tools

2

The model form represents the dimensions of the manufacturer's sample size. Terms define key landmarks for measuring the form. Measurements, including personal arm measurements, are taken with draper's tools and recorded on the Measurement Chart (page 15).

The configuration of the various forms were developed by using measurements closely representing those of the human figure within each size. Model forms are available in all standard sizes and shapes for both males and females. Forms can be purchased with attachable arms and attachable legs for draping or drafting pants. Forms can also be ordered to specifications to satisfy the manufacturer's target market or for individual figures.

Industrial forms are partially made by hand; therefore, they are subject to error. A form may differ slightly from side seam to the center front and/or to center back. The shoulderlines and/or side seams may be out of alignment, causing fitting problems in the hang of the sleeve. The model form should be checked for accuracy at the time the sleeve is set. The correction(s) may require that the side seams and/or shoulderlines be repositioned, and the new locations drawn on the form.

The silhouette of the form can be changed or modified to adapt to figure differences with the use of padding for special designs (for example, to enlarge the bust, waist, or hips). The padding is covered with a soft gauze or muslin fabric. Shoulder pads are added to the form for garments requiring them. (See later in this chapter for instructions on creating the relaxed arm and the straight arm for specific types of garments.)

Reference points on the form are identified by the same names as on the human figure. These reference points are guides when measuring the form.

Reference Points of the Model Form

The numbers refer to both the front and back form. Areas of the form are identified by the following terms (Figure 2.1):

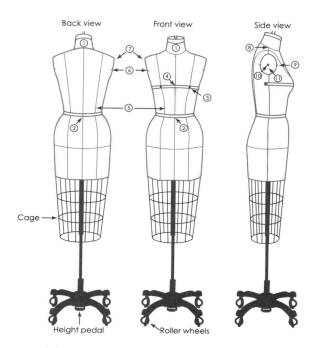

Figure 2.1

Symbol Key

Use these symbols on the model form if necessary.

CF = Center front
CB = Center back
SS = Side seam
SW = Side waist
BP = Bust Point
SH = Shoulder
SH-Tip = Shoulder Tip
HBL = Horizontal Balance Line

1. Center front neck
   Center back neck

2. Center front waist
   Center back waist

3. Bust points

4. Center front bust level

5. Side front (Princess)
   Side back (Princess)

6. Mid-armhole front
   Mid-armhole back
   (at level with plate screw)

7. Shoulder tip

8. Shoulder at neck

9. Armhole ridge or roll line

10. Plate screw

11. Armhole

Preparing the Model Form
for Measurements

Figure 2.2

Waistline Replace the waistline tape if damaged.

Bust bridge Cut a strip of cloth 1 1/2″ × 26″, fold edges to the center, and then fold again. Press. Place folded strip across bust points, ending just beyond side seams and pin. Mark center line of the form on the bust bridge. Thrust pins through bust point.

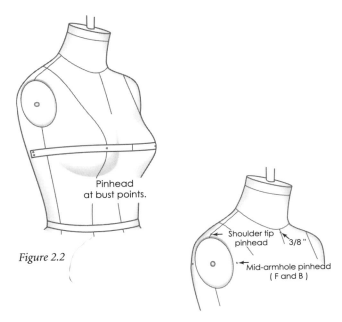

Pinhead
at bust points.

Figure 2.2

Figure 2.3

Additional pinhead guides Thrust pins through the ridge line of the armhole at the shoulder tip, the mid-armhole at a point level with the plate screw, and 3/8″ below neck at the center front.

Shoulder tip
pinhead   3/8 ″

Mid-armhole pinhead
(F and B)

Figure 2.3

Figure 2.4

Armhole depth From the chart below, choose the measurement that applies to the form size, and measure down from the plate to determine the armhole depth. Thrust a pin through the form at the location.

Size	Inches	Size	Inches
6	5 1/2	5	5 3/8
8	5 5/8	7	5 1/2
10	5 3/4	9	5 5/8
12	5 7/8	11	5 3/4
14	6	13	5 7/8
16	6 1/8	15	6
18	6 1/4		

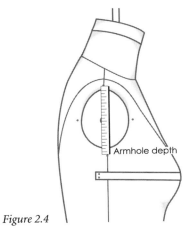

Armhole depth

Figure 2.4

Figure 2.5

Personal fit Mark 3/4″ down from the armhole at the side seam of the leotard.

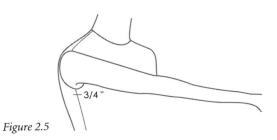

3/4 ″

Figure 2.5

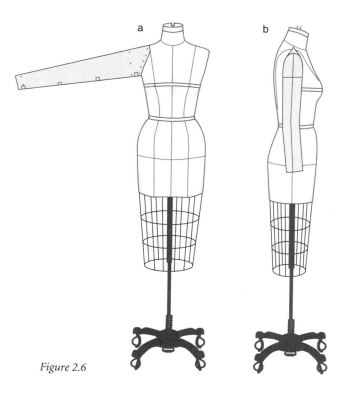

Additional Form Preparation

Figure 2.6

Attachable arms are useful to draper/designers. If unavailable, construct them by following the directions given on pages 9–12.

Figure 2.6

Padding for Special Designs

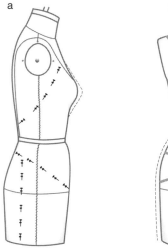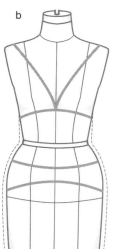

Figure 2.7

Materials needed

Wadding or poly filler for stuffing
Cotton fabric for cover

Steps *(Figure 2.7)*

To enlarge the bust, place layers of padding over the bust mound to the desired cup size (a bra with the correct bust cup size can be placed on the form filled with padding).

To enlarge the waist and hip, place strips of padding around the waist and/or hipline until the desired dimensions are reached. The padding should blend well (avoid lumps).

To secure the padding temporarily, drape a cotton fabric over the padded section(s) and pin. For a permanent padding, drape and stitch a basic bodice or torso cover for the form.

Shoulder Pads

Place the shoulder pads to the form for designs requiring them (jackets, coats, dresses) and for personal fit correct shoulder slope difference.

Style Marking the Form

Place style tape or pins on the form in order to outline the desired stylelines as a guide for the drape (Figure 2.7a,b).

Preparing Attachable Arms

Attachable arms can be ordered from the model form company. However, the following instructions are useful to create the relaxed arm for fitting garments and the straight arm for draping kimono and raglan sleeves.

Relaxed Attachable Arm

Figure 2.8

Trace the basic sleeve. If seamless, add seams after the modification.

Mark 3/8″ in from the underarms. Draw new underseams.

Raise the biceps 1/2″, lower the cap 1/4″, and blend.

Measure capline and record.

Measure wrist and record. (Adjust wrist measurement to whole numbers. For example, 8 1/4″ should be recorded as 8″.)

Figure 2.9 (wrist circle with 1/2″ seams included)

Use the radius measurement of the wrist level:

Radius: 7″ wrist = 1 5/8″

8″ wrist = 1 3/4″

Fold paper in half, and fold in half again. Corner is A.

Draw a circle with the compass from A using the desired radius measurement.

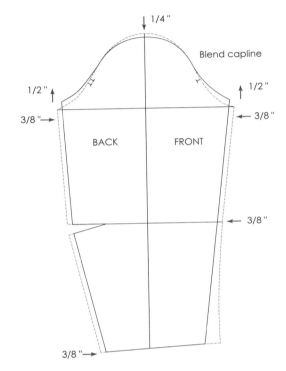

Figure 2.8

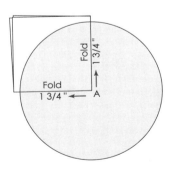

Figure 2.9

Figure 2.10 (armhole pad with 1/2″ seams included)

Fold paper in half, and fold in half again. Corner is (A).

Measure up and out from A using measurements given. Mark.

Square lines up and out from each mark.

At the intersection, draw a line to A. Mark 5/8″ down.

Draw a smooth curved line touching this mark.

Figure 2.11 (shoulder support with 1/2″ seams included)

Fold paper in half.

A-B = 5″. Mark on foldline.

B-C = 4″. Square a line from B to C.

Draw a line from A to C. Mark center and square up 5/8″. Draw a smooth curved line from A to C.

Measure up 5/8″ from B and draw a curved line to C.

Cut from paper.

Figure 2.12 (finished sleeve)

Machine stitch the marked sleeve part way down from the top and up from the bottom of the underseam.

Stitch wrist pad to hem of sleeve, and the armhole pad with the stitched shoulder support to the armhole.

Stuff filler through the opening. Hand stitch to close opening.

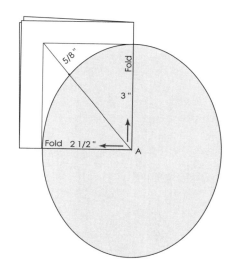

Figure 2.10

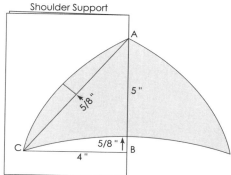

Figure 2.11

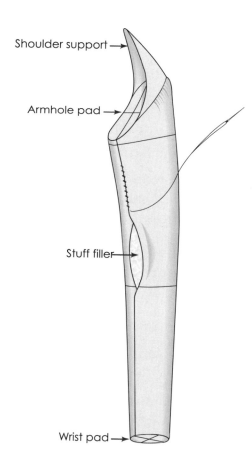

Figure 2.12

Straight Attachable Arm

A straight attachable arm is an excellent tool for draping a kimono or other extended sleeve design.

Figure 2.13

Cut a rectangle, 30″ × 20″ from stiff paper and fold the paper in half lengthwise.

Measure 6″ down and fold the paper. Corner is A.

A-B = 1″. Mark on foldline.

A-C = 3 1/2″. Mark and square a line 7 1/2″, D.

C-E = 23″. Mark and square a line 4″, F.

Fold paper on E-F line.

Draw one line from F to D and another 1″ from the F-D line.

Draw a slightly curved line from D to B.

Cut arm from paper.

Figure 2.14

Unfold on vertical line and trim 1″ of the underseam on the right side.

Staple the folded sections.

Add strips of tape as shown.

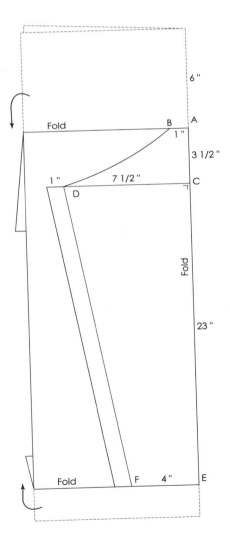

Figure 2.13

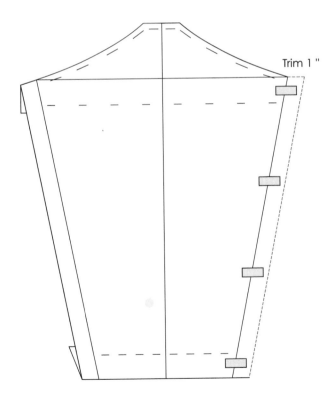

Figure 2.14

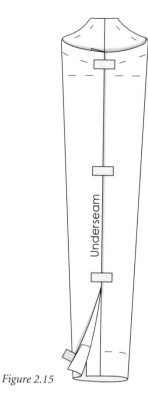

Underseam

Figure 2.15

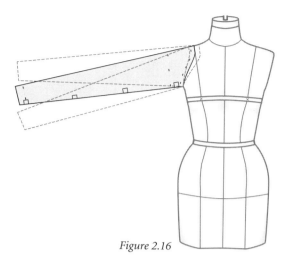

Figure 2.16

Figure 2.15

Lap the right underseam to the D-F line, and tape.

Figure 2.16

Place arm on the form and adjust to the desired angle. Tape to the shoulder or use pins to secure to the shoulder.

To store, lay flat or make a hole at wrist level for hanging.

Measuring the Model Form and the Human Figure

Measurements of the form are important to the designer/draper, who uses them as a reference when trueing the draped or paper pattern. Measurements are a time-saving device only when taken accurately. It requires concentration and patience to measure the form or the human figure. Record the measurements on the Model Form Measurement Chart (page 15).

For personal fit, the model should wear a bodysuit that defines neckline, shoulder, and side seams. With the exception of the circumference measurements of the bust/back level, waist, abdomen, and hip, only one half of the form will be measured, and it is always the same half of the

form. The stitched, or draped garment is placed on the same side of the form that was measured.

When measuring the form, place the metal-tipped end of the measuring tape at one reference point and extend it to the other reference point. Numbers in parentheses correspond to those on the Model Form Measurement Chart.

Note: Arc measurements refer to measurements taken from the centerlines of the form to the side seam.

Measure to the mid-tape or bottom of the waistline tape. Once established be consistent.

Figure 2.17 (circumference measurements)

Record all of the following measurements on the Model Form Measurement Chart.

Bust/back level (1): Measure with tape over the bust point and across the back. Tape is held parallel to the floor.

Waistline (2): Measure with tape around the waistline.

Abdomen (3): Measure with tape held 3″ below the waist and parallel to the floor.

Hip level (4): Measure around the widest part of the hips with tape held parallel to floor. Pin-mark center front at hip level. This is referred to as the X point.

Figure 2.18 (horizontal balance line)

Measure from pin-mark (X) to the floor.

Using this measurement, measure up from the floor and pin-mark locations at the center back and at the right and left sides of the form.

Recheck the measurements for accuracy.

Draw a line around the hip level using a flex ruler and crossing over the pin-marks to establish the horizontal balance line (HBL).

Figures 2.19 and 2.20 (vertical measurements)

Side length (11): Pin-mark below armplate at side seam to waist.

Shoulder length (13): Shoulder tip to neck.

Side hip depth (26): Side waist to HBL, on side of form being measured.

Bust radius (9): Measure from bust point ending under bust mound.

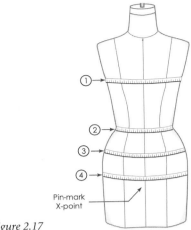

Pin-mark
X-point

Figure 2.17

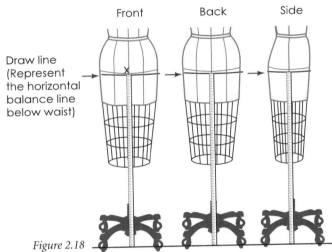

Front   Back   Side

Draw line
(Represent
the horizontal
balance line
below waist)

X

Figure 2.18

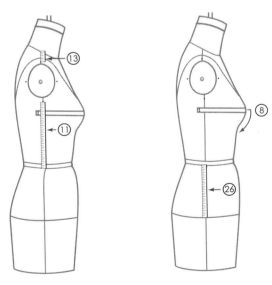

Figure 2.19   *Figure 2.20*

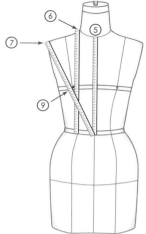

Figure 2.21

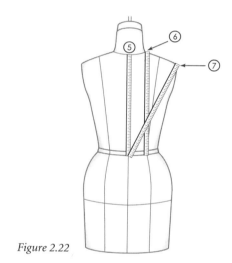

Figure 2.22

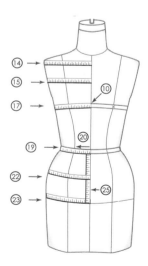

Figure 2.23

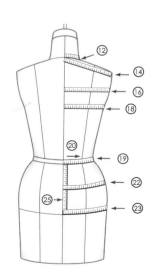

Figure 2.24

Figure 2.21 (front bodice) and Figure 2.22 (back bodice)

Center length (5): Neck to waist (over bust bridge).

Full length (6): Waist to shoulder at neck, parallel with center lines.

Shoulder slope (7): Center of waist to shoulder tip (pin-head mark).

Bust depth (9): Shoulder tip to bust point.

Figure 2.23 (horizontal measurements: front bodice)

Across shoulder (14): Shoulder tip to center front neck.

Across chest (15): Center front to mid-armhole (pinhead mark), plus 1/4″.

Bust arc (17): Center front over the bust point, ending 2″ below the armplate at the side seam.

Bust span (10): Place tape across bust points and divide in half for measurement.

Waist arc (19): Center front waist to side waist seam.

Dart placement (20): Center front to side front (Princess line).

Abdomen arc (22): Center front to side seam, starting 3″ down from the waist.

Hip arc (23): Center front to side seam on HBL.

Hip depth (25): Center front to HBL.

Figure 2.24 (horizontal measurements: back bodice)

Back neck (12): Center back neck to shoulder at neck.

Across shoulder (14): Shoulder tip to center back neck.

Across back (16): Center front to mid-armhole at ridge (pinhead mark).

Back arc (18): Center back to bottom of armplate.

Waist arc (19): Center back waist to side waist seam.

Dart placement (20): Center back waist to side back (Princess line).

Abdomen arc (22): Center back to side seam, starting 3″ down from the waist.

Hip arc (23): Center back to side seam on HBL.

Arm measurements for personal fit (see page 50).

Standard measurements for sleeve draft (see page 51).

This chart can be duplicated without permission from the publisher.

Measurement Chart

CIRCUMFERENCE MEASUREMENTS

1. Bust: _____, plus 2″ ease _____
2. Waist: _____, plus 1″ ease _____
3. Abdomen: _____
4. Hip: _____, plus 2″ ease _____

UPPER TORSO (BODICE)

5. Center length: F_____, B_____
6. Full length: F_____, B_____
7. Shoulder slope: F_____, B_____
8. Bust radius: F_____
9. Bust depth: F_____
10. Bust span: _____
11. Side length: _____
12. Back neck: _____
13. Shoulder length: _____
14. Across shoulder: F_____, B_____
15. Across chest: _____
16. Across back: _____
17. Bust arc: _____
18. Back arc: _____
19. Waist arc: F_____, B_____
20. Dart placement: F_____, B_____
21. Omit

LOWER TORSO (SKIRT/PANT)

22. Abdomen arc: F _____, B_____
23. Hip arc: F _____, B_____
24. Crotch depth:
25. Hip depth: CF_____, CB_____
26. Side hip depth: _____
27. Waist to ankle: _____
    Waist to knee: _____
    Waist to floor: _____
28. Upper thigh: _____
29. Knee: _____
30. Calf: _____
31. Ankle: _____

PERSONAL ARM MEASUREMENTS
Standard measurements on page 50

32. Overarm length: _____
33. Elbow length: _____
34. Biceps: _____
35. Wrist: _____
36. Around hand: _____
37. Cap height: _____

Set form at desired height and measure the following length:

C.F. waist to floor _____, C.B. waist to floor _____, C.B. neck to floor _____

Tools and Supplies for Draping

The designer/draper needs tools and supplies to work efficiently. It is important to know the names and the function of each. Tools may be purchased from apparel supply companies or from art, fabric, or student bookstores. Space is provided to check off each tool as it is purchased.

1. Straight pins
   __Dressmaker silk # 17 for draping and fittings.

2. Straight pin holder
   __Pincushion, or magnetic holder for wrist or table.

3. Scissors
   __Paper scissors
   __Fabric scissors

4. Pencils and pens
   __Mechanical pencil and sharpener (use # 4-H lead for patternwork).
   __Red and blue colored pencils to identify pattern changes. Black, green, red, and blue felt tip markers for pattern information.

5. Rulers
   __Flex general ruler: 1/2″ × 12″ (very accurate).
   __36″ ruler
   __18″ × 2″ plastic ruler (flexible for measuring curves).
   __Tailor's square: 24″ × 14″ metal ruler with two arms that form a 90º angle (measures, rules, and squares simultaneously).
   __Triangle with measurements for square lines.

6. Curved rulers
   __French curve: Deitzgen # 17 is one of several curves used for shaping armhole and neckline.

   __Hip curve rule: shapes hipline, hem, and lapels.
   __Vary form curve: blends and shapes armhole necklines.

7. Measuring tape
   __Metal-tipped, linen or plastic for measuring form and figure (not very accurate).
   __Metal tape: 1/4″ width in a dispenser. Convenient and flexible for measuring form or figure (very accurate).

8. Hanger hooks or ringers
   __Hold sets of patterns on hooks or rods.

9. Pushpins

10. Notcher
    __Cuts 1/4″ × 1/16″ from pattern's edge to indicate seam allowance, centerlines, and ease notches to identify the front and back pattern parts.

11. Tracing wheels
    __Pointed wheel that transfers muslin pattern to paper.
    __Blunted wheel, which is used with carbon paper.

12. Awl
    __Pierces a small hole within the legs of a dart indicating how much further the seamstress should sew to dart point. Other uses are to indicate pocket and trim placements and for buttonhole locations.

13. Tracing paper
    __Transfer muslin pattern to fabric or to the other side of the pattern.

14. Stapler and remover
    __Prevents pattern slippage when cutting several thicknesses of paper.

15. Scotch Magic Tape
    __To mend pattern work.

16. Black and white twill tape
    __To indicate placement of stylelines on the form.

17. Tailor's chalk
    __Clay, chalk, chalk wheel, or chalk marking pencils in black and white. Use a disappearing chalk suitable for fabrics. Wax chalk leaves decrease marks, but can be used for marking woolens.

18. Elastic
    __3/8″ wide for the control excess in the legline, cutout neckline, armhole of the bodysuit and leotard. Also used to define the waistline of the human figure.

Pattern Paper

Pattern paper is available through suppliers in a variety of weights and colors for special purposes. Heavy pattern papers are commonly referred to as tag board, manila, or hard paper, whereas lighter weights are called marking paper. If a supplier is not available, use butcher paper or any other paper suitable for making patterns.

Draping fabric

Purchase as required.

Draping Principles and Techniques

3

Fabric is often the source of inspiration for the creation of designs, but it is the draper's skillful hands that manipulate shapeless pieces of cloth into beautiful garments.

The first version of most garments is draped in muslin, because it is an economical fabric. Ideally, a garment should be draped in the design fabric or a substitute that is closely related in texture and weight. Although this may be too expensive for the manufacturer, it may be appropriate when draping for private clientele. At completion, the drape should be critiqued for styleline placement, proportion, balance, and fit before removing it from the form or model.

After the critique, the pins are removed from the draped design. The marked stylelines and seams are trued. Trueing a draped garment requires that all markings placed on the muslin indicating stylelines and seams be straightened and curved lines blended. Measurements should be compared with those on the measurement chart. These steps are necessary if an accurate outline of the pattern shapes is to be achieved. The cloth patterns can be stitched and placed on the form, or model, for a test fit, or transferred to paper, cut, and stitched in the design fabric for fitting.

The beginning draper is often surprised to learn that the pinned drape that looked near perfect on the form can still have fitting problems when cut and stitched in the design fabric. This is to be expected for two reasons:

1. The design fabric, which has a different texture and weight from that of draped muslin, can result in a garment that hangs differently on the figure, thereby creating fitting problems.

2. Inaccurate marking and trueing of muslin patterns that were then transferred to paper also cause fitting problems.

Beginning drapers are greatly tempted to put fabric on the form to create wonderful designs, but draping is not that simple. Every accomplished artist knows that it takes hard work and determination to achieve perfection. Draping depends on controlling the straight and crosswise grainlines when manipulating the fabric on the form to create the desired design effect, and the balance of the garment. It also involves an understanding of the principles that guide the draper in choosing the correct draping techniques required by the design. Finally, the draper must have knowledge of the characteristics of fabrics and the ability to choose a fabric that will be compatible with the design. The identification of fitting problems and their solution is an ongoing learning experience. To go forward, remember that perseverance is the key, as is the love for draping beautiful garments.

Garments that are designed for the retail market require production patterns. The garment may go through several test samples to assure that the fit and patterns are perfect before being released for production.

Designers who create one-of-a-kind garments for private clientele often drape in the design fabric. In some cases after the drape has been completed, the garment is removed and basted for a fitting. Adjustments are made, and the garment is stitched. It is ready for wear without the creation of a pattern for the design because it will not be made again.

Draping Plan

A draping plan assists the draper in achieving a successful drape. Without establishing a plan, the draper would not know where to begin or how to proceed.

The plan begins with an accurate analysis of the design. This process involves the identification of the creative elements of the design and the draping technique(s) required to achieve the drape. Next the information should be recorded on the fashion drawing. It becomes the schematic, which offers a visual guide to the draper by providing the following information:

1. Planned sequence of the drape.

2. Location of stylelines on the form.

3. An estimate of fabric required.

4. Grainline placement for proper hang of the garment.

5. The draping techniques required.

Three Draping Techniques

Manipulating Dart Excess

Moving the dart excess to designated places on the drape and using the excess to create varying design effects.

Adding Fullness (not to be confused with ease added for comfort)

Adding fullness to a design in greater amounts than the dart excess can provide—within the garment and/or to the outer dimension of the figure.

Contour Draping

Fabric is draped to the contour of the figure above, below, and in between the bust and other mounds of the figure. These draping techniques will be introduced in design projects throughout the text. The following is an example of a draping plan.

Design Analysis

Preparing a Design Schematic

Figure 3.1

With knowledge of the basic dress foundation, the draper will be able to identify the root on which designs are based. The creative elements and identification of the draping technique(s) to be applied are noted on the sketch. The draping plan should be applied to all draped designs. To establish a schematic of the fashion drawing, the following questions need to be asked and answered.

Manipulating Dart Excess

Question: Where is the dart excess located and how is it used—as a dart(s), gathers, pleats, flare, cowl, drape, styleline (over the bust), or to enlarge the armhole of casual garments?

Answer: Princess styleline above an empire styleline.

Adding Fullness

Question: Is the fullness indicated by the sketch greater than the fullness provided by the dart? If so, where is the fullness located? What type of fullness—gathers, flare, pleats? What is the ratio of fullness? Does the garment extend beyond the outer dimensions of the form?

Answer: Yes. Five tuck darts emanate from the empire styleline and end with fullness 3″ below the waist. A flared sleeve with a "puff" gathered at the cap (based on the flat pattern system).

Figure 3.1

Contour Draping

Question: Does the design reveal the contour shape of the figure? Where—below, above, between the bust mound, other mounds?

Answer: Yes, under the bust, above the bust, at the cutout neckline and at the tapered hemline of the skirt.

Figure 3.2

Draping Short Cuts

Figure 3.2

The following information may not be appropriate for the beginning draper because it is important that they have practice in draping to perfect their skills in manipulating fabric. The information will be relevant later in their development, when there is demand for fast turnover of designs in industry. It is also useful for the designer who creates garments for private clientele—especially if personal fit patterns have been previously developed. Tracing parts of an existing pattern that closely relate to certain elements of the design can help to develop patterns that must be generated quickly. The related pattern(s) are traced on muslin in preparation of the drape. Draping and flat patternmaking are often combined in industry to produce designs.

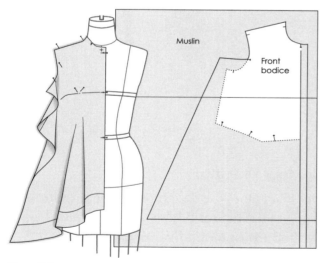

Figure 3.3

Figure 3.3

Through design analysis it was determined that the basic pattern could be traced from the neckline to the armhole. The prepared muslin is cut and placed on the form or figure to be draped in completing the design.

Methods for Joining Seams

Several pinning methods can be used to join the seams of a drape. Pins not only connect two joining seams, but also provide a guide for pencil or chalk markings to outline the pattern shape.

Lapped Seams

Figure 3.4

A folded seam is lapped to the marked line of the joining seam. Excess folds toward the center-lines. Pins are placed perpendicular to the seam, or at an angle to it.

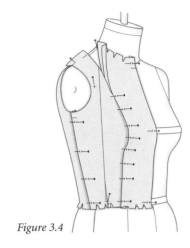

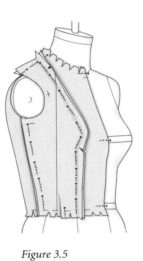
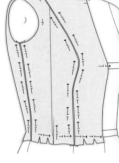

Figure 3.4

Raw Seams Out

Figure 3.5 and Figure 3.6

The raw seams are pinned right side out. This method may be preferred when draping to the contour of the bust. Pins are placed parallel with the seamline. The seams are marked, trued, turned, and then stitched or pinned to check the fit.

Not Recommended

Avoid pinning each fold of the seam to the form, rather than to the joining seams. It will interfere with the hang, fit, and critique of the drape.

Figure 3.5   *Figure 3.6*

Basic Dress Foundation 4

An introduction to draping begins with the drape of the basic dress foundation (Figure 4.1). It is draped to replicate the shape and dimension of the form, or model with ease added for comfort. Although the basic dress has no particular style or design, it is related to every garment in your clothing collection, to every design created, and to every pattern developed. It represents the very foundation on which design, patternmaking, and fit is based. After you have mastered the procedures and techniques, other chapters will build on these applications to illustrate variations and the draping of more complex garments.

The basic dress fits the outer lines of the figure, bridging the hollow areas around the bust, abdomen, buttocks, and between the shoulder blades. The garment has sufficient ease for comfortable movement without the appearance of stress. The sleeve hangs in perfect alignment with the relaxed arm and has the correct amount of looseness and cap ease. The skirt hangs

Figure 4.1

in the introduction to draping, a waist/shoulder dart (illustrated on page 70), and a waist/side dart (illustrated on page 68). The choice of which bodice to drape for the foundation is left to the instructor, or the designer/draper.

At the completion of the drape of the dress foundation there will be five pattern parts: (a) front and back bodice, (b) front and back straight skirt, and (c) basic mounted sleeve. The pattern shapes have straight and curved lines with wedges (darts) that lead into the patterns from the cut edges (Figure 4.2).

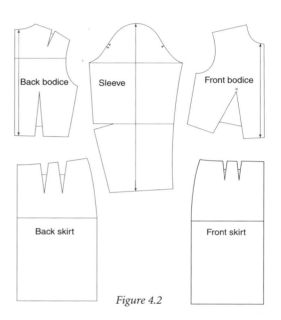

Figure 4.2

straight from the hipline with the hem parallel to the floor. The fit of the dress is controlled by darts. Darts take up excess while gradually releasing fullness where it is needed. The drape of the basic dress foundation introduces the relevant information about balance, ease, and fit.

The following illustrations show the bodice with a single dart (the location where the original fullness hangs below the bust) as illustrated

Basic Dress Drape

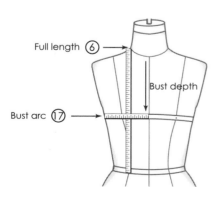

Figure 4.3

The bodice may be draped with a single waist dart, as illustrated, or with a waist and side dart (page 69) or shoulder dart (page 70).

Preparing Muslin

Figure 4.3

Measure the front length and width as illustrated, or use #6 and #17 from the Model Form Measurement Chart. (Measurements also apply to the back form.)

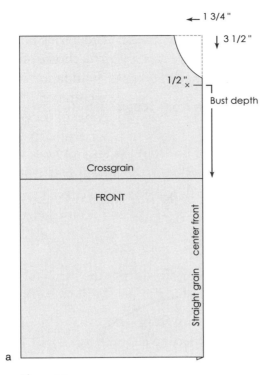

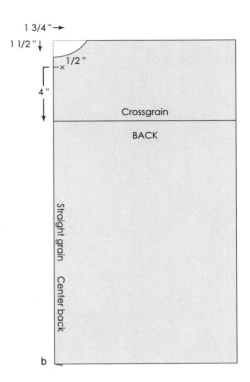

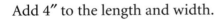

a

Figure 4.4

Add 4″ to the length and width.

Measure bust level. Record.

Cut muslin for the front and back bodice using length and width measurements. Refer to Chapter 1 for instructions on correcting the bowing and skewing of the fabric, if necessary.

Figure 4.4a and Figure 4.4b
Fold muslin 1″ along the length of the straight grain, and press without steam!

Draw temporary necklines with a French curve, using the measurements given. Cut excess away.

Mark 1/2″ down from front and back neck (X).

From (X), mark measurements given and square a crossgrain line across the muslin at bust level and across the back.

Front Bodice Drape

To establish an accurate outline of a draped garment, mark the muslin clearly and accurately with pencil or tailor's chalk in the form of dots, crossmarks, or solid lines. These marks are essential guides for trueing the cloth pattern and transferring the drape to paper. Slashes along the neckline and waistline are necessary to release tension in the fabric. Slashes should never extend past the outline of the form or they will affect the shape and fit of the draped garment. Be sure that the pinhead indicating the armhole depth is marked on the form (see page 7, Figure 2.4).

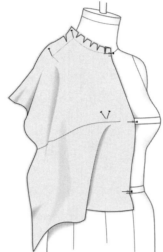

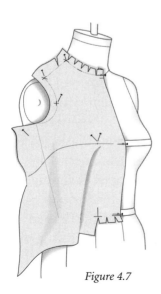

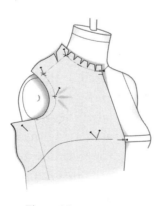

Figure 4.5

Figure 4.6

Figure 4.7

Figure 4.8

Figure 4.5

Place the fold of the muslin at center front and pin the following: neck at pin-mark, bust bridge, and the waistline (midtape).

Smooth muslin from center front to bust point (cross-pin).

Smooth muslin up from the bust and over the shoulder. Pin.

The crossgrain of the side falls downward creating a flare under the bust.

Figure 4.6

Smooth muslin upward from the bust and along the neckline, slashing to the shoulder/neck. Pin.

Smooth muslin up from the bust and along shoulder from neck to shoulder tip. Slash 1″ from neck. Pin.

Figure 4.7 and Figure 4.8

Smooth muslin from shoulder tip down along roll line of the armhole to the pinhead of mid-shoulder. Allow the fabric to bridge the hollow area between the shoulder and the bust (Figure 4.7). If stress folds are noticed (Figure 4.8), un-pin and relax the fabric. Repin.

Smooth and slash muslin along the waist to Princess line. Crossmark Princess at bottom of waist tape for dart leg.

Mark the following:
Bust point
3/8″ below CF neck
Mid-neckline curve
Shoulder/neck intersection
Shoulder tip
Mid-armhole at
    pinhead mark
CF at bottom of waist tape

Trim excess to within 1/4″ at neck, 1″ at shoulderline, and 1/2″ or more around armhole and waist, ending at Princess line.

Figure 4.9

Ease is added at the curve of the armhole between the mid-armhole and the side seam. Ease allows room for the muscle and fleshy connect between the body and the arm when the arm is in forward motion.

Remove holding pin from the side. Lift fabric upward pivoting from bust point and pin a 1/4″ ease tuck (1/8″ on the fold). Direct ease tuck toward the bust point.

Smooth muslin around armhole just past the side seam. Pin.

Smooth muslin downward along side seam to bottom of the tape. Pin.

Pencil rub side seam with the lead end.

Remove pin from the ease tuck.

Figure 4.10 (armhole depth and side ease)
Draw a short, curved line of the bottom armhole plate.

Draw a line down from the armhole plate to the pinhead indicating the armhole depth on side seam.

Measure out 1/2″ for side seam ease.

Optional: Draw side seam with ruler.

Smooth, slash, and trim muslin from side waist to Princess line, and pin a 1/4″ ease tuck (1/8″ on the fold) between the waist and the Princess line.

Crossmark the Princess line at the bottom of tape for the location of the other dart leg.

Dart Excess

The excess left hanging as flare from the bust mound (its natural location) is the result of the difference in measurement between the circumference around the bust/back and that around waist. The excess is a part of any design in which

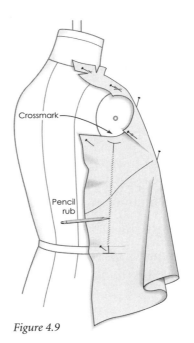

Figure 4.9

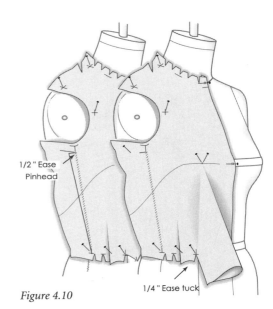

Figure 4.10

a mound exists. In the basic garment, the excess is stitched as a dart, but can also be used as flare gathers, pleats, and cowls, or as stylelines that cross over the bust mound. The result of using the dart excess creatively is referred to as dart equivalents, because they function as darts.

Figure 4.11

Fold the dart excess toward the center front. If the dart excess overlaps the centerline as illustrated by broken lines, trim excess to within 1″ of the dart legs.

Figure 4.12

Crease-fold seam of the dart inward, and lap to other dart leg. Place pins perpendicular to the foldline of the dart legs. Do not pin to the form!

Trim excess from waistline of the dart.

For accuracy, recheck all marks and measurements with those recorded on the Model Form Measurement Chart.

Figure 4.13

Fold the seam allowance (with thumbnail) along the shoulderline and side seam using guide marks.

Figure 4.14

The front drape may be removed or peeled back. Pin the shoulder and side seam, making room for the back bodice drape.

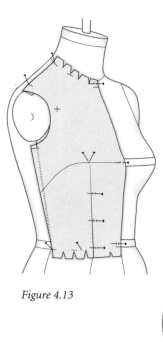

Figure 4.13

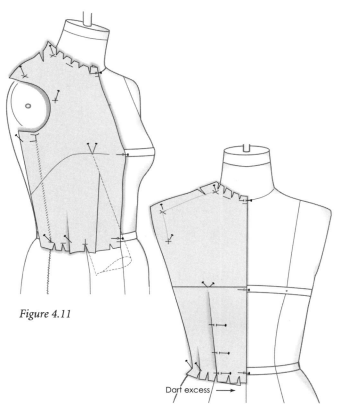

Figure 4.11

Figure 4.12

Dart excess →

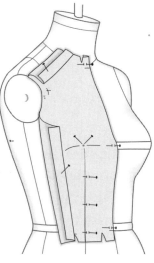

Figure 4.14

Back Bodice Drape

Figure 4.15

Place the fold of the muslin at center back and pin the neck, crossgrain line, and waist (mid-tape).

Smooth muslin along the crossgrain from center back to the pinhead location of the mid-armhole.

Smooth muslin over shoulder and pin.

Figure 4.16

Smooth and slash muslin along the neckline. Pin at shoulder/neck.

Smooth muslin along the shoulder to the Princess line, and mark for dart leg.

Draw a 3″ line along the Princess line to direct the angle of the dart leg.

Dot mark 1/2″ from Princess line for dart intake.

Slash 1″ from neck.

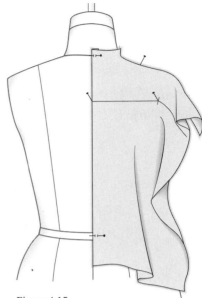

Figure 4.15

Figure 4.17

To form the shoulder dart, fold fabric from crossmark to meet dot mark with excess toward centerline. Pin perpendicular to fold. Do not pin to the form.

Smooth muslin to shoulder tip. Mark and pin.

Smooth muslin along roll line of the armhole to the crossgrain pin. Release pin to adjust if looseness or tightness appears.

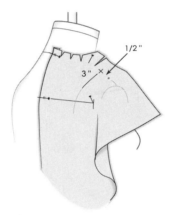

Figure 4.16

Mark the following:

Center back neck	Line across shoulder dart
Curve of the mid-neckline	Shoulder tip
Shoulder/neck intersection	Mid-armhole pin-mark

Trim excess approximately to within 1/4″ of the neckline, 1″ or more of the shoulderline and armhole to the crossgrain.

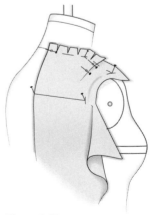

Figure 4.17

Figure 4.18

Smooth, slash, and trim muslin from center back waist to Princess line. Crossmark at bottom of tape for dart leg.

Dot mark 1 1/2″ from Princess line for dart intake. (Mark 1″ for junior size).

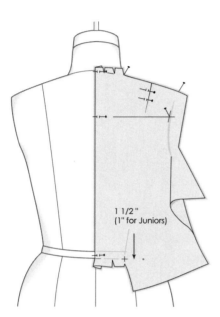

1 1/2 "
(1" for Juniors)

Figure 4.18

Figure 4.19

Fold waist dart from crossmark to dot mark with excess toward centerline.

Place pins perpendicular to foldline. Do not pin to the form.

Smooth, slash, and trim muslin along waist, pinning a 1/4″ ease tuck (1/8″ on the fold).

Smooth muslin beyond side seam. Pin.

Pencil rub along the side seam.

Mark bottom of waist tape at: Side waist
Midwaist
Across dart
CB waist

Figure 4.20

Release holding pins. Lap front shoulder and side seam over back seams matching guide marks very carefully. Place pins perpendicular to the foldlines. Do not pin to the form.

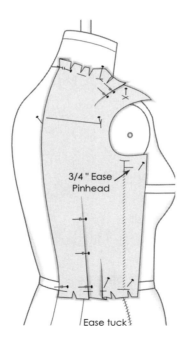

3/4 " Ease
Pinhead

Ease tuck

Figure 4.19

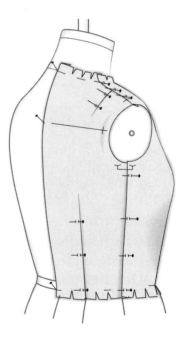

Figure 4.20

Armhole Depth and Side Ease

Draw a short, curved line of the bottom armhole plate.

Draw a line down from the armhole plate to pinhead, indicating the armhole depth on side seam.

Measure out 3/4″ for side ease (guide for shaping the armhole).

Optional: Draw the line for the side seam with a ruler.

Trim excess to within 1/2″ of the armhole and 1″ or more of the side seam.

Make a final check for marks and of the length of the shoulder, side seam, waistline, and centerline with those recorded on the Model Form Measurement Chart (Table 2.1).

Fit Analysis of the Bodice Drape

A well-fitting drape aligns with the form when the holding pins are removed from the centerlines of the front and back drape. There should not be any appearance of stress lines, gapping, or looseness around the neck, armhole, or body of the garment except for the ease added. Adjust the garment if fitting problems are noticed and mark the adjusted area with red pencil for blending later. If, after analyzing the fit of the bodice drape by comparing it with the following illustrations, and there are too many fitting problems, redrape the garment.

Armhole

A well-shaped armhole fits smoothly over the shoulder without the appearance of stress lines or gapping, and it moves away evenly from the side seam of the form. If stress or gaps appear anywhere around the armhole, as illustrated in the examples, follow instructions to correct the problem.

A well-balanced sleeve depends on the accurate shape of the armhole and correct placement of the shoulder and side seam of the form. All adjustments should be marked on the muslin with a red pencil.

Gap above Mid-Armhole

Figure 4.21

Release pins and smooth excess over the shoulder of the front and/or back bodice.

Re-mark shoulder tip. Repin.

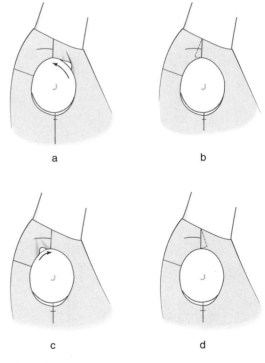

a   b

c   d

Figure 4.21

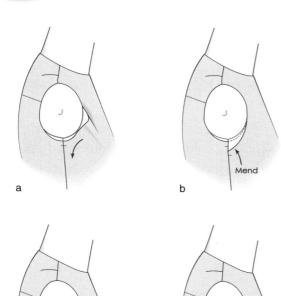

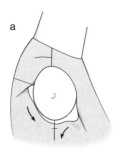

a   b

c   d

Figure 4.22

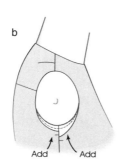

a   b

Figure 4.23

Gap below Mid-armhole

Figure 4.22

Release pins, and smooth excess past the side seam of the front or back bodice.

Re-mark armhole depth and side waist locations. Repin.

Gap below Mid-Armhole at Front and Back

Figure 4.23

Release pins and smooth excess past the side of the front and back bodice.

Re-mark armhole depth, side ease, and side waist. Repin.

Center Alignment of the Bodice

Figure 4.24 (perfect alignment)

No other fitting problems noticed. No correction required.

Figure 4.25 (imperfect alignment)

Front or back garment swings inside the centerline of the form.

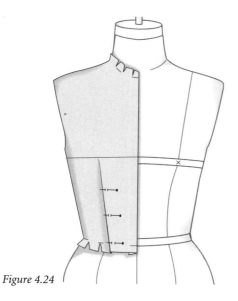

Figure 4.24

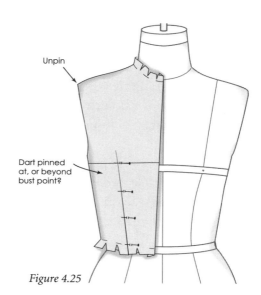

Figure 4.25

Possible causes:
Careless marking or handling of the drape.
Dart pinned beyond the bust point.

Possible solution:
Repin dart leg.
Release pins at shoulder and align to center.
Redrape and mark shoulder tip. Pin.

Figure 4.26 (imperfect alignment)

Front or back bodice overlaps the centerline of the form.

Possible cause
Careless marking or handling of the drape.

Possible solution
Raise shoulder tip.

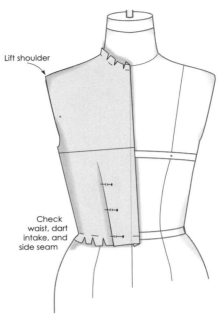

Figure 4.26

Trueing Front and Back Bodice

The basic bodice is corrected and stitched (to check the fit) before the skirt is attached. An unbalanced bodice or skirt affects the hang of the garment. To prepare the drape for trueing, unpin (except for pins holding darts) and draw connecting lines around the pattern. Cup the patterns when drawing the darted waist and shoulderlines. (Remember that the excess of the darts is folded toward the center front and back of the bodice.) While pinned, all folded darts are traced across with the tracing wheel to help determine their shape. The French curve is used for shaping the neckline, armholes, and waistline.

Verify all bodice measurements using the Model Form Measurement Chart (page 15) and correct any errors. Muslin patterns can be stitched for the fitting or be transferred to paper. To transfer muslin patterns to paper, either use pushpins thrust through the center of each mark (as illustrated) or use a tracing wheel crossing each corner.

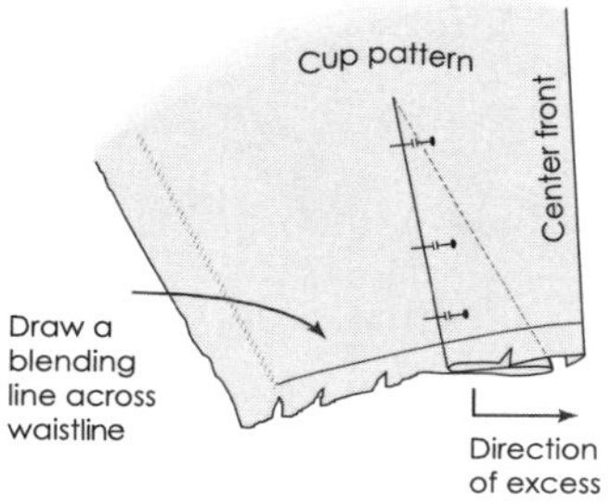

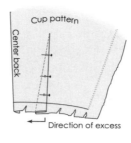

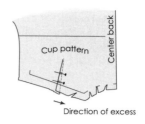

Figure 4.27   *Figure 4.28*   *Figure 4.29*

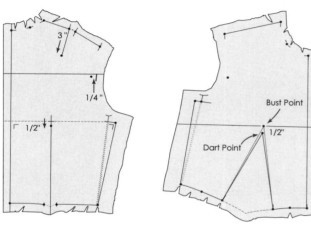

Figure 4.30   *Figure 4.31*

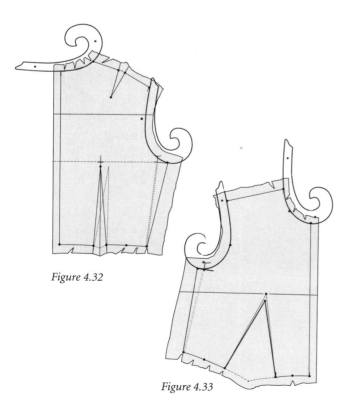

Figure 4.32

Figure 4.33

Figure 4.27 and Figure 4.28 (waist darts)

Folded darts are traced after a blending curved line is drawn across the front and back waistline. Unpin darts.

Figure 4.29 (back/shoulder dart)

Draw a line across the shoulderline with the dart folded, and trace. Unpin dart.

Figure 4.30 (back)

Draw the side seam line.

Draw shoulder dart (follows Princess line) 3″ to 3 1/2″ long.

Center a straight grainline through waist dart parallel with center back, ending 1/2″ below the armhole depth level.

Mark 1/4″ out from mid-armhole pin-mark.

Figure 4.31 (front)

Draw the side seam line.

Draw dart legs to bust point first. Mark dart point centered 1/2″ down from bust point, and draw dart legs to dart point.

Figure 4.32 (back)

Draw the neckline and armhole curves touching marks with the French curve.

Figure 4.33 (front)

Draw the neckline and armhole curves touching marks with the French curve.

At this point the muslin may be stitched for a fitting, if preferred.

Transferring Front and Back Bodice to Paper

Figures 4.34 (back) and Figure 4.35 (front)

Draw a line 2″ from edge of paper.

Place center back on line and front on fold.

Place pushpins where indicated.

Remove pins and muslin from paper.

Figure 4.36 (back) and Figure 4.37 (front)

Draw shoulderline 1/16″ above shoulder.

Draw side seams and square a short line at each end.

Square short lines at shoulder ends, center lines, and waist. Square a line at armhole depth. Draw dart legs to dart points.

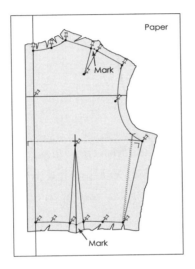

Figure 4.34

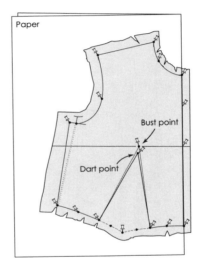

Figure 4.35

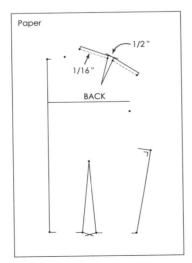

Figure 4.36

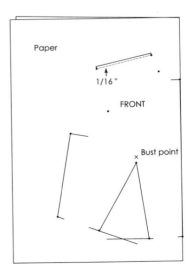

Figure 4.37

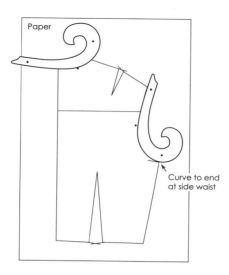

Figure 4.38

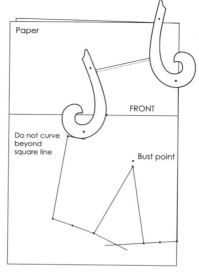

Figure 4.39

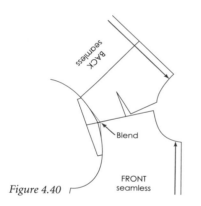

Figure 4.40

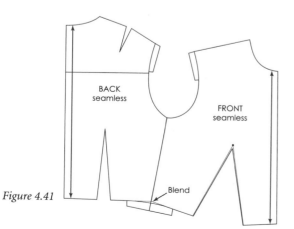

Figure 4.41

Figure 4.38 (back) and Figure 4.39 (front)

Back: Draw neckline and armhole touching the three guidemarks with the French curve. Draw waistline curves.

Front: Repeat steps.

Blend Waistline and Shoulderline

Figure 4.40 and Figure 4.41

Cut patterns allowing the excess paper at the waistline and armhole area for blending, if necessary.

To blend, match the seams and draw blending curve lines across the waistline and shoulder. After blending is completed, trim away excess.

Seamless and Seamed Patterns

It is suggested that two sets of basic patterns be completed. Use the seamless pattern set when making patterns through the flat pattern-making method; use the seamed pattern for draping projects quickly.

Seamless Patterns

Figure 4.42 and Figure 4.43

Cut a short distance up each of the dart legs. With the awl, place a hole at the dart point and mark bust point.

Seamed Patterns

Figure 4.44, Figure 4.45, and Figure 4.46

Two front bodice patterns are illustrated: one with a cutout dart and one with a full dart.

Seam allowance: 1/4″ at the neckline, 1/2″ at shoulder and waist. The side seam and centerline can vary from 1/2″ to 1″.

Notches: All seams and dart legs. No notches indicating seam allowance around the neck, armhole, or waistline.

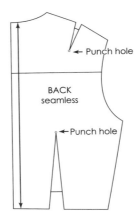

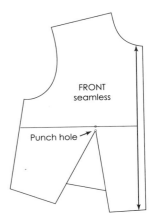

Figure 4.42

Figure 4.43

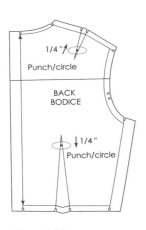

Figure 4.44

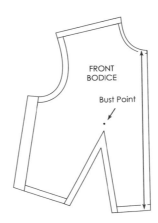

Figure 4.45

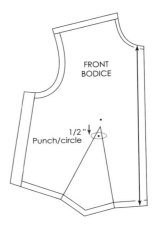

Figure 4.46

Basic Skirt Drape

The key to a balanced skirt lies in the accurate placement of the horizontal balance line (HBL) on the form and on the muslin (crossgrain) in preparation for the drape. If the HBL placed on the muslin or form are inaccurate, fitting problems will occur. The basic skirt can function as an attachment to the bodice as a dress or, with a waistband, as a separate skirt.

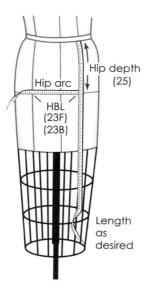

Figure 4.47

Preparing Muslin

Figure 4.47

Use the Model Form Measurement Chart #23
F_____ B_____ , #25 F_____ B_____, or measure the
front and back form.

Figure 4.48 and Figure 4.49

Width: Hip arc, plus 2 1/2″.
Length: As desired.

Fold muslin 1″ on straight grain. Press (without
steam).

Hip depth: Plus 1̶/̶2̶″ measured down on foldline. Mark and square a line across the muslin
(HBL—the crossgrain).

Hip arc: Measure from center front across HBL,
and crossmark.

Mark 1/2″ for ease, and draw lines through the
straight grain for the side seam.

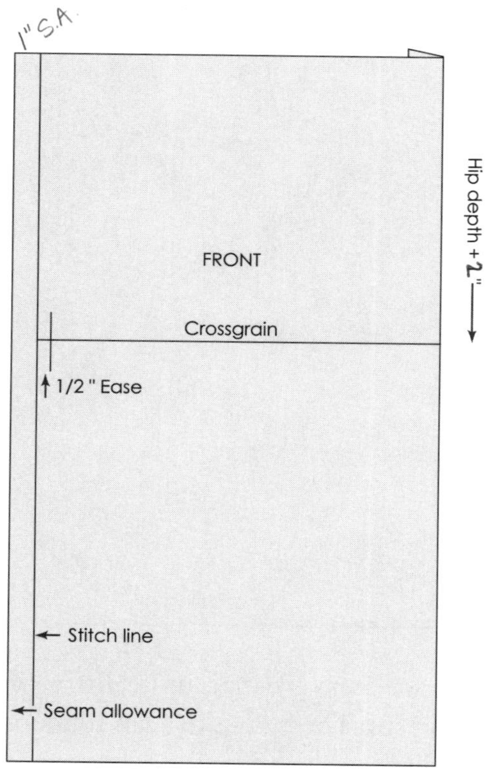

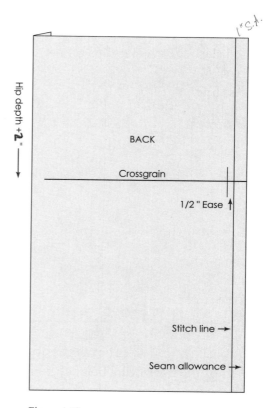

Figure 4.48

Figure 4.49

Front Skirt Drape

Figure 4.50

Place fold of muslin to center front aligning HBL (crossgrain). Pin to the HBL of the form.

Pin at center front waist and below waist on the centerline.

Smooth muslin on crossgrain from center front to side seam, aligned with the HBL.

Smooth and slash muslin from center front waist to Princess line. Crossmark at bottom of the waistline tape at Princess line (dart leg location) and at the center front waist.

With your hand on the hip and your fingers on the crossgrain of the HBL at the side seam, smooth muslin upward to side waist. Crossmark at side waist.

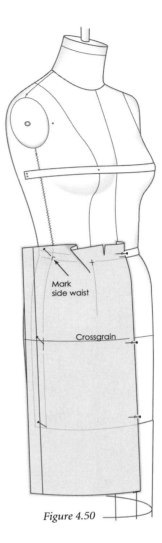

Mark side waist

Crossgrain

Figure 4.50

Figure 4.51

Smooth and slash muslin along waistline. Pin an ease tuck 1/4″ (1/8″ on fold) between side seam and Princess line.

Crossmark Princess line at bottom of waist tape (dart leg) and mark mid-waistline.

Figure 4.52

Remove pin at crossgrain of the side hip and move muslin to the stitchline for ease allowance. Repin on the stitch line.

Smooth muslin upward along side seam to waist, and pencil rub muslin as a reference when pinning front to back hiplines.

Trim side seam to within 1″ of the pencil-rub line.

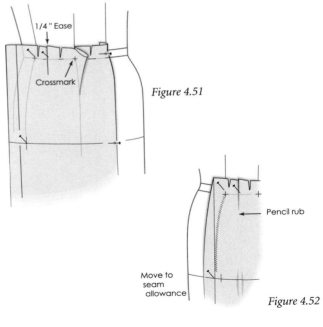

1/4″ Ease

Crossmark

Figure 4.51

Pencil rub

Move to seam allowance

Figure 4.52

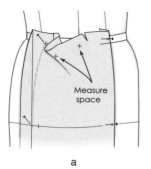

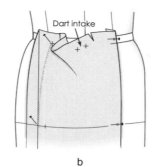

a

b

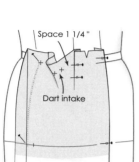

c

d

Figure 4.53

Figure 4.53

Measure the distance between crossmarks (Figure 4.53a). (The excess will be divided between two 3″ to 3 1/2″ long darts.)

Mark intake of the first dart (Figure 4.53b).

Fold the dart at Princess line, with excess toward the center front. Pin.

Mark dart space 1 1/4″ (1″ for juniors) (Figure 4.53c). (The second dart takes up remaining excess.)

Fold second dart and pin.

Mark at center front and across darts at bottom of tape. Trim excess to within 1/2″ of waistline (Figure 4.53d).

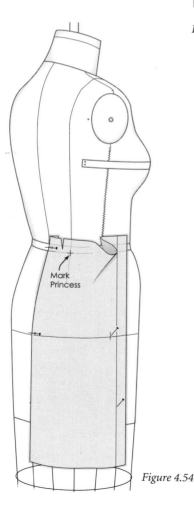

Figure 4.54

Back Skirt Drape

Figure 4.54

Place the fold of the muslin to center back aligning HBL (crossgrain). Pin to the HBL of the form.

Pin at center back waist and below waist on the centerline.

Smooth muslin on crossgrain from center back to side seam aligned with the HBL. Pin.

Smooth and slash muslin from center back waist to Princess line. Crossmark at bottom of the waistline tape at Princess line (dart leg location), and mark the center back at the waist.

With your hand on the hip and your fingers on the crossgrain of the HBL at the side seam, smooth muslin upward to side waist. Crossmark at side waist.

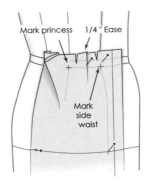

Figure 4.55

Smooth and slash muslin along waistline. Pin an ease tuck 1/4″ (1/8″ on fold) between side seam and Princess line.

Crossmark Princess line at bottom of waist tape (dart leg) and mark mid-waistline.

Figure 4.55

Figure 4.56

Remove pin at the crossgrain of the side hip and move muslin to the stitchline for ease allowance. Repin on stitch line.

Smooth muslin upward along seam line to side waist and pencil rub muslin as a reference when pinning front to back hiplines.

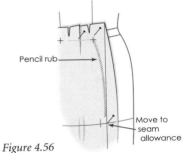

Figure 4.56

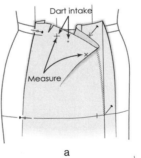

Darts

Darts can be arranged in the following two ways:

1. Darts of equal intake and length, as shown.

2. Darts of unequal intake and length.

> First dart intake, 1/2″ and length 3″.
> Second dart takes up remaining excess and is placed at the Princess line, with a length of 5 1/2″.

Do not pin darts to form!

Figure 4.57

Measure the distance between crossmarks and divide the excess between two darts.

Mark intake of first dart out from Princess line (Figure 4.57a).

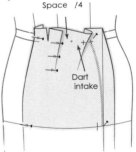

a

Fold dart excess toward the center back. Pin. Space the second dart 1 1/4″ from first dart (Figure 4.57b). Fold second dart excess toward the center back. Pin. Trim excess to within 1/2″ or more of the waistline (Figure 4.57c).

b

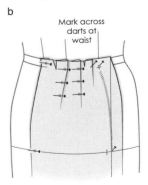

Figure 4.57   c

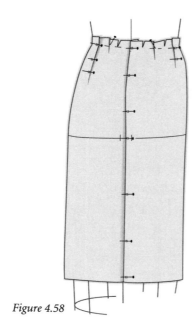

Figure 4.58

Figure 4.58

Fold side seam along rub line of the front skirt and place on top of rub line of the back skirt and pin.

Pin from HBL to hemline.

Fit Analysis of the Draped Skirt

To allow the skirt to hang freely from the waist, remove all holding pins at the HBL and below. Which example applies to the hang of your draped skirt? The fit of the skirt resulting from the drape accompanies each drape. Make appropriate adjustments to the drape.

The Hang of a Balanced Skirt

Figure 4.59

The skirt aligns with the centerlines of the form and hangs straight from the hip to hemline, indicating that the crossgrain is parallel with the floor (Figure 4.59a). Figure 4.59b illustrates a well-balanced skirt. If the skirt is misaligned, the following problems will occur and need to be corrected. Mark adjustments with a red pencil.

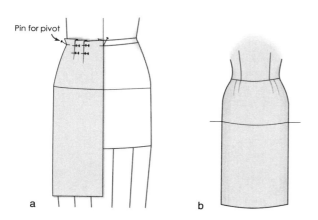

Figure 4.59

Figure 4.60 (imperfect alignment)

Skirt overlaps center, resulting in a stitched skirt that will flare at the centerline.

Possible causes:
    Insufficient dart intake and/or the side
        waist incorrectly marked.
    HBL not marked horizontal to the floor.

Possible solution:
    Unpin side seam and lift the side waist
        until the skirt aligns with the centerline
        of the form.
    Mark new side waist location.
    If required increase dart intake.
    Check location HBL of the form and
        muslin when trueing.

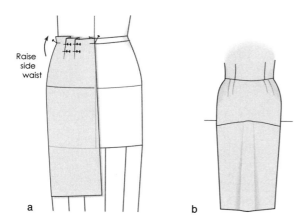

Figure 4.60

Figure 4.61 (imperfect alignment)

Skirt swings away from the center. As a result, the stitched skirt will press against the thigh of the model and will move up the legline when walking.

> Possible causes:
> Too much dart intake and/or side waist incorrectly marked.
> HBL not marked parallel to the floor.

> Possible solutions:
> Unpin side seam and lower the side waist until the skirt aligns with the centerline of the form.
> Mark new side waist location.
> Decrease dart intake.

Recheck location of the HBL of the form and muslin when trueing.

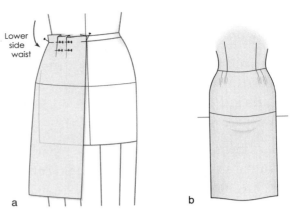

Figure 4.61

Pinning Draped Bodice to the Skirt

Figure 4.62

Pin bodice to skirt along the waistline.

Recheck alignment of the center front and back with the centerline of the form. Adjust if necessary. The waist dart bridges the hollow between bust and waist.

Note: A paper pattern or a trued-and-stitched muslin prepares the basic dress for the sleeve.

Trueing Front and Back Skirt

Prepare the drape for trueing by drawing connecting lines around the pattern. Verify all skirt measurements using the Model Form Measurement Chart, correcting any errors. Muslin patterns can be transferred to paper with pushpins thrust through centers of each mark, as illustrated, or with a tracing wheel that crosses each corner. Remove all pins so that the muslin skirt pattern lays flat. If muslin is wrinkled, press with warm iron (no steam).

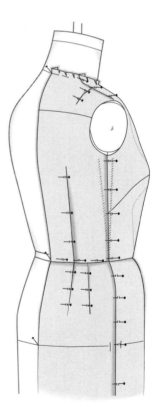

Figure 4.62

Skirt Drape on the Open

Figure 4.63

Verify that the intake of both darts is equal. If not, correct dart intake. Verify the space between the darts at 1 1/4″. Adjust side waist to preserve the waist arc measurement, if necessary.

Draw a line in the center of each dart that is parallel to the centerline of the skirt ending at dart point level. Re-mark dart intake to be equal and of equal length down from the waist.

Figure 4.64

Dart Legs and Hip Curve.

Draw front and back dart legs and hip curve.

Waistline and Dart Fold

Figure 4.65

Run tracing wheel over the folded darts. The perforated markings help to shape the dart when it is open. Draw the waistline with a French curve.

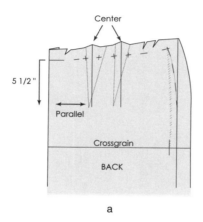
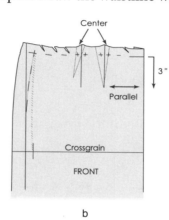

Figure 4.63

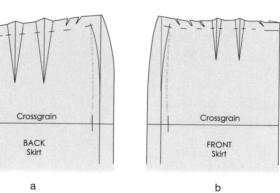

Figure 4.64

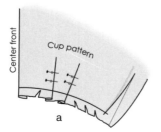
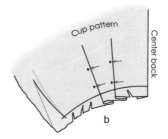

Figure 4.65

Preparing Paper for Front and Back Skirt

Figure 4.66

Width: Hip arc plus 5″.

Length: As desired, plus 5″.

Draw a vertical line 1″ from the edge of the paper equal to the skirt length and add 3″.

On the vertical line, measure the hip depth and add 3″. Square a line across equal to hip arc plus 1/2″ for ease and 1/2″ to 1″ for seam allowance. Square a line down from hip arc (side seam) to skirt length. Square a line from side seam to centerline.

Transferring Front and Back Skirt to Paper

Figure 4.67

Place muslin on paper, with the center front and back matching the vertical line of the paper and the HBL (crossgrain) on the square line.

Place pushpins through the HBL and the center. Smooth the muslin across the paper and place the pushpins where indicated. It is not necessary to pin the bottom part of the skirt because the outline has already been drawn. Remove the pushpins.

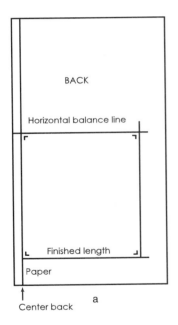
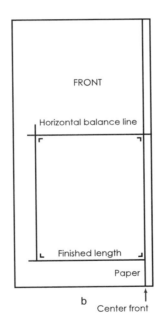

Figure 4.66

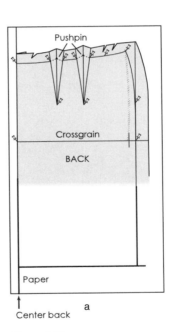
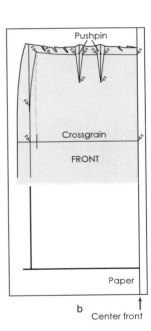

Figure 4.67

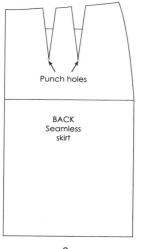

Punch holes

BACK
Seamless
skirt

Punch holes

FRONT
Seamless
skirt

a

b

Figure 4.68

BACK
Skirt
Horizontal Balance Line

Finished length

a

Center back

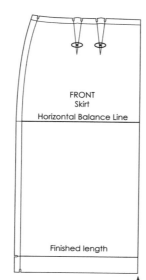

FRONT
Skirt
Horizontal Balance Line

Finished length

b

Center front

Figure 4.69

Outlining Front and Back Skirt: Seamless Pattern

Figure 4.68

Draw the outline of the skirt, using the hip curve ruler to shape the side hip.

Cut partially into each dart leg and, with the awl, penetrate the dart points.

Label the patterns.

Outlining Front and Back Skirt: Seamed Pattern

Figure 4.69

Fold paper to cut front skirt.

Draw outline of the patterns.

Add 1/2″ seam allowance to waist, 1/2″ to 1″ at side seam, and 1″ for hem.

Center punch holes 1/4″ to 1/2″ up from dart points.

Place zipper notch at center back or the side seam.

Place two notches at the center back. Identify the pattern parts.

Basic Sleeve

The basic sleeve, also referred to as a mounted sleeve, is drafted to fit the armhole of the basic dress foundation. The basic sleeve is used to help develop all other sleeves, which will be discussed in later chapters.

The arm is one of the most efficient and mobile parts of the human anatomy. It functions in a forward motion, but is capable of moving in every direction. This flexibility places a burden on the sleeve, making it one of the most difficult parts of the garment to fit. A well-balanced sleeve will hang at, or slightly forward of, the side seam. The sleeve will have sufficient ease around the biceps and the elbow area. The capline will be smooth without puckers or stress lines.

In the basic sleeve, the front and back cap are drafted with approximately the same measurements. The hang of the sleeve can be affected if the shoulder and/or side seam of the form is incorrectly placed or if the model has slouched shoulders or an upright military stance. It is best that the sleeve be rotated until the centerline of the sleeve aligns with, or is slightly forward of, the side seam of the form. However, a sleeve should be in balance with the model's stance and with the angle of the arm regardless of its alignment with the side seam. Rotating a sleeve may require relocation of the shoulder and/or side seam of the form.

Therefore developing the sleeve is accomplished by drafting. The draping of the basic sleeve is time consuming and the results are doubtful.

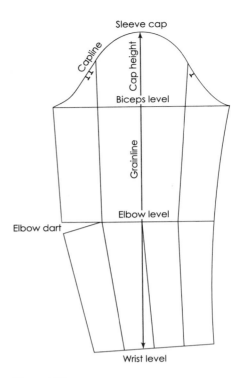

Figure 4.70

Sleeve Terms

Figure 4.70

Communicating in terminology that is familiar to those in the design and production room helps to avoid misunderstanding when problem solving. The following terms clarify the parts of the sleeve and the sleeve draft.

Cap ease Difference between cap and armhole measurement (ranging from 1 1/4″ to 1 1/2″).

Cap height The distance from biceps to cap at center.

Biceps level The widest part of the sleeve dividing cap from lower sleeve.

Elbow level The location of the dart at level with the elbow.

Sleeve ease Additional allowance at biceps, elbow, and wrist levels accommodating the circumference of the arm. Ease permits freedom of movement.

Grainline Center of the sleeve from the top of the cap to wrist level—straight grainline of the sleeve.

Notches One notch indicates the front part of the sleeve, and two notches indicate the back sleeve. Cap notch is often shifted to equalize the cap ease.

Sleeve cap The curved top of the sleeve from front to back.

Wrist level The bottom (hemline) of the sleeve at level with the wrist.

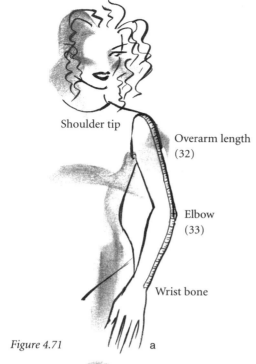

Shoulder tip

Overarm length
(32)

Elbow
(33)

Wrist bone

Figure 4.71 a

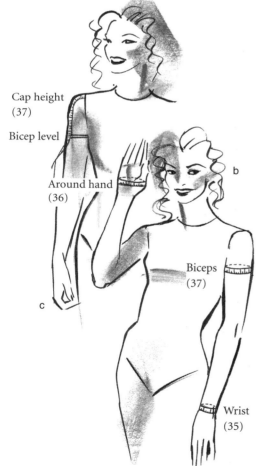

Cap height
(37)

Bicep level

Around hand
(36)

Biceps
(37)

Wrist
(35)

b

c

Measuring the Model's Arm for Personal Fit

Figure 4.71

Measurements are taken with the arm slightly bent so that the sleeve will not appear too short when the arm is fully bent or too long when the arm is relaxed. Numbers in parentheses correspond to those on the Model Form Measurement chart (page 15).

Vertical Measurements

Figure 4.71a

Overarm length (32): Shoulder tip over elbow to mid-wrist bone.

Elbow depth (33): Shoulder tip to elbow.

Circumference Measurements

Figure 4.71b

Biceps (widest area) (34): Add 2″ for ease. If biceps are very large, add 1 1/2″ (to avoid too much cap ease).

Wrist (35): Around wrist bone.

Around hand (36): Place thumb across palm; measure around the knuckle and hand. Add 1″ (varies) for ease.

Cap Height

Figure 4.71c

Cap height (37): Place a measuring tape or a piece of elastic around the biceps level with the mark for armhole depth placed on the side seam (see page 7). The tape should be parallel with the floor or tabletop. Mark biceps level. Measure from shoulder tip to top of the tape.

Sleeve Measurement Chart

Choose the measurements that apply to the form size (ease included):

Grade	1″			1 1/2″			2″
Sizes	6	8	10	12	14	16	18
Overarm length	22 1/4	22 5/8	23	23 3/8	23 3/4	24 1/8	24 1/2
Cap height	5 3/4	5 7/8	6	6 1/8	6 1/4	6 3/8	6 1/2
A-E measurement	___	___	___	___	___	___	___
Biceps	12 1/4	12 5/8	13	13 1/2	14	14 1/2	15 1/8
Wrist	8 1/4	8 5/8	9	9 1/2	10	10 1/2	11 1/8

Cap Ease

Measurements on forms vary among forms of the same size and among the companies that develop them. Because of these variations, it is difficult to determine which set of measurements apply to the size of the form. Generally, the sleeve cap ease for size 12 and larger is 1 1/2″; for size 10 and smaller, approximately 1 1/4″. Cap ease can be controlled by the A-E measurement of the draft and is discussed below.

Use a flexible plastic ruler instead of a measuring tape to measure the curve of the armholes. Measure front and back bodice armholes. Record the measurements on patterns. Add them together, divide in half, add 1/4″, and record the result in A-E space of the Sleeve Measurement chart.

The A-E Measurement

Figure 4.72, Figure 4.73, and Figure 4.74

The A-E measurement is used as a guide for comparison of the biceps placement in the sleeve draft. The adjustment of the biceps enables the cap ease to be in better proportion to the armhole of the bodice. Practice using a thin plastic ruler to measure the curved lines of the armhole and sleeve cap.

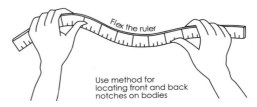

Figure 4.72

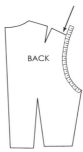

Measure and record on pattern

BACK

Figure 4.73

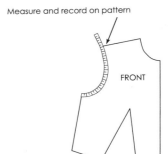

Measure and record on pattern

FRONT

Figure 4.74

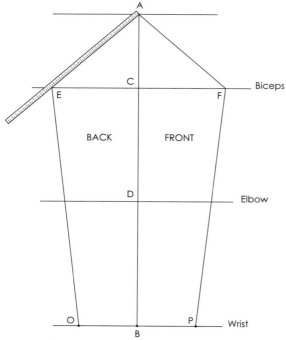

Figure 4.75

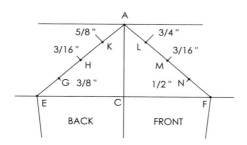

Figure 4.76

Sleeve Draft

Sleeve Frame

Figure 4.75

Draw a line on paper. Mark and label:

A-B = Overarm length.

A-C = Cap height. Mark.

C-D = One half of C-B, less 3/4″. Square lines from A, C, D, B.

A-E measurement

Place edge of ruler at A and pivot ruler until A-E measurement touches biceps line. Place temporary mark.

C-E = One half of biceps measurement. Compare placement of biceps with A-E mark. Re-mark biceps between the two marks. Label (E).

A-F same length as A-E. Mark.

B-O = One half of wrist measurement.

B-P = Same as B-O.

Draw a line from O to E and P and F.

Back and Front Sleeve

Figure 4.76

Divide A-E line into fourths.

Label G, H, K.

Divide A-F line into fourths for front sleeve.

Label L, M, N.

Square out from the following marks:

Back sleeve:

G = in 3/8″

H = out 3/16″

K = out 5/8″

Front sleeve:

L = out 3/4″

M = out 3/16″

N = in 1/2″

Front and Back Caplines

Figure 4.77

Front capline:

Use the French curve to shape the capline by touching A, L, and M. Draw curve beyond M for blending.

Change position of the curve rule touching F and N, blending with M line.

Back capline:

Place curve rule so that A, K, and H touch.

Draw curve past the H line for blending.

Change position of curve so that E and G touch. Draw curve blending with H line.

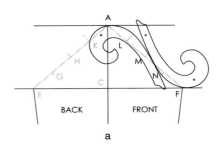

a

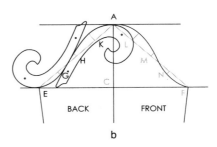

b

Figure 4.77

Finished Sleeve

Figure 4.78

Label elbow S, with R extended 1/4″. Draw a line from R to E.

Elbow dart:

R-T = One half of R-D.

R-U = 1″

T-U = T-R

O-V = 3/4″

Draw a line from U through V equal to R-O. Label W.

W-X = O-P, ending on line.

Draw a line ending at wrist level.

Draw line from X to S.

Ease control notches:

Back: Center notch between H-G with second notch 1/2″ below.

Front: Center notch between M-N (see instructions on page 54).

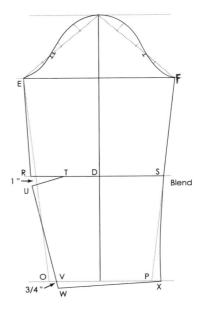

Figure 4.78

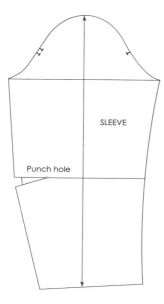

Figure 4.79

Seamed and Seamless Sleeve Patterns

A seamless sleeve, or a seamed pattern (as illustrated), can be used to "walk" the sleeve around the bodice armhole. Walking the sleeve has three purposes: (1) to place the front and back armhole notches, (2) to help determine the amount of cap ease, and (3) to determine if the center cap notch must shift from its original location to distribute the existing excess equally on both sides of the front and back bodice armholes.

Seamless Sleeve Pattern

Figure 4.79

Cut the sleeve from the paper as a seamless pattern. The seamless pattern is useful as a base for correcting the pattern before seams are added. However, seams are added to the muslin for the test fit when tracing the seamless pattern. (This method is optional.) It is also useful for generating patterns through the Flat Patternmaking Method, as all illustrations are based on a seamless pattern.

Cut a short wedge shape into the elbow dart legs.

Place a punch hole at dart point.

Seamed Sleeve Pattern

Figure 4.80

Trace a copy of the seamless pattern. Add the following seam allowances:

1/2″ around the sleeve

1″ to 1 1/2″ for hem turnback

Notches:

- Two notches for back sleeve
- One notch for front sleeve
- Seam allowance for underseams
- Hem foldback

Center cap notch may shift to equalize cap ease on the front and back bodice armhole.

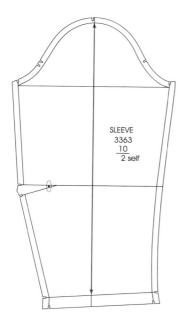

Figure 4.80

Sleeve Cap Ease and Notch Placements

The amount of cap ease varies with the size of the armhole and the style of the sleeve. Generally, cap ease of the basic sleeve is from 1 1/4″ for sizes 10 and smaller and 1 1/2″ for sizes 12 and larger. Cap ease of the casual sleeve is about 1/2″. There are other sleeve designs with differing ease requirements. Cap ease should be known before stitching the sleeve into the armhole. To measure around the front and back sleeve cap, use the flex rule (see page 51 for guidance). Subtract the measurement from the armhole or walk the sleeve cap around the front and back armhole.

Walking the Sleeve Cap to the Armhole

Figure 4.81, Figure 4.82, and Figure 4.83

The sleeve can be walked with or without seams. It is best to use two pushpins, one to pivot the pattern and one to hold the next location for pivoting.

Front: Place the sleeve on the armhole aligning with the side seam of the stitchlines. The sleeve and armhole curves should have the same shape for the first few inches. If not, redraw armhole curve. Then, place a pushpin into the stitchline of the sleeve every 1/8″ marking the ease control notch, as the sleeve is pivoted to the shoulder tip of the armhole. Mark the location of the shoulder tip on the sleeve cap.

Repeat the process for the back sleeve and armhole.

Placement of the Cap Notch

Measure the distance between the marks.

If cap ease is sufficient, go to page 57 for instruction. If the excess is too much, or not enough, see Figures 4.84 through 4.89 for suggestions on how to correct the problem.

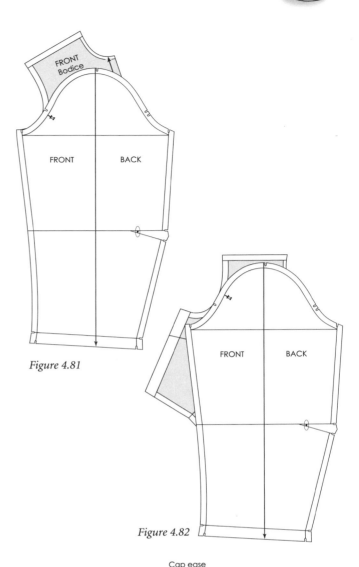

Figure 4.81

Figure 4.82

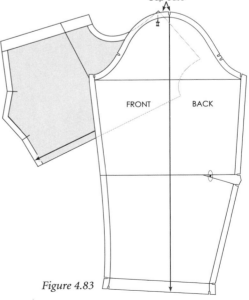

Figure 4.83

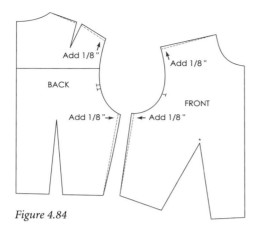

Figure 4.84

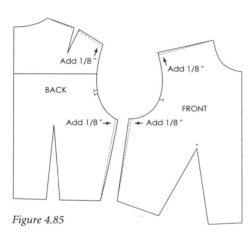

Figure 4.85

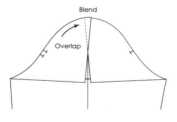

Figure 4.86

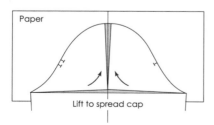

Figure 4.87

Increase and Decrease Cap Ease

Cap ease creates room for the ball of the arm. However, too much cap ease causes puckers, and too little cap ease causes strain lines along the cap of the sleeve. Both fitting problems spoil the look of the garment. To help control the cap ease, use one or more of the suggestions given.

Adjustment to the Armhole

Figure 4.84

To redistribute cap ease:

Lower the bodice notches from 1/8″ to 1/4″. This will redistribute cap ease above and below the armhole.

Figure 4.85

To enlarge the armhole to allow room for cap ease:

Add 1/16″ to 1/8″ at shoulder tips and/or the side seams to zero at the shoulder/neck, and waistline.

Adjust Sleeve Cap to Decrease Ease

Figure 4.86

Cut through the pattern from the center sleeve grainline and out to each side along the biceps up to, but not beyond, the underseam corners.

Overlap the amount of cap ease to be removed.

Retrace the adjusted sleeve and blend the cap. The biceps remain the same.

Adjust Sleeve Cap to Increase Ease

Figure 4.87

Repeat the cutting direction above.

Place on paper and spread the pattern to increase cap ease. Tape and blend the cap. The biceps remain the same.

Adjustment to Increase Biceps Width

Figure 4.88

To increase biceps, trace sleeve and extend biceps to needed amount.

Place the sleeve at the extended line.

Place a pushpin at the corner stitchline and pivot the pattern upward touching the traced sleeve. Draw a blending line. Pivot the sleeve downward to edge of the hemline and trace. Repeat to the other side.

Adjustment to Decrease Biceps Width

Figure 4.89

To decrease biceps, trace sleeve and mark a point inside the corner of the biceps to needed amount.

Place a pushpin at the corner of the sleeve to the mark and pivot the pattern upward touching the traced sleeve. Draw a blending line. Pivot the sleeve downward to edge of the hemline and trace. Repeat to the other side.

Rotate Sleeve for Alignment

The sleeve is ready to be placed into the armhole. What is not known is if the sleeve will align with, or be slightly forward of, the side seam or the angle of the arm. The sleeve can be stitched long into the armhole for assessment or can be rotated into the armhole before stitching to the armhole.

Figure 4.90

To prepare the sleeve, cut in the fabric of choice. Either crimp excess or place two rows of stitching—one on the stitchline and the other 1/4″ above (from notch to notch).

Pull the threads until the gathered section equals the same measurement as from notch to notch.

Sew the underseam (press) and steam mold cap on sleeve.

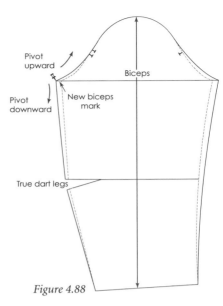

Figure 4.88

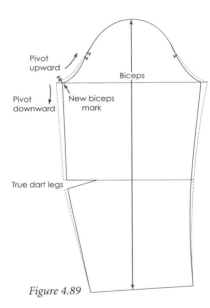

Figure 4.89

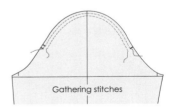

Figure 4.90

Evaluate the Hang of the Sleeve

Figure 4.91

If the sleeve hangs forward or backward of the side seam, remove the sleeve from the armhole, and rotate it until the center grain of the sleeve aligns with, or is slightly forward of, the side seam. The instructions will help in this process.

Imperfect alignment: Sleeve that hangs forward of the side seam.

Move the underseam of the sleeve about 1/4″ toward the back armhole or until the centerline of the sleeve aligns with, or is slightly forward of, the side seam of the bodice (see Figure 4.92).

Pin or baste the sleeve around the armhole for evaluation.

The centerline of the cap is notched at a location that equalizes the cap ease between front and back armhole.

Imperfect alignment: Sleeve that hangs to the back of the side seam.

Reverse the process illustrated in Figure 4.92, so that the cap ease is equalized (see Figure 4.93).

Pattern Corrections

Correct the side seam and/or shoulder of the front and back bodice patterns (Figure 4.92).

Correct the side seam and/or shoulder of the bodice patterns (Figure 4.93).

Figure 4.92

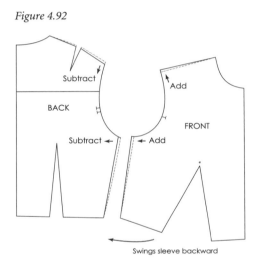

Figure 4.93

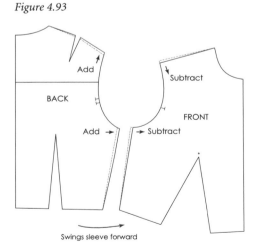

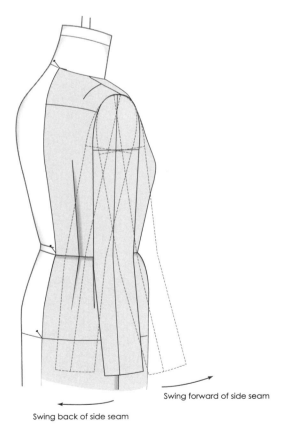

Figure 4.91

Seam Allowances of the Basic Pattern Set

Follow the suggested instructions for seam allowance as a guide for all patterns.

Seam Allowance

Figure 4.94

Seam allowance varies with each company. The following measurements are general guidelines:

Add 1/4″ to:

   All faced areas
   Narrow spacing
   Extreme curves
   Sleeveless armholes

Add 1/2″ to:

   Armhole with sleeves
   Waistlines
   Centerlines (varies)
   Stylelines
   Side seams can vary from 1/2″ to 1 1/4″
   Seam for zipper varies from 1/2″ to 1″

Overlock Seams:

   3/8″ seam allowances

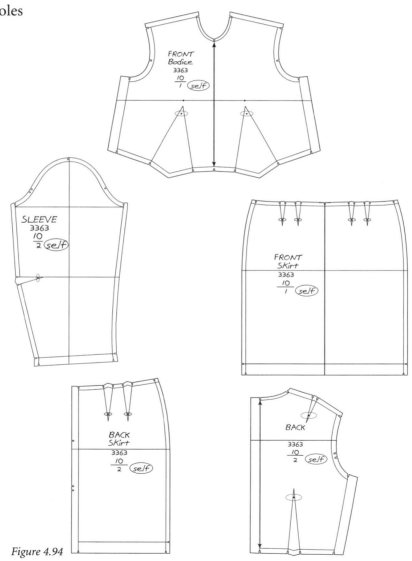

Figure 4.94

Completing the Pattern Information

After the pattern has been transferred to paper, it is important to add patternmaking symbols and special marking to guarantee the smooth flow of producing the desired garment. The general information below should be used as a guide to completing patterns. If the information differs from that of a particular company, defer to company standards.

Grainline

Always draw the grainline through the length of the pattern. The grainline is finished with an arrow at both ends (indicating that the fabric of choice does not have a nap) or at either end. The latter indicates which end of the pattern is head up on the straight grain for those fabrics having a nap, such as velvet, corduroy, or sheen, so that shading in the garment parts can be prevented.

Pattern Size

The sample size is marked on all pattern pieces. When the pattern is graded, the sample size is used as the basis for the grade. Each of the graded patterns is marked to appropriate size.

Style Numbers

Each design is coded with a number. For example, #3363 may be broken down to mean a top (#33) and a type of fabric (#63). The significance of the numbers is determined by each company.

Identify Pattern Parts

Each pattern is a part of the whole and should be identified. For example, sleeve, front and back bodice, skirt, and pocket should be labeled.

Number of Pattern Pieces

Mark the number of pattern pieces for each specific pattern required to complete the desired garment.

Markings

The "cut" symbol can be indicated with a horizontal line drawn between the size and number of cut pieces. The word "cut" can be written instead of the drawn line. The number of pieces can follow with the word "self" (circled).

Information can be centered on the pattern part, or written on line with the grainline. Use a black felt tip pen to mark pattern information for self-fabric. Red, blue, and green are often used to identify which patterns are cut in special fabrics for the lining and the interconstruction.

Manipulating Dart Excess

Chapter 4 discussed the control of the excess through darts when draping the basic dress. However, the following bodice designs illustrate how this excess is also used to create fashion features.

Dart manipulation begins with an understanding of the underlying principles involved in creating and interpreting designs. The principles state that a dart, or its equivalent, is always directed to the bust from which it radiates and to which it ends (Figure 5.1) and that the dart excess in one form or another is a permanent part of the bodice design.

The dart excess that hangs as a flare from the bust can be manipulated to any location of the form's outline in creating designs. The excess can be adapted and used as a dart equivalent in the form of gathers, tuck dart(s) or pleat(s), flares, flanges, and cowls, and for stylelines that pass over the bust mound (or any mound). The excess is also used to enlarge the armhole of casual garments.

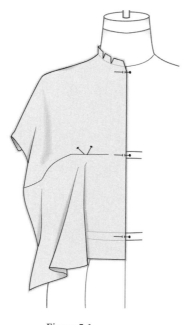

Figure 5.1

The designer/draper is to identify the location of the excess, and how the excess is utilized before draping the project.

In a fashion sketch, the dart is identified as a line directed to a mound (bust mound in the following projects). In a garment, the dart is a seamline directed to and ending near the bust.

Stripes are used in these drawings to illustrate the changes in the position of the grainlines as the dart excess is draped to various locations of the garment. In preparing the muslin, the straight and crossgrain is drawn to show the rise and fall of the grain in manipulating the fabric.

Knowledge gained from draping the basic bodice should be applied to the following projects. To complete the practice design projects, drape or trace a copy of the basic back pattern. Use the instruction on page 45 for trueing the muslin pattern.

Dart Excess

Shoulder Dart

Figure 5.2

Design Analysis

Question: Where is the dart excess, and how is the excess utilized?

Answer: The dart excess is draped to the shoulder/Princess, and pinned as a dart (Figure 5.2).

Preparing Muslin

See pages 26 and 27.

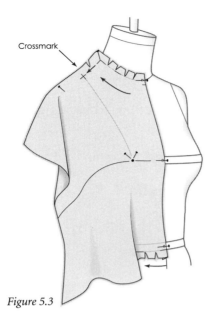

Crossmark

Figure 5.3

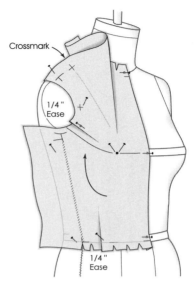

Crossmark

1/4"
Ease

1/4"
Ease

Figure 5.4

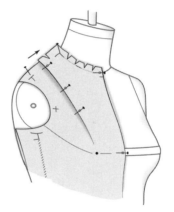

Figure 5.5

Draping Steps

Figure 5.3

Pin muslin to the form.

Drape muslin to the Princess line of the shoulder and waist.

Crossmark dart leg at the shoulder. Trim excess.

Figure 5.4

The crossgrain is lifted as the muslin is draped around the bust mound in the direction indicated by the arrow.

Continue until the excess reaches the Princess line of the shoulder.

Crossmark the dart leg.

Figure 5.5

Fold dart with excess toward the center front. Pin. Mark a line across the fold of the dart legs.

Remove and true the pattern.

Finished Pattern

Figure 5.6

Study pattern shape with that of the design.

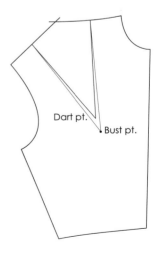

Dart pt.

Bust pt.

Figure 5.6

Armhole Dart

Figure 5.7

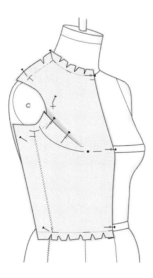

Figure 5.8

Design Analysis

Figure 5.7

Question: Where is the dart excess, and how is the excess utilized?

Answer: The draper answers the question.

Preparing Muslin

See pages 26 and 27.

Draping Steps

Figure 5.8

Pin the muslin to the form. Smooth muslin around neck and shoulder, ending at pinhead of mid-armhole. Mark dart leg.

Figure 5.9

Crossgrain is lifted upward until the dart excess reaches the pinhead of the armhole (mark arm plate, and pin 1/4″ ease). Mark the dart leg.

Figure 5.10

Fold dart excess toward the waistline. Pin. Mark a line across the fold of the dart legs. Remove and true the pattern with dart folded when drawing armhole.

Finished Pattern

Figure 5.11

Compare pattern shape with that of the design.

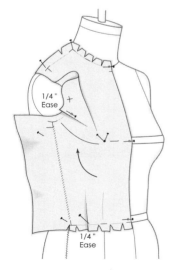

Figure 5.9

Figure 5.10

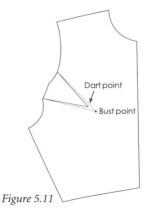

Figure 5.11

French Dart

Design Analysis

Figure 5.12

Question: Where is the dart excess, and how is the excess utilized?

Answer: The draper answers the question.

Preparing Muslin

See pages 26 and 27.

Draping Steps

Figure 5.13

Pin the muslin to the form.

Drape the fabric in the direction indicated by the arrows, first around the neck and shoulder, and then along the waist to Princess line.

Figure 5.14

Continue draping along waistline and side seam to the location for the French dart. Mark the dart leg.

Pin 1/4″ ease at mid-armhole, and then mark arm plate and side seam.

Continue the drape to the dart location. Mark dart leg.

Figure 5.15

Fold dart excess toward the waistline. Pin. Pencil rub the side seam. Mark a line across the fold of the dart legs. Remove and true the pattern.

Finished Pattern

Figure 5.16

Compare pattern shape with that of the design.

Figure 5.12

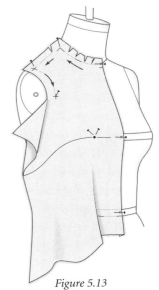

Figure 5.13

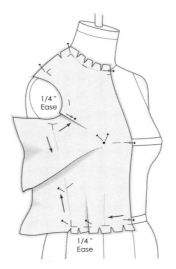

1/4" Ease

1/4" Ease

Figure 5.14

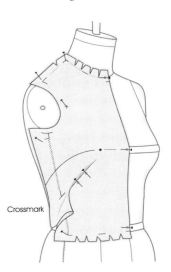

Crossmark

Figure 5.15

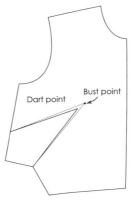

Dart point   Bust point

Figure 5.16

Center Front (Bust Dart)

Design 1

Figure 5.17

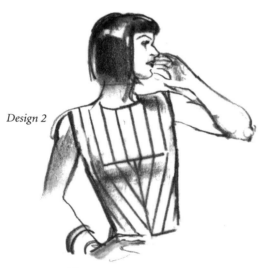

Design 2

Figure 5.18

Design Analysis

Figure 5.17 and Figure 5.18

Design 1 illustrates one of two designs; design 2 is a thought problem.

Question: Of the two designs illustrated, which does the pattern represent? What would the pattern shape of the other design look like?

Answer: The draper answers the question.

Preparing Muslin

See pages 26 and 27.

Do not cut out the neckline, as it is draped later in the design.

Draping Steps

Figure 5.19

Slash the extension (below bust level), and unfold. Excess is moved in the direction indicated by the arrow.

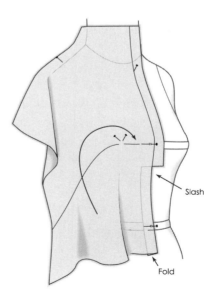

Slash

Fold

Figure 5.19

Figure 5.20

Continue the drape around the bust mound until the dart excess reaches the center front bust level (mark arm plate, and pin 1/4″ ease at mid-armhole).

Figure 5.21

Fold dart with excess toward the waistline. Pin.

Mark a line across the fold of the dart legs.

Remove and true the pattern.

Finished Pattern

Figure 5.22

Compare pattern shape with that of the design.

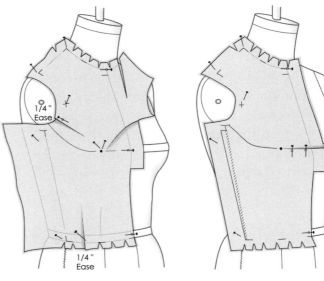

Figure 5.20   Figure 5.21

Figure 5.23

Figure 5.24

Figure 5.25

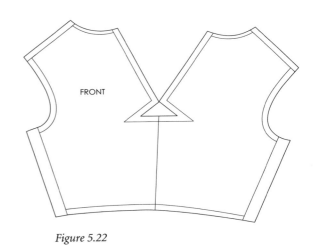

FRONT

Figure 5.22

Design Analysis

Figure 5.23, Figure 5.24, and Figure 5.25

Question: Where is the dart excess, and how is the excess utilized?

Answer: The draper answers the question.

Dividing Dart Excess

Dividing Dart Excess

Fullness released from two darts improves the fit around the bust mound. Therefore, the excess is more often shared between two darts. Two popular bodice foundations that share the dart excess are the waist/side and waist/shoulder combinations. Both are the basis of many design variations. When the excess is divided between the waist and side seam or shoulder, the crossgrain is at bust level from center front to the side seam and parallel to the floor. By raising and lowering the crossgrain, the excessed between the darts can be increased or decreased.

Waist/Side Dart

Figure 5.26

Draping Plan

Question: Where is the dart excess, and how is the excess utilized.

Answer: The dart excess is shared between the waist and side seam.

Crossgrain guidelines are needed at the bust and waist level in the preparation of the muslin to control the distribution of the dart excess (Figure 5.26).

Preparing Muslin

Figure 5.27

See pages 26 and 27.

Add to the preparation a squared line across the muslin at the waistline.

Use #5 from the Model Form Measurement Chart or measure from center neck to waist.

Figure 5.27

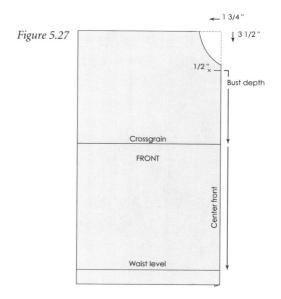

Draping Steps

Figure 5.28

Pin the muslin to the form.

Drape the neckline and shoulderline, ending at the pinhead at the armhole, and trim.

Figure 5.29

Continue the drape around the armhole. Pin ease and armhole depth. Pencil rule the cross-grain line at the side seam. Pin.

Lift the crossgrain until the guideline of the waist is level with the side waist. Pin.

Pin dart excess at waist. Adjust intake if guideline is not at side waist.

Smooth the muslin upward at side seam. Pin.

Figure 5.30

Fold dart on the crossgrain with excess toward the waistline. Pin. Pencil rub the side seam.

Mark a line across the fold of the dart legs.

Remove and true the drape. Make a pattern.

Finished Pattern

Figure 5.31

Compare the shape of the pattern with the foundation.

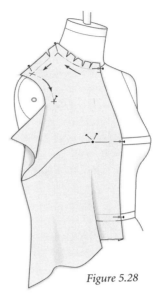

Figure 5.28

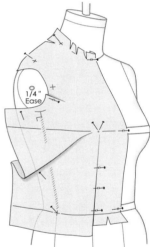

Figure 5.29

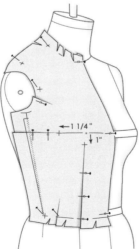

Figure 5.30

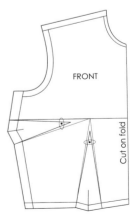

Figure 5.31

Waist/Shoulder Dart

Figure 5.32

Design Analysis

Question: Where is the dart excess, and how is the excess utilized?

Answer: The dart excess is shared between the waist and shoulder at the Princess line. Cross-grain guidelines are needed at the bust and waist level in the preparation of the muslin to control distribution of the dart excess (Figure 5.32).

Preparing Muslin

See pages 26 and 27.

Add to the preparation a squared line across the muslin at the bust and waistline. Use #5 from the Model Form Measurement Chart or measure from center front neck to waist.

Draping Steps

Figure 5.33

Pin muslin to form.

Drape neckline to shoulder at Princess, and waist to Princess. Crossmark for dart legs.

Figure 5.34

Lift the crossgrain until the waist guideline is at level with the side waist. Pin.

Smooth the excess to the shoulder tip. Pin.

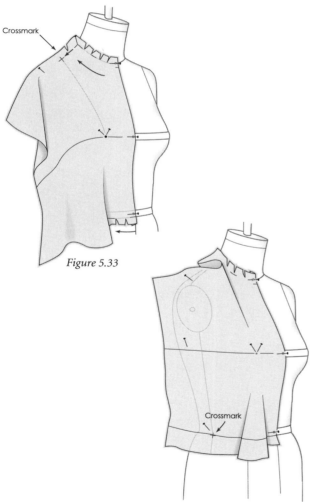

Figure 5.33

Figure 5.34

Figure 5.35

Continue the drape along the waist, side seam, armhole, and shoulder.

Crossmark dart legs.

Figure 5.36

Fold dart with excess toward the centerline. Pin.

Pencil rub the side seam, and mark armhole depth and ease. Mark bust point.

Mark a line across the fold of the dart legs.

Remove and true the drape and make the pattern (see pages 35–39).

Finished Pattern

Figure 5.37

Compare the pattern shape with the foundation.

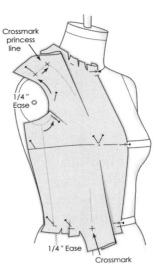

Figure 5.35

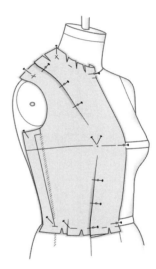

Figure 5.36

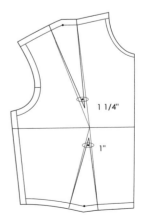

Figure 5.37

Dart Equivalents: Gathers, Pleats, and Tuck Darts

The following examples are dart equivalents and illustrate how the shared excess is adapted as gathers, pleats, and tuck darts. Flare is already known as the natural fall of the grain when the fabric is placed on the form. Other dart equivalents are given in a later chapter. The finished patterns are included.

Gathers

Space allowance for shirring is marked between 3/4″ and 1 1/4″ out from each dart leg. The gathers can be pinned or taped with elastic across gathered section to the form.

Draw a pencil line across the gathered sections as a guide for blending (Figure 5.38).

Trueing and Marking the Pattern

Figure 5.39

The guidelines are unevenly marked across the gathered sections.

Blend by drawing a line through the markings.

The drawn shape is rounded.

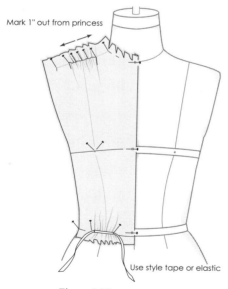

Figure 5.38

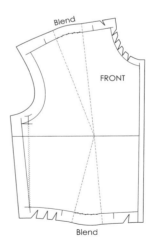

Figure 5.39

Finished Pattern

Figure 5.40

Dart equivalents are in the general shape of dart legs.

Control notches are placed on the shoulderline of the joining pattern.

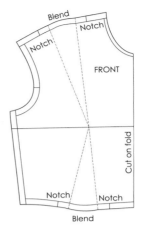

Figure 5.40

Pleats

Notches are placed at the dart legs of the seam.

The fabric is folded as a dart without stitching the dart legs (Figure 5.41).

Figure 5.41

Tuck Dart (or Half-Dart)

Notches are placed at the dart legs. The dart is folded and traced before marking its shape. Follow the angle of the dart legs and mark a point where the stitching ends. Place and punch a circle 1/8″ in from the dart leg, ending 1/2″ above the finished stitch (Figure 5.42).

Place another punch at the center of the dart space. The unstitched part of the dart releases fullness giving the appearance of a pleat.

Tuck dart

Figure 5.42

Curved Dart

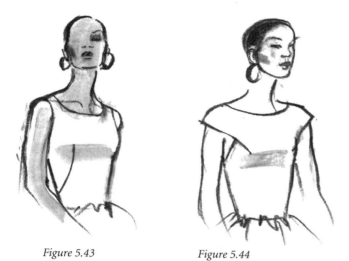

Figure 5.43   Figure 5.44

Dart legs can be designed as curves, combined with straight and curved legs, or jagged. Stylized darts are cut to within seam allowance for easy manipulation when being stitched. A curved French dart is the prototype for stylized darts. The front bodice is illustrated (Figure 5.43 and Figure 5.44).

Design Analysis

The French dart is placed approximately 3″ up from the side waist and directed to the bust point. The neckline is scooped from a depth of about 3″ below the front, ending at the Princess line of the shoulder. Drape a basic back bodice with a higher scoop neckline.

Preparing Form

Figure 5.45

Pin-mark the shape of the scoop neckline.

Pin-mark the curve line of the French dart.

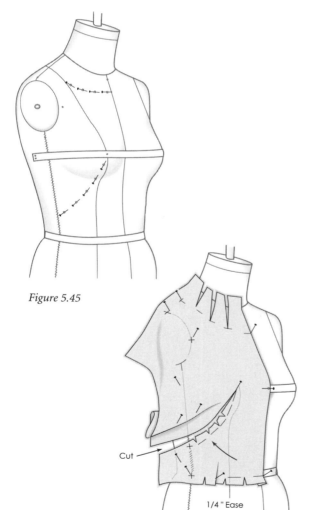

Figure 5.45

Cut

1/4 " Ease

Figure 5.46

Preparing Muslin

See pages 26 and 27.

Draping Steps

Figure 5.46

Place fold of the straight grain to center of the form. Pin.

Smooth, slash, and mark along the waistline, and pin waist ease.

Smooth excess to side waist, and crossmark.

Lift crossgrain upward along the side seam to the location of the French dart.

Pencil rub along pin-marks of the dart and trim to allow 1/2″ or more for seam. Slash along the seam of the dart leg.

Smooth and slash muslin along scoop neckline. Pencil rub pin-marks of the neckline. Pin.

Smooth, and mark shoulder tip, mid-armhole, and arm plate/side seam.

Figure 5.47

Trim excess around the neckline, armhole, and side seam.

Peel back the dart leg and pin.

The crossgrain drops as the dart excess is draped to the location of the French dart.

Pencil rub along the dart leg pin-marks.

Trim excess.

Figure 5.48

Fold lower dart leg on marked seamline.

Pin dart together, matching seamlines to within 1/2″ of bust point.

Remove the drape and true. To complete the pattern, see pages 35 to 39.

Finished Pattern

Figure 5.49

Cut a 1/16″ slit to within 1/8″ of the dart point.

Compare the pattern shape with that of the design.

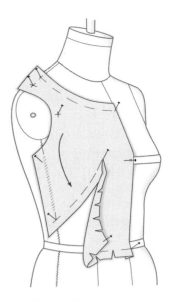

Figure 5.47

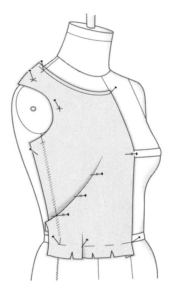

Figure 5.48

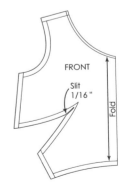

Figure 5.49

Intersecting Darts

Darts can be draped to intersect with one another. Intersecting darts allow for greater flexibility in creating designs. The draping technique is also applied. The design is accompanied by a form prepared with pin-markings to guide the draper (Figure 5.50 and Figure 5.51).

Design Analysis

Question: Where is the dart excess, and how is the excess utilized in the development of the design?

Answer: The excess of the right dart is draped to the left side of the form, passing the centerline and ending at the shoulder/Princess line. The excess of the left dart is draped to intersect with the first dart at the centerline of the form. The dart excess is trimmed (Figure 5.52).

The crossgrain is lifted as the darts are draped at their new locations, but all other draping procedures remain the same.

Manipulating the dart excess creates a different pattern shape from that of the basic pattern.

Figure 5.50

Figure 5.51

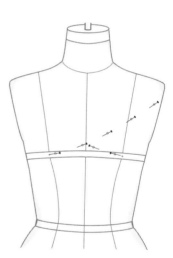

Figure 5.52

Preparing Muslin

Figure 5.53

See pages 26 and 27 for muslin required and double the width.

Draw straight grain in center of muslin, and fold. Mark 4″ down. Measure down for bust level, and square a line.

The neckline is not cut out.

Draping Steps

Figure 5.54

Place straight grainline of the muslin on the centerline of the form. Pin. The dart excess is noted as A and B for clarity of instruction.

Slash center front to waist.

Figure 5.55

Drape excess (A) upward around the bust and along the stitchline of the form to the shoulder/Princess on the right side. Pencil rub the pin-marks to transfer the styleline to the muslin. Trim 1/2″ of the rub line.

Crossmark dart legs. The crossgrain is lifted in the process.

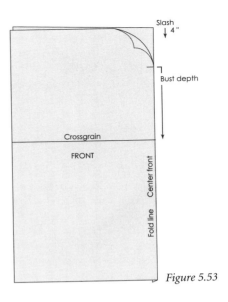

Figure 5.53

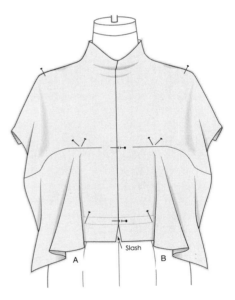

Figure 5.54

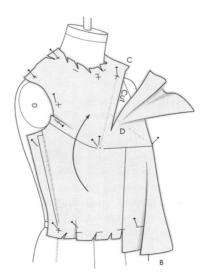

Figure 5.55

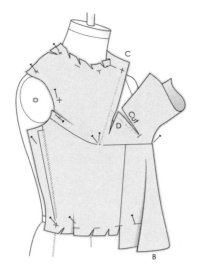

Figure 5.56

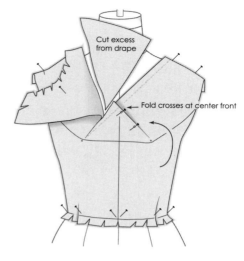

Figure 5.57

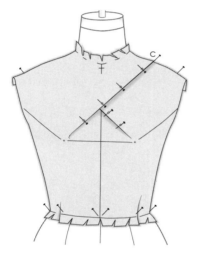

Figure 5.58

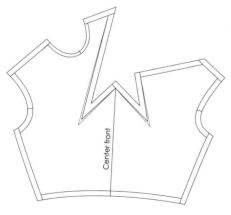

Figure 5.59

Figure 5.56

Slash to within 1/2″ of the intersecting dart leg (D), ending above the bust point.

Figure 5.57

Peel back muslin from neck area.

Drape excess upward around the bust and along the stitchline of the form to the shoulder Princess line.

Fold excess into the intersecting dart (D), and trim excess. The crossgrain is lifted in the process.

Figure 5.58

Fold dart (C). Pin to finish the drape.

Finished Pattern

Figure 5.59

Mark dart points 1/2″ from bust points and draw dart legs.

Compare the pattern shape with that of the design.

Asymmetric Darts

Designs that are created with seamlines that cross the centerline of the garment are referred to as asymmetric darts (garments that differ on each side of center). The front drape is an example of how the dart is utilized in creating asymmetric designs (Figure 5.60).

Design Analysis

The squared neckline is pin-marked approximately 3″ below neck and ends at the Princess (can vary). Pin-marks are placed to form a square armhole that is level with the armhole depth at side seam.

Asymmetric designs require a full front muslin.

The waist dart excess from both bust points is draped to the side waist and completed as tuck darts. An attached bow completes the bodice.

Preparing Form

Figure 5.61
Pin-mark the square neckline and armhole.

Preparing Muslin

See pages 26 and 27.

Cut the muslin twice the width to cover the front form.

Draw straight grain at the centerline.

Figure 5.60

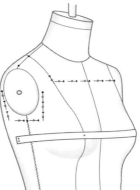

Figure 5.61

Figure 5.62

Figure 5.63

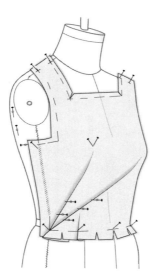

Figure 5.64

Draping Steps

Figure 5.62

Place the center straight grain at center of the form and smooth muslin over both shoulders.

Pin centerline, bust points, and shoulders.

Slash up to waist at center. The waist dart excess hangs from both bust points.

Figure 5.63

Instruction applies to both sides of center.

Pencil rub pin-marks of the square neckline.

Smooth and slash muslin along square neckline. Pencil rub pin-marks at the square armhole. Trim excess.

Smooth muslin along side seams. Crossmark and pencil rub.

Waist Dart A

Drape the dart excess to the side waist.

Pin and mark the foldline of the dart and side waist. Pin.

Waist Dart B

Figure 5.64

Smooth, slash, and mark along the waistline, as the dart is draped across the form to the side waist corner.

Pin and mark the foldline of the dart.

Crossmark tuck lengths.

Trim excess from waistline.

Remove drape from the form and true.

To complete the design, drape a basic back with squared neckline.

Finished Pattern

Figure 5.65

The excess of the darts can be trimmed to within 1/2″ seams to avoid the bulk when darts end at one location. The fullness remains to form the tuck dart.

Compare the pattern shape with that of the design.

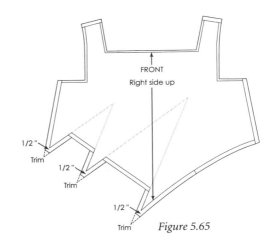

Figure 5.65

Multiple Darts

The dart excess can be divided into multiples for design variations (Figure 5.66). The excess can be equally or unequally shared as stitched darts, tuck darts, or pleats. Armhole ease is optional for sleeveless designs.

Design Analysis

The excess from the waist dart is divided equally among 3 tuck darts. The center dart is directed to the bust point. The first and third darts are spaced about 1″ from the bust point and 3/4″ apart at the waist.

Preparing Muslin

See pages 26 and 27.

Draping Steps

Figure 5.67

Pin the fold to centerline. Cross pin the bust point.

Smooth muslin from center to the front waist Princess line. Trim excess.

Smooth, mark, slash, and trim muslin around neck, shoulder, and mid-armhole and mark armhole depth.

Figure 5.66

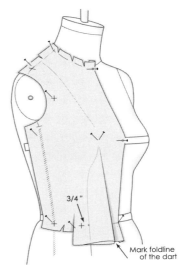

Figure 5.67

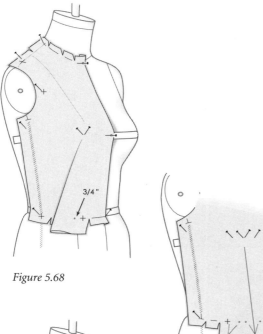

Figure 5.68

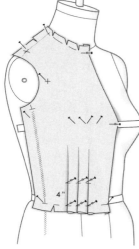

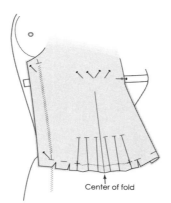

Figure 5.69

Figure 5.70

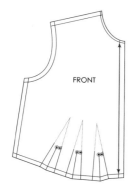

FRONT

Figure 5.71

Figure 5.72

Pencil rub side seam and crossmark side waist. Pin.

Pin 1/4″ ease at waistline.

Dot mark at Princess, and crossmark 3/4″ out from the dot for dart leg.

Figure 5.68

Dot mark at Princess line and crossmark 3/4″ out from the dot for dart leg.

Figure 5.69

Measure from crossmark to crossmark. Subtract 1 1/4″ from this measurement (allowance for dart space). The remaining excess is divided among the three tuck darts.

To help direct the dart excess, place pins approximately 1″ out from each side of the bust point.

Figure 5.70

Pin the excess as normal darts in the direction of the pin-marks.

Draw a guideline across each dart 4″ to 5″ up from the waist and at waist.

Pencil rub each dart.

Remove from form. Do not unpin darts.

Trace across the pinned darts at waistline.

Figure 5.71

Remove from form, unpin the darts, and true the dart legs. Return to form.

Figure 5.72

Notch each dart leg.

Punch/circle 1/8″ in from stitchline and 1/2″ down from the finish tuck.

Compare the shape of the pattern with that of the design.

Dart Excess Draped to Armhole Banding

A variety of insets were created using the excess of the dart as dart equivalents (gathers, pleats, and three radiating darts). Prototypes for related designs are illustrated (Figure 5.73).

Design Analysis

The bodice is held by a banding that encircles the front and back armhole. The depth at center front and back neck is about 3″. The excess is draped level with the mid-armhole and is divided equally among three darts radiating toward and away from the bust mound.

Preparing Form

Figure 5.74

Pin-mark the inset banding a width of approximately 1 3/4″. The banding is parallel with the curve of the front, and back armhole.

Pin-mark front and back necklines.

Preparing Muslin

Cut 2 pieces 12″ × 16″ for front and back bodice and allow 1″ for a foldback.

Cut 2 lengths 8″ × 12″ for front and back banding. Draw straight grain through centers of each length.

Draping Steps

Figure 5.75

Place the straight grain of the muslin to the armhole allowing sufficient fabric at the shoulder, and the side seam.

Smooth, slash, and pencil rub the pin-marking of the front armhole banding.

Figure 5.73

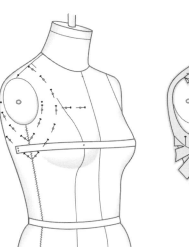

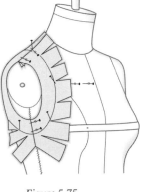

Figure 5.75

Figure 5.74

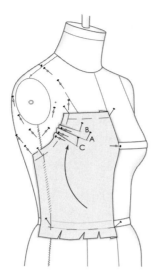

Figure 5.76

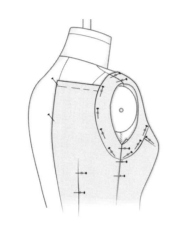

Figure 5.77

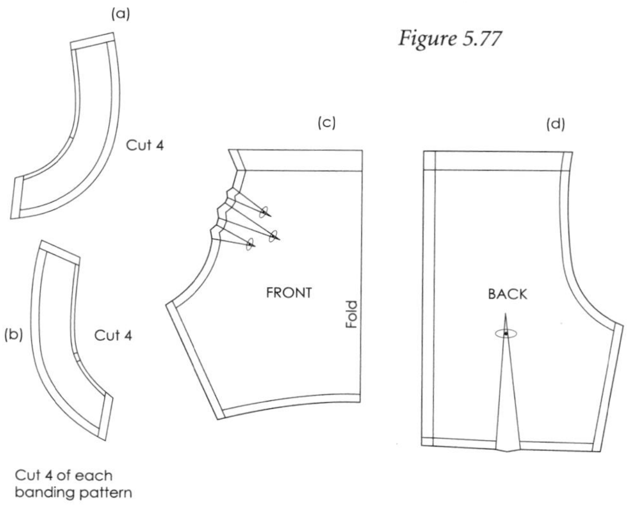

(a)

Cut 4

(b)   Cut 4

Cut 4 of each
banding pattern

Figure 5.78

(c)

FRONT

Fold

(d)

BACK

Repeat for the back drape.

Pin together to match seams.

Remove drape, and true seamlines.

Figure 5.76

Pin the fold of the muslin to the centerline 1″ up from the pin-marks of the neckline.

Smooth the muslin across the bust to the armhole banding.

Smooth the muslin 1 1/4″ down the armhole band. Pin and mark for dart leg.

Smooth the muslin along the waist and side seam and along the inset.

Pencil rub the outline of the design. Trim excess.

The excess is divided and pinned into three radiating darts spaced approximately 3/8″ apart at the seam and 3/4″ apart at dart points.

Figure 5.77

Pin the fold of the muslin 1″ up from the pin-marks of the neckline.

Drape the back to the pin-marks of the armhole band and pencil rub.

Drape a back waist dart.

Pin the armhole banding to the front and back bodice.

Remove drape and true patterns. For guide to completing the patterns, see pages 35 to 39.

Finished Pattern

Figure 5.78

The banding should be self-faced. Cut four of each.

Compare the pattern shapes with that of the design.

Dart with Gathered Leg

Designs with fullness in greater amounts than that which can be provided by the dart excess will require added fabric when draping the garment. The dart excess is included with the added fullness only if the excess is directed to the bust. Fullness directed away from the bust will not include the dart excess (Figure 5.79).

Added fullness can be draped as gathers, pleats, and flares. Fabric is also added when the silhouette of the garment is designed beyond the dimensions of the figure.

There are three distinct types of added: (a) fullness draped on one side of the garment, (b) fullness draped in equal amounts on both sides of the garment, and (c) fullness draped in unequal amounts on both sides of the garment.

Figure 5.79

Design Analysis

Question: Where is the dart excess located, and how is the excess utilized?

Answer: The excess is utilized as a dart. The dart is directed to the center front approximately 3″ to 4″ below bust level.

Question: Does the design require added fullness?

Answer: Yes. Gathers are draped on one side of the dart leg and at center front. The dart excess is not a part of the added fullness.

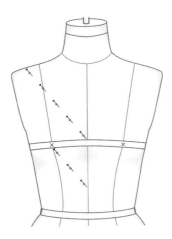

Figure 5.80

Preparing Form

Figure 5.80

Pin-mark from bust point ending 3″ up from center front waist for the dart location.

Pin-mark V neckline so that the line is parallel with the dart. Adjust dart leg if necessary.

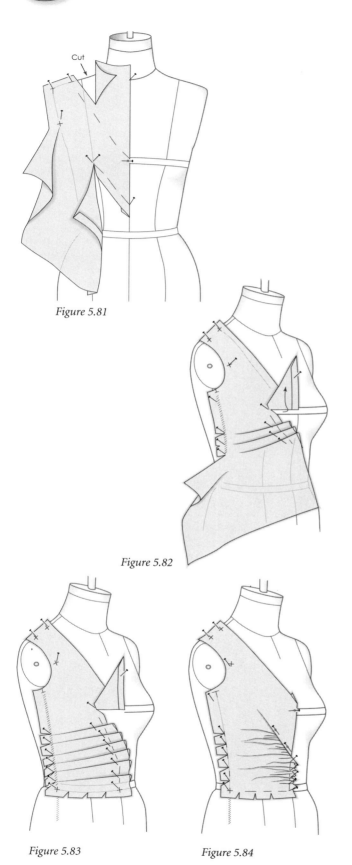

Figure 5.81

Figure 5.82

Figure 5.83   *Figure 5.84*

Preparing Muslin

See pages 26 and 27.

Add 8″ to length and 5″ to width.

Fold 1″ on straight grain.

Draping Steps

Figure 5.81

Pin the fold to center front neck.

Pencil rub pin-marks of the V neckline, and the pin-marks from bust to center front.

Trim neckline, and cut to bust point allowing 1/2″ for seams.

Drape the shoulderline to mid-armhole.

Figure 5.82

Smooth, trim, and mark muslin to the armhole depth, and about 4″ down the side seam.

Peel back the front dart leg, and pin.

Slash to the seam, and pin.

Lift the crossgrain, and fold a 3/4″ pleat (3/8″ on fold).

Pin past the pin-marks of the dart leg.

Repeat the process about every inch smoothing the muslin along the side seam between the slash points.

Figure 5.83

Continue the process to the waistline.

Pencil rub pin-marks from bust point to center-line and trim.

Figure 5.84

Pin dart legs. At the same time distribute fullness of the gathers as evenly as possible. For gathers that join each other (the centerline below the dart legs), it will be necessary to secure by stitching a tape to the seamline that is the length of the section from point of dart legs to waistline.

Draw a pencil line across the gathers on the pin-marks of the dart leg. The line will be blended at the time of trueing.

Remove the drape and true. To complete the pattern, see pages 35 to 39.

Finished Pattern

Figure 5.85

Compare the pattern shape with that of the design.

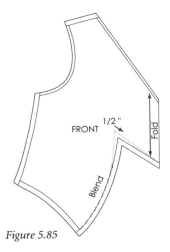

Figure 5.85

Bodice Styles

6

O f the many bodice stylelines, four are prototypes: the Princess, armhole Princess, the empire, and panel stylelines. They are the foundations for related features. Each of the prototypes is also foundation for the drape of the torso (dress), and jacket in later chapters. Other bodice styles included in this chapter are the surplice, off-shoulder, and halter. Bodice stylelines when attached to a skirt create a dress, and when attached to pants create jumpsuits.

Classic Princess Drape

Figure 6.1

Design Analysis

Figure 6.1

The styleline follows the princess line over the bust and shoulder blade of the front and back form.

Question: Where is the dart excess, and how is the excess utilized?

Answer: The dart excess is shared between the waist and shoulder at the princess line. The dart legs (excess trimmed) are the underlying control of stylelines crossing over the bust point and shoulder blade (dart equivalent). The straight grain of the side panels is perpendicular to the waistline.

Preparing Muslin

Figure 6.2

Measure length, and add 3″.

Measure centerline to bust point, and add 3″.

Measure bust point to side seam, and add 3″.

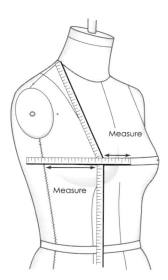

Figure 6.2

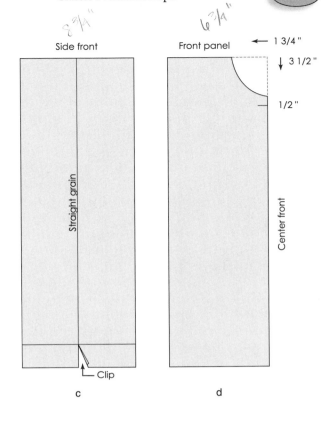

Back panel   Side back   Side front   Front panel

2″ →   1 3/4″   7″   2 3/8″   8 3/4″   6 3/4″   ← 1 3/4″

3 1/2″ ↓   ↓ 3 1/2″

1/2″   1/2″

Center back   Straight grain   Straight grain   Center front

21″8″   20 3/4″

Clip   Clip

a   b   c   d

Figure 6.3   fold back 1″ CF & CB

Figure 6.3

Follow illustration for the cutout necklines.

Draw straight grain in center of side panels.

Draw a line 1″ up from bottom of side panels, and slash.

Draping Steps

Figure 6.4

Place fold of straight grain to centerline. Pin.

Smooth, slash and mark around neckline, shoulder, waist, and Princess line.

Mark notches 2″ up and down from bust point. Notches control distribution of bust ease.

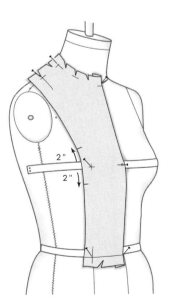

2″

2″

Figure 6.4

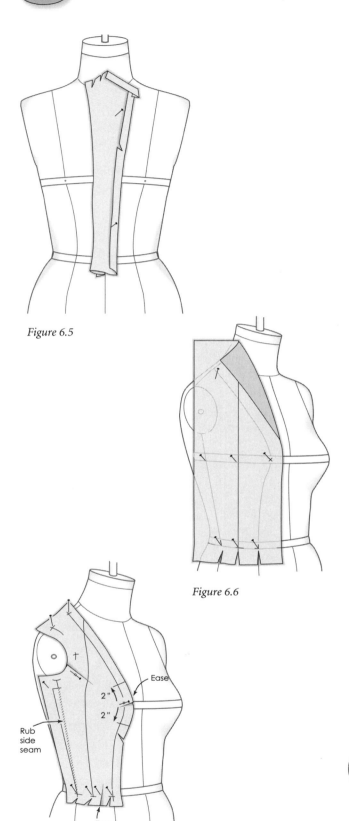

Figure 6.5

Figure 6.6

Figure 6.7

Figure 6.5

Peel back and pin or remove from form making room for the side panel.

Side Front Panel

Figure 6.6

Place side panel on form so that straight grain is centered and perpendicular to waistline. Pin.

Figure 6.7

Smooth, slash and mark muslin along the Princess line, shoulder, and waist.

Excess will appear at bust point. Pin excess. Mark 2″ up and down from pinned excess for ease distribution.

Smooth muslin around armhole, and pin 1/4″ ease (1/8″ on fold).

Mark armhole depth.

Pencil rub side seam. Allow 1/2″ for ease.

Pin 1/4″ ease at waist, and mark side waist.

Back

Figure 6.8

Place fold of straight grain at the centerline. Pin.

Smooth, slash, and mark muslin around neckline, shoulder, waist, and Princess line. Pin.

Peel back or remove for side panel drape.

Side Back Panel

Figure 6.9

Place side panel on form so that straight grain is centered and perpendicular to waistline.

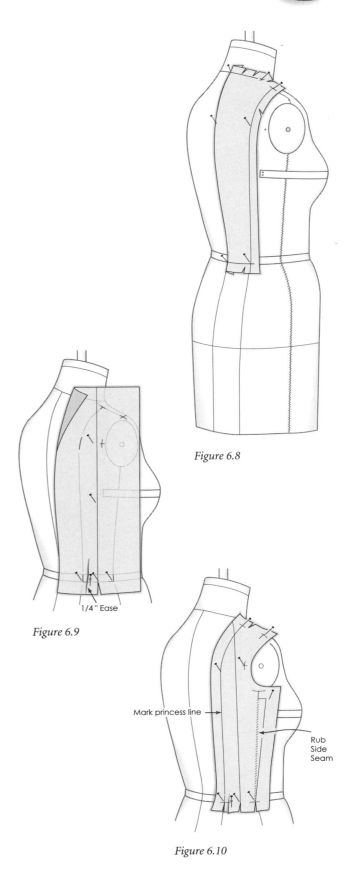

Figure 6.8

Figure 6.10

Smooth muslin and mark along princess line, shoulder, and waist. Some excess may appear at the shoulder blade area. It may be eased into the back panel.

Pin 1/4″ ease at waist. Mark and pin.

Pencil rub along side seam. Mark armhole depth and side seam ease (3/4″ ease for sleeved garments and 1/2″ ease for sleeveless designs).

1/4″ Ease

Figure 6.9

Mark princess line →

Rub Side Seam

Figure 6.10

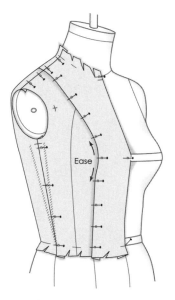

Figure 6.11

Figure 6.11

Crease-fold the seam of the front panel and lap over the side front Princess line.

Spread ease between the marks.

Repeat for back and side back panels.

Crease-fold shoulder and side seam of the front panels. Lap and pin to back.

Check fit of the armhole and alignment of the drape (see pages 33–35).

Remove from the form. True and stitch, or transfer to paper first to recheck fit.

To complete the patterns, see pages 59 and 60.

Finished Pattern

Figure 6.12

Compare the pattern shape with that of the design.

For facing guide, see Chapter 16.

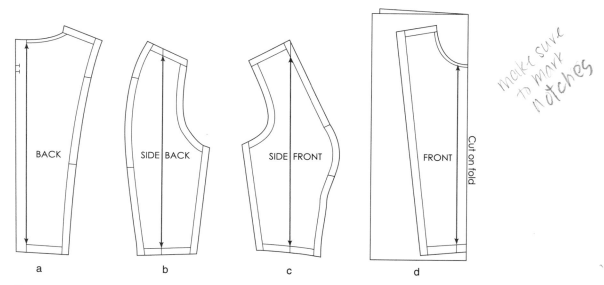

Figure 6.12

Design Variations

Figure 6.13

The following design projects are based on the princess foundation (styleline crossing the bust point). Apply the principle of dart manipulation by transferring the dart excess and sharing the excess among the locations. The trimmed dart legs provide the styleline.

Figure 6.13

Armhole Princess

Design variations based on the draping procedures of the armhole princess follow the drape project.

Design Analysis

The styleline follows the princess line from waist to bust point and curves up to the mid-armhole (Figure 6.14).

Question: Where is the dart excess, and how is the excess utilized?

Answer: The dart excess is shared between the waist at the princess line and the mid-armhole. The dart legs (excess trimmed) are the underlying control of stylelines crossing over the bust point (dart equivalent). The straight grain of the side panels are perpendicular to the waistline.

Figure 6.14

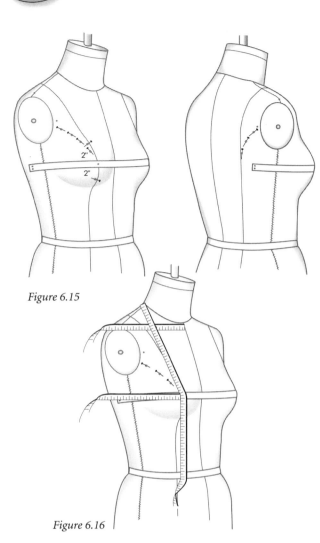

Figure 6.15

Figure 6.16

Preparing Form

Figure 6.15

Place pins or style tape curved from the bust to mid-armhole of the front and back form.

Measuring the Form

Figure 6.16

Length: Full length, plus 4″.

Width: Across shoulder, plus 3″.

Side panel:

Width: Bust point to side seam, plus 3″.

Length: Cut 4″ less than full length.

Preparing Muslin

Figure 6.17

Cut muslin to measurements given.

Cut front and back necklines.

Draw straight grainlines through center of side panels.

Fold 1″ along straight grain. Press without steam.

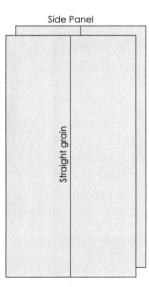

1 3/4″   Back Panel

1 ″

1/2 ″

Center back

Side Panel

Straight grain

Front Panel   1 3/4 ″

3 1/2 ″

1/2 ″

Center front

Figure 6.17   a   b   c

Draping Steps

Figure 6.18

Place fold of the straight grain at centerline of the form, and pin.

Allow muslin to bridge the hollow between shoulder tip and bust.

Smooth, mark, pin, and trim muslin.

Pencil rub pin-markings for the armhole princess styleline and continue to waist.

Mark 2″ up and down from bust point for notch placement.

Trim excess from princess line to bust point.

Figure 6.19

Trim excess along styleline.

Mark 2″ up and down from bust point for notch placement.

Figure 6.20

Place side panel on the form with straight grain centered and perpendicular to waistline.

Pencil rub side seam and mark armhole depth and side ease.

Pin 1/4″ (1/8″ on the fold) ease at armhole and waist.

Pencil rub pin-markings for styleline.

Pin ease at the bust mound.

Mark 2″ up and down from bust point for notch placement.

Figure 6.21

Crease-fold and slash seam allowance of the front panel and lap over side panel. Pin. Excess at bust point will be eased in to provide room for the bust.

Peel back the drape, or remove.

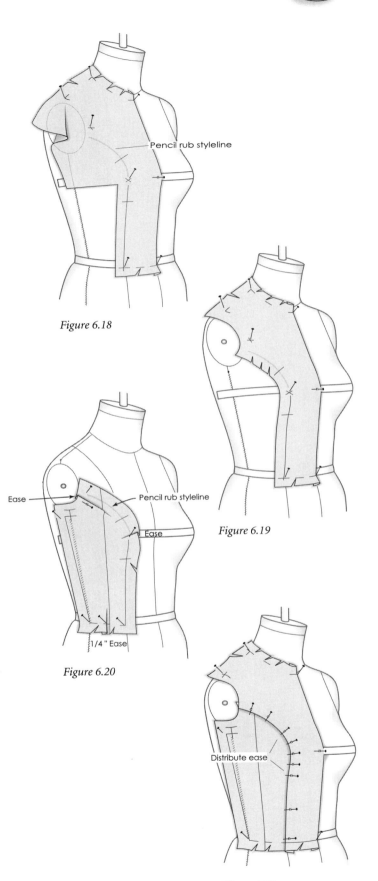

Pencil rub styleline

Figure 6.18

Figure 6.19

Ease

Pencil rub styleline

Ease

1/4″ Ease

Figure 6.20

Distribute ease

Figure 6.21

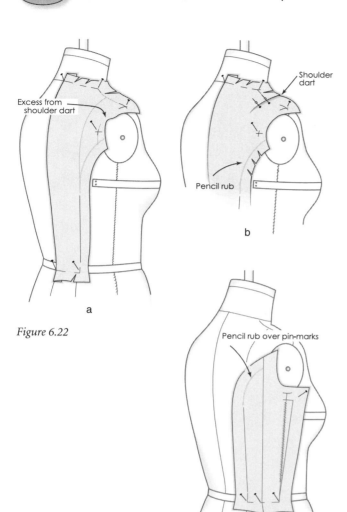

Figure 6.22

Figure 6.23

Figure 6.22

Place fold of the straight grain at centerline. Pin.

Smooth, slash, mark, and pin muslin around neckline and shoulder.

Pencil rub pin-markings of the styleline.

Shoulder Dart

The excess at shoulderline can be distributed among neck, armhole, and shoulder or smoothed to the armhole (slight gap will appear). It can also be pinned as a dart.

Peel back the panel, or remove from the form for the side panel drape.

Figure 6.23

Place side panel on the form with straight grain centered and perpendicular with waist.

Pencil rub pin-marking of the styleline and side seam.

Mark armhole depth and allow 3/4″ ease for sleeved garments or 1/2″ for sleeveless designs.

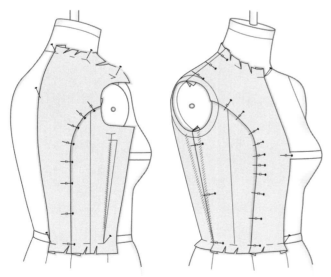

Figure 6.24   *Figure 6.25*

Figure 6.24

Crease-fold and slash seam allowance of the back panel and lap over side panel. Pin.

Figure 6.25

Crease-fold shoulder and side seam of front bodice. Lap over the back panel and pin.

Check fit of the armhole and alignment of the drape (see pages 33–35).

Figure 6.26

Remove drape from the form.

Unpin princess to approximately 2″ of the front and back armhole.

Lay the garment flat before drawing the armholes. (Separated, the armhole would be too difficult to draw.)

True and stitch the bodice or transfer to paper first before the fitting. To complete the pattern, see page 60. For facing guide, see Chapter 16.

Finished Patterns

Figure 6.27

Compare the patterns shape with that of the design.

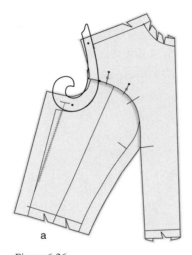

a

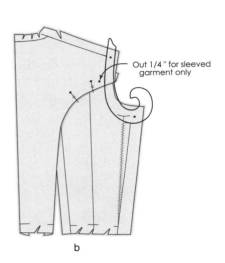

Out 1/4″ for sleeved garment only

b

Figure 6.26

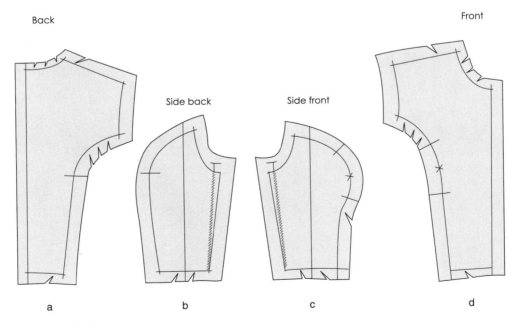

Back

Side back

Side front

Front

a

b

c

d

Figure 6.27 (a-d)

Design Variation on the Armhole Princess: The Basic Empire

The basic empire is a popular foundation and is a prototype for empire design variations. Design variations follow the drape project. The empire foundation introduces the technique of contour draping. Unlike draping garments that bridge the hollows of the figure, the designer/draper smoothes the fabric to fit into the contour of the bust—under, above, and in between where contouring most often occurs. Contouring emphasizes the silhouette of the figure. A careful analysis of designs will direct the draper to areas of the figure requiring contour draping (Figure 6.28 and Figure 6.29).

Design Analysis

The styleline of the classic empire crosses under the bust sloping downward to the center back. The midriff part of the design fits to the body, rather than bridging the hollow area from bust point to waist. The dart excess below the bust can be stitched as a dart or be gathered (dart equivalent). The remaining dart excess of the back is draped as darts at shoulder and above the midriff. The centerlines are straight grain.

Figure 6.28

Figure 6.29

Measuring the Form

Figure 6.30

Use #6 and #17 from the Model Form Measurement Chart.

Measure length, add 5″.

Measure width, add 3″.

Place style tape from center front and gradually slope downward to the center back.

Preparing Muslin

Figure 6.31

Cut muslin and cut out front and back necklines using measurements given.

Fold 1″. Press without steam.

Separate muslin 7″ up from the bottom.

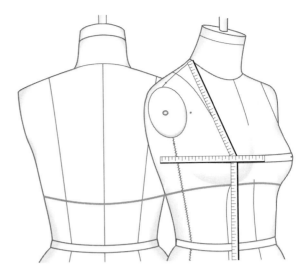

Figure 6.30

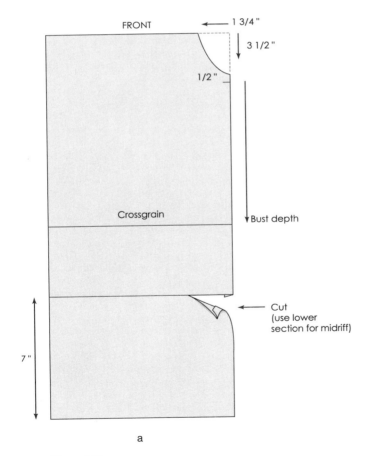

a

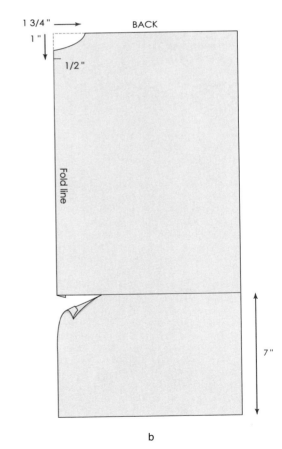

b

Figure 6.31

Draping Steps: Midriff

Figure 6.32

Place fold of the straight grain at centerline. Pin.

Smooth, slash, pin, and mark the muslin.

Pin 1/4″ ease at waist (1/8″ on fold).

Draw empire styleline, and pencil rub side seam.

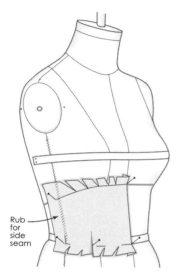

Rub for side seam

Figure 6.32

Figures 6.33

Place fold of straight grain to centerline of form. Pin.

Smooth, slash, mark, and trim muslin around neckline, shoulder, and to mid-armhole.

Pin 1/4″ ease at the armhole. Smooth muslin along the side seam.

Mark armhole depth and pencil rub side seam.

Pin a tentative dart at princess line under bust. The dart intake is greater than the basic dart; this is a result of fitting into the hollow under the bust rather than bridging it.

Draw the empire styleline and pencil rub side seam (see Figure 6.33a).

The excess can be draped as a dart (see Figure 6.33b) or as gathers. Mark 1″ out from each side of the pinned dart legs to allow space for gathers, if desired (see Figure 6.34).

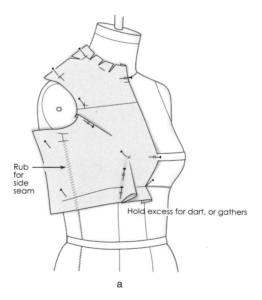

Rub for side seam

Hold excess for dart, or gathers

a

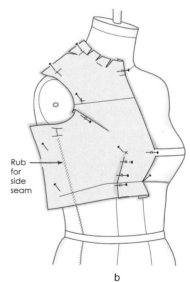

Rub for side seam

b

Figure 6.33

Draping Steps: Gathers

Figure 6.34

Distribute and pin excess as gathers in a space of 2″ (more or less as desired).

Figure 6.35

Crease-fold on the marked styleline of the midriff.

Pin empire styleline to midriff.

Draping Steps: Back Midriff

Figure 6.36

Place fold of straight grain to center back. Pin.

Smooth, slash, trim, mark, and pin muslin around the outline of the form.

Figure 6.37

Place fold of straight grain to center back. Pin.

Smooth muslin around the form. Slash, mark, pin, and trim.

Pin shoulder and back darts.

Mark armhole depth.

Draw empire styleline and pencil rub side seam.

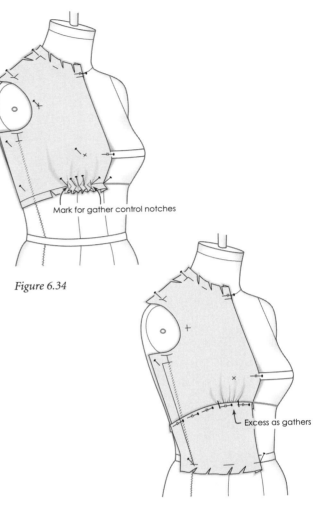

Figure 6.34

Figure 6.35

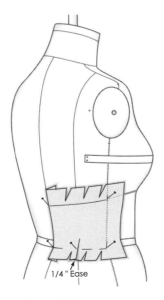

Figure 6.36

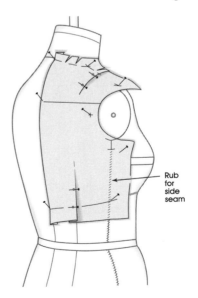

Figure 6.37

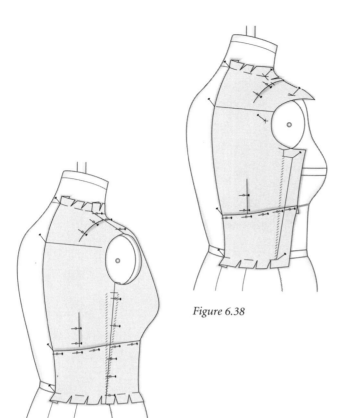

Figure 6.38

Figure 6.39

Figure 6.38

Crease-fold seam of the empire styleline and pin to upper bodice.

Figure 6.39

Crease-fold side seam and shoulder of front bodice and lap over seams of back bodice matching empire stylelines.

Check fit of the armhole and the alignment of the front and back drape (see pages 33–35). Adjust if necessary.

Remove the drape from the form.

Figure 6.40

True the draped patterns and stitch, or transfer to paper for the test fitting. To complete the patterns, see page 60. For facing guide, see Chapter 16.

Compare the pattern shape with that of the design.

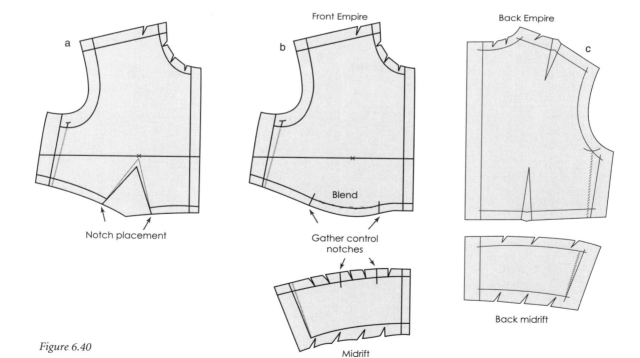

Figure 6.40

Design Variations on the Empire Styleline Foundation

Panel Bodice

The styleline of a traditional panel design does not cross over the bust point. Therefore, excess will radiate from the bust requiring a small dart. The dart intersects with a panel styleline. The dart excess can be gathered or transferred to other locations for design variation. The panel design is a prototype for designs with similar features. Design variations based on the panel design follow the drape project (Figure 6.41 and Figure 6.42).

Design Analysis

The front and back are connected by a side panel that does not have a side seam. The panel styleline does not cross bust point. This leaves part of the dart excess on the front panel.

Question: Where is the dart excess, and how is the excess utilized?

Answer: The excess is draped to intersect with the panel styleline and pinned as a dart. The grain is straight at the centerlines and in the center of the side panel.

Figure 6.41

Figure 6.42

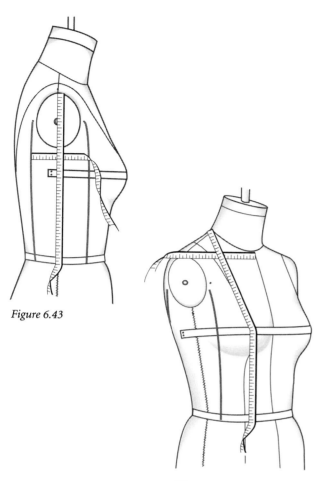

Figure 6.43

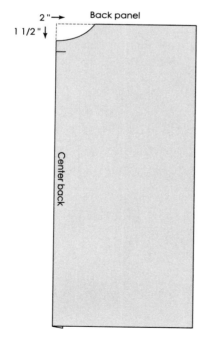

Figure 6.44

Preparing Form

Figure 6.43

Place style tape just below the mid-armhole of the front and back form. Curve the tape slightly outward from the armhole, then straight downward to the waistline. (For design variation the styleline can be of any shape providing that it does not cross the bust point.)

Measuring the Form

Panel (Figure 6.43)
Length, as is.
Width, add 2″.

Figure 6.44
Length, add 3″.
Width, add 3″.

Preparing Muslin

Figure 6.45

Cut muslin and the front and back necklines using measurements given.

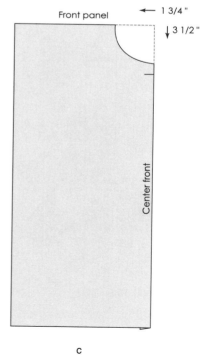

Figure 6.45

a

b

c

Draping Steps: Front

Figure 6.46

Place fold of straight grain to centerline. Pin.

Slash, mark, trim, and pin as muslin is smoothed around the outline of the form. The excess hanging from the bust mound is lifted raising the crossgrain. The excess is draped to the side bust and folded into a french dart with excess toward the waistline.

Draw panel styleline.

Peel back or remove for back drape.

Draping Steps: Back

Figure 6.47

Place fold of straight grain to center back. Pin.

Slash, mark, trim, and pin as muslin is draped to the styleline.

Draw panel styleline.

Peel back or remove.

Draping Steps

Figure 6.48

Place slit of the panel at bottom of the side seam at waist, with straight grain pinned on side seam.

Mark armhole depth, and measure out from straight grain for side ease—1/2″ (front) and 3/4″ (back) or 1/2″ if sleeveless.

Figure 6.49

Fold ease allowance marks together at the straight grain guide. Pin.

Pin 1/4″ ease (1/8″ on the fold) on each side of centerline at waist.

Draw panel stylelines.

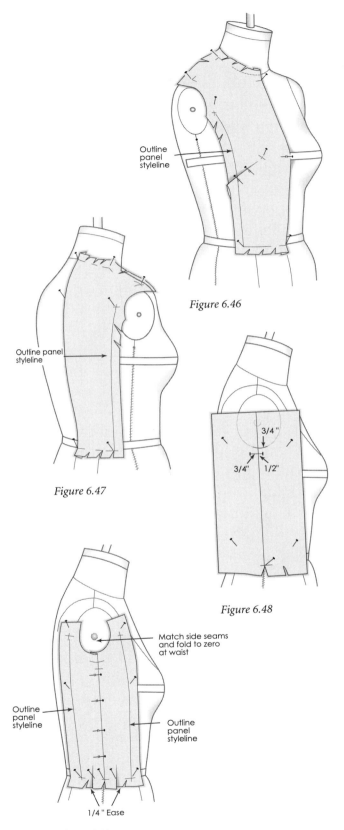

Figure 6.46

Figure 6.47

Figure 6.48

Figure 6.49

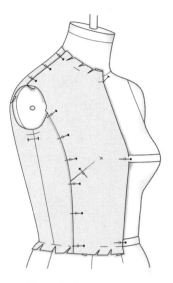

Figure 6.50

Figure 6.50

Crease-fold seam allowance of the front and back panels. Lap over seamlines of the panels.

Check the fit of the armhole and the alignment of the centerline (see pages 33–35).

Figure 6.51

Remove muslin and unpin the panel without separating the panels around the armhole.

Draw the shape of the front armhole and neckline.

Figure 6.52

Draw the shape of the back armhole and neckline.

True remaining pattern and stitch, or transfer to paper first for the test fitting.

To complete the pattern, see page 60.
For facing guide, see Chapter 16.

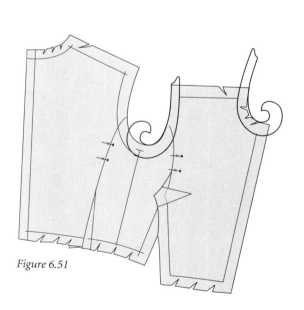

Figure 6.51

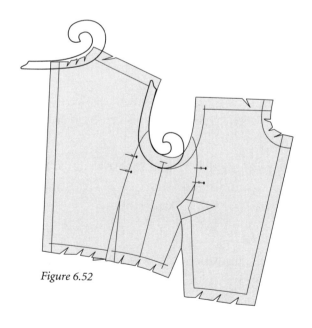

Figure 6.52

Finished Pattern

Figure 6.53

Compare the pattern shape with that of the design.

Design Variations

Figure 6.54

Each design is based on the panel drape.

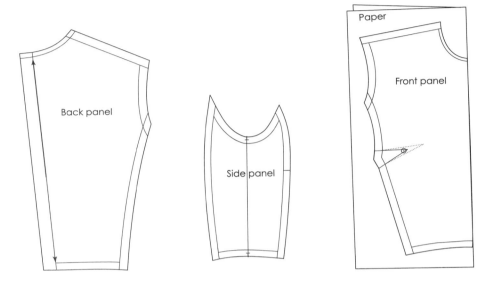

Figure 6.53

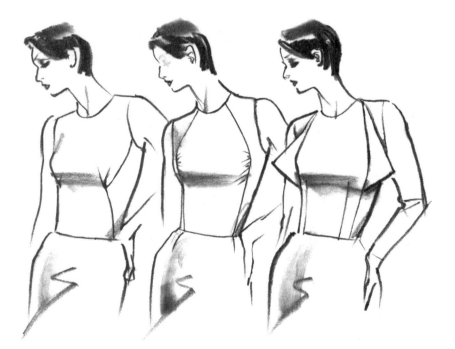

Figure 6.54

Halter Stylelines

A halter style is described as having part of the shoulder, and armhole cut away from the garment exposing the shoulders of the figure. The halter is anchored around the neckline with a variety of design options: as a jewel neckline, a V neck, built-up neck, banded, or with straps; and can be secured with buttons, hooks, ties, or drawstring. The dart excess can be used to create gathers, pleats, style darts, flare, or other combinations. The back can be designed to the neckline, or cut low (Figures 6.55 and 6.56).

Design Analysis

As shown in Design 1, the V neckline of the halter is created when the centerline of the front is tied at the back neck. The halter styleline crosses the side seam approximately 3″ below the arm plate and ends approximately 5″ up from the center back waist. Center back is extended 3/4″ for button/button- holes. The dart excess is draped toward the side seam and stitched as a tuck dart. The back is cut low. Finishing options: Tie can be folded and stitched 6″ to finish the ends or trimmed and curved. To finish, narrow facings can cover the remaining raw edges, or the raw edges can be overlocked and stitched back or lined.

Design 1

Figure 6.55

Design 2

Figure 6.56

Halter with V Neck

Preparing Form

Figure 6.57

Use style tape or pins to indicate the styleline of the halter.

Preparing Muslin

Measure length at shoulder/neck to waist, and add 13″.

Measure across bust, and add 3″.

Measure width and length of the back, and add 5″.

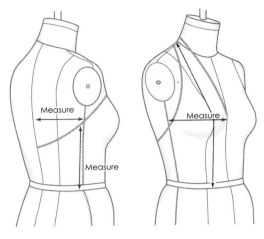

Figure 6.57

Front

Figure 6.58

Cut muslin and draw a straight grainline 1/2″ in from the straight grain at the muslin edge.

Follow measurements given for length of A, width of B, and lengths of C and E. Mark.

Square a 4 1/2″ line from A to D.

From D draw a line to E, and curve a line to C.

Cut away unneeded fabric.

Back

Draw a straight grain 3 1/4″ in from muslin edge.

Fold 2 1/2″, and press without steam.

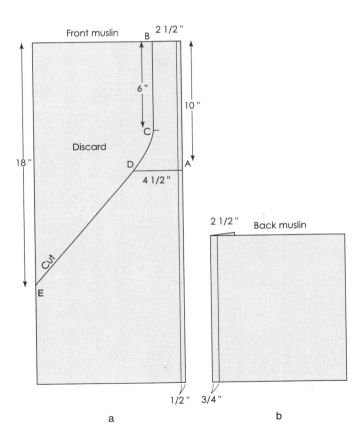

Figure 6.58

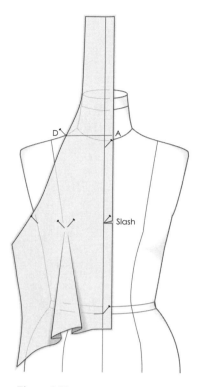

Figure 6.59

Draping Steps

Figure 6.59

Pin the muslin on the form with the straight grainline on center.

Pin D at shoulder tape.

Slash in at center front at bust level.

Mark center waist.

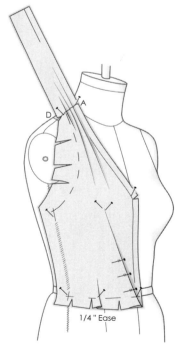

Figure 6.60

Figure 6.60

Remove holding pin at center front neck at A, and move the muslin to the style tape at neck (gathers will appear). Pin.

Smooth, mark, and slash muslin along the halter style tape. Pin.

Pencil rub side seam and mark the side waist.

Smooth, mark, slash, and add 1/4″ ease at waistline.

The dart excess is draped to the center front waist. The excess is folded toward the side seam, marked, and pinned as a tuck dart.

Figure 6.61

Bring tie to the back. Pin.

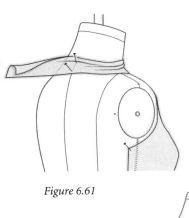

Figure 6.61

Figure 6.62 (back)

Place the straight grainline 1″ below the waist at the center back, and pin.

Smooth, mark, slash, and add 1/4″ ease to the muslin along the waist.

Pencil rub side seam.

Mark styleline, and trim excess.

Mark locations for button and buttonholes.

Remove drape from the form, and true. Stitch muslin, or transfer to paper first for the test fitting. To complete the pattern, see page 60.

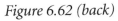

Mark locations
for button/buttonhole

Figure 6.62

Finished Pattern

Figure 6.63

Mark for button/buttonhole placements.

Facing is noted by broken lines.

Compare the patterns shapes with that of the design.

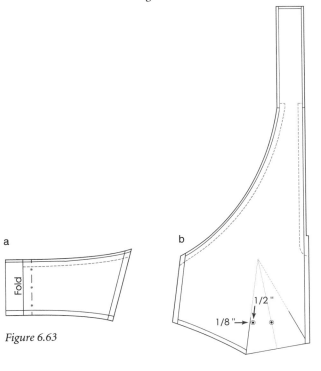

a

b

Fold

1/2 ″

1/8 ″→

Figure 6.63

Torso Halter

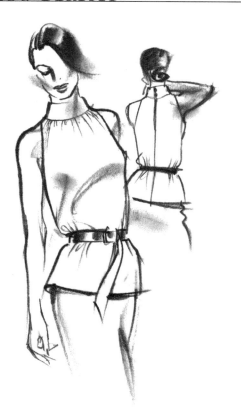

Design Analysis

The halter design extends 5″ below the waistline, with a 4″ opening at the sides. The dart excess is shared with the neckline as gathers spaced approximately 2″ apart. The opening for the head entry is approximately 5″ made down the center of the back neck. A banded turtle collar is draped around the neckline. Loops and buttons are suggested for closure. A separate tie gathers the waist. The torso halter is based on the torso foundation (see page 264).

Preparing Form

Figure 6.64

Pin-mark the halter styleline 1/2″ from neck at shoulder and 5″ below the waist.

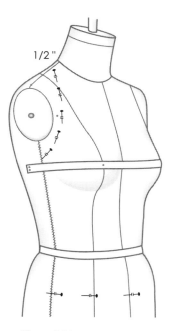
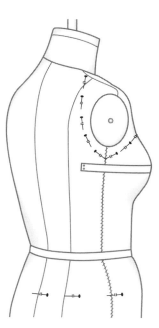

1/2 ″

Figure 6.64

Preparing Muslin

See page 27.

Add 6″ to the length of the back and front measurements.

Measure around neckline, and record.

Figure 6.65 (front and back)

Cut muslin to the measurement given. Square a line 6″ up from muslin edge for waist level.

Press fold 1″ on both front and back muslin.

Draping Steps: Turtle Neck Band

Figure 6.65

Use neck measurement, plus 2″.

Cut bias strip 3″ wide for collar.

Cut bias for button loops.

Figure 6.66 (back)

Place fold of the straight grain at center back 1″ below pin-marks at hip. Pin and mark.

Smooth crossgrain along pin-marks at hip, and pin 1/4″ ease (1/8″ on fold). Continue smoothing muslin to side seam. Pin.

Mark 1/2″ for ease at side hip.

Smooth muslin upward along side seam and continue to the shoulder. Mark, and slash muslin around the neckline.

Mark shoulder.

Pencil rub halter styleline to side seam.

Add 1/2″ ease at armhole.

Trim excess.

Remove the drape from the form, and true.

Figure 6.65

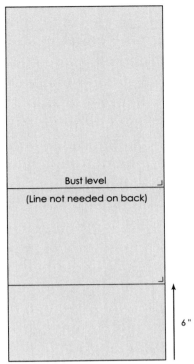

Bust level
(Line not needed on back)

6″

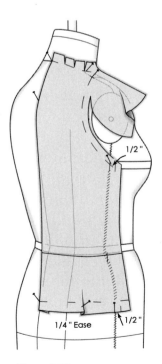

1/2″

1/4″ Ease   1/2″

Figure 6.66

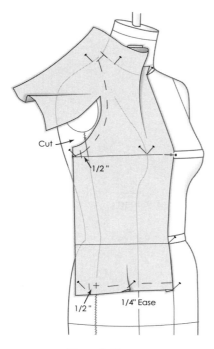

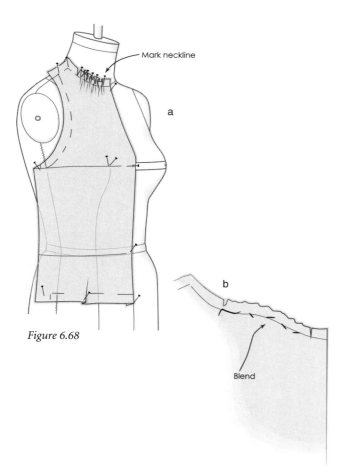

Figure 6.67

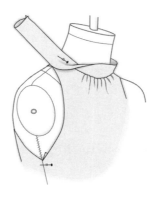

Figure 6.68

Figure 6.67 (front)

Place fold of the straight grainline to the centerline 1″ below pin-marks. Pin and mark.

The crossgrain is draped along pin-marks at the hipline. Pin 1/4″ ease (1/8″ on fold). Continue smoothing muslin to side seam. Pin.

Mark 1/2″ for ease at side hip.

The crossgrain is lifted as the dart excess is draped to the neckline.

Pencil rub pin-marks of the halter styleline.

Add 1/2″ for ease at the side seam. Trim excess.

Figure 6.68

Allow a 2″ space for gathering the excess. The gathers start 1″ from the center front neck mark.

Draw a guideline around the pinned gathers of the neck.

Remove the drape from form and draw a blending line across the random markings (Figure 6.68b), and true.

Run two rows of gathering stitches; pull the threads to gather. Stitch to back bodice drape.

Figure 6.69

Pin bias band around the neck stretching slightly. Trim excess from the turtle collar allowing for seams.

To complete the patterns, see page 60.

Figure 6.69

Finished Pattern

Figure 6.70

Allow 1/2″ to 1″ for the fold back of the side slit.

Trace facing patterns as indicated by the broken lines.

Mark notches for loops.

Compare the pattern shape with that of the design.

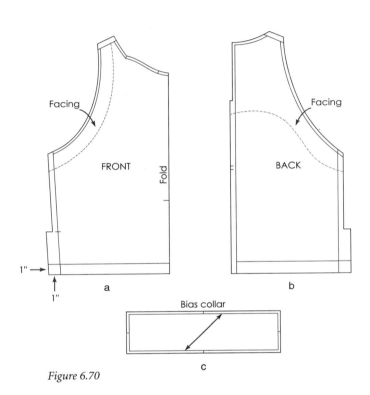

Figure 6.70

Surplice

A surplice design has two fronts that cross each other on the way to the opposite side. The sides may be identical or different. The surplice can be designed to be attached to a skirt, pant, or separate, as a top. The excess from the waist dart can be utilized as gathers, pleats, or as stylelines (Figure 6.71).

The surplice styleline can be cut on straight grain, with the rest of the design draped on the bias. However, the garment can also be draped with the straight grain at the centerline of the form causing the styleline of the surplice to be on the bias. A facing would be cut with the straight grain running lengthwise to hold the bias from stretching. A variation is based on the halter drape (see page 112).

Figure 6.71

Design Analysis

The right side drapes across the front to the left side on the straight grain. The dart excess is draped as a pleat first, and then gathers. The left side crosses underneath to the right side on the straight grain. The dart is pinned to follow the contour of the bust, and the excess is cut away. The neckline of the back bodice is cut approximately 2″ below the center back neck (see Figure 6.71).

Preparing Form

Figure 6.72

Front

Remove bridge band to allow for contouring between the busts.

Place pinheads 1″ from shoulder tips and 2″ up from the side waist on the opposite side of the form.

Back

Place pins from shoulder pin mark curving to 1 1/2″ below center back.

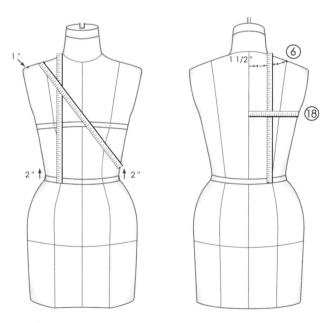

Figure 6.72

Preparing Muslin

Front: Measure the princess at shoulder to pinhead at side seam, and add 5″.

Measure the shoulder/neck to waist, and add 3″.

Back: Measure the shoulder/neck to waist, and add 3″.

Measure across the back to side, and add 3″.

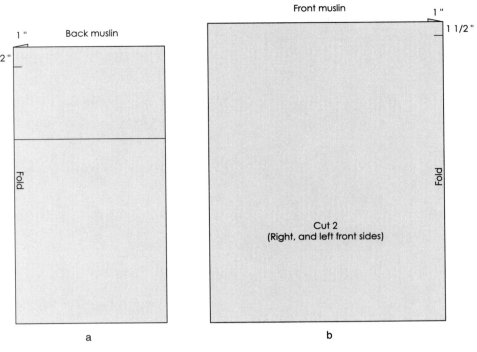

Figure 6.73

Figure 6.73 (front and back)

Fold and press 1″ on the straight grain.

Draping Steps: Front (Right to Left side)

Figure 6.74

Pin the fold of the straight grain at shoulder/princess (crossing just below the bust point) to the pinhead at the side seam. A pleat is folded at the pin-mark of the side seam.

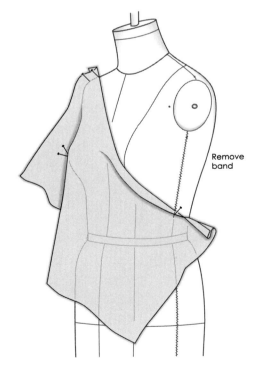

Figure 6.74

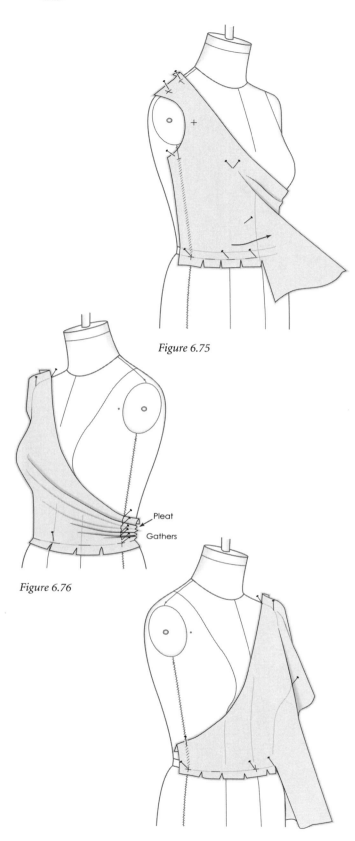

Figure 6.75

Figure 6.76

Figure 6.77

Figure 6.75

Drape, mark, slash, and trim muslin along the shoulder and around the armhole and side seam.

Smooth muslin along the side seam and waist. Drape dart excess toward the left side of the form.

Pencil rub side seam and crossmark side/waist.

Figure 6.76

Smooth the dart excess to the side seam.

Fold a 1″ pleat (2″ underlay) approximately 3/4″ down from the pinhead.

Gather the remaining excess with pins and draw a line at the side seam along the gathers.

Remove the drape. Do not unpin the pleat. Blend across the gather marks and run a tracing wheel across the pleat to transfer the shape of the inside fold.

Draping Steps: Front (Left to Right)

Figure 6.77

Place fold of the straight grain on the left side of the form at shoulder/princess (crossing just below the bust point) to the pinhead of the right side seam. Pin.

Drape, mark, slash, and trim muslin along the shoulder, side seam, and waistline ending at the princess line of the opposite side.

Figure 6.78

Drape, mark, slash, and trim the muslin along the armhole side seam and waist.

Pin a contour dart at the princess line. Trim excess.

Peel back or remove the drape from the form.

Draping Steps: Back Drape

Figure 6.79

The back bodice is draped, with a scoop neckline ending at the pinhead at shoulder.

Remove the drape from the form and true stitch, or transfer to paper first for the test fitting. To complete the pattern, see page 60.

Finished Pattern

Figure 6.80

Front or back patterns that differ in shape on each side are labeled "right side up." The label assists the marker maker in placing the patterns correctly on the fabric for cutting.

Compare the pattern shape with that of the design.

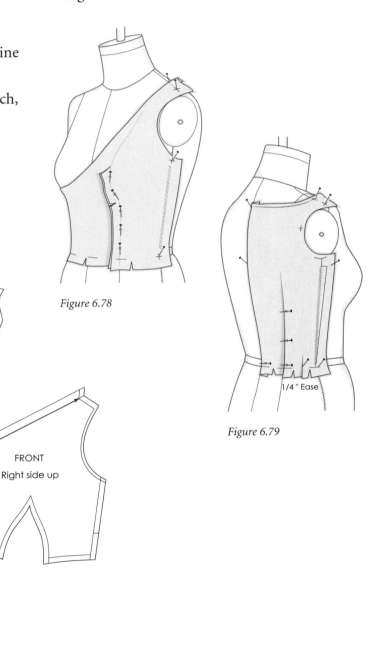

Figure 6.78

1/4" Ease

Figure 6.79

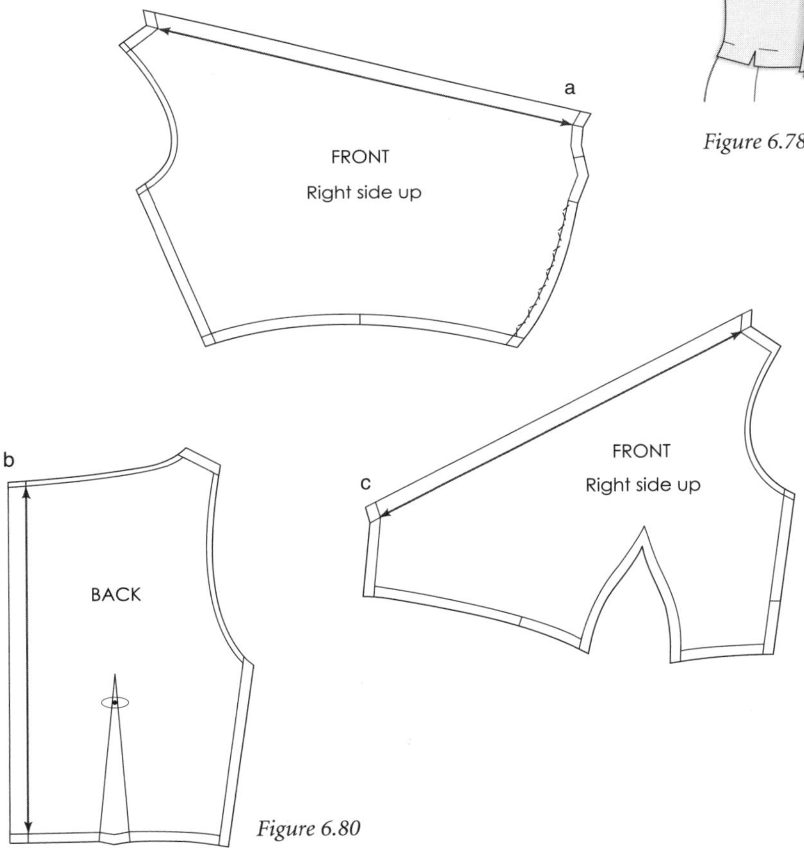

a

FRONT
Right side up

b

BACK

c

FRONT
Right side up

Figure 6.80

Off-Shoulder Designs

Off-shoulder designs reveal part of the shoulder on one side of the figure. The other side may be designed with or without a sleeve, or draped as a kimono (a possible influence by the traditional Buddhist garment called the Kasaya). Off-shoulder designs are created for the bodice, tops, dresses, gowns, and jumpsuits (Figure 6.81). Design 1 is illustrated. Figure 6.82 is a thought problem.

Figure 6.81

Figure 6.82

Design Analysis

Figure 6.82

The straight grain of the fabric lies across the form from the right shoulder to the underarm of the left side, creating an off-shoulder garment. The hemline falls at an angle parallel with the neckline. Side seams are of equal length. The dart on the right side follows the contour of the princess line from under bust to the hemline. The dart excess on the left side is controlled by a double-ended tuck dart pinned at princess. Fullness is released from the inverted box pleat at the waist, and under the bust. The back is buttoned for entry.

Preparing Form

Place pinheads 2″ from shoulder tip (right side) and approximately 2″ below armhole plate at the side seam (left side).

Preparing Muslin

Figure 6.83

Front: Length, 32″. Width, 22″.

Back: Length, 25″. Width, 26″.

Fold 1″ on the straight grain.

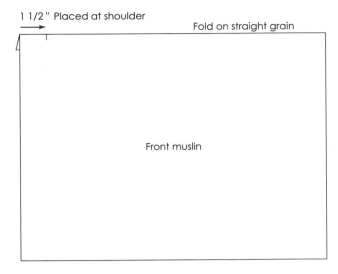

1 1/2 ″ Placed at shoulder

Fold on straight grain

Front muslin

Figure 6.83

Draping Steps

Figure 6.84

Pin fold of the straight grain 1/2″ past pinhead at right shoulder. Drape muslin across the form to pinhead on left side.

Pin and mark at the center of the waist and hem.

Cross-pin bust points.

Smooth muslin over right shoulder. Mark and pin at shoulder tip.

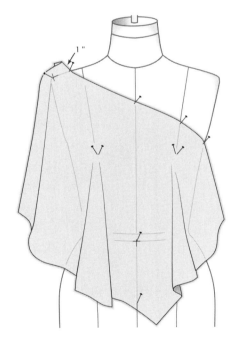

Figure 6.84

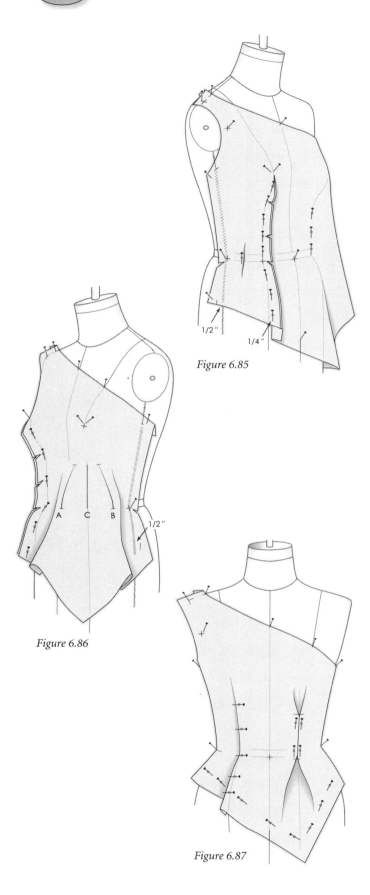

Figure 6.85

Figure 6.86

Figure 6.87

Figure 6.85

Drape, mark, and trim muslin around the armhole. Mark at the pinhead of the armhole depth and at the side seam. Pin.

Right and Left Side:

Smooth the muslin downward on the side seam to the waist. At waist, slash to within 1/2″ of the form (fit adjusted later).

Pin 1/4″ ease (1/8″ on fold) at waist.

Smooth muslin over hipline and pencil rub side seam. Allow 1/2″ for ease at the hip.

Pin a contour dart along the princess line of the form. Do not pin so close to the waistline as to cause stress lines.

Pencil rub the pins that secure the dart. Trim to within 1/2″.

Slash the dart leg at the waist level and under the bust.

Pin the dart excess on the left side from under bust to waist on the princess line. Pencil rub the pin guides.

Draping Steps: Tuck Dart

Figure 6.86

Unpin the tuck dart on the left side.

Open the dart excess. The dart legs are labeled (A) and (B); the center is labeled (C) for clarity.

Figure 6.87

Fold dart legs (A) and (B) to the center (C), and pin each side to the centerline from waist to just under bust.

Unpin the contour dart, and repin with excess folded under.

Pin-mark desired length of the hemline.

Peel drape back, and pin, or remove from form.

Draping Steps: Back Drape

Figure 6.88

Drape the back as one piece, and separate at center back when making the patterns. With exception of the tuck dart, follow instructions given for the front drape.

Trim hemline to match with side seams of the front drape.

Pin front to back, adjust ease allowance at waist, and hip, if necessary.

Remove drape from the form, and true. Stitch or transfer to paper first to test fitting. To complete the pattern, see page 60.

Separate back at centerline. When making the patterns, add 3″ to each side of the center back and 3/4″ for the extension. Fold back.

Finished Pattern

Figure 6.89

Trace facing noted by broken lines.

Compare the pattern shape with that of the design.

Tuck Dart Markings:

Put punch holes 1/8″ in from dart stitchlines, and at center.

Place them 1/2″ from the finish lengths at top and bottom.

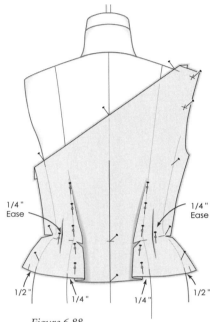

Figure 6.88

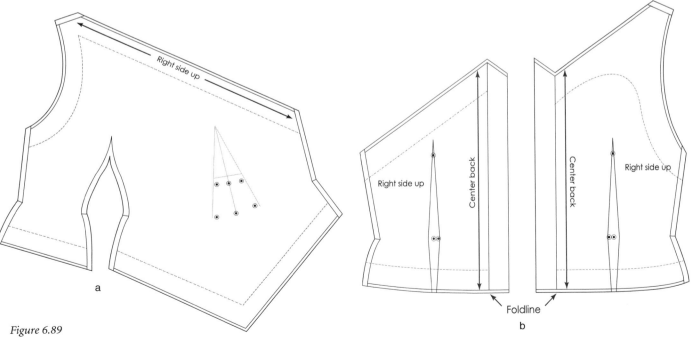

Figure 6.89

Skirts

The silhouettes of skirts (their outer shapes) are used by designers to change the look and direction of fashion. The silhouette of the basic straight line may be radically altered by moving the skirt away from or closer to the figure. The hemlines are constantly changing from mini length to floor length, with the waist at, above, or below the natural waistline (Figure 7.1).

• The sweep of a skirt is the amount of width at its hemline.

• The movement depends on the fullness of fabric in a skirt.

• The break point is the location where the flare of the skirt breaks into fluid movement.

Figure 7.1

Four Skirt Prototypes

The amount of deviation from the basic straight line skirt determines the new silhouette. The four skirt prototypes are identified by their silhouettes and are the basis for an infinite number of designs (Figure 7.2).

Straight, or rectangular, silhouette   fits around the abdomen and buttocks to the widest area of the hip. From there, the skirt hangs straight from hip to hemline.

A-line, or triangle, silhouette   fits around the abdomen and buttocks flaring out at the hemline

increasing the sweep (includes circular and flare skirts).

Peg, or inverted triangle, silhouette   side seam tapers, or the waist area has fullness, creating a peg silhouette.

Bell silhouette   clings to the contour of the hipline at varying distances from the waist before breaking into fluid movement at the hemline.

Straight   A-line   Peg   Bell

Figure 7.2

Waistband

The waistline of a skirt (or pant) may be finished with an attached waistband, facing, or belting. The waistband can be extended for a button/buttonhole (standard 3/4″) or end flush with the end of the waist of the skirt. In this instance, the zipper could be stitched to the top of the waistband. The extension can be pointed or rounded. The waistband finishes 1/2″ longer than the waist measurement, with 3/4″ added for the extension. The skirt is draped with 1″ ease at the waistline, therefore 1/2″ will be eased into the waistband.

Preparing Muslin

Measure the waist of the form, or use #2 from the Form Measurement Chart.

Drafting Steps

Figure 7.3a

Fold paper lengthwise.

Square a line 1 1/4″ down from fold and square a line that equals waist. Mark and mark again for center of band. Continue for another 3/4″ and square up to fold.

Add 1/2″ for seam allowance.

Figure 7.3b

Mark for button/buttonhole.

Cut waistband from paper.

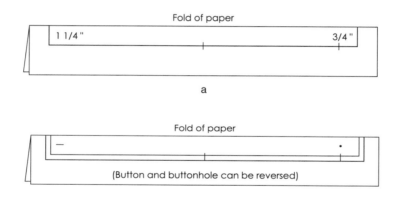

Figure 7.3

Flare Skirts: The A Silhouette

Skirts designed with flare have an A-shaped silhouette. The silhouette is created by adding extra fabric to the side of the skirt drape, thereby changing the silhouette from a "straight line" to an A-line. By manipulating the dart excess to the hemline as flare (dart equivalents) and adding additional flares, the sweep of the hemline will increase (Figure 7.4). Within the silhouette, designer/drapers can create many design variations. The following A-silhouette skirt projects include the modified A-line flare, the basic flare, the added flare, and the circular skirt series.

Figure 7.4

The A-Line Skirt with Modified Flare

Design Analysis

The flare of an A-line skirt is created by draping half the original waist dart excess to the hemline for a modified hemline sweep. The crossgrain falls as the flare is formed. To create the A-sil-houette, fabric is added to the side seam to bal-ance the flare skirt. The A-silhouette starts at the outermost part of the hipline and ends at the hem. The A-line flare skirt can be converted to a four-gore skirt by adding a seam at the front and back.

Preparing Muslin

Figure 7.5

Length: skirt length, plus 3″ and 1″ for hem.

Width: half of the fabric width for the front skirt and half for the back skirt drape.

Fold 1″. Press without steam.

Mark 14″ down from the top to mark the hip level and square the HBL crossgrain line for the front and back skirt.

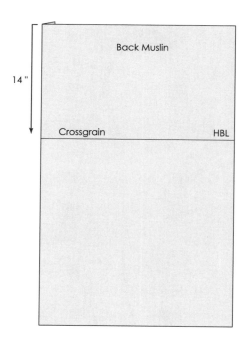
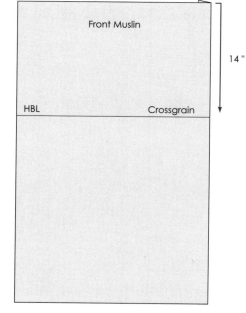

Figure 7.5

Draping Steps: Front Skirt

Figure 7.6

Place fold to centerline of the form and pin the following:

- HBL line (crossgrain): match to the HBL of the form.
- Center front waist.
- Bottom of form base.
- Holding pins at side seam.

Smooth and trim muslin to Princess line at waist and crossmark. Mark 1/2″ for dart intake.

Figure 7.7

Fold and pin the dart intake.

Remove holding pins.

Slash, trim, and pin 1/4″ ease along the waistline, as the remaining excess is smooth across the waist/abdominal area.

The muslin is smoothed downward along the side seam and as the crossgrain falls, a flare is created at the hemline.

At the base of the form, pin the flare together and measure the width (A-B).

Mark base of the form at side seam.

Dot mark A-B measurement out from the cross-mark. (The other part of the flare is made up by the back flare.)

Pencil rub side seam from waist to the HBL of the hip.

Figure 7.8

Trim excess 1″ from side seam approximately 3″ down and clip to within 1/8″ from the pencil rub.

Fold muslin touching the dot mark at side seam for A-line flare.

Trim muslin to within 1 1/2″ of the fold for adjustment, if needed when pinned to back skirt.

Peel back and pin.

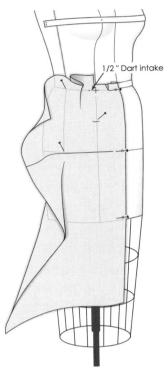

Figure 7.6

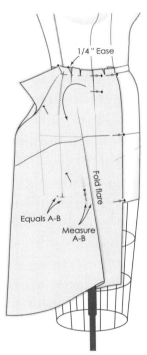

Figure 7.7

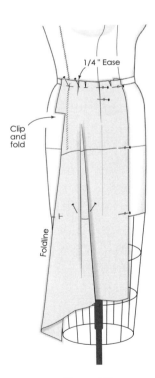

Figure 7.8

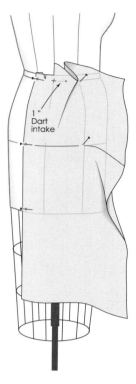

Figure 7.9

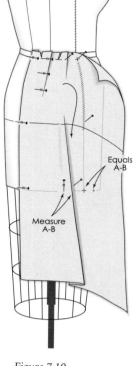

Figure 7.10

Draping Steps: Back Skirt

Follow the instruction given for the drape of the front skirt, except that the dart intake is 1″.

Figure 7.9

Crossmark at Princess and 1″ for dart intake.

Figure 7.10

Fold and pin dart with 1/4″ for ease. Smooth muslin to side waist.

Smooth excess downward along side seam. Flare is created as crossgrain falls. Measure flare as illustrated.

Figure 7.11

Clip and fold muslin touching the dot mark.

Trim allowing 1 1/2″.

Figure 7.12

Unfold back flare and place the fold of the front flare on top, pin.

Evaluate the hang and balance of the skirt. Adjust side flare, if needed.

Pin-mark for skirt length parallel with floor and trim hem along the pinline.

Remove skirt and true the seams, stitch muslin or transfer to paper before the test fit.

Equalize side seams.

Complete the pattern (see pages 35–39).

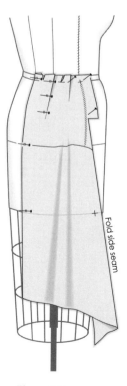

Figure 7.11

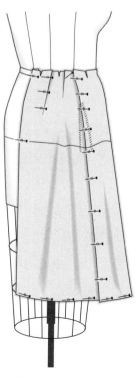

Figure 7.12

Draping Steps: Equalize the Hemline Sweep

Figure 7.13

To prevent the bias of the front and back side seams from hanging unevenly, equalize the angle of the flares.

Place the back skirt on top of the front skirt, matching at the centerlines. (The even and un-even broken lines indicate front and back side seam.)

Center a mark between the front and back side seam at hem and draw the new side seams blending at hiplines.

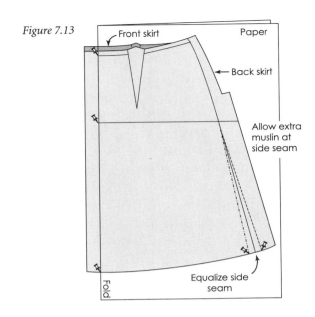

Figure 7.13

Front skirt

Paper

Back skirt

Allow extra muslin at side seam

Fold

Equalize side seam

Finished Pattern

Figure 7.14

Finished patterns with front cut on fold and two backs (zipper opening).

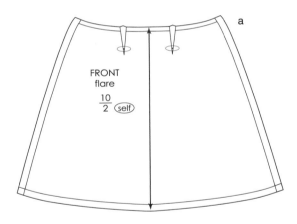

a

FRONT flare
$\frac{10}{2}$ self

Figure 7.14

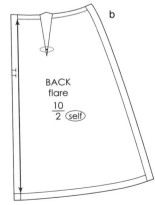

b

BACK flare
$\frac{10}{2}$ self

Figure 7.15

To create a four-gore skirt, place a seam at the center front. To drape this skirt on bias, see Chapter 14 for guidance.

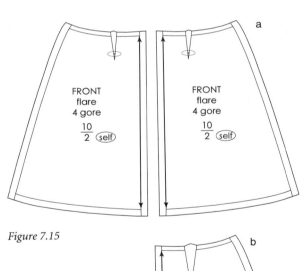

a

FRONT flare 4 gore
$\frac{10}{2}$ self

FRONT flare 4 gore
$\frac{10}{2}$ self

Figure 7.15

b

BACK flare
$\frac{10}{2}$ self

Full Flare Skirt

Figure 7.16

Design Analysis

The full flare skirt is created by draping all of the original waist dart excess to the hemline, thereby increasing the sweep of the skirt more than for the A-line flare skirt. The crossgrain falls as the flare is formed. To create the A-silhouette, fabric is added to the side seam. The skirt can be converted to a four-gore skirt by adding a seam at the center front (Figure 7.16).

Preparing Muslin

Figure 7.17

Length: Skirt length, plus 5″ and 3/4″ for hem allowance.

Width: Half of the fabric width. Cut to length for front and back skirt.

Fold 1″. Press without steam.

Mark 5″ down from the top and 9″ from this mark, square the HBL crossgrain line for front and back skirt.

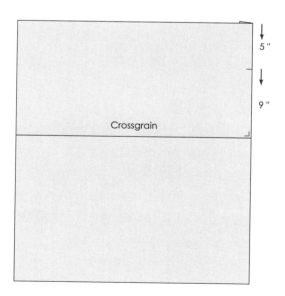

Figure 7.17

Draping Steps: Front Skirt

Figure 7.18

Place fold to centerline of the form and pin the following:

- HBL line (crossgrain): match to HBL of the form.
- Center front waist, at mid-tape.
- Bottom of form.
- Holding pins at side seam.

Smooth muslin to Princess line.

Slash and trim.

Figure 7.19

Release holding pins.

Slash, trim, and pin 1/4″ ease along the waistline, as excess is smoothed across the waist/abdominal area. The excess is directed downward along the side seam creating a flare.

At the base of the form, pin the flare together and measure the width of half (A-B).

Crossmark the base of the form at the side seam.

Dot mark A-B measurement out from the crossmark. (The other part of the flare is made up by the back flare.)

Pencil rub side seam to ~~the HBL of the hip~~. 3″ below waist

Trim to within 1 1/2″ of side seam approximately 3″ down.

Clip to within 1/8″ from pencil rub.

Crease-fold to the dot mark at the side seam.

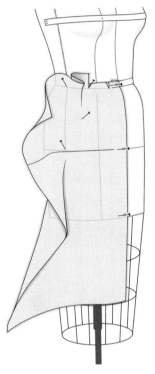

Figure 7.18

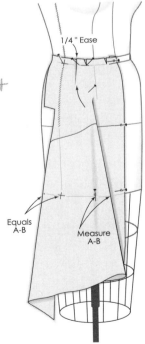

1/4″ Ease

Equals A-B

Measure A-B

Figure 7.19

Figure 7.20

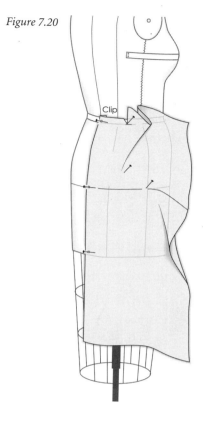

Draping Steps: Back Skirt

Follow the instruction given for the drape of the front skirt.

Figure 7.20

Pin muslin to the form. Smooth muslin to Princess and trim excess.

Figure 7.21

Smooth, trim, and slash muslin along waist/ abdomen to side seam.

Smooth excess downward as crossgrain falls to create flare. Pinch and measure flare (A-B).

Trim excess, clip and fold muslin for flare touching the dot mark.

Figure 7.22

Unfold back flare and pin front side seam flare to back flare.

Let the skirt hang overnight so that the bias can stretch. Evaluate the fit and balance before marking the hemline.

Pin-mark hemline parallel with the floor. Trim.

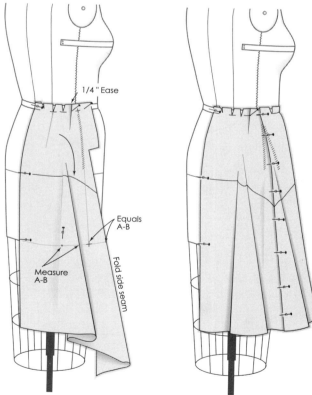

Figure 7.21   *Figure 7.22*

Figure 7.23

Remove the skirt drape and true. Stitch muslin or transfer to paper first for the test fit.

Equalize the side seam (see page 135).

To complete the pattern, see pages 35 to 39.

To drape this skirt on bias, see Chapter 20, for guidance.

Figure 7.24

To create a four-gore skirt, add a seam at the center front of the skirt.

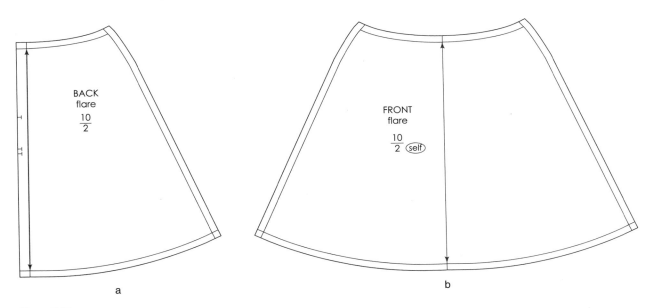

Figure 7.23

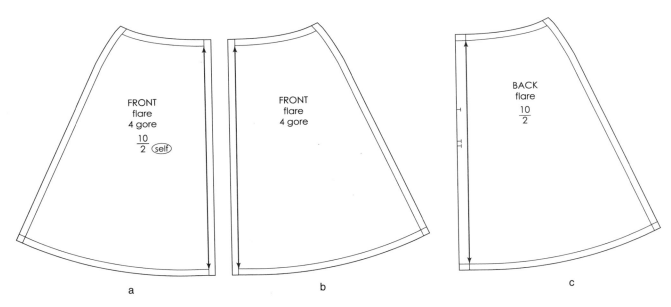

Figure 7.24

Flared Skirt with Increased Hemline Sweep

Design Analysis

Figure 7.25

The skirt has a greater hemline sweep than does the basic flared skirt. To increase the hemline sweep, the muslin is slashed along the waistline and the crossgrain is dropped to create flare. Each flare increases the sweep of the hemline. The back skirt can be draped or a copy of the front skirt can be traced and adjusted.

Preparing Muslin

Length: Skirt length plus 7″ and 1/4″ to 1/2″ for hem.

Width: Use one half the fabric width. Allow more for a wider sweep.

Figure 7.25

Draping Steps: Front Skirt

Figure 7.26

Place fold to the centerline of the form, and pin the following:

- HBL line (crossgrain) at centerline.
- Center front, at mid-tape.
- Bottom of form.

Smooth muslin along waist to Princess line.

Trim excess to within 1/2″ of the waist, and slash where flare is placed.

Place holding pins at Princess and side seam.

Figure 7.27

Pivot muslin downward from the slash/pin-mark, dropping the crossgrain to the desired amount of flare. Smooth muslin flat against the flare. Place holding pins at the side of the flare.

Pin to measure the flare (A-B). Release pin.

To control the width of each flare, repeat the process.

Figure 7.28

Smooth muslin along the waist to the next flare. Slash and pin.

Figure 7.29

Pivot muslin downward from the slash/pin-mark, dropping the crossgrain until the flare equals the A-B measurement (on fold). Place holding pins at the side of the flare.

Crossmark at the base of the form at side seam.

Mark A-B measurement out from crossmark.

Pencil rub the side seam.

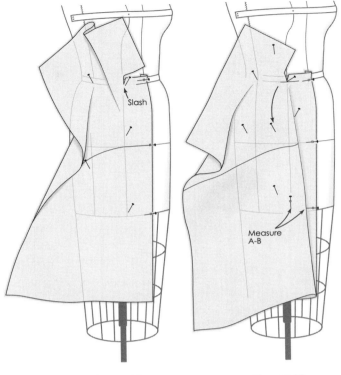

Figure 7.26   *Figure 7.27*

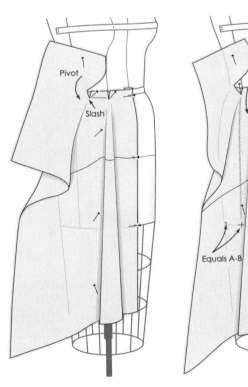

Figure 7.28 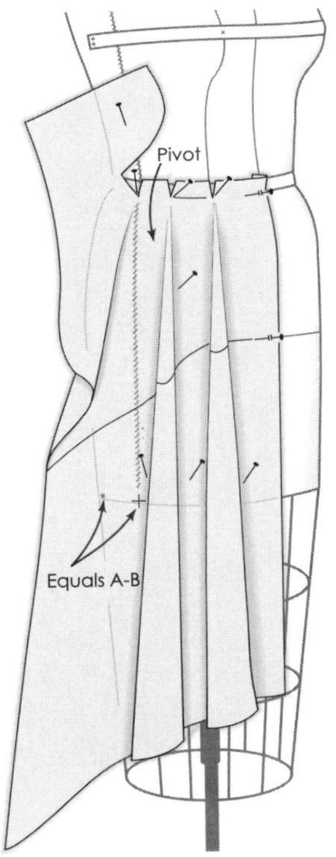   *Figure 7.29*

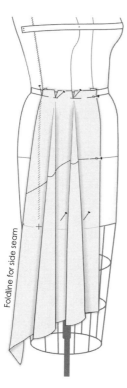

Figure 7.30

Foldline for side seam

Figure 7.30

Fold excess passing through the A-B mark to the waistline. The foldline establishes a temporary side seam.

Trim excess to within 1 1/2″ of the foldline.

To use front skirt for the back pattern, see Figure 7.32, Figure 7.33, and Figure 7.34.

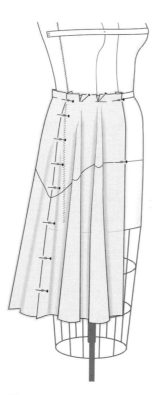

Figure 7.31

Draping Steps: Back Skirt

Drape the back skirt using the instructions given for the front drape.

Figure 7.31

Pin front seam over back seam. The crossgrains should meet at the flare of the side seam. If they do not, refold the seams until they do. Pin.

Hang skirt overnight to allow bias to stretch. Evaluate fit and balance before pin-marking hemline and trim the excess.

Draping Steps: Back Skirt Developed from the Front Skirt

Remove the front skirt drape. True all marked lines, and blend the hemline. Trim excess to within 1″ of the side seam.

Preparing Muslin

Figure 7.32

Draw a line 1″ in from muslin edge (to represent the center back).

Square a crossgrain line 15″ from the top.

Align the front skirt with the centerline and the crossgrain. Pin to secure, and cut from the muslin.

Place the back skirt on the form, and adjust the location of center back waistline, ending at the side waist.

Place front skirt on the form and pin side seams together. If the crossgrains do not match, take in or let out the side seams until they do.

Let drape hang overnight.

Pin-mark hemline, measuring up from the floor.

Make adjustments with a red pencil in trueing the back pattern.

The front skirt can be cut on the fold or with a seam for a four-gore skirt.

Add seam allowance and place notches. Cut skirts from the paper and recut to test fit.

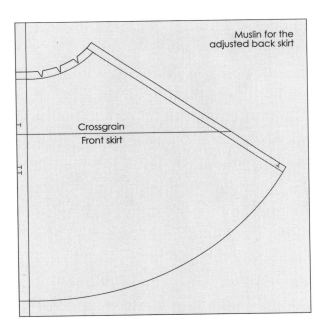

Figure 7.32

Circle: Skirts, Radius Chart

Circular skirts can be draped following the instructions given on pages 141 and 142, or the fabric can be prepared so that the desired type of circle is created by using the Circle/Skirt Radius Chart. The chart provides measurements for the radius when drawing the waist arc for specific types of circle skirts. The radius measurements are always drawn on the quarter section of a circle. It is the perfect shortcut for designing skirts with circularity.

Grainlines, Bias, and Flare

Figure 7.33 and Figure 7.34

Circular skirts have grainlines that are bias, straight, and crosswise—all interacting within the skirt. Flare falls along the side of the straight grain, flaring out gracefully along its bias. The designer/draper can control the location of flares at the hemline by changing the position of the grain on the fabric (pattern). The three grainline

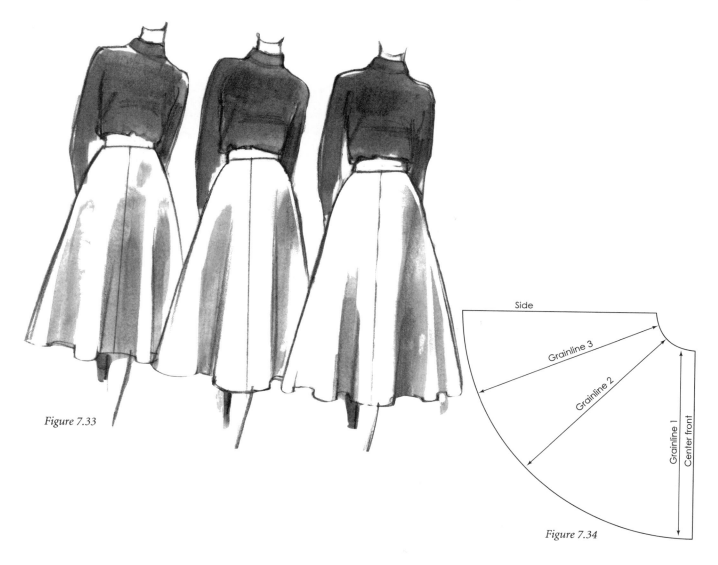

Figure 7.33

Figure 7.34

placements (center, middle, or three-quarter from center) illustrate the effect on the flares of the skirts.

Grainline 1 (center front of pattern) has two flares: one falls toward the side front, and one at the side.

Grainline 2 (between front and side) has two flares: one falls at the center front, and one toward the side.

Grainline 3 (between side and grainline) has three flares: front, side, and middle.

Circular skirts tend to stretch on the bias section of the hemline. The skirt should be left on the form or pinned on the straight bar of a hanger overnight. This allows the bias fibers to stretch creating an uneven hemline. The hem-

line is re-marked by pins or chalk measuring up from the floor so that it will be parallel with it. The skirt is taken from the form, and the pin-marks are pencil rubbed. Pins are re-moved, and the rubbed or chalk lines are blended along the hemline. The hemline is trimmed, and the skirt is placed on paper and traced. If a paper pattern was made, the skirt is placed on top of the pattern, and the corrected hemline is traced.

Parts of the Circle

Figure 7.35

Think of the circle skirt as having four quarter sections. Each quarter section helps make up the whole (a complete circle) (see Figure 7.35). Re-

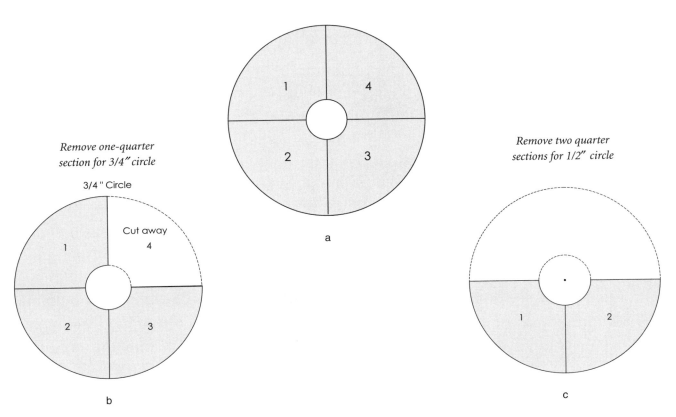

Remove one-quarter section for 3/4″ circle

3/4 ″ Circle

Cut away

a

b

Remove two quarter sections for 1/2″ circle

c

Figure 7.35

move one quarter section for a 3/4 circle skirt (see Figure 7.36). Remove two quarter sections for a 1/2 circle skirt (see Figure 7.37).

The measurement of the circle must always equal the waist measurement. This measurement is the basis for selecting the radius for each of the different circles. The radius is always drawn on a quarter section of the whole. The radius increases each time a quarter section is removed in order to retain the original waist measurement.

Circle/Skirt Radius Table

Table 7.1 provides the correct radius for establishing the waistline for the type of circle skirt desired. To select the radius, measure the waistline and modify as instructed. Select the type of circle required by the design. Modifications are given with preparation of the fabric or paper pattern.

Column 1 provides a selection of waist measurements.

Columns 2, 3, and 4, provides the correct radius measurements for each circle. Select the column indicating the circle of choice.

Sample Plan

- Waist measurement: 26″
- Subtract 1″ for stretch.   25″*
- Add for 2 seams (varies)   2″**

                        Total 27″

Based on 27″, select the radius that applies to the type of circle skirt desired. Seam allowance at waistline is provided by subtracting 1/2″ from the radius measurement.

- Radius for half circle   8 5/8-″
- Radius for three-quarter circle   5 3/4-″
- Radius for full circle   4 3/8-″

The (+) and (-) means add or subtract 1/16″.

*For loosely woven (chiffon) skirts, cut a sample of the radius and stretch it along a ruler to measure the correct amount of stretch.

** For measurements in between whole numbers, use the whole number that is the closest.

Full Circle Skirt

Figure 7.36

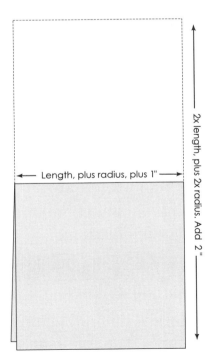

Length, plus radius, plus 1"

2x length, plus 2x radius. Add 2"

Figure 7.37

Follow the steps and record the measurements in preparing the muslin or paper for the full, three-quarter, and one half circle skirts. A full circle skirt is the sample given as a guide for using the chart. Use the formula to develop a 3/4, and 1/2 circle skirts (page 148).

Formula

Waist measurement minus 1".
- Example: Waist 26" minus 1" for stretch equals 25".

Number of seams. Examples:
- Two seams (1/2" allowance) equals 2".
- Three seams (1/2" allowance) equals 3".
- Four seams (1/2" allowance) equals 4".

Total measurement:
- Column 1. Example: 25" plus 2" for seams equals 27"—Locate in column.

Radius:
- Example: Full circle using 27". The radius is 3 7/8" minus 1/2", which equals 3 3/8".

Length:
- Example: Skirt length and hem allowance equals 25".

Preparing Muslin or Paper

Use measurement given, or use personal measurements for waist and skirt length.

A half circle is drafted and traced to complete a full circle skirt with 2 seams, using the technique discussed.

Length: Twice the skirt length plus twice the radius plus 2".

Width: Skirt length, plus the radius, plus 1".

Fold in half and mark corner X.

Table 7.1   CIRCLE/SKIRT RADIUS CHART

Column 1 Waist Measurement	Column 2 1/2 circle	Column 3 3/4 circle	Column 4 Full circle
1	0 1/4+	0 1/4-	0 1/8+
2	0 5/8	0 1/2-	0 3/8-
3	0 7/8+	0 5/8	0 1/2-
4	1 1/4+	0 7/8-	0 5/8
5	1 5/8-	1 1/8-	0 3/4+
6	1 7/8+	1 1/4+	0 7/8+
7	2 1/4-	1 1/2	1 1/8
8	2 1/2+	1 5/8+	1 1/4+
9	2 7/8	1 7/8+	1 3/8+
10	3 1/8+	2 1/8	1 5/8-
11	3 1/2	2 3/8-	1 3/4
12	3 3/4+	2 1/2+	1 7/8+
13	4 1/8	2 3/4	2 1/8-
14	4 1/2-	2 7/8+	2 1/4-
15	4 3/4+	3 1/8+	2 3/8
16	5 1/8-	3 3/8+	2 1/2+
17	5 3/8+	3 5/8-	2 3/4-
18	5 3/4+	3 3/4+	2 7/8
19	6 1/8	4 1/8-	3
20	6 3/8	4 1/4	3 1/8+
21	6 5/8+	4 1/2-	3 3/8-
22	7	4 5/8+	3 1/2
23	7 1/4+	4 7/8	3 5/8+
24	7 5/8	5 1/8-	3 3/4+
25	7 7/8+	5 1/4+	3 7/8+
26	8 1/4+	5 1/2+	4 1/8
27	8 5/8-	5 3/4-	4 3/8-
28	8 7/8+	5 7/8+	4 1/2-
29	9 1/4-	6 1/8+	4 5/8
30	9 1/2+	6 3/8	4 3/4+
31	9 7/8	6 5/8-	4 7/8+
32	10 7/8+	6 3/4+	5 1/8-
33	10 1/2	7	5 1/4
34	10 3/4+	7 1/4-	5 3/8+
35	11 1/8	7 1/2-	5 1/2+
36	11 1/2-	7 5/8	5 3/4-
37	11 3/4+	7 7/8-	5 7/8
38	12 1/8-	8 1/8-	6 1/8-
39	12 3/8+	8 1/4+	6 1/4-
40	12 3/4-	8 1/2	6 3/8
41	13 1/8-	8 5/8+	6 1/2+
42	13 3/8	8 7/8+	6 5/8+
43	13 5/8+	9 1/8	6 7/8-
44	14	9 3/8+	7
45	14 1/4+	9 1/2+	7 1/8+
46	14 5/8+	9 3/4	7 3/8-
47	14 7/8+	9 7/8+	7 1/2-
48	15 1/4+	10 1/8+	7 5/8
49	15 5/8-	10 3/8+	7 3/4+
50	15 7/8+	10 5/8	7 7/8+

Technique for Drawing Circles

Figure 7.38

Use an awl to punch holes in an old measuring tape at the 1″ mark (X).

Add 1″ to the following:
- (X) to (Y) = Radius measurement.
- (Y) to (Z) = Skirt length.

Figure 7.39a

With a pushpin through (X), place at the corner (X) of the folded paper.

Place a pencil in the hole (Y) and draw an arc for the waistline.

Figure 7.39b

With a pencil through hole (Z), draw the hemline of the circle skirt.

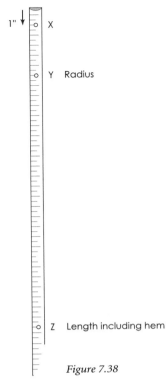

Measuring Tape
Use awl to make following tools:

1″ → X

Y   Radius

Z   Length including hem

Figure 7.38

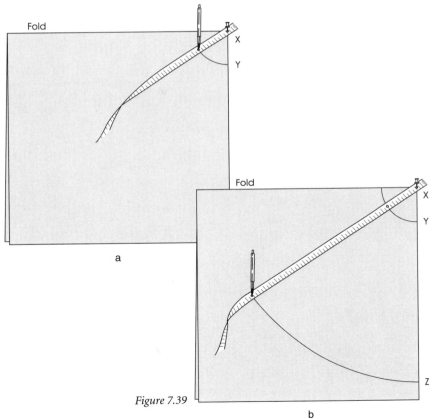

Fold

X
Y

a

Fold

X
Y

Z

Figure 7.39

b

Figure 7.40

Cut the skirt from the fabric or paper.

Trace a duplicate copy for the other half of the circle. Notch for seams, hem, zipper, and grain-line placement.

Option

Raise center front 1/4″, blending to the side seam line to flatten the center front of the skirt. Trim 1/4″ at the center back blending to the side to accommodate the slope of the back waist.

Hang skirt overnight. Mark hemline parallel to the floor.

Variation: Circle Skirts with Uneven Hemlines

Uneven hemlines create drama in fashion. The hemlines can vary in a number of ways, some of the most popular is the handkerchief (square corners), uneven hemlines caused by allowing the bias to hang lower than the parts of the skirt that are on the straight and crossgrain, or the graduated hemlines created by an offset inner circle.

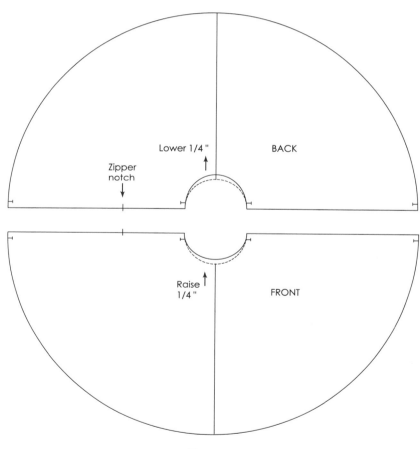

Figure 7.40

Circular Skirt with Offset Circle

Preparing Muslin or Paper

Figure 7.41

Measure the waist and skirt length.

Compute the following:

- Waist, less stretch
- Seam allowance

    Total _____

- Radius,
- Skirt lengths:

    Longest _____
    Shortest _____
    Total _____

length and width: Twice the length plus twice the radius.

Fold paper, and fold again.

Technique for Marking

Figure 7.42

The hemline is drawn before the waist arc.

Mark the following:

- Hem at fold (Z)
- (Z) to (Y) equals shortest hem length.
- (Y) to (X) equals radius.

Cut along the curved hemline.

Figure 7.41

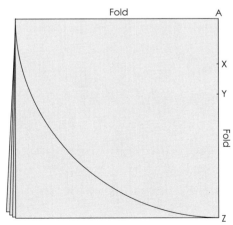

Figure 7.42

Figure 7.43

Refold paper on (X).

Draw waist arc from (Y).

Draw a cutaway line (broken lines).

Cut waist arc from paper.

Figure 7.44

Trim the new curved line.

Open the pattern and separate along the fold-line.

For a tiered look trace and shorten lengths as many times as tiers desired (broken lines).

Variation: Circle Skirts with a Gathered Waistline

Gathers can be added to circular skirts by adding to the waist measurement. The fullness should be computed as a ratio of the whole measurement. For example, a waist of 26″ can be increased by 1 1/2 or more times its measurement to provide for gathers.

Variation: Skirts with Two or More Circles

Circle skirts cut in chiffon and other soft fabrics often need more fullness. Increase the number of circles by dividing the waist measurement into the number of circles planned. To this measurement, add for seam allowance. Locate the measurement in column 1, and record the radius measurement, less 1/2″. See page 146 for fabric or paper preparation, and page 149 for preparing the tape measure to draw the waist and hemline arc.

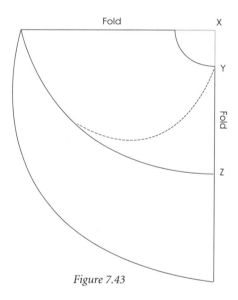

Figure 7.43

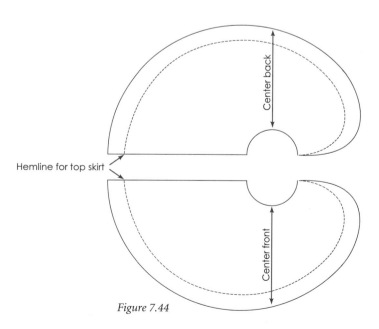

Figure 7.44

Variation: Skirt Lengths Wider Than the Width of Fabric

Long circular skirts may require a set-in piece when the fabric is not wide enough to accommodate the length of the skirt. The set-in pieces are seen on gowns, loungewear, and wedding dresses.

Figure 7.45

An example for adding a section of the pattern to complete the length of the garment.

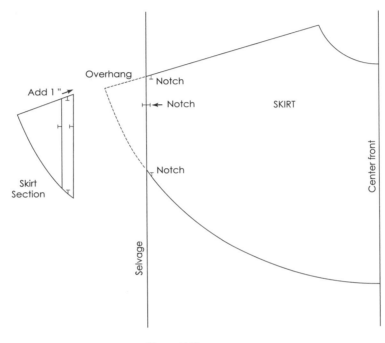

Figure 7.45

Skirts with Pleats

A pleat is a fold in the fabric that overlays itself. It is either stitched at one end releasing fullness at the other, or confined at both ends for special design detailing (Figure 7.46). Pleats can be functional or can be used creatively on skirts, bodices, sleeves, dresses, and jackets. They can be equally or unequally spaced and can be pressed or left unpressed, stitched or unstitched, grouped together or as single pleats. Skirt designs in this section illustrate the versatility of pleats.

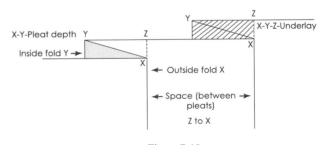

Figure 7.46

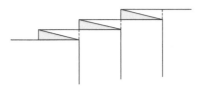

Figure 7.47

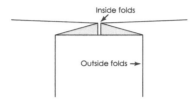

Figure 7.48

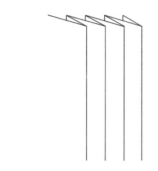

Figure 7.49

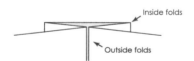

Figure 7.50

Figure 7.51

Skirts with Pleats

Figure 7.46

Pleat depth The distance from the outside fold of the pleat (labeled X) to the inside fold (labeled Y). X to Y is the shaded area of the first pleat.

Pleat marking Notches are placed from point X (outside fold) to point Z to complete the underlay of the pleat. Z to X is the distance between the pleats.

Pleat spacing The distance between pleats.

Pleat underlay (forms the pleat) This measurement is always twice the pleat depth (X to Y to Z). For example, a 2″ pleat depth equals a 4″ underlay (lined area illustrated at second pleat).

Types of Pleats

Knife or side pleats (Figure 7.47).

Pleats grouped and facing in one direction.

Box pleats (Figure 7.48).

Pleats that fold away from each other on the right side of the garment.

Accordion pleats (Figure 7.49).

Folded pleats that resemble the bellows of an accordion. Pleats are close and tend to overlap.

Inverted pleats (Figure 7.50).

Pleats folded to meet each other on the right side of the garment.

Sunburst pleats (Figure 7.51).

Pleats that fan out and graduate from the waist. Sunbursts are pleated on circular skirts. To sustain the pleating, fabric should be either all synthetic or a blend with more than 50 percent synthetic fibers.

All-Around Pleated Skirt

The all-around pleated skirt (Figure 7.52) can be created by using the pleat formula or may be pleated by professional pleaters. Generally, it is less expensive for a manufacturer to send a skirt out for pleating than to pleat it in the factory. Professional pleaters will conform any pleating arrangement to fit waist and hip measurements for all graduated sizes and to any length desired. Pleating services for garments designed for private clientele and for personal fit should contact yardage or notion departments for information.

Design Analysis

The skirt has 20 pleats that encircle the hips and are stitched 7″ from waist. The depth of the pleat is determined at hip level (widest part of the hip) and graduated to fit the waistline. This type of pleated skirt is best planned on the fabric laid out on the table rather than draped on the form.

Measurements Needed

- Waist (2) _____ Example: 30″
- Hip (4) _____ Example: 40″
- Length: _____ Example: 29″
  (include hem and waist seam).

Decide on the number of desired pleats. Example: 20 pleats.

Determine the depth of pleat, which can be any amount desired. Example: 1 1/2″ × 2″ = 3″ pleat underlay.

Determine the spacing between the pleats by dividing the number of pleats (20) by the hip circumference (40″). In the example, the pleats are 2″ apart.

Figure 7.52

Planning Pleats

Figure 7.53

Start pleat series with seam allowance (labeled A) and mark.

Measure and mark pleat depth (labeled A to B), which equals one half the pleat underlay. B to C equals the space between pleats. Mark.

Measure and mark pleat underlay (labeled C to D).

Repeat the process until the last pleat. The last pleat (the other half of the pleat underlay

A to B) ends with G to H, plus the seam allowance.

Pleats should always be planned with the joining seam connecting the pleat depth at each end of the fabric width.

After seam allowance trim excess fabric from the skirt.

Figure 7.54

Example of the joining seams of the pleated panels. The underlays are notched.

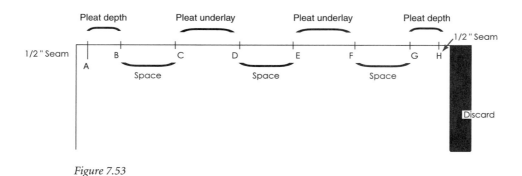

Figure 7.53

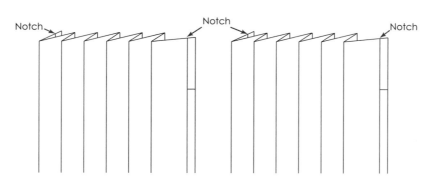

Figure 7.54

Pleats Adjusted to the Waistline Measurement

Figure 7.55

Pleats are first formed to fit the circumference of the widest part of the hip and then adjusted to fit the waist by subtracting the waist measure- ment from hip measurement. For example, if the waist is 30″ and the hip is 40″, the difference is 10″. Divide 10″ by 20 pleats, and the result is 1/2″ (1/4″ out from X and Z).

Figure 7.56

Example of stitched pleat from waist to hip.

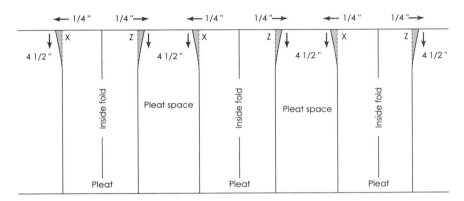

Figure 7.55

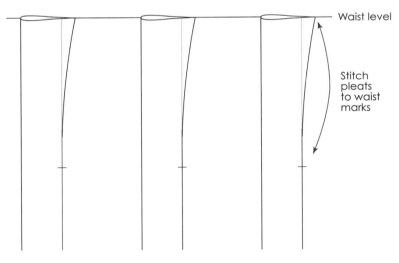

Figure 7.56

Skirts with Yokes

Skirt yokes are the upper part of the skirt. They are connected to the bottom section by a seamline. The connected section can be draped as a fitted, gathered, or flared skirt. Yokes are fit close to the body and can be draped without the waistline darts to a width of about 3 1/2″ to 4″. Yokes that are wider will either be draped with waistline darts or the dart excess will be draped as flare at the yoke's edge. Yokes can be designed in many variations, being parallel with the waistline to uneven levels below the waist. Yokes are also used as a base to support overlays of gathers (design 3) and pleats and connected to a bodice (design 2) (Figure 7.57).

Design 1

Design 2

Design 3

Figure 7.57

Stylized Yoke with Pleat and Flare

Design Analysis

The skirt has six flares in the front and back. There is a box pleat at the center front which is wider at the hemline than at the yokeline. (The Circle Skirt Radius Chart is not used to draft a circular skirt for stylized yokes. The flares at the hemline would hang unevenly.)

Preparing Form

Figure 7.58

Pin-mark or use style tape to mark the front and back yoke styleline.

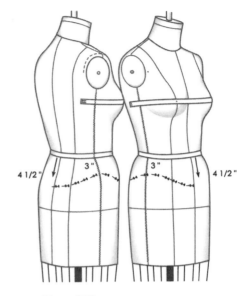

Figure 7.58

Preparing Muslin

The following measurements apply to both the front and back skirt drape.

- Yoke: Front width at the widest plus 2″ and length from center front to side seam, plus 2″.
- Skirt length: plus 9″ and 3/4″ for hem.
- Width: Three fourths of fabric width.

Preparing Muslin: Yoke

Figure 7.59 and Figure 7.60

Cut 2 muslins for front (**Figure 7.59**) and back (Figure 7.60) drape.

Fold 1″ at the centerlines, and press without steam.

Pin muslin to form and drape yoke.

Smooth, slash, and trim muslin along the waist, and pin 1/4″ ease.

Pencil rub side seam.

Dot mark 1/8″ for ease.

Repeat drape instruction for the back yoke.

Remove front and back yokes.

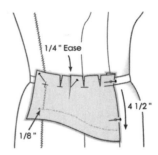

Figure 7.59

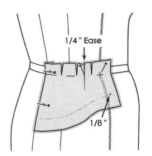

Figure 7.60

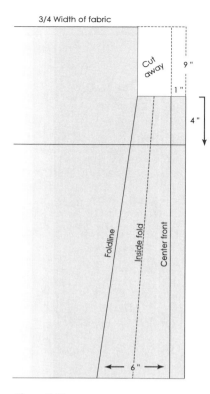

Figure 7.61

Preparing Muslin: Box Pleat

Figure 7.61

Length, plus 11″.

Width of muslin.

Cut a 5 × 9 section from corner of muslin.

Square a line out 4″ down from top.

Draw a line 1″ in from muslin edge.

Measure and mark 6″ space at hem.

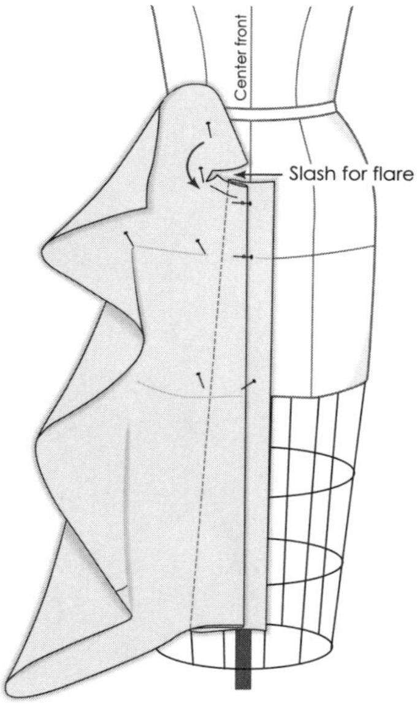

Draping Steps

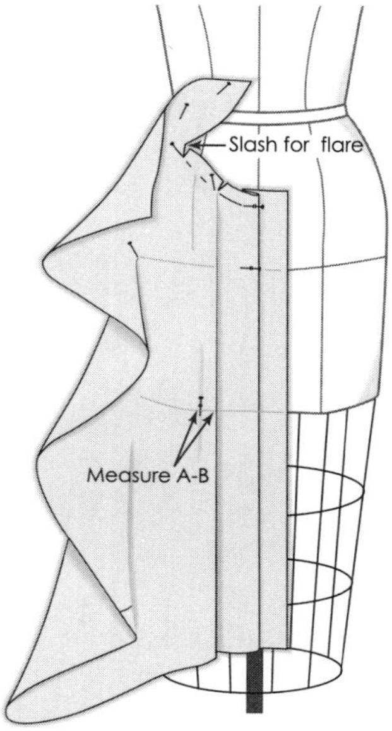

Figure 7.62

Fold pleat to centerline and pin.

Place pleat 1/2″ above the yokeline with pleat at the center front. Pin.

Smooth the muslin along the yokeline.

Figure 7.63

Slash where the first flare is to be placed. Pivot the crossgrain downward to create the first flare.

Pin the flare together at the base of the form and measure (A-B). Use this measurement for each flare to balance sweep of the hemline.

Figure 7.62

Figure 7.63

Figure 7.64

Smooth muslin along the yokeline and slash for the second flare to equal (A-B) measurement.

Smooth muslin to the side seam.

At the base of the form, dot mark for A-B measurement.

Pencil rub the side seam.

Crease-fold the side seam from yoke to hemline touching the A-B dot mark. The addition creates half the flare and the A-silhouette. The back drape will complete the flare.

Figure 7.65

Drape back skirt using front drape as a guide (without box pleat). (A flare can be draped at center back.)

Pin front over back skirt at side seams and evaluate flare placement. Allow skirt to hang overnight.

Pin-mark the hemline by measuring up from the floor.

Trim hemline along pin-marks.

Transferring Muslin to Paper

Figure 7.66 and Figure 7.67

Place front yoke (Figure 7.66) on fold of the paper, and trace.

If fabric is wide enough, place skirt on the center of fold. If not, add seam allowance to the center-line and cut two fronts (Figure 7.67).

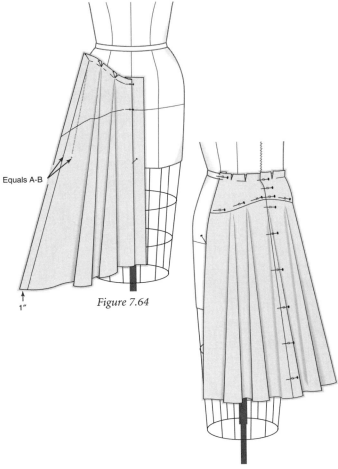

Equals A-B

1"

Figure 7.64

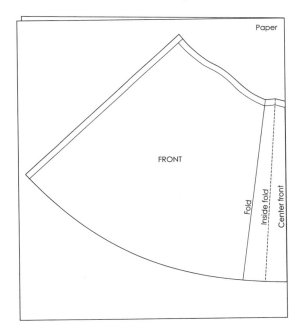

Figure 7.65

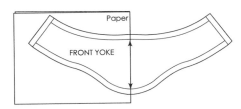

Figure 7.66

Figure 7.67

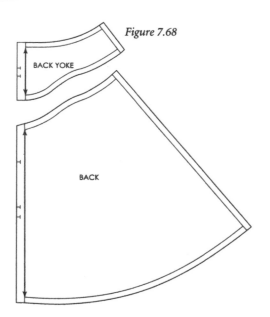

Figure 7.68

BACK YOKE

BACK

Figure 7.68

Trace back yoke and skirt.

Add seams and cut from paper.

High-Waisted Skirt

Skirts designed without a seamed waistline allow for many creative variations. The top of a skirt can be designed to heights above or depths below the natural waistline. The high-waisted skirt can serve as a prototype for such designs (Figure 7.69 and Figure 7.70).

Figure 7.69

Figure 7.70

Design Analysis

The dart excess of the basic skirt is combined and draped as a one-dart front and one-dart back. The dart intake extends 2″ above the waist. Dart points end below the waistline as in the basic skirt. High-waisted skirts can be designed as a yoke, with an attached bottom of any design (see page 162).

Preparing Muslin

Measure the form or take from the Model Form Measurement Chart:

- Hip arc (23)
  Front _____
  Back _____
- Hip depth (25) _____
- Length: as desired plus 1 1/2″ for hem plus 3 1/2″ extension above

Figure 7.71

Length: Cut two skirt lengths.

Width: Cut two widths

- Front: Hip measurement, plus 2″
- Back: Hip measurement, plus 2″

Press a 1″ fold without steam.

Measure down at fold that equals hip depth plus 3 1/2″, and square a line across the muslin (crossgrain).

Crossmark for hip measurement. Measure out 1/2″ for ease, and draw a line parallel to fold.

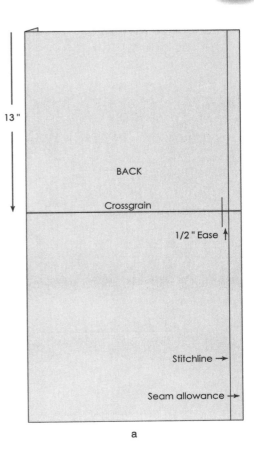

a

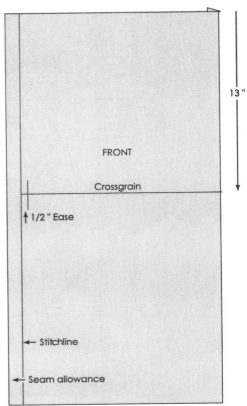

Figure 7.71

b

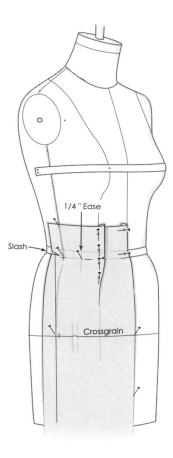

Figure 7.72

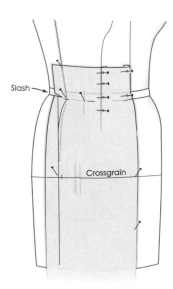

Figure 7.73

Draping Steps

Figure 7.72

Place fold of muslin to centerline matching crossgrain with the HBL line of the form. Pin the crossgrain, waistline at center, and top of the extension. Smooth the crossgrain along the HBL line to the side seam, and pin.

Smooth muslin up from the crossgrain to the side waist. Slash and pin. Continue smoothing muslin upward, and pin.

Ease Allowance at Hip

Move the pin to the ease line at the hip HBL.

Pin 1/4″ ease at the waist.

Pin an outward dart at the Princess line taking up the remaining excess. Dart point should end approximately 3″ below the waist.

Slash at an angle to within 1/8″ of waist.

Pencil rub the side seam, and mark dart intake along pinning.

Figure 7.73

Unpin dart, fold excess under, and repin.

Peel skirt back or remove from form.

Figure 7.74

Place fold of muslin to center back matching crossgrain with the HBL of the form. Pin the crossgrain, waistline at center, and top of the extension.

Continue with the drape, using the front drape as a guide.

Dart length is approximately 5 1/2″ below the waist.

Figure 7.75

Fold dart under, and pin.

Figure 7.76

Pin front and back skirt along the side seam.

Allow ease at the extended side waist.

Mark hipline shape along the pin-marks.

Remove and true the pattern. Trim side seam to within 1/2″ or 3/4″. Stitch muslin, or transfer to paper first for the test fit.

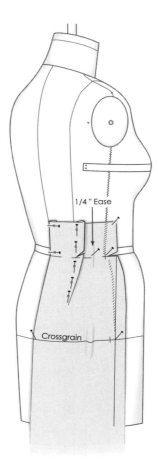

Figure 7.74

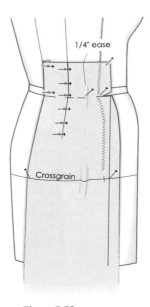

Figure 7.75

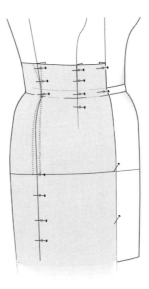

Figure 7.76

Figure 7.77

Complete the pattern.

Place punch/circles at the center fold of the dart at the waist at 1/8″ in from stitchline and 1/4″ from dart point centered.

Making the Facing Patterns

Place paper under the patterns and trace extended section to 1/2″ below waist level.

Close darts and trace.

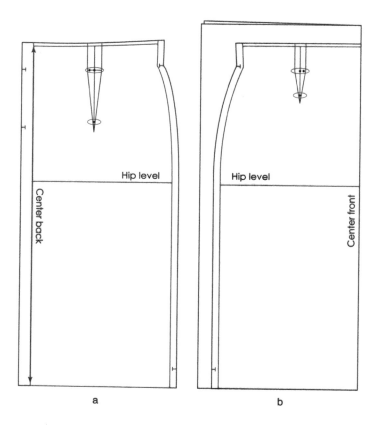

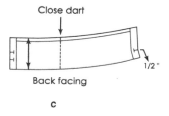

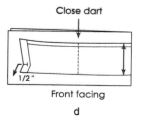

Figure 7.77

Gore Skirts: Six-Gore and Eight-Gore Flare

Skirt gores are multiple panels that taper to the waist. Gore panels can be designed in a variety of ways—equally spaced or in clusters; hanging straight or flared at any point along the way to the hemline; pleated; with uneven hemlines; or angled panels for interest (Figure 7.78). Because gore panels tend to look alike, notches are needed to identify the correct joining panels. The four-gore skirts of the A-line and full flare skirts are discussed on pages 135 and 139.

Design Analysis

The skirt has six flared gore panels, with the front and back panels cut on the fold. To convert the six-gore to an eight-gore skirt, add seams and flare to the front and back centerlines. The amount of flare is estimated at 1 1/2″ on each side of the gore panels, but add an extra inch (2 1/2″) for experimentation. The zipper is placed at the left side seam or at the side back panel.

Figure 7.78

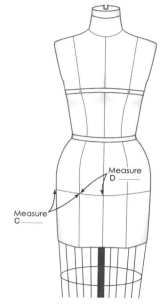

Figure 7.79

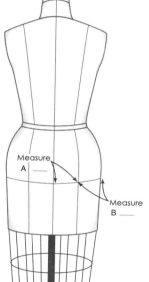

Figure 7.80

Preparing Muslin

Figure 7.79 and Figure 7.80

Measure the space between the Princess panels of the front and back form at the HBL line. Record for A, B, C, and D. These measurements are the widths of the gore panels.

Length: As desired.

Figure 7.81

Cut skirt length plus 2 1/2″ across half the width of the fabric.

Draping Steps

Back and Front Gore Panels: A and D

Fold fabric to equal measurement A plus 2 1/2″.

Measure 2 1/2″ in and draw a line parallel with the foldline.

Draw a line from hem to 1″ at waist.

Repeat for panel D of the front panel.

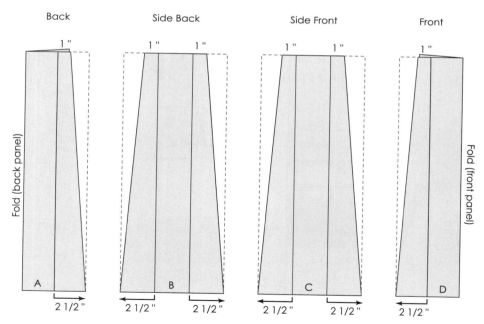

Figure 7.81

Side Gore Panels: B and C

Cut two panels using measurements B, which is the side back panel, and C, which is the side front panel. Add 5″.

Measure 2 1/2″ in from each side and draw lines parallel with each other.

Draw lines from hem to 1″ at waist.

Front Panel

Figure 7.82

Place the center of the unfolded gore panel to the center line of the form 1″ above the waistline. Pin to form.

Crossmark Princess at waist, and pencil rub Princess line to 5″ (can be higher or lower) below waist.

Mark 1/8″ out from this point and clip.

Peel back or remove for the drape of the side panel.

Front Side Panel

Figure 7.83

Center side panel to form 1″ above waist.

Pin 1/4″ ease at waist.

Smooth muslin along the Princess and side seam. Pin.

Pencil rub Princess line and side seam from waist to 5″ below the waist.

Front Side Panel

Figure 7.84

Pin front gore panel to the side front gore panel at the Princess line from waist to the 1/8″ mark of the slash line.

Fold front panel to the desired width of flare at the hemline. Crease this line.

Pin to side front panel flare at an equal distance from the gore line at hem.

Adjust the amount of flare until satisfied.

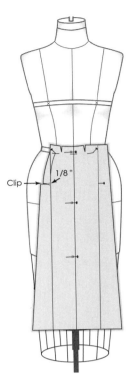

Figure 7.82

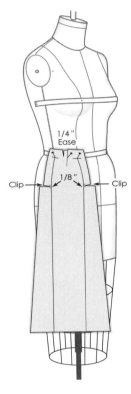

Figure 7.83

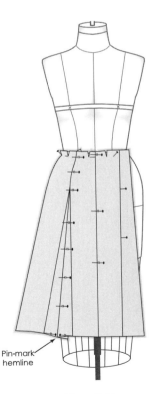

Figure 7.84

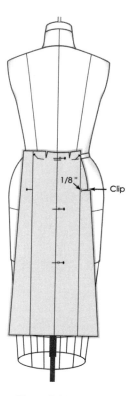

Figure 7.85

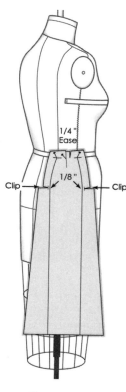

Figure 7.86

Back Panel

Figure 7.85

Drape back panel using instruction for the front panel.

Side Back Panel

Figure 7.86

Drape side back panel using instruction for the side front panel.

Figure 7.87

Pin side seam from waist to the 1/8″ mark at the slash line. Pin the flare at hemline equal to the measurement of the front panel. Pin.

Check the silhouette from the front view. If necessary, increase or decrease the side flare to improve symmetry.

Finished Pattern

Figure 7.88

Remove panels from the form, and true the gore seamlines. Stitch muslin, or transfer to paper first for the fitting.

Place the gore panels on paper. Trace and add seams and notches where shown.

Figure 7.87

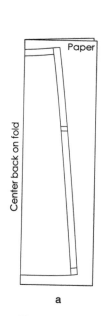

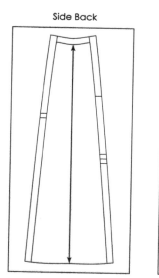

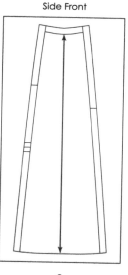

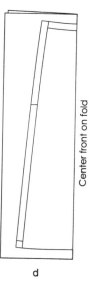

Figure 7.88

Eight-Gore Inverted Box-Pleated Skirt

Side pleats, box pleats, or triple pleats can be added to the gore lines for design variations (Figure 7.89). To review pleats, see pages 153 and 154.

Design Analysis

The skirt has eight gores with an A-line silhouette. The length is above the knee or to the length desired. The gore panels include box pleats except at the A-line of the side seams. The depth of each pleat is 1 1/2″. The box pleats are stitched at an angle to prevent flopping. A zipper is placed at the side seam. Muslin preparation for the gore panels include pleats and a 1/2″ seam allowance. Ease of 1/8″ is added when draped at the hipline of the form.

Preparing Muslin

Figure 7.90

See page 168. Record A, B, C, and D.

Length: Cut a width of fabric equal to the desired length, plus 2 1/2″ for hem and waist seam. Draw crossgrain 7″ down from the top of the muslin.

Panel widths: Cut each panel equal to the recorded measurements for A, B, C, and D,

Figure 7.89

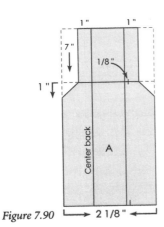

Figure 7.90 2 1/8″

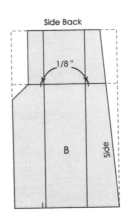

Side Back

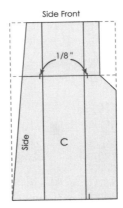

Side Front

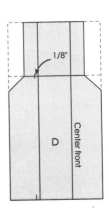

plus 4 1/4″. Panel A: Draw lines through length of the panel 2 1/8″ in from each side. Mark 1/8″ out from hip for ease. Mark at hem, as shown. Repeat for panel D. Repeat for panels B and C, except at side seam the line connects from hem to waist for the A-line silhouette.

Trim the panels as indicated by the broken lines on page 171.

Draping Steps

Front Panel

Figure 7.91

Fold center front of the muslin.

Place fold to the center front of the form 1″ above waistband. Pin at the centerline.

Smooth, slash, and mark muslin along waist to Princess line.

Smooth muslin along the Princess line and pencil rub to crossgrain line. Trim.

Peel back or remove from the form.

Side Front Panel

Figure 7.92

Center the side panel to the form 1″ above waistline. Pin.

Pin 1/4″ ease at the waist.

Smooth, slash, and mark muslin along the waist.

Smooth muslin along the curve of the Princess line and side seam to the crossgrain line. Pencil rub, trim, and remove from the form.

Figure 7.91

Figure 7.92

Back and Side Back Panels

Figure 7.93 and Figure 7.94

To drape the back and side back panels, follow the instructions given for the front skirt panels.

Figure 7.95

Use a curve rule to reshape the hipline from the waist, ending at the 1/8″ mark at the crossgrain line. All panels must line up with the crossgrain line. If not, adjust the waistline so that they do.

Add 1/2″ seams. Cut panels for a full skirt.

Figure 7.93

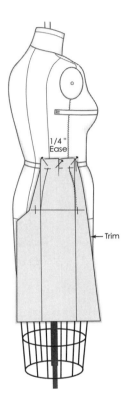

Figure 7.94

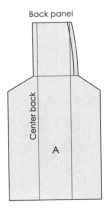
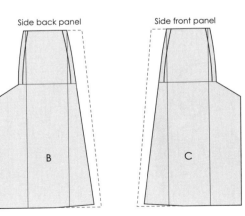

Back panel Side back panel Side front panel Front panel

A B C D

Center back Center front

Figure 7.95 Adjust A-Silhouette

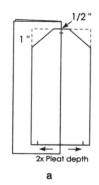

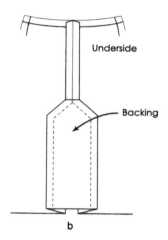

Figure 7.96

Pleat Backing

Figure 7.96a

Draw a line on paper equal to the length of the pleat. Fold on this line.

Square a 2″ line out from top and bottom of the pleat, and connect.

Draw a line 1/2″ out from the top, ending 1″ down. Mark a 1/2″ seam allowance at hemline of backing.

Cut backing for six pleats.

Figure 7.96b

Stitch seams and pleat backing to each panel.

Do not stitch side seams.

Finished Pattern

Figure 7.97

Place skirt on the form, and pin side seam allowing sufficient ease at the hipline. If necessary, raise the center back so that the hemline is parallel with the floor. Pin side and adjust side flare, if necessary, when viewing the front and back skirt for fit and balance.

Remove skirt and make paper patterns.

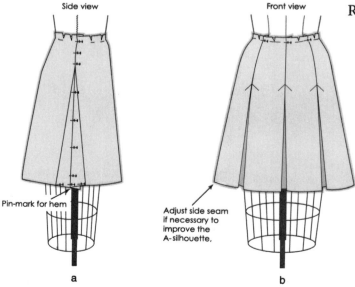

Figure 7.97

Skirts with Gathered Waistlines

Gathers are computed by ratio or by width of the fabric. An example of the amount of fabric gathered is shown in Figure 7.98:

- Width = 26″
- 1 1/2 times the width of the fabric = 39″ (13″ added to the width)
- 2 times the width of the fabric = 52″ (26″ added to the width)
- 2 1/2 times the width of the fabric = 65″ (39″ added to the width)

The ratio of gathers may be difficult to visualize. It is suggested that a gathered sample of each fullness be stitched and used as a reference for added fullness. Cut and stitch a 5″ sample of each.

An example of width computed by the ratio is shown in Figure 7.99, which illustrates one-and-a-half widths, or two or more widths of fabric. Lightweight fabrics may require more gathers and heavy fabrics less.

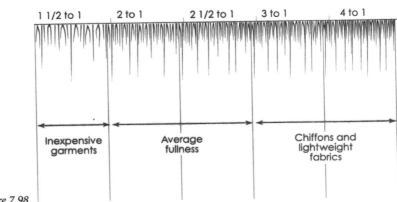

Figure 7.98

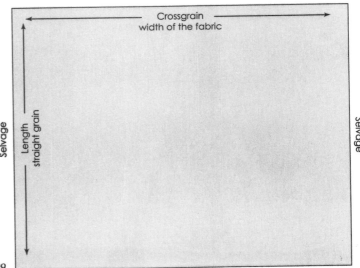

Figure 7.99

Dirndl Skirt

Design Analysis

The dirndl skirt has as much fullness at the waist as at the hemline. The fabric is cut into the number of widths required for fullness. The rectangular shape is cut to length—generally, two panels of 36″ widths, or from one-and-a-half to two panels of 45″ widths of fabric. The waist gathers into the waistband (Figure 7.100).

Figure 7.100

Preparing Fabric or Paper

Cut the required panels to length.

Measure hip depth (#25) using the Form Measurement Chart.

Subtract front from the back hip depth to mark center back.

Draping Steps

Figure 7.101

Use this measurement and mark at center back drawing a curved line ending at the side seam. Trim.

Optional

The center back can be cut on the fold or with a center back seam. The zipper can be placed at the center back or at the side seam.

Gathered skirts are sometimes cut to gather along the selvage placing the straight grain around the skirt.

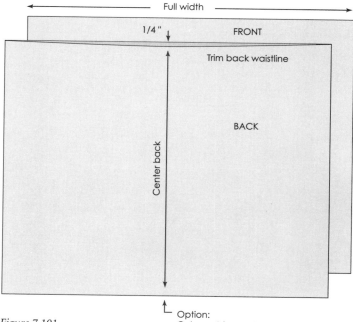

Figure 7.101

Tiered Skirts

A tier is one of a series of rows placed one above the other in the form of gathers, pleats, or flares (Figure 7.102). A tiered skirt can be designed with the tiers stitched in rows that connect one row to the other, or stitched within the seams of panels of a straight or flared skirt. Tiers may be the same width, graduated, stitched horizontally, or on an angle for a skirt or dress. To determine the proportion of tiers, the designer/draper has several options:

Drape the full flare skirt and pin-mark tier locations.

Trace a copy of a basic skirt or flare skirt on marking or tissue paper. Place on the form and pencil mark tier locations (see Figure 7.103 and Figure 7.104).

Pin-mark or use style tape directly on the form to mark tier locations.

Design 1

Design 3

Design 2

Figure 7.102

Separated Tiers

This example is based on a draped front and back basic skirt.

Design Analysis

The basic skirt is draped and used for two purposes:

1. To mark the visual location and underlay of each tier to determine yardage.

2. To establish a skirt frame to which the tiers will be stitched into seams. The seam of the underlay is marked at least 1″ up from each tier to cover stitches. This measurement is added to the length of each tier after the first. Each of the tiers has a 1/2″ seam and hem allowance. The third panel (C) of the frame is discarded for Designs 1 and 2, but needed for Design 3, which is a thought problem.

Tier Proportions

Figure 7.103

Drape the front and back skirt to the desired length.

Pin-mark the level of each tier (A, B, and C).

Figure 7.104

Pencil mark (use a red pencil) 1″ up from pin-marks of panels B and C.

Measure the length of each tier

- Tier A: Length, plus 1/2″ seam for waist and hem. Record.
- Tiers B and C: Length, plus 1″ for the underlay plus 1/2″ for seam and hem. Record.

Skirt Frame

Figure 7.105

Cut panels along the red lines of the underlay.

True panels A and B.

Discard panel C.

Trace on paper, adding seam and hem allowances as indicated.

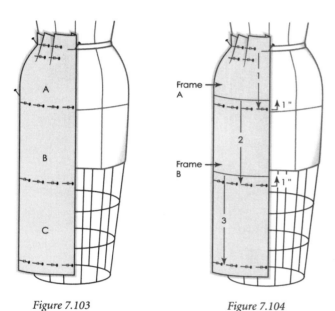

Figure 7.103

Figure 7.104

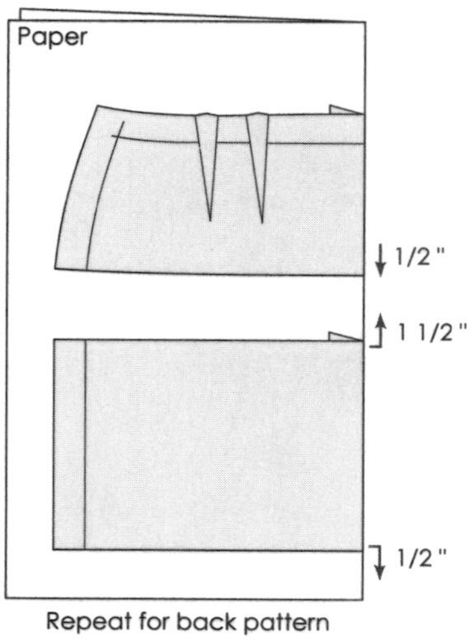

Figure 7.105

Gathered Tiers: Design 1

Figure 7.106

Yardage suggested for each tier:

- Tier 1: Recorded length, plus full width of fabric.
- Tier 2: Recorded length, plus two widths of fabric.
- Tier 3: Recorded length, plus three widths of fabric.

Join and gather tiers 1, 2, and 3. Pin or stitch tiers to panels A and B of the front and back skirt. Critique fullness and proportion of the tiers.

Flared Tiers: Design 2

Figure 7.107

The flare of the first tier is created by smoothing the excess of the waist (dart) to the hem. For greater flare, slash and drop the crossgrain.

Tiers 2 and 3 are created by dropping the crosswise grain and adding flare to the side seams.

Stitch the flared tiers to the frames of A and B.

Critique flared tiers.

Pattern shapes accompany the draped skirt.

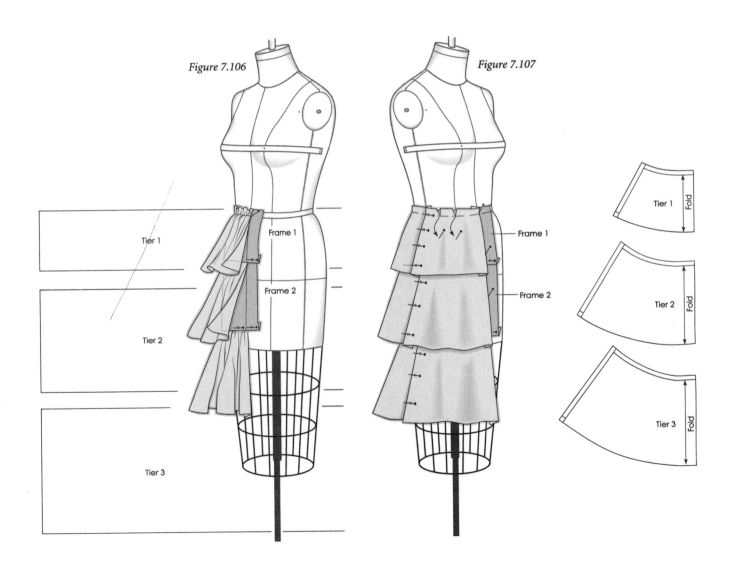

Figure 7.106

Figure 7.107

Tiered Rows Stitched Together

Design 4

Figure 7.108

Design 4 is illustrated. It is a prototype for other tiered variations that are joined together (Figure 7.108).

Design Analysis

A copy of the basic skirt pattern is cut in marking paper (Figure 7.109), pinned, and placed on the form and marked for tier placement. After the tiers are marked (use example given or mark your own), the amount of fullness allotted for each row should be determined. The first tier is cut to the width of the fabric (36″ or 45″), and each subsequent row will be from 1 1/2 to 2 times the previous row. The waist of the first tier is tapered from the side to the center back waist. This allows the skirt to hang parallel to the floor.

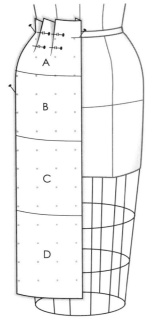

Figure 7.109

Tier Proportions

Figure 7.109

Length: 29″

Note the length of each tier:

- Tier A: 6 1/4″
- Tier B: 6 3/4″
- Tier C: 7 1/4″
- Tier D: 8 3/4″

To these measurements, add 1/2″ seams.

Add 1″ for the hem to the last tier.

Yardage suggested for each tier (Figure 7.110):

- Tier 1: One width. Trim 3/8″ at center back waist to zero at side waist.
- Tier 2: Two widths.
- Tier 3: Four widths.
- Tier 4: Eight widths.

Add 1/2″ to tiers A, B, and C for seams and hem allowance.

Cut the panels apart 1/2″ and trim center back.

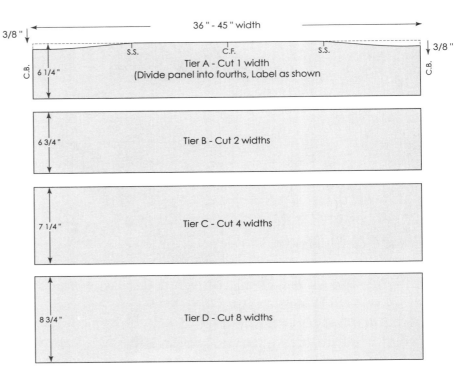

Figure 7.110

Wrap Skirt with Asymmetric Drape

Figure 7.11

Design Analysis

Figure 7.111

A four-pleat, asymmetric drape wraps a basic skirt (and can also be attached to a bodice with a zipper back). The front under the skirt continues to the side seam, where it is secured with a tie string or a hook and eye. The waistband is attached to the draped section continuing around the back, and front skirt ending at the location where the front drape overlaps it. The waistband is secured with a button or Velcro. The excess from the waist dart is draped to the hemline as flare and is then lifted, thereby providing excess for the asymmetric pleats. This design is the prototype for other designs with pleated drapes.

Follow the instructions for draping the basic skirt on page 39 or trace a copy of the basic skirt pattern. The right side seam is not stitched to the back side seam. The back side seam is stitched to the asymmetric drape.

Preparing Muslin

Figure 7.112

Measure as needed:

- Width: Across front hip or use double #23 on the Form Measurement Chart and add 10".
- Length: As desired, plus 5".

Draw a grainline in the center of the muslin and slash 3" down from this line.

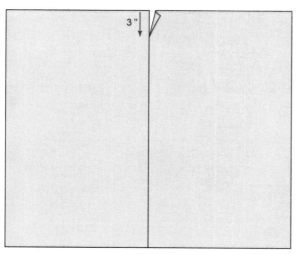

Figure 7.112

Draping Steps

Figure 7.113

Place guideline to the center of the form, pinning the slash line at bottom of waist tape.

Pin down the centerline to secure.

Smooth, clip, and mark the muslin along the waistline and abdomen to the side seam.

Smooth the muslin along the side seam and pencil rub. Pin. The flare will appear at the hemline.

Smooth, clip, and mark muslin 1″ past the centerline for placement of the first pleat. Pleats can be folded in either direction as desired.

Figure 7.114

Trim to within 1″ of the side seam.

To fold the first pleat, lift the crossgrain and fold a pleat depth of approximately 1 1/2″ (3″ on the open). The fold of the pleat should not twist, but should roll smoothly to the waist where it is pinned. Fabric should lie smoothly below the drape and be pinned temporarily.

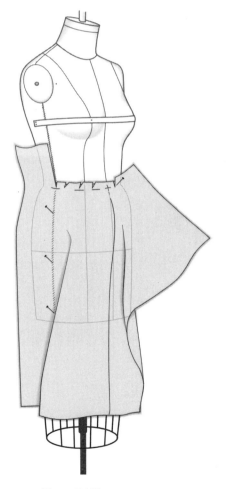

Figure 7.113

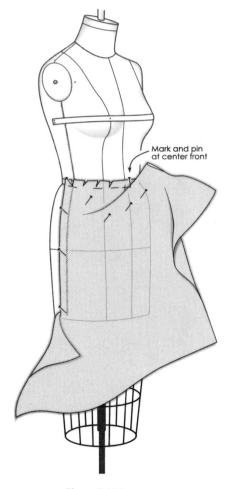

Mark and pin at center front

Figure 7.114

Figure 7.115

The second pleat is placed 1/2″ from the first pleat. Lift the crossgrain and fold a pleat depth of approximately 2″ (4″ on the open). Pin.

Figure 7.116

Repeat the process for the third pleat.

Figure 7.117

Smooth the side seam, and pin to the cage to secure.

Trim excess to within 1″ of the side seam.

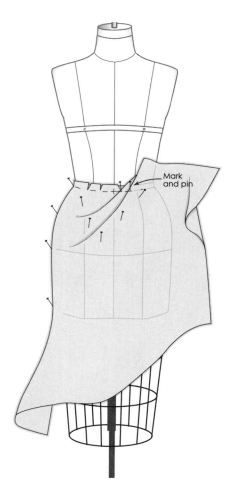

Figure 7.115

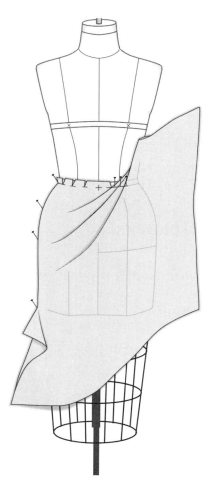

Figure 7.116

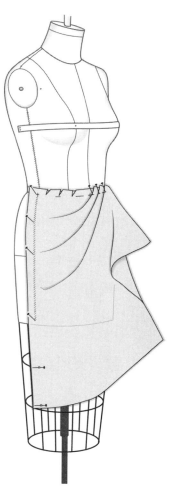

Figure 7.117

Figure 7.118 and Figure 7.119

Repeat the process for the fourth pleat.

Draw a continuous line across the pleated drape at the bottom of the waist tape.

Trim to 1/2″ along the waistline.

Continue trimming approximately 8″ to 10″ beyond the last pleat to create a cascade of folds.

Trim the curve line of the cascade to the desired length of the skirt.

Clip the muslin 1″ past the last pleat to establish the drop of the cascade. Pin-mark at the waist tape for button placement of the waistband, which will end 1″ past the pin-mark. Repin across the foldline to secure the angle of the underlay of each pleat or use masking tape.

Remove the drape for trueing.

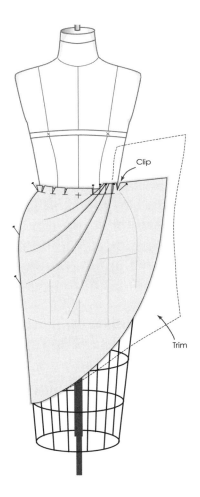

Figure 7.118

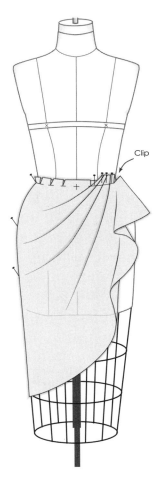

Figure 7.119

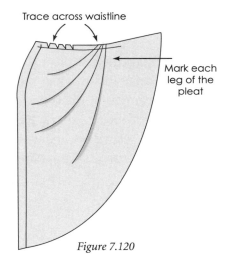

Figure 7.120

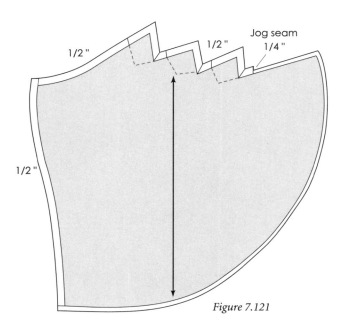

Figure 7.121

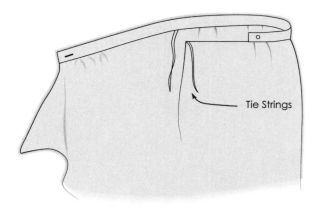

Figure 7.122

Figure 7.120

Lay the pinned drape on the table, allowing the pleats to lay flat.

With a curved ruler, draw the waistline with a red pencil.

Mark the location of each pleat leg.

To transfer the shape of the pleat underlay, trace across the waistline.

Figure 7.121

Unpin and draw the underlay of each pleat (broken lines are used for pleats folded downward; the bold lines are for the shape of the pleat folded upward). Draw and true the line of the side seam. Stitch muslin or transfer to paper first for the test fit.

Transfer to paper, and notch each pleated drape and side seam. Recut.

Fold and stitch across each pleat.

Stitch the basic skirt together with the draped overlay stitched to the back side seam. (The cascade can be merrow edged, baby hemmed, or faced.)

Types of Wrap Closure

Figure 7.122

The waistband starts at the cascade and extends about 1″ past the pin-mark on the waist tape of the form for button placement.

Tie strings are placed at the side waist. At the end of the wrap, hooks and eyes or Velcro can be used. The belt can be buttoned or can use Velcro.

Side Cowl Draped Skirt

Review the theory of the cowl drape given in Chapter 12. Cowls drape best when on true bias (Figure 7.123 and Figure 7.124).

Design Analysis

The four pleated cowls draped at the sides of the skirt create a peg silhouette. The dart excess at the front and back waist are incorporated into the pleats of the cowl. The pleat intake of the back cowls will be greater than that of the front cowls. The front cowls will be draped first, taking up all the excess so that the straight grain of the center front aligns with that of the form. The back cowls are draped in sequence with those of the front, with the center back seam on the bias grain. (The center front may be cut on fold if the fabric has sufficient width.) The skirt should be draped in a softly woven fabric, or knit.

Figure 7.123

Figure 1.124

Preparing Muslin: Front and Back Skirt

Figure 7.125

Measurements needed:

Width

Back Hip arc: #23 _____
Length: 20 to 25″ _____

Fold fabric so that the crossgrain aligns with straight grain of the selvage. Mark the foldline (true bias). Cut folded section from the fabric. Pencil rub guidelines on bias fold.

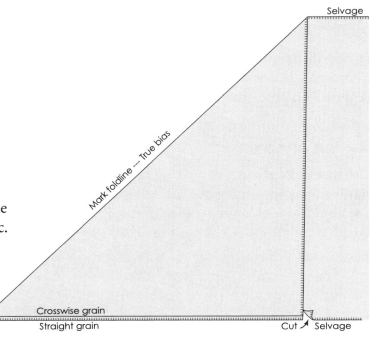

Figure 7.125

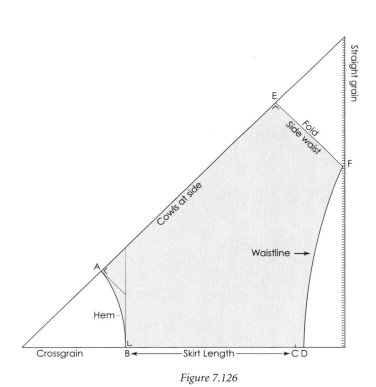

Figure 7.126

Draping Steps

Front Drape

Figure 7.126

Square up from crossgrain equal to hip measurement plus 3″ and mark 2″ down. Square a line from fold and draw a curved line that equals hip arc plus 1/2″ for hemline of the skirt (A-B).

Measure up from (B) for the skirt length, plus 1″ for the hem (C). Add 1–1/2″ (D).

Square an 8 1/2″ line from the fold (E to F). This is the first fold of the cowl (E) to (F).

Draw a soft curve line from (D) to (F) for the waistline. Measure this line. To determine the pleat intake, subtract the front waist from (D-E). Divide into the number of cowls desired.

Repeat for the back waist. The centerlines of the front and back skirt are on the grain.

Cut skirt section from the fabric (darkened section).

Draw guideline on bias fold.

First Cowl

Figure 7.127

Unfold the fabric, and fold across the muslin (E-F).

Pin 1″ down from the fold on each side of the side seam at the waistline.

Place holding pins to secure the fabric as the drape proceeds.

Bring together the front points to form first cowl.

Second Cowl

Figure 7.128

Second cowl: Fold a cowl pleat and pin approximately 3/4″ from the first cowl. The bias guideline must align with the side seam of the form throughout the drape. Adjust the pleat to shift the alignment, if necessary.

Mark across the pleat at waist and on each side of the fold of the pleat.

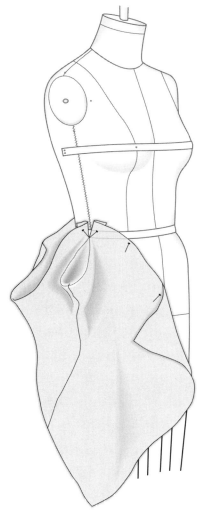

Figure 7.127

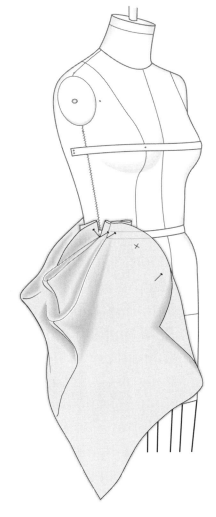

Figure 7.128

Third Cowl

Figure 7.129

Repeat the instruction.

Fourth Cowl

Figure 7.130

Pin center front with fabric extending 1″ beyond center front and parallel with it. Remaining excess is folded for the last pleated cowl. (Excess should be shared about equally among the pleated cowls if possible.) Adjust, if necessary.

Back Drape

Figure 7.131

Repeat the instructions for the front drape. The center back line should be parallel to the center back of the form and extend 1″ beyond. Recheck so that the bias guideline is on the side seam of the form. Check for twisting of the cowls by placing a finger at the guideline fold of each cowl and pressing down. If twist occurs, adjust the pleat intake. (See Chapter 12.)

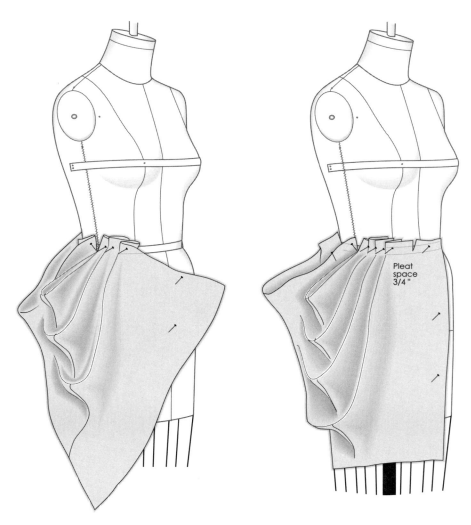

Figure 7.129   Figure 7.130   Figure 7.131

Finished Pattern

Figure 7.132

Pin through each pleat to secure before removing the drape from the form.

Lay the drape on the table and draw a blended front and back waistline.

Run the tracing wheel along the pinned waistline to transfer the exact shape of the pleat underlay.

Figure 7.133

Unpin pleats and pencil in the preferred pleat underlay of each cowl.

True the remaining drape.

Make the paper pattern. Cut and test fit. (A) to (B) can be stitched together or left unstitched.

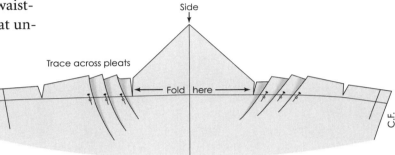

Figure 7.132

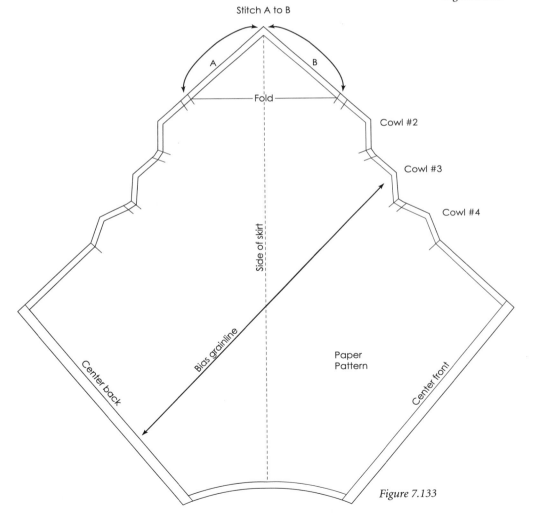

Figure 7.133

Collars

The draper/designer has freedom to create the design of the collar's width, length, height of stand, and direction in which it will lie (see Figure 8.1). This is the advantage of draping collars. The choice of collar design should always compliment and enhance the style and purpose of the garment. The shawl collar is illustrated in Chapter 17.

Figure 8.1

Collar Terminology

Figure 8.2

Collar edge: The design part of a collar.

Collar stand: The height at which a collar rolls over itself. There are three basic stands:

- 1″ stand, a full roll.
- 1/2″ stand, a partial roll.
- 1/8″ stand, a flat roll.

The height of the stand limits a collar's width from the center back to the shoulder. From the shoulder to the front, a collar can be of any width and shape.

Neckline edge: Stitches to the neckline of the garment.

Roll line: The point at which a collar rolls over itself, creating the collar stand.

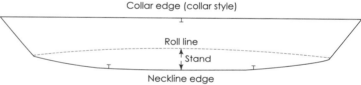

Figure 8.2a

Two Basic Neckline Edges

Regardless of the collar design, the neckline edge which controls the collar stand has one of two basic shapes:

- Contrary to the curved neckline of the garment (unbuttoned, the collar springs open) (see Figure 8.2b).
- Following closely to the curved neckline of the garment (unbuttoned, the collar stays in place) (see Figure 8.2c).

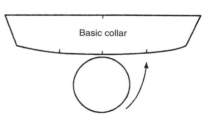

Figure 8.2b

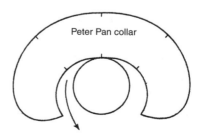

Figure 8.2c

Basic Collar

The basic collar ends at a point and is designed for shirts and garments requiring a casual look. The front collar can be of any shape providing that it blends to the shoulderline. The collar will open when unbuttoned rather than stay at its original location (Figure 8.3).

Principle

The neckline edge of a collar, in opposition to the curve of the form's neckline, will cause the collar to open when unbuttoned.

Design Analysis

The basic collar has a 1″ collar stand (full roll). However, a wider collar, will increase the height of the stand.

Preparing Muslin

Figure 8.4

Cut muslin as follows:

- Length: 12″
- Width: 3″

Draw straight grain 1″ from edge.

Draw crossgrain 1/2″ up from muslin length.

Figure 8.3

Figure 8.4

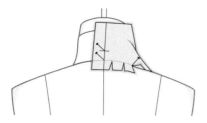

Figure 8.5a

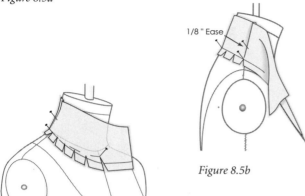

Figure 8.6

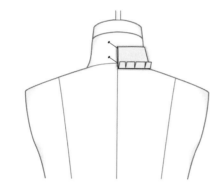

1/8 " Ease

Figure 8.5b

Figure 8.8

Draping Steps

Figure 8.5a

Place straight grain at the center back, with the crossgrain guideline at the neckline.

Pin at neck, and from 1 to 1 1/2″ (for higher stand) up from neckline for collar stand.

Smooth the crossgrain guideline along the back neckline to the shoulder/neck. Slash and pin.

Figure 8.5b

Pin 1/8″ approximately 1″ up from the shoulder/neck.

Figure 8.6

As the muslin is smoothed around the neck to the center front, the crossgrain lowers.

Mark the neckline curve to the pinhead guide at center front.

Slash to, but not past, the marked neckline. Pin.

Trim excess to within 1/4″ of the front neckline.

Figure 8.7

Fold the back collar over from the pin-mark at the stand.

Fold muslin upward approximately 1/4″ below the neckline of the form. Slash down to the collar edge. Trim excess.

Figure 8.8

Draw the front basic collar (or any design) ending at and blending with the shoulder/neck. The broken lines show other possible designs. Add to muslin preparation for design variations.

Remove draped collar and true.

Transfer Collar to Paper

Figure 8.9

Place collar on folded paper.

Use pushpins or a tracing wheel to transfer the upper collar to paper.

Remove traced collar.

Pencil the collar's outline and add 1/4″ seams.

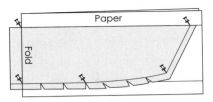

Figure 8.9

Finishing Pattern

Figure 8.10

Mark notch placement at the center back and shoulder. To complete the undercollar, trace and trim 1/8″ to zero at point of collar. Use also for inner support.

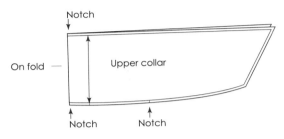

Figure 8.10a

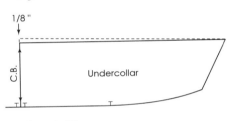

Figure 8.10b

Mandarin Collars

Inspiration for the mandarin collar as a fashion style is taken from traditional Chinese wear. The mandarin can be described as a standing band that fits around the neckline at varying heights (Figure 8.11). The center front of the mandarin can be rounded, straight (military effect), or winged for design variation. It can be extended for button/buttonholes and be part of the stand for the tailored shirt collar. The mandarin can also be draped on fold at center front with the opening in back. The collar can be draped at the basic neckline or at a distance from it.

Principle

The neckline edge is the same as that of the basic collar. The mandarin does not have a fold over collar (with exception of the collar/stand shirt collar) and will not open to same extent as the basic collar when unbuttoned.

Figure 8.11

Design Analysis

The mandarin collar has the traditional rounded shape. The basic height of a mandarin collar is from 1 1/4″ to 1 1/2″. It can be wider, but may be uncomfortable if the collar rubs against the turn in the back neck.

Preparing Muslin

Figure 8.12

Cut muslin as follows:

- Length: 10″
- Width: 2 1/4″

Draw straight grain 1″ from edge. Draw cross-grain 1/2″ up from muslin length.

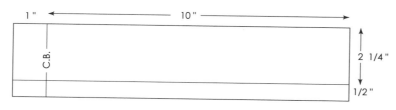

Figure 8.12

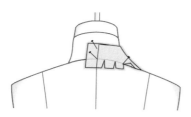

Figure 8.13

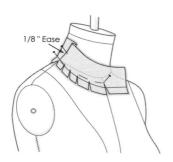

Figure 8.14

Draping Steps

Figure 8.13

Place straight grain at the center back and cross-grain at the neckline. Pin at the neck and 1 1/2″ up from the neckline.

Slash to, but not past, the neckline, as the muslin is smooth to the shoulder/neck. Pin.

Figure 8.14

Pin 1/8″ approximately 1″ up at the shoulder/neck.

Smooth fabric around the neck to the center front, slashing to release tension. Pin.

Draw a neckline curve from the pinhead guide to the shoulder/neck.

Trim excess to within 1/2″.

Figure 8.15

Draw style curve of the mandarin. (The broken lines show the mandarin with a straight line for a military effect.)

Figure 8.16

Remove the collar, true, and transfer to paper. The upper and undercollar can be the same size.

Finished Pattern

Variation: Winged Mandarin

Figure 8.17 (the design), Figure 8.18, and Figure 8.19

Refer to Figure 8.13 and Figure 8.14 for draping instruction.

The excess is cut to a point. The point is folded and pressed to hold its position.

Finished Pattern

Variation: Mandarin with Extension

Figure 8.20, Figure 8.21 (the design), and Figure 8.22

Drape past the center front an amount equal to the width of the extension of the garment. The extended end is rounded. The back mandarin is stitched to the back neck of the vest. Mark for button/buttonhole.

Finished Pattern

Figure 8.22

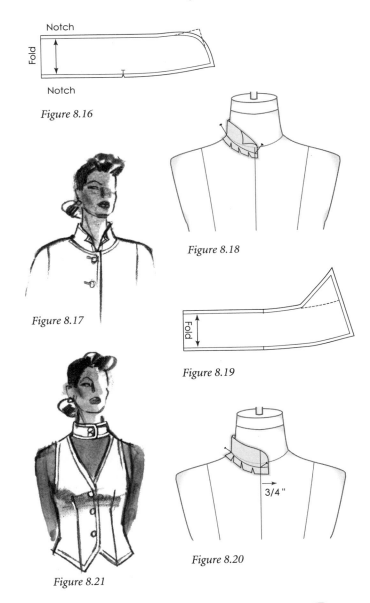
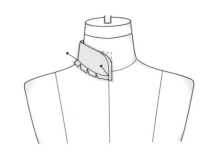

Figure 8.15

Figure 8.16

Figure 8.18

Figure 8.17

Figure 8.19

Figure 8.21

Figure 8.20

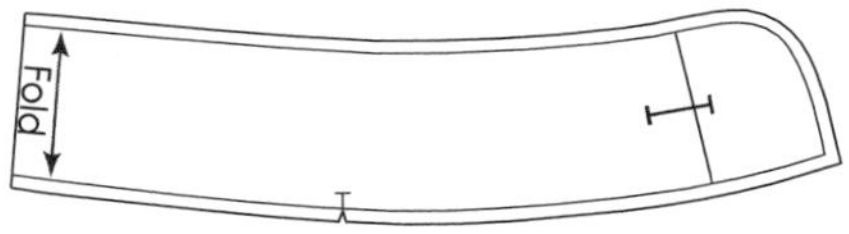

Figure 8.22

Peter Pan Collars

The Peter Pan introduces the principle of the full roll, partial roll, and flat roll collars (illustrated as a sailor collar) (see Figure 8.23). Apply this principle to all designs in which the collar is to stay in place when unbuttoned.

Figure 8.23

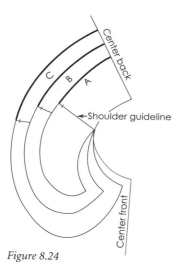

Figure 8.24

Principle

The neckline edge of collars that stay in place when unbuttoned must be similar in shape to the curve of the form's neckline. The closer the similarity, the lower the stand of the collar; the less the similarity, the higher the stand.

By applying a pivotal technique of the flat patternmaking method, called the 4 to 1 rule, the designer/draper will be able to drape a full roll (1″ stand), a partial roll (1/2″ stand), or a flat roll (1/8″ stand). The degree to which the neckline edge curves controls the height of the collar stand and the collar's width.

Relationship of Neckline Stand, and Width

Figure 8.24

Compare the curve of the neckline edge of each collar to that of the basic neckline. Compare the width of each collar to the height of the collar stand.

- Full roll: 1″ stand; 2 3/4″ wide, example A.
- Partial roll: 1/2″ stand; 3 1/2″ wide, example B.
- Flat roll: 1/8″ stand; any width, example C.

By design, the Peter Pan has a rounded collar's edge. Figure 8.23 illustrates the three basic types by the shape of the neckline, height of the stand and width of the roll-over collar. The front part of a collar can be designed to any length and width, but must blend with the back collar at or near the shoulder.

Peter Pan Collar: Full Roll

Design Analysis

Figure 8.25

The collar has a 1″ stand, and a finished width of 2 3/8″. The draping formula is to follow the back neckline to shoulder. Pivot the back drape 4″ to the front to complete the collar. The collar edge of the Peter Pan is drawn parallel with the neckline.

Figure 8.25

Preparing Muslin

Figure 8.26

Cut muslin 12″ × 12″.

Fold muslin 1/2″ for the center back.

A-B = 3″ for collar width. Mark.

B-C = 2″ squared from B. Square up 1″, mark, and continue through the length of the fabric. Draw a curve line from B to C.

Cut from B to C and continue through the length of the straight grain.

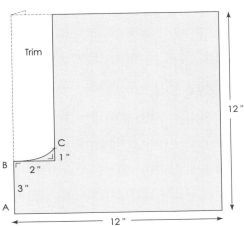

Figure 8.26

Draping Steps

Figure 8.27

Place fold (B) 1/2″ up at the center back neck. Pin.

Slash to, but not past, the neckline as muslin is being draped to the shoulder/neck, and cross-mark.

Thrust a holding pin upright at the shoulder/neck.

Crossmark (x) shoulder-tip. Remove all pins except shoulder/neck to allow muslin to pivot forward.

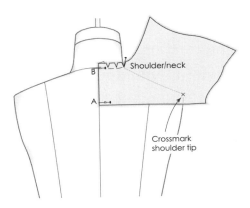

Figure 8.27

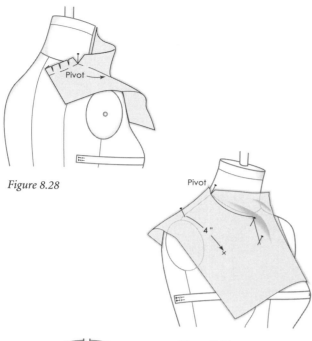

Figure 8.28

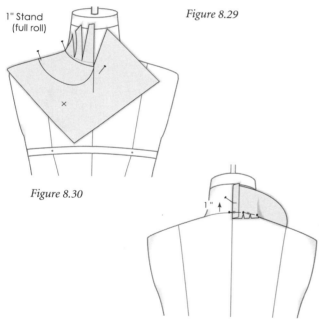

Figure 8.29

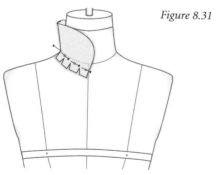

Figure 8.30

Figure 8.31

Figure 8.32

Draping Steps: Pivoting Collar Forward

Figure 8.28

Illustrates the muslin pivoted forward at the shoulder/neck.

Continue with the instructions to complete the full roll collar. To complete the partial roll collar, see page 204, and the flat roll, page 206.

Figure 8.29

Pivot (x) 4″ past the shoulder-tip. Pin at the shoulder-tip.

Smooth muslin around the neck. Pin.

Draw the curve of the neckline to center front pinhead.

Figure 8.30

Slash to, but not past, the neck guideline.

Draw collar 2 1/2″ wide and parallel to the neckline, rounding to the center front. (Any design can be created.)

Remove collar from the form and complete the shape of the back collar.

Trim excess to within 1/4″ around neckline.

Repin Collar to Neckline

Figure 8.31

Pin at the back neck and 1″ up for foldover.

Pin along neckline to the shoulder/neck.

Figure 8.32

Pin along the pin guide of the front neckline.

Back

Figure 8.33

Roll collar over. Pin.

Front

Figure 8.34

Roll collar to the center front. Adjust if necessary.

Remove to complete the collar patterns.

Completing Pattern

Trueing and Transferring the Collar

Figure 8.35

Adjust the neckline edge of the collar using the measurements given. (The point at shoulder/neck is less noticeable on the partial and flat roll collars.)

Mark notches at the shoulder and collar's edge.

Secure back collar to the fold of the paper.

Transfer collar on stitchline with a tracing wheel, and mark notches.

Remove paper tracing.

Upper Collar

Figure 8.36

Pencil in traced collar shape and notches.

The collar should be approximately 1/8″ longer than the neckline of the design pattern (that is, 1/16″ on each side of the notch) to compensate for the thickness of the collar construction.

Measure and mark the collar width from neckline edge.

Add 1/4″ seam around the collar.

Cut from paper and recheck fit by walking to the neckline of the design pattern.

Cut from paper. Notch the center back, shoulder and collar edge, as noted.

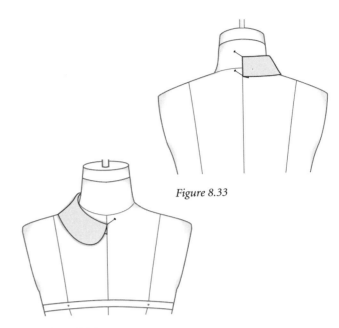

Figure 8.33

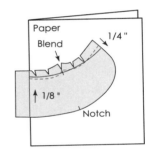

Figure 8.34

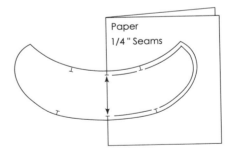

Figure 8.35

Figure 8.36

Undercollar and Interfacing Pattern

Figure 8.37

Place back collar on fold. Trace neckline and mark at the center back of the collar edge.

With a pushpin at the center front, pivot the collar until the back collar is raised 1/8″ from the mark. Trace the collar and mark notches. The undercollar is shorter in width and length (along the stitchline). The bias stretches to length when stitched.

Cut from paper, and double notch center back of collar's edge, and where noted.

If interfacing is fused by the yardage, the undercollar pattern is used. If not, trace the undercollar and remove seam allowance for fusing.

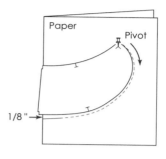

Figure 8.37

Peter Pan Collar: Partial Roll

Figure 8.38

Design Analysis

Figure 8.38

The collar has a 1/2″ stand, and a finished width of 3 1/2″. The collar is draped to follow the back neckline and pivots 2″ to the front to complete the drape. The collar edge is drawn parallel to the neckline.

Preparing Muslin

To prepare the muslin, see the instructions on page 201, Figure 8.26, using 4″ for the A-B measurement and the draping instructions in Figure 8.28 and Figure 8.29.

Draping Steps

Figure 8.39

Pivot (x) 2″ past shoulder-tip. Pin at shoulder-tip.

Smooth muslin around the neck. Pin.

Draw guideline for the neckline shape.

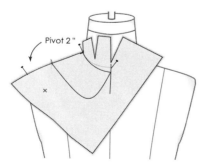

Figure 8.39

Slash to, but not past, the neck guideline.

Draw the collar 3 1/2″ wide parallel to the neckline and rounding to the center front neck. (Any design can be created.)

Trim excess to within 1/4″ around the neck.

Remove the collar from the form and complete the shape of the back collar.

Trim collar edge.

Pin Collar to Neckline

Figure 8.40a
Pin at back neck and 1/2″ up for foldover.

Pin along the neckline to the shoulder/neck.

Figure 8.40b
Pin along front neckline guide.

Back

Figure 8.41
Roll collar over. Pin.

Front

Figure 8.42
Roll collar over. Pin.

Remove collar. To complete the collar, see the instructions on page 203, Figures 8.35 through 8.37.

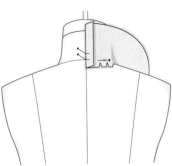

Figure 8.40a

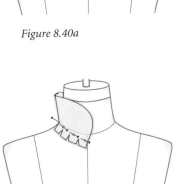

Figure 8.40b

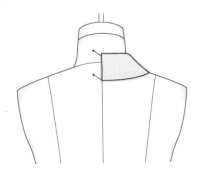

Figure 8.41

Figure 8.42

Sailor Collar

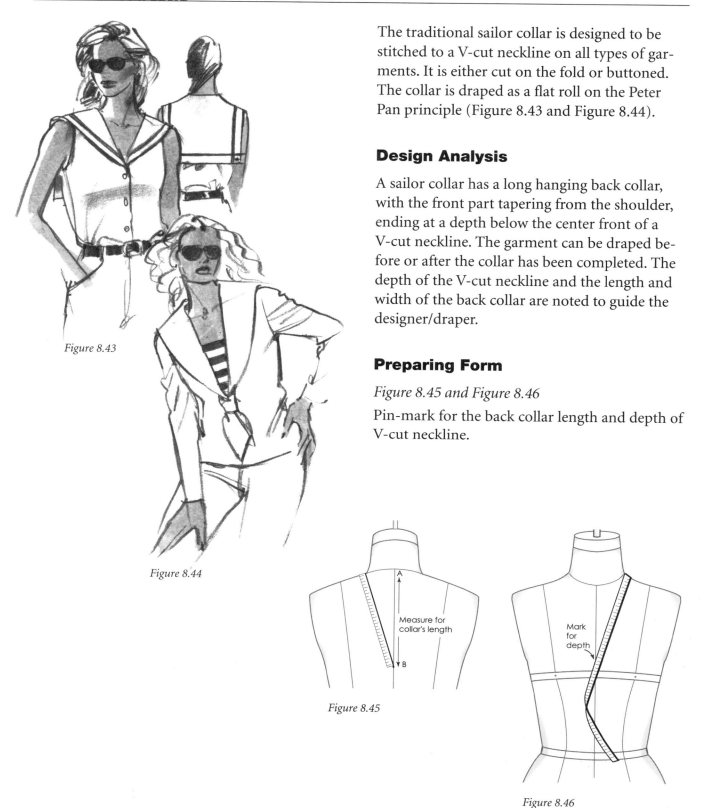

Figure 8.43

Figure 8.44

The traditional sailor collar is designed to be stitched to a V-cut neckline on all types of garments. It is either cut on the fold or buttoned. The collar is draped as a flat roll on the Peter Pan principle (Figure 8.43 and Figure 8.44).

Design Analysis

A sailor collar has a long hanging back collar, with the front part tapering from the shoulder, ending at a depth below the center front of a V-cut neckline. The garment can be draped before or after the collar has been completed. The depth of the V-cut neckline and the length and width of the back collar are noted to guide the designer/draper.

Preparing Form

Figure 8.45 and Figure 8.46

Pin-mark for the back collar length and depth of V-cut neckline.

A

Measure for collar's length

B

Figure 8.45

Mark for depth

Figure 8.46

Preparing Muslin

Figure 8.47

Length: Measure from the back mark to the shoulder/neck to the depth at the centerline. Add 6″.

Width: 12 1/2″.

Measure the back collar length and width. Add 1/2″ (reference measurement).

Cut muslin to equal length and width.

A-B equals the back collar length. Mark and square in 2 1/2″ and up 3/4″ (C).

Cut a curve line from B to C. From C, cut to the end of the muslin 1″ in from the corner.

Fold 1/2″ on the straight grain.

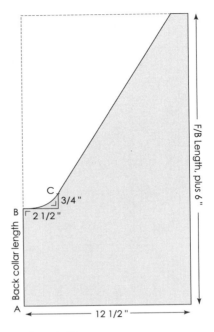

Figure 8.47

Draping Steps

Figure 8.48

Place fold of the straight grain to the center back 1/4″ above neck. Pin.

Smooth muslin across the back. Pin.

Slash to, but not past, the neckline as the muslin is smoothed around the back neckline.

Trim the neckline to within 1/4″ of the neckline.

Thrust a pin upright through the shoulder/neck.

Crossmark shoulder-tip.

Remove all pins except at the shoulder/neck.

Figure 8.49

Pivot 1/2″ past shoulder-tip. Pin shoulder-tip.

Draw the V-cut line and collar edge of the sailor (can be stylized for variations). Remove from the form to true.

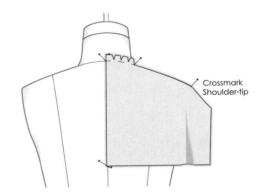

Figure 8.48

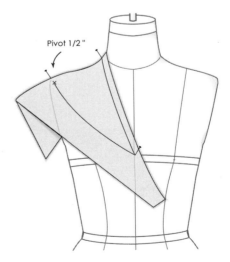

Figure 8.49

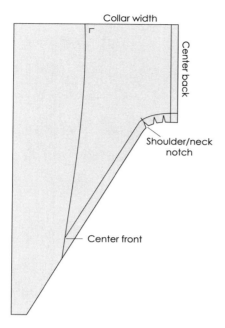

Figure 8.50

Trueing the Collar

Figure 8.50

Mark the width of the back collar and square a line, blending with the front sailor at the shoulderline. Cut sailor collar from the muslin.

Figure 8.51

Pin collar to the back neckline.

Pin 1/8″ up from the back.

Figure 8.52

Fold collar over, and pin along the center back.

Figure 8.53

Fold under the seam allowance of the V-cut, and pin at the depth of the collar.

Remove the collar and transfer to paper. True to neckline of the garment.

For instructions for undercollar and interfacing, see page 197.

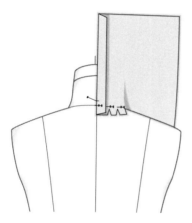

Figure 8.51

Figure 8.52

Figure 8.53

Cascade Collar

A cascade is created using the flat roll principle. Other design variations follows this project (Figure 8.54).

Design Analysis

The cascade collar is based on the flat roll principle. The collar is stitched to the styleline of the panel garment and falls as a cascade. The panel garment to which the collar is stitched can be a bodice or a dress, and it can be draped before the collar. The panel will be illustrated as a completed drape. See page 107 for the draping guide. A bishop's sleeve completes the design.

Preparing Form

Figure 8.55

Use style tape or pins to establish the panel styleline, using measurements given.

The shoulder/neck is labeled (x). Pin (y) at level with the armhole depth.

Preparing Muslin

Figure 8.56a

For the panel dress or bodice panel, see pages 26 and 27.

Cut muslin 12″ × 12″.

A-B = 5 1/2″. Square in 2 1/2″and up 3/4″. Mark and continue line through the length of the muslin.

Draw a curveline from B to C.

Cut unneeded section.

Fold 1/2″ on the straight grain.

Figure 8.54

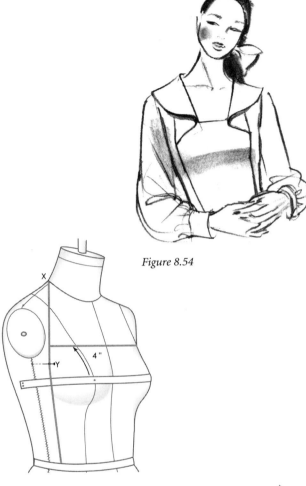

Figure 8.55

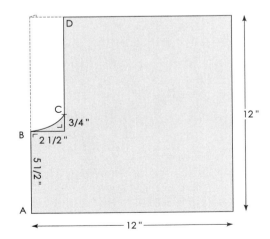

Figure 8.56a

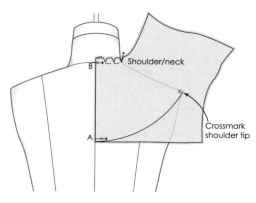

Figure 8.56b

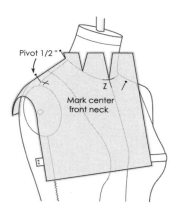

Figure 8.57

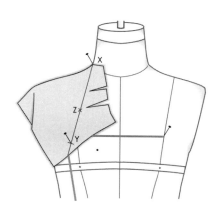

Figure 8.58

Draping Steps

Figure 8.56b

Place fold 1/2″ up from neck.

Drape neckline to shoulder/neck. Thrust pin upright at this point.

Draw a curve of the collar's edge parallel to the neckline.

Crossmark shoulder-tip. Remove all pins except at the shoulder/neck.

Figure 8.57

Pivot crossmark 1/2″ past shoulder-tip. Pin shoulder-tip.

Smooth and slash muslin around neck.

Crossmark center front neck (Z).

Figure 8.58

Pivot muslin downward from neck so that crossmark (Z) aligns with the X-Y styleline tape. Pin.

Draw styleline from X to Y. Pin and slash.

Figure 8.59

Remove drape from the form and draw shape of collars's edge. Add 1/2″ seam allowance X to Y.

Figure 8.60

Pin the collar to the garment from center back neckline to the front, ending in the seam of the panel line X to Y.

Figure 8.61

Front view of the drape.

Remove from form, true. Stitch muslin, or transfer to paper first for the test fit. To complete the collar, see pages 203 and 204. For facing instructions, see Chapter 14 .

Design Variations

Through design analysis, the designer/draper should be able to determine whether a collar is based on the full roll, partial roll, or flat roll principle.

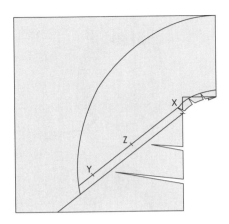

Figure 8.59

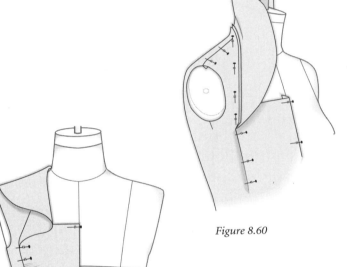

Figure 8.60

Figure 8.61

Turtleneck Collar

The drape of the bias band follows the neckline of the garment to which it will be stitched. The bias band should stretch as it is pinned or stitched to the neckline of the garment. Stretching the bias allows the band to fit closer to the neckline and prevents puckering. The turtleneck pattern will measure less than the neckline of the garment. An opening at the center back will be necessary if the garment is not cut in a stretchable fabric. A zipper, button/buttonhole, or loops and buttons are suggested for closures.

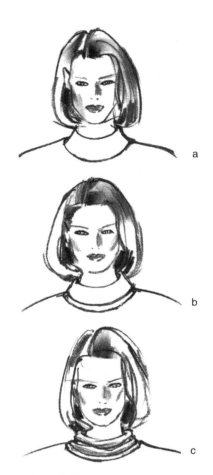

Figure 8.62

Design Analysis

Figure 8.62

Single-fold Turtleneck (Figure 8.62a): Draped to follow the basic neckline. The finished width is illustrated as 1 1/2″; however, it may be of any width.

Double-Fold Turtleneck (Figure 8.62b): Draped to follow the basic neckline. Double the finished width desired.

Wide Crush Neck (Figure 8.62c): Draped to follow an open neckline. The wide turtleneck falls in a crush-like effect around the neckline.

To avoid puckering, the bias band should be stretched as it is being pinned or stitched to the neckline. The banding pattern will measure less than the neckline of the garment.

Single-Fold and Double-Fold Turtlenecks

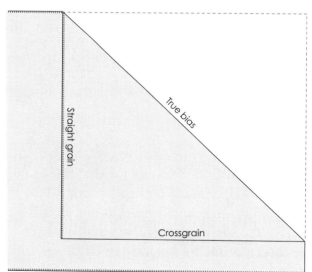

Figure 8.63

Preparing Muslin

Measure around the neckline. Add 1″.

Cut a 20″ square for Figure 8.62a (see Figure 8.63).

Cut a 22″ square for Figure 8.62b (for foldover).

Fold straight grain to crossgrain for true bias.

Figure 8.64

Square a line up from the fold equal to the banding width.

Mark length from this line and square again. Draw a connecting line.

Draw a 1/2″ parallel line for seam.

Cut band from fabric.

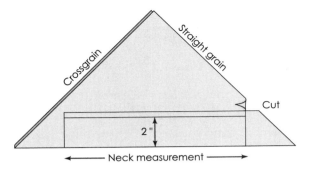

Figure 8.64

Draping Steps

Figure 8.65

Place fold side up. Pin center back and along the neck to the shoulder, stretching slightly.

Figure 8.66

Slightly stretch the banding as the bias is draped around the front neck.

Pin the 1/2″ seamline at the marked neckline.

Slash to, but not past, the neckline.

Figure 8.67

Pin banding together at the center back.

Remove the drape, true, and transfer to paper.

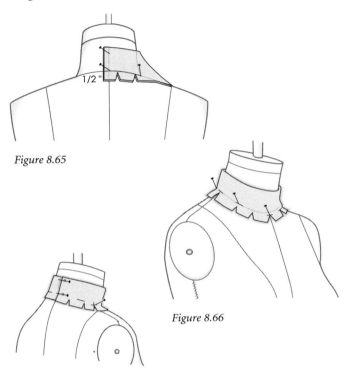

Figure 8.65

Figure 8.66

Figure 8.67

Bias Collar Pattern

Figure 8.68

Cut and stitch to garment.

If additional stretching occurs when stitching the bias collar to the garment, adjust collar pattern for notch locations and length.

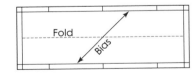

Figure 8.68

Wide Crush Turtleneck

Design Analysis

The drape of the bias band follows an open neckline. The wide turtleneck falls in a crush-like effect around the neckline (see page 212, Figure 8.62c).

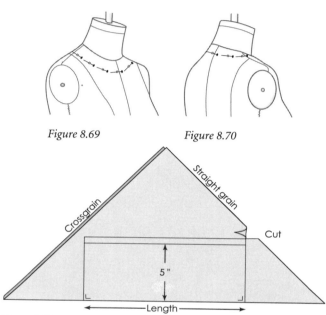

Figure 8.69   Figure 8.70

Figure 8.71

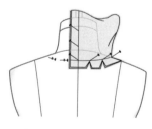

Figure 8.72

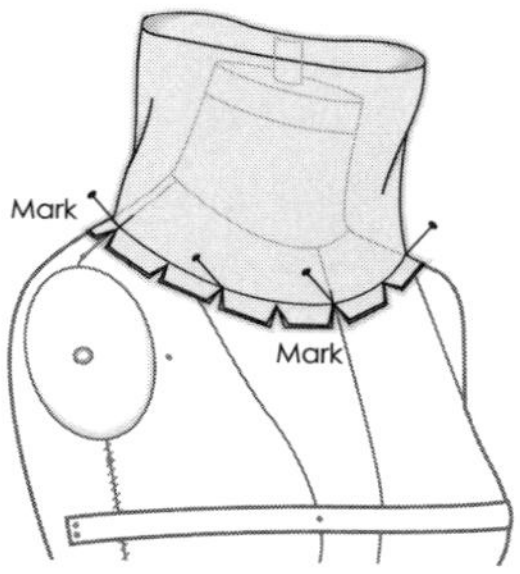

Figure 8.73

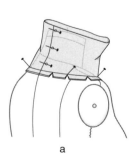

a   b

Figure 8.74

Preparing Form

Figure 8.69 and Figure 8.70

Pin-mark 1″ parallel to the front and back necklines. The shape of the neckline can vary.

Measure pin-marks from front to back. Add 1″.

Preparing Muslin

Figure 8.71

Cut a 22″ square and fold.

Square a 5″ line. From this point, square a 5″ line.

Draw a connecting line and a 1/2″ seam allowance line.

Draping Steps

Figure 8.72

Drape back neck, stretching slightly.

Mark a notch at the shoulder.

Figure 8.73

Drape across the front neck, stretching slightly.

Mark a notch at the center front.

Figure 8.74

Pin back neck.

Remove, and make paper pattern.

Cut in fabric and stitch to garment.

Figure 8.74b

If additional stretching occurs when stitching bias collar to the garment, adjust collar pattern for notch placement and collar length.

Variation: Draped Banding Inset

Design Analysis

Figure 8.75

The bias band is pinned into a style neckline, with a wrap at the center back to hold the excess as folds. The drapery effect ends in a V-neckline.

Figure 8.75

Preparing Form

Figure 8.76

Remove tape across bust. Pin-mark style neckline. Measure the styleline to the center back neck.

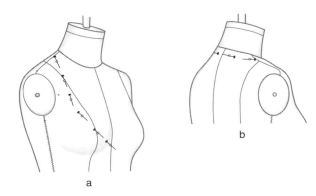

Figure 8.76

Preparing Muslin

Figure 8.77

Cut a 40″ square, and fold cross grain to the straight grain for a bias folsline.

Mark banding width, as desired, plus 1/2″ for seam guide.

Cut banding from muslin.

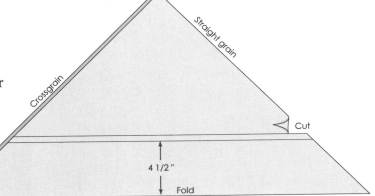

Figure 8.77

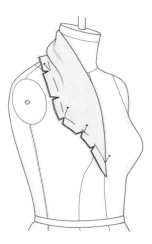

Figure 8.78

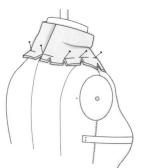

Figure 8.79

Figure 8.80

Draping Steps

Figure 8.78

Pin corner fold at the mark of the center front.

Slash and pin along the pin guide to the shoulder.

Figure 8.79

Pin across the back to the center neck.

Options: Continue draping to the other side or remove the drape and fold at the center back. Trim to the draped length.

Figure 8.80
Return drape to the form to check fit.

Figure 8.81

To control the folds at the center back, place a 1/2″ folded band over the gathers. The band is stitched to the design garment (on page 213).

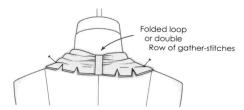

Folded loop or double
Row of gather-stitches

Figure 8.81

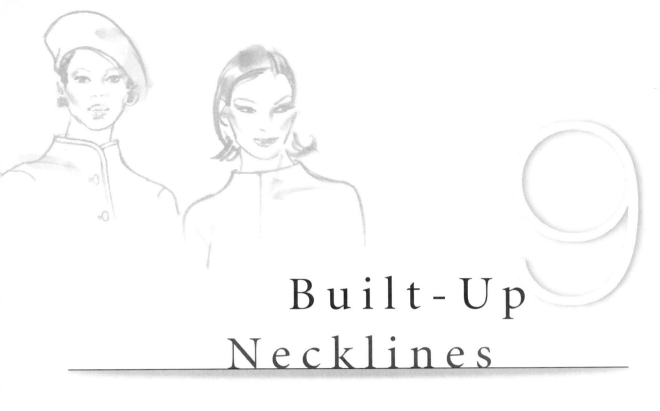

Built-Up Necklines

B uilt-up necklines extend above the base of the neck and should be draped to accommodate the forward position of the neck. There are two types: all-in-one with the garment and set-in bands. Built-up necklines are designed for blouses, shirts, jackets, and coats. Facings are included because of their special features.

Stovepipe Neckline

Figure 9.1

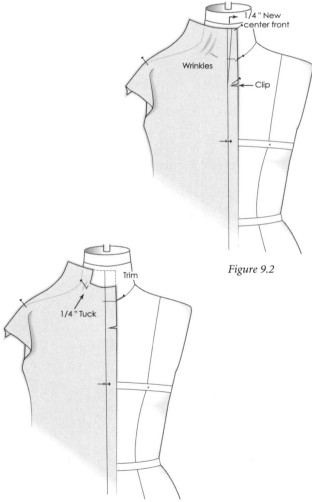

Figure 9.2

Figure 9.3

Design Analysis

Figure 9.1

The stovepipe extends to any height above the neckline (comfort must be considered). Ease of about 1/4″ is draped at the front neck; the back neck has a dart.

The design is draped using the same instructions, but the stovepipe line is curved, thereby blending into an extension for the button/buttonholes.

Preparing Muslin

Add 4″ to the length of the design garment.

Draw a center grainline 1″ from the muslin edge.

Draping Steps

Figure 9.2

Place the centerline of the muslin 4″ up from the center front neck.

Pin waist at and above bust level.

Move centerline 1/4″ to 1/2″ out in from the centerline of the form and mark. Slash at 3″ to 4″ down and mark new centerline. Wrinkles will appear in curve of the neckline.

Figure 9.3

Mark the neckline and trim 1″ above the neck (indicated by broken lines).

Pin a tuck to hold the wrinkle at the curve of the neckline.

Figure 9.4

Smooth the muslin around the neck to the shoulder.

Remove pin tuck at the neck.

Mark neckline and shoulder.

Mark 3/4″ from the neck on the shoulderline.

Slash to this mark.

Mark 1/2″ out from the shoulder/neck.

Trim excess.

Complete the drape of the front drape.

Back

Figure 9.5

Place the straight grain 2″ up from the center back neck. Pin.

Pin 1/4″ dart at the neckline.

Mark the neckline and shoulder

Mark 3/4″ from the neck on the shoulderline.

Slash to this mark.

Figure 9.6

Mark 1/2″ out from the shoulder/neck.

Trim excess to the height of the stovepipe.

Complete the drape of the back garment.

Figure 9.7

Pin the shoulders together from the slash to the shoulder-tip.

At slash point, pin out to the 1/2″ mark to the top of the stovepipe.

Remove, true, and allow 1/2″ seam at center front. Make pattern.

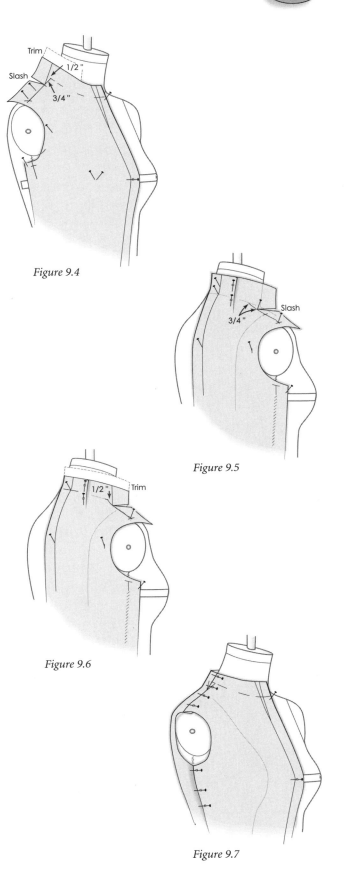

Figure 9.4

Figure 9.5

Figure 9.6

Figure 9.7

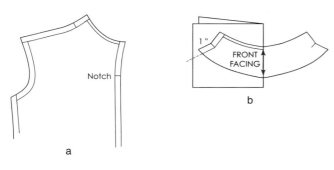

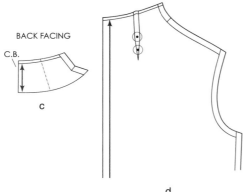

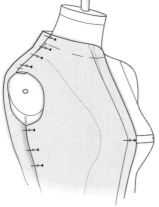

Figure 9.8

Front Facing

Figure 9.8

Place folded paper under the front pattern and align with the center front.

Trace upper part of the stovepipe to 1″ below the notch.

Back Facing

Trace back facing to the center back to 1″ below the notch.

Figure 9.9 and Figure 9.10

The curveline of the stovepipe is blended into the front extension.

Mark for button/buttonhole placement.

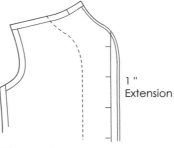

Figure 9.10

Figure 9.9

Bateau Neckline

A bateau neckline extends beyond and away from the neckline. Two styles of the bateau are given: one with a tuck dart in front; the other without a dart (Figure 9.11).

Design Analysis

Design 1: The dart excess is shared and draped to the neckline and pinned as a tuck dart. The back shoulder excess can be incorporated into the bateau neckline, or the excess can be stitched as a dart.

Design 2: Follow the draping instructions of Design 1, but pin 1/2″ of excess at the front neckline. The excess is ease and not a dart.

Preparing Muslin

Add 4″ to length of the draped garment. Draw a center grainline 1″ from the muslin edge.

Draping Steps

Figure 9.12

Place the centerline of the muslin 3″ up from the center front neck. Pin.

Crosspin bust point.

Raise crossgrain parallel with floor pin at side.

Smooth excess to the neckline and pin a dart 2″ from the center neckline.

Mark both sides of the pinned dart.

Figure 9.13

Trim 1 1/4″ above the neckline to dart location.

Mark 1/4″ out from each dart leg at the neck and 1/8″ out from each dart leg 2″ down.

Trim to within 1/2″ from both marks for the seam allowance. Discard this section.

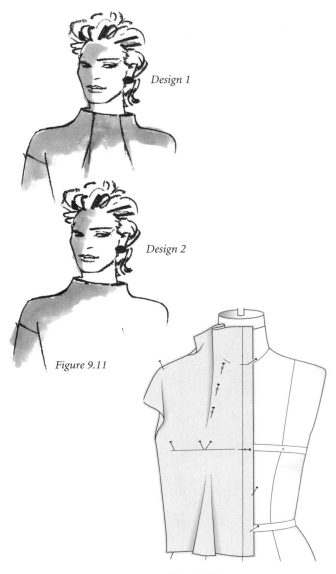

Design 1

Design 2

Figure 9.11

Figure 9.12

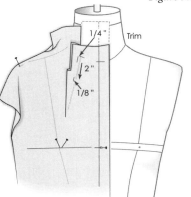

Figure 9.13

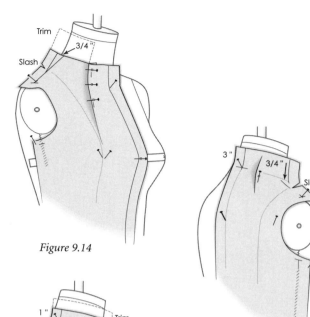

Figure 9.14

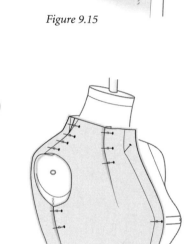

Figure 9.15

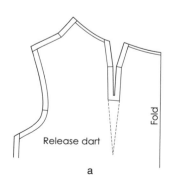

Figure 9.16

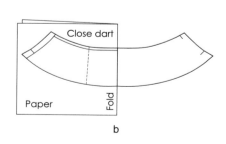

Figure 9.17

Figure 9.14

Draw the shoulderline.

Slash on the shoulder princess line.

Mark 3/4″ out from the shoulder/neck.

Pin on marks of the dart legs.

Trim the excess to within 1″ of the shoulder and trim bateau styleline.

Figure 9.15

Place straight grain 3″ up from the center back neck. Pin and mark the neckline.

Pin stress excess at the neck (not a dart).

Draw shoulderline.

Slash just to the princess line.

Mark 3/4″ out from the shoulder/neck.

Figure 9.16

Remove pin that held excess.

Trim excess to within 1″ of the shoulder and bateau line (a temporary line).

Figure 9.17

Pin front shoulder over back shoulder.

Adjust bateau to a desired height, and distance from neck.

Complete the drape, remove, true, and make the patterns.

Finished Pattern

Figure 9.18

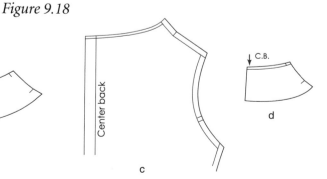

Figure 9.18

Set-In Bands

Set-in bands lift upward from stylelines of any design.

Design Analysis

Regardless of the styleline to which a band is draped, 1/4″ ease is pinned at three locations on the front and back neckline. At the shoulder/neck location 1/2″ is added to help lift the banding from the form (Figure 9.19).

Preparing Form

Figure 9.20

Pin-mark or use style tape to mark 1 1/4″ at the front to the princess line and to 1″ down at the center back neck.

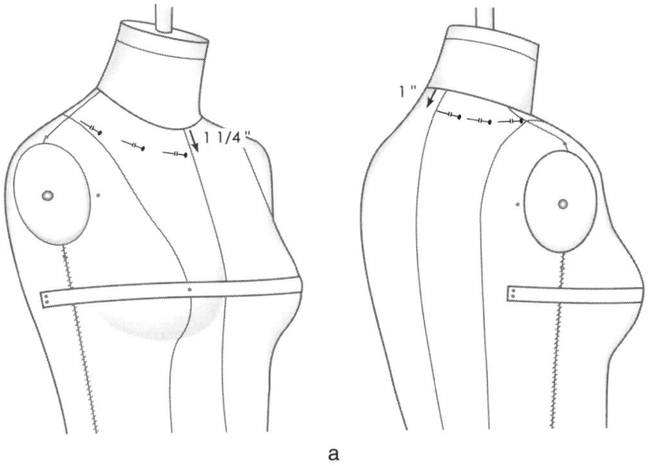

Figure 9.19

Figure 9.20

Preparing Muslin

Cut muslin to the length and width required for the design (example 10″ × 5″).

Draw the center grainline 1″ from the muslin edge.

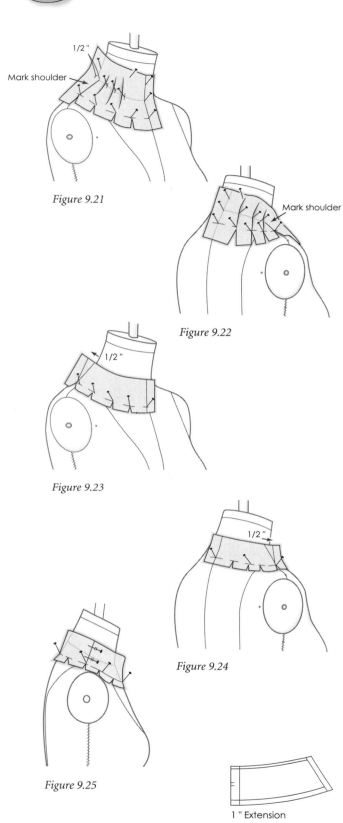

Figure 9.21

Figure 9.22

Figure 9.23

Figure 9.25

Figure 9.24

Draping Steps

Figure 9.21

Place the muslin 1 1/2″ below the pin-mark and the straight grain on the centerline.

Smooth muslin around the styleline.

Pin 1/4″ tucks at three locations.

Mark the shoulderline and mark 1/2″ out from the shoulder/neck.

Figure 9.22

Repeat the draping procedure.

Figure 9.23

Add 1/2″ to the shoulderline.

Release holding pins and trim to desired height.

Figure 9.24

Repeat the procedure for the back drape.

Figure 9.25

Pin the front shoulder to the back shoulder.

Adjust the neckline, if necessary.

Complete the drape. Remove, true, and make pattern. The front set-in band is made on a fold.

Test fit and make adjustments to the band, if necessary.

Finished Pattern

Figure 9.26

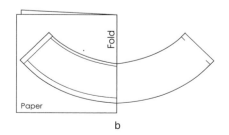

1 ″ Extension

a

Fold

Paper

b

Figure 9.26

Cowls

owls are folds created by allowing fabric to fall to
desired depths from secured ends of a bias triangle.
Cowls drape best on true bias, and when cut in soft,
loosely woven fabrics, such as crepe, silk, gauze, rayon, satin,
chiffon, and certain knits. The bodice cowl depends on excess
taken from the basic dart—the lower the depth of the cowl,
the greater the amount of excess needed—an application of
dart manipulation.

Figure 10.1

Types of Cowls

Cowls can be draped with or without pleats/ gathers and with few or many folds. They can fall at varying depths, creating a soft look to any garment. Cowls are designed to fall from the shoulders, neckline, armholes, or waist of dresses, gowns, blouses, pants, jackets, and coats. With the help of a brooch or clip, the cowl can be pulled in any direction to create interesting design effects (see Figure 10.1).

Cowls are either draped in one with the garment or set in to save fabric. Garments cut on the bias use more fabric than garments cut on the straight grain and are therefore more expensive. The first three cowls that are illustrated are prototypes for variations.

Bias: Location of the Straight Grain and Crossgrain

The fabric is folded so that the crossgrain is lying on the straight grain or is parallel with it. The foldine is marked with tailor's chalk or hand-stitched to indicate "true bias." The bias guideline must align with the center of the form as the folds of the cowl fall into place (Figure 10.2).

The straight and crossgrain run in opposite directions when the cowl is pinned at its ends to the shoulders of the form. The straight grain angles downward, and the crossgrain angles upward on the bias cut triangle. On one side of the drape, the fold of the cowl follows more closely to the straight grain, and on the other side the fold follows more closely to the crossgrain (Figure 10.3). The yarn of the straight grain is twisted more firmly than the crossgrain. This difference may cause the fold of the cowls to roll differently, and often is the reason for twisting (Figure 10.4).

The alignment of the straight grain and crossgrain become distorted as the bias fabric stretches in creating the shape of the design patterns. The grains do not completely align after the drape is removed from the form. The patterns that are made from the drape are cut in fabric that has not yet been stretched. Therefore, the fabric will stretch as it is being refitted. All changes are marked on the fabric. The differences are removed from the patterns. The final patterns will be smaller than the originals, which allows the bias to stretch to shape when the final garment is cut again.

Twisting

Figure 10.4

A well-draped cowl will not twist along the foldline. Twisting occurs when the grain is out of alignment with the location in which it has been draped. To test for twisting, place a finger in the center of the cowl drape and press downward gently. If the fold of the cowl(s) twists even slightly, unpin the twisting side, and redrape until the grain allows the fold of the cowl to roll smoothly. Recheck the fit of the garment and cowl after it has been cut and stitched. As a result

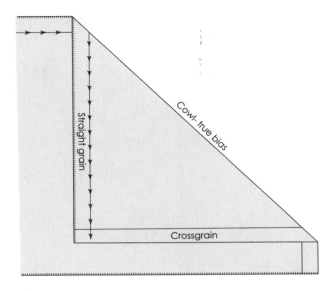

Figure 10.2

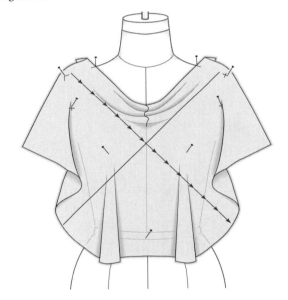

Figure 10.3

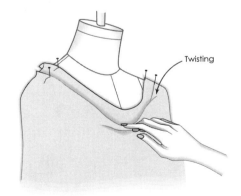

Figure 10.4

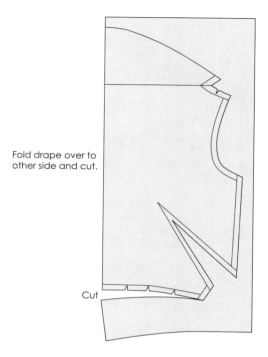

Fold drape over to
other side and cut.

Cut

Figure 10.5

of this fitting, the corrected pattern may differ
on each side of center.

Facing of cowls are in one with the draped
garment; they are not a separate facing stitched
to it. The shape of the foldback facings vary
greatly—parallel to the foldline, rounded,
pointed, or as an all-in-one facing covering the
shoulder and armhole area. A small weight can
also be attached to the end of a deep facing to
hold it in place.

Except for the drape of the cowl, one side of
the bodice may be draped (Figure 10.5). The
drape is marked along the shoulder, armhole,
side seam, and waist. It is removed from the
form, and the seam markings trued. The drape is
folded on the bias guideline, pinned, and traced,
using carbon paper to transfer it to the other
side of the fabric. Return the drape to the form.
Pin and check the fit. This method is optional
and not illustrated in the cowls designs that follow. For additional information, see Chapter 19.

High Relaxed Cowl

Figure 10.6

Design Analysis

The cowl falls slightly relaxed 3/4″ from the
shoulder/neck with very little excess taken from
the waist dart (Figure 10.6). The location of the
French darts should be on the grain directed to
bust, if possible. If draped in crepe, follow special instructions. The basic back is draped on the
straight grain unless otherwise desired.

Preparing Form

Figure 10.7

Place a pinhead on each side of the shoulder 3/4" from shoulder/neck.

Measure from pinhead to center front neck. Record (A-B). Add 4".

Pin-mark at side waist for location of the French dart.

Preparing Fabric

Figure 10.8

Fold the fabric so that the crossgrain meets, or is parallel to, selvage.

Mark the fold as a guideline.

Square a line from the fold and mark using the A-B measurement and continue the line an additional 4".

Draw a line 1 1/2" up from the A-B line (fold-back facing).

Measure down 20" from (A) and square a line across the fabric.

Cut away the excess where indicated (see page 236, Figure 10.27).

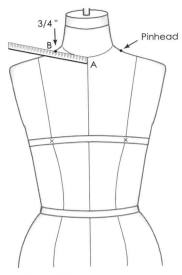

Figure 10.7

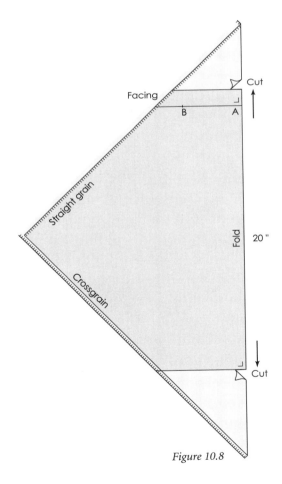

Figure 10.8

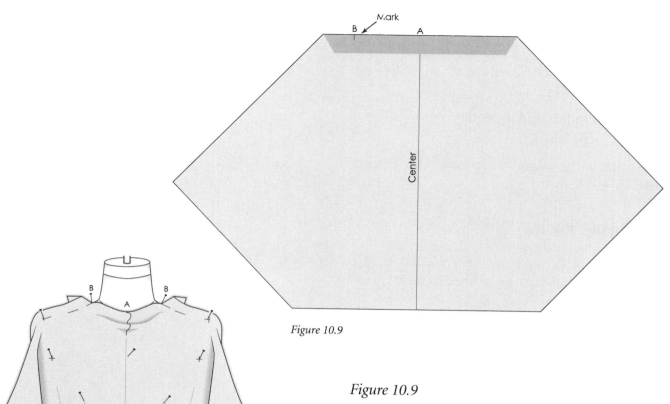

Figure 10.9

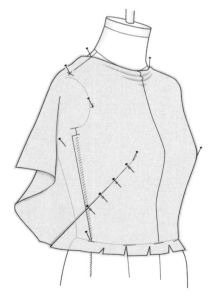

Figure 10.10

Figure 10.11

Figure 10.9

Unfold the fabric and fold facing on A-B line.

Mark location of (B) on other side of the center guideline.

Draping Steps

Figure 10.10

Pin each end of the fabric to the pinhead locations (B). Guideline (A) aligns with center front. (Approximately 1/2″ of the dart excess is draped into the fall of the relaxed cowl. The remaining excess hangs as flare from the bust mound.)

Pin bust points and the waist at center.

Smooth fabric over both shoulders. Pin.

Figure 10.11

Drape and mark the garment from shoulder to the French dart location.

Smooth fabric from the center front waist moving the excess beyond the side waist. Pin.

Smooth fabric upward along the side seam to the French dart location and mark the dart leg.

Fold the dart excess in direction of bust point, preferably on grain. The dart on the other side should also be on grain, or close to it. Mark both sides of the folded dart.

Mark the shoulder, mid-armhole, arm plate/side seam, armhole depth, side waist, and along the waistline. Crossmark all corners.

Pencil rub the side seam. Add 1/2″ for ease.

If draped in muslin, trim the excess. Remove the drape from the form and true the muslin. Make a paper pattern and cut in design fabric. Go to Figure 10.15 to complete the instructions.

If draped in crepe, do not trim excess. Remove and true. Continue with the following instructions.

Figure 10.12

Paper: Measure 28″ × 28″, cut, and fold a triangle. One side of the drape is transferred to paper.

Place the fabric's straight grain and crossgrain at the corner of the paper and pin along the paper's edge to control the bias.

Gently smooth the fabric toward the fold of the paper. The center guideline may extend beyond the fold of the paper because of the bias stretch. Let it. Pin the cowl to the paper carefully. Use push-pins or a tracing wheel to transfer drape to paper.

Remove fabric from the paper and draw the cowl pattern.

Facing Pattern

Fold A-B line and trace the shoulder (Figure 10.13).

Unfold, and cut pattern from the paper (Figure 10.14).

Cut in fabric, stitch, and check the fit. Thread line center as a guide.

Continue instructions on page 232, Figure 10.15, Figure 10.16, and Figure 10.18.

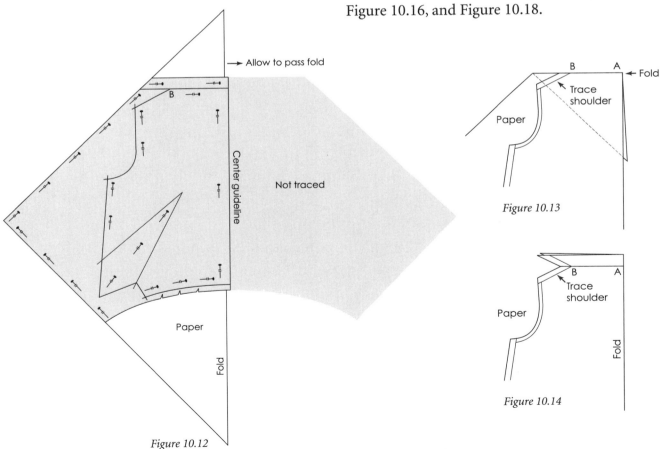

Figure 10.12

Figure 10.13

Figure 10.14

Figure 10.15

Pin cowl to the form to recheck fit. Mark the shoulder, mid-armhole, armhole depth, side seam, and waistline.

Remove from the form, true and measure the distance between the new marks and stitch line. Remove this amount to make corrections to the paper pattern.

Back Bodice

Figure 10.16

Drape or trace a copy of the back bodice or drape the back according to the instruction on page 31.

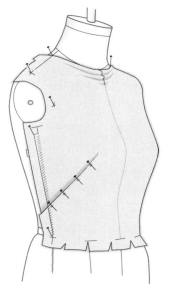

Figure 10.15

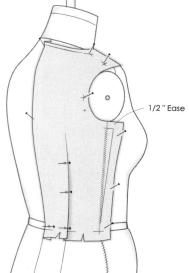

Figure 10.16

The curved neckline ends at the pin-mark (B) on the shoulder.

After the back drape is completed, pencil rub the side seam and add ease.

Remove the drape from the form, and true the drape. Make paper patterns.

Finished Patterns

Figure 10.17 and Figure 10.18

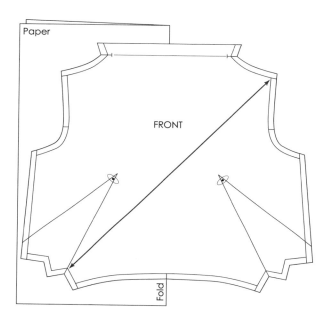

Paper

FRONT

Fold

Figure 10.17

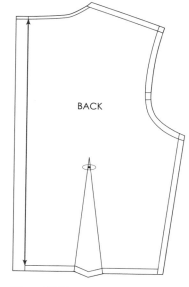

BACK

Figure 10.18

Mid-Depth Cowl

Design Analysis

Figure 10.19

Two cowls and a fold will appear between the busts when the bias is pinned to the shoulder. The cowl will fall midway between neck and bust level, indicating that half of the excess from the waist dart is taken up by the cowl. The foldline of the drape is the first cowl. To control the location of the second cowl, a slash is made in the fabric at the shoulder, and the grain is raised. The cut out neckline of the back bodice ends at mid-shoulder in line with the front cowl drape. The location of the French dart should be on the grain that is directed to bust, if possible.

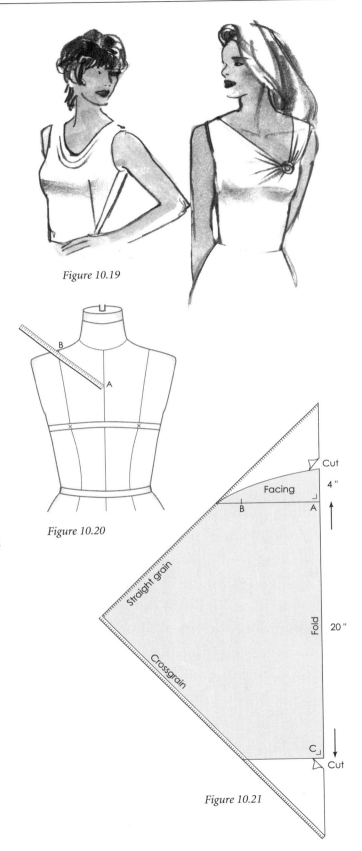

Figure 10.19

Preparing Form

Figure 10.20

Measure from the mid-shoulder to a point half the distance between shoulder/neck and the bust level. Record (A-B).

Pin-mark 1 1/2″ up from the side waist for the location of the French dart.

Preparing Fabric

Fold fabric so that crossgrain meets, or is parallel to, selvage.

Mark the fold (true bias) for a guideline.

Figure 10.20

Figure 10.21

Square a line from the fold using the A-B measurement. Mark and continue the line for 4″ to selvage.

Draw a curved line 4″ up from (A) and ending past (B) for the foldback facing.

Measure down 20″ from (A) and square a line across the fabric.

Cut away the excess fabric where indicated.

Figure 10.21

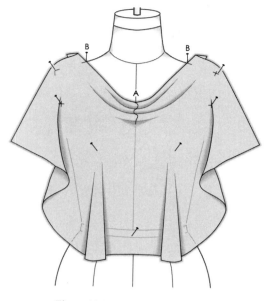

Figure 10.22

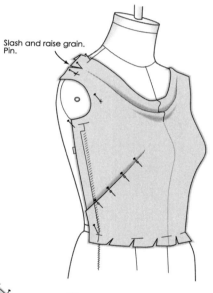

Slash and raise grain.
Pin.

Figure 10.23

Figure 10.24

Draping Steps

Figure 10.22

Unfold the fabric, and fold on the A-B line.

Mark B on other side of the center guideline.

Place fabric to form and pin (B) at each end of the mid-shoulders and shoulder-tips.

Guideline (A) falls (and remains) at the center front, as a mid-depth cowl, which takes up one half of the dart excess. Pin at bust points and waist. If draped in crepe, see page 231, where there are also instructions for transferring the pattern to paper.

Figure 10.23

Smooth the fabric over the shoulder, around the armhole, side seam, and waistline. Mark armhole depth.

To bring the second cowl closer to the shoulder, slash and raise grain. Pin.

Check for twisting (see page 227, Figure 10.4).

If draping in crepe or equivalent, do not trim excess. Instructions for transferring drape to paper are given in Figures 10.12 through 10.14 and in Figure 10.25.

Figure 10.24

Drape, or trace, a copy of the back bodice. The neckline is about 1 1/4″ at center back neck and ends at pin-mark (B).

Finished Pattern

Figure 10.25

The French dart may be cut to within seam allowance, as shown, or it may not, as shown on the high cowl on page 231.

Test for Fit

Cut a sample of the cowl from the design fabric for the test fit.

Make corrections to the drape following instructions on page 232, Figure 10.15 and make the pattern.

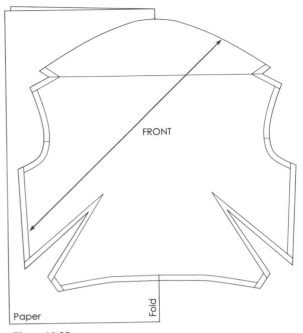

FRONT

Paper   Fold

Figure 10.25

Low Cowl

Design Analysis

Figure 10.26

Two cowls and a fold appear between the busts when the bias is pinned to the shoulders 1″ from the princess line. The cowls will fall to a depth of bust level indicating that all of the excess from the waist dart is draped into the cowls. The cut-out neckline of the back ends at the drape of the front cowl. The front fold-back facing includes the armhole. The back armhole is faced or the back bodice can be fully lined.

Figure 10.26

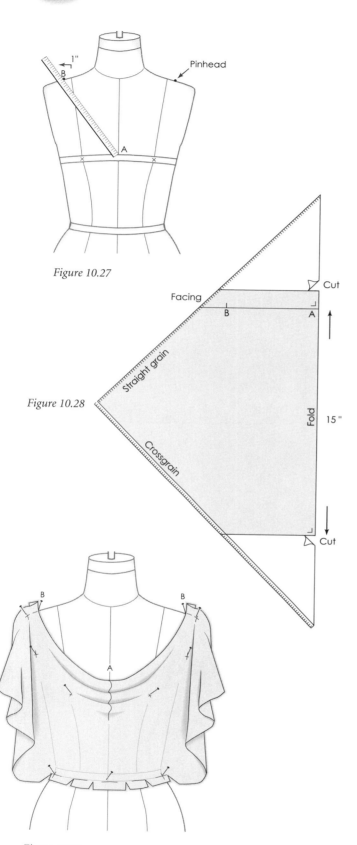

Figure 10.27

Figure 10.28

Figure 10.29

Preparing Fabric

Figure 10.27

Measure from the center of the bust bridge to 1″ past mid-shoulder. Record (A-B).

Fold fabric so that crossgrain meets, or is parallel to, selvage.

Mark the fold (true bias) for a guideline.

Figure 10.28

Square a line from the fold at the point of the A-B measurement, and continue the line an additional 2″, touching the selvage. Mark (B) on the line.

Draw a parallel line 1 1/2″ up from the A-B line for the facing.

Measure down 15″ from A, and square a line across the fabric.

Cut away the excess fabric where indicated.

Draping Steps

Figure 10.29

Unfold the fabric and fold on A-B line.

Place the fabric to the form and pin each end of (B). Guideline (A) falls (and remains) at center front, using all the dart excess. Pin at the bust point and waist.

Smooth, slash, and mark fabric along the waistline.

Figure 10.30

Continue to drape up from the side seam along the armhole to the shoulder. If excess is left over, smooth the excess along the shoulder and fold under with the facing at pinhead mark. To bring the second fold closer to the shoulder, clip and raise the grain.

Mark the shoulder, mid-armhole, armhole depth, and side waist.

Test for twist. If draping in crepe, do not trim excess. For instructions on transferring the drape to paper, see page 231, Figure 10.12 through Figure 10.14.

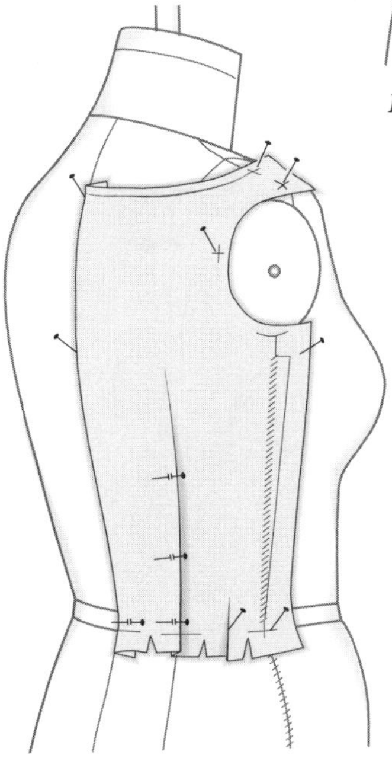

Figure 10.31

Drape the back bodice, with the neckline ending in line with the front drape.

Remove, true, and make the pattern.

Finished Pattern

Figure 10.32

The facing is traced on the fold to include the armhole.

Test for Fit

Cut a sample of the cowl from the design fabric and pin (or baste) the armhole facing to the garment for the test fit.

Make corrections to the drape and make the pattern using the instruction on page 232, Figure 10.15.

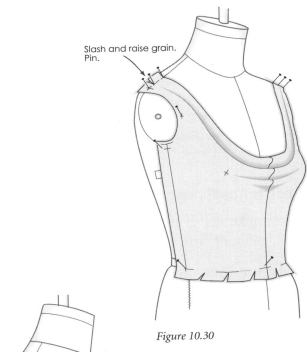

Figure 10.30

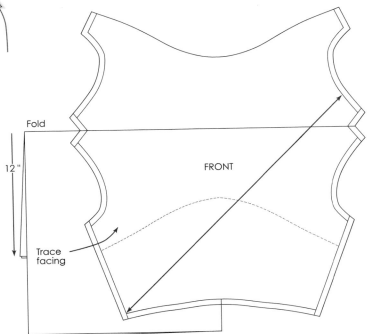

Figure 10.31

Figure 10.32

Deep Cowl with Bustier

Figure 10.33

Design Analysis

Figure 10.33

The cowl falls below the bust level. A Princess bustier shows above the cowls. The bustier is attached to the side seams of the bodice and stitched to the back. The back is draped with a cutout neckline. This design is for a short or long evening dress.

Preparing Form

Figure 10.34

Pin-mark or use tape to outline the bustier location.

Pin mark 1″ from shoulder-tip.

Preparing Fabric

Measure for depth of the cowl 3″ below the bust level, ending 1″ from the shoulder-tip. Record (A-B).

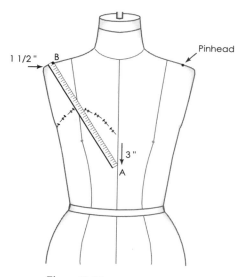

Figure 10.34

Figure 10.35

Fold fabric so that crossgrain meets, or is parallel to the selvage.

Mark the fold (true bias) for a guideline. Draw a square line from the fold at the point where the A-B measurement, plus 4″ touches the selvage. Mark (B) on the line.

Draw a parallel line 1 1/2″ up from the A-B line, a temporary facing.

Measure down 18″ from A, and square a line across the fabric.

Trim the excess fabric where indicated. Use discarded fabric to drape bustier.

Draping Steps: Bustier

For instructions to drape the front Princess bustier, see page 294. Drape to waist. For instructions on the choices of inner support for the bustier, see page 313.

Figure 10.36

After the drape, true, and make the pattern. Stitch, and pin to the form. Cut four front and side panels (self-lined).

Figure 10.37

Pin cowl drape (B) 1″ in from shoulder-tips. Guideline (A) will fall to (and remain at) the centerline of the form. Adjust depth, if required.

Pin waist.

Smooth fabric along the armhole and side seam. Slash along the waist.

Mark the shoulder, mid-armhole, armhole depth, side waist to match bustier, and waistline of one or both sides.

Remove the cowl drape from the form and true. (If draping in crepe or equivalent, do not trim excess. For instructions on transferring the drape to paper, see page 231.)

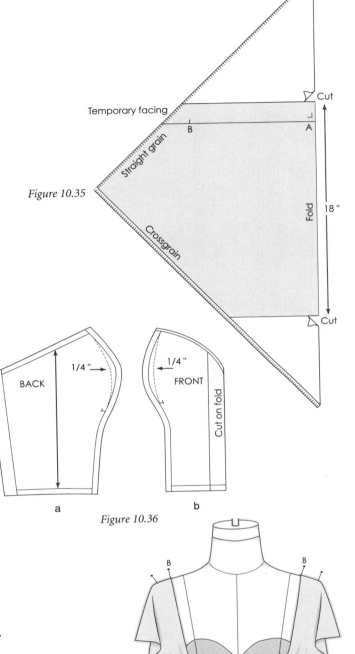

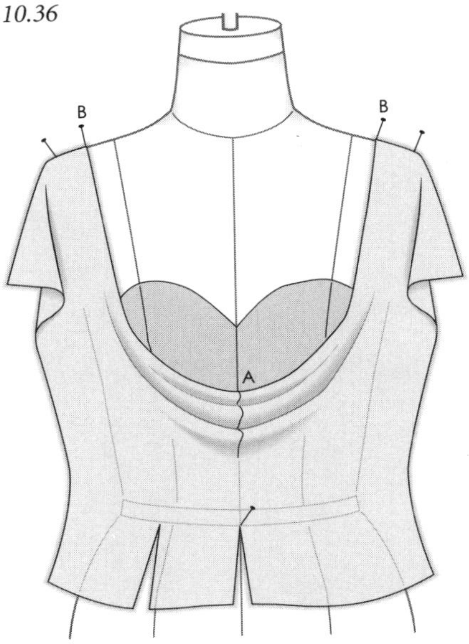

Figure 10.35

Figure 10.36

Figure 10.37

Back Drape

Figure 10.38

Drape back or trace a copy of the basic back pattern (cut on straight grain). The neckline depth is 2″ below the center neck and 1 1/2″ from shoulder-tip.

Complete the back drape, and pin to bustier to check fit.

Figure 10.39

Place the cowl drape on the garment pin and check fit.

Make the adjustments to the drape.

Remove from the form. True and correct pattern using instructions on page 232, Figure 10.15. Make the patterns.

Finished Patterns

Front Cowl

Figure 10.40

One side is traced when transferring pattern to folded paper. The front facing on fold includes the armhole.

Fold back facing includes the armhole.

Back Pattern

Figure 10.41

If lined, mark Cut 4″ or trace a facing (see Chapter 11).

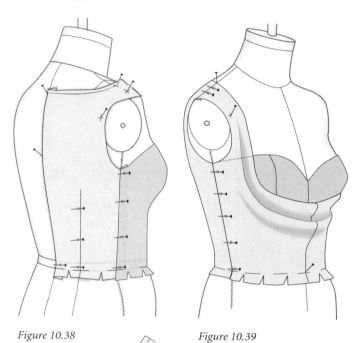

Figure 10.38   *Figure 10.39*

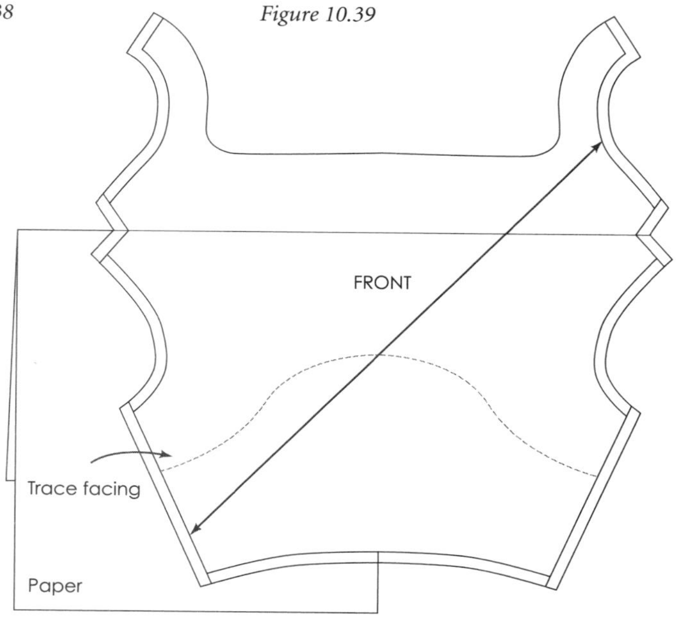

FRONT

Trace facing

Paper

Figure 10.40

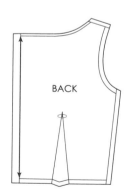

BACK

Figure 10.41

Pleated Cowls

Two versions of pleated cowls are illustrated. Design 1 is draped with three pleated cowls, with French darts taking up the remaining excess. Design 2 is draped with pleated cowls and continues with pleating to the waistline (Figure 10.42). Both designs are draped with the same instructions for the first three pleated cowls. The examples given are prototypes for pleated cowls of skirts, back cowls, and armhole cowls. Both designs are for evening wear with short or long skirts.

Design Analysis

Design 1: Three pleated cowls are draped to mid-depth. The first cowl is placed 1/2″ past the princess line of the shoulder. The pleat depth is from 3/4 to 1″. The back is draped with a cut-out neckline ending at the shoulder of the front cowl. The back drape is the same for both designs.

Design 2: The three pleated cowls at the shoulder are draped by the same method as in Design 1. Pleating continues around the armholes, side seams, and ends at the waist. A lining (draped as a princess style) supports pleats and finishes the raw edges of the seams.

Preparing Form

Figure 10.43

Measure for cowl depth from mid-shoulder to a point half the distance between the neck and bust point. Record (A-B).

The location of the French darts should be on grain directed to bust, if possible.

Styleline for the undersupport is marked 1″ below the center front. Mark with pins or use style tape.

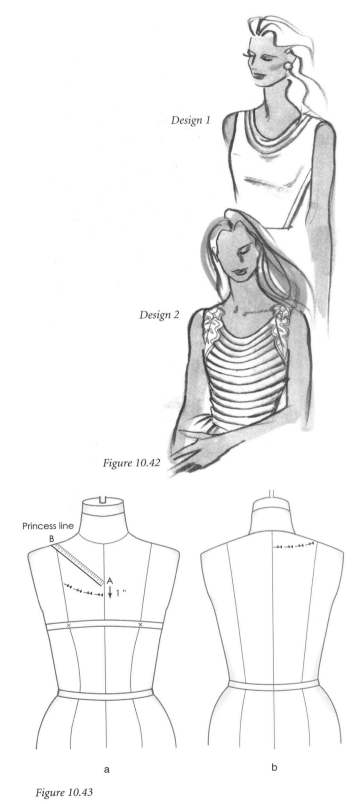

Design 1

Design 2

Figure 10.42

a   b

Figure 10.43

Three-Pleated Cowl

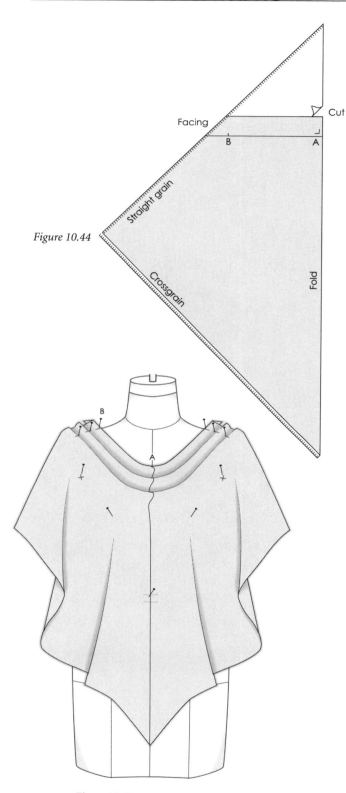

Figure 10.44

Figure 10.45

Figure 10.44

Fold fabric so that crossgrain meets, or is parallel with straight grain.

Draw a square line from the fold at the point where the A-B measurement, plus 2″, touches the selvage. Mark (B) on the line.

Mark fold and cut excess from the fabric where indicated.

Figure 10.45

Open muslin and fold facing back. Mark (B) on other side.

Pin (B) to pin-marks at each shoulder. Fold pleats 3/4″ to 1″ depth. Pleats are placed approximately 1/2″ apart. Pin through the pleats to hold. Place other pins to secure at shoulders.

Drape pleats from shoulder to shoulder, with the guideline remaining at the center of the form throughout the drape.

Drape to shoulder-tip and trim excess.

Check twist of each cowl.

Mark each side of the pleat fold.

Draw a line across the shoulder.

For Design 1, continue the drape.

For Design 2, continue on page 245.

Figure 10.46

Drape from the shoulder-tip, around the mid-armhole to about 2″ above waist at the side seam.

Move the excess along the waist to the side seam. Mark.

Move the excess upward along side seam and pin excess. Find the grain leading to bust. Change dart location at side seam if necessary. Mark and fold dart excess, pinning in direction of the bust.

Crossmark dart point.

Pencil rub along the side seam. Mark armhole depth and add 1/2″ ease (ease not required if designed as a sleeveless evening dress).

If draping in muslin, trim excess; if draping in crepe or equivalent, do not trim excess.

Figure 10.47

Remove drape from the form.

Remove pins from only the French darts.

Lay pleats flat on the table.

Run tracing wheel across shoulderline to transfer the underlay of the pleats (Figure 10.47a).

Unpin and pencil the perforated lines (Figure 10.47b). If draping in crepe, see page 231 for instructions on transferring the drape to paper.

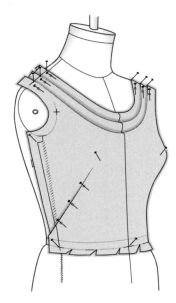

Figure 10.46

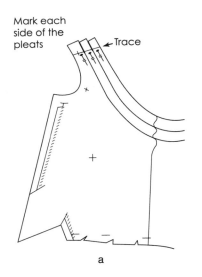

Mark each side of the pleats

← Trace

a

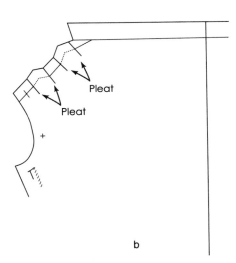

Pleat

Pleat

b

Figure 10.47

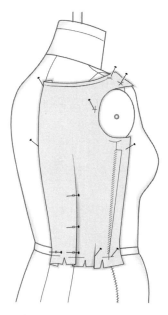

Figure 10.48

Figure 10.48

Complete the back drape with the cutout neckline ending at the shoulder mark of the front drape as illustrated.

Remove from the form, and true. Stitch muslin, or transfer to paper for a test fit.

Finished Patterns

Figure 10.49 and Figure 10.50

Secure patterns to paper with one side of the front on fold (see page 231).

Use pushpins or tracing wheel to transfer patterns to paper.

For facing instructions, see Chapter 11.

Figure 10.49

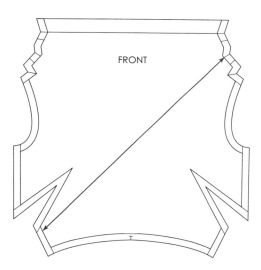

Figure 10.50

Multiple Cowls and Pleats

Draping Steps

The drape continues from the instructions on page 242, Figure 10.44, and Figure 10.45. For instructions for the back drape, see page 244, Figure 10.48.

Figure 10.51

If draping in crepe or equivalent, do not trim excess throughout the drape. After marking pleats, see pages 231 and 232, Figures 10.13 through 10.15, to transfer to paper.

Trim excess to within 1/2″ of the shoulders.

Continue the pleats along both sides of the armhole and side seams to just below the armplate. Trim excess to within 1/2″ of seam allowance. The excess of the waist dart is lifted and taken up with the pleat that crosses nearest to the level of the bust point. This increases the pleat underlay. It is suggested that pleats of equal intake and intervals be pinned along the centerline to the waist to help simplify the drape.

Test for twisting.

Figure 10.52

Pin through the pleats, and mark each side of the folded pleats at the seamline. Place other pins to secure to the form.

Pencil rub the side seam or use the ruler. Side ease is not needed for bodices that fit close to the body. Remove drape from the form.

Figure 10.53

Before unpinning, lay the pleats flat on the table.

Run the tracing wheel across the penciled lines on one side of the drape at the shoulder, armhole, and side seam. The tracing wheel transfers the pleat underlay for trueing, when using carbon paper. The other side will be duplicated when the pattern is transferred to paper.

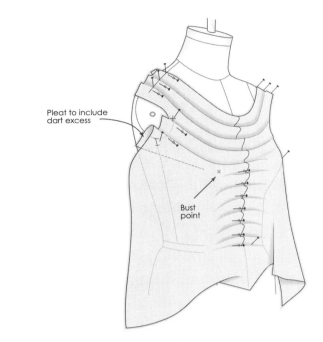

Pleat to include dart excess

Bust point

Figure 10.51

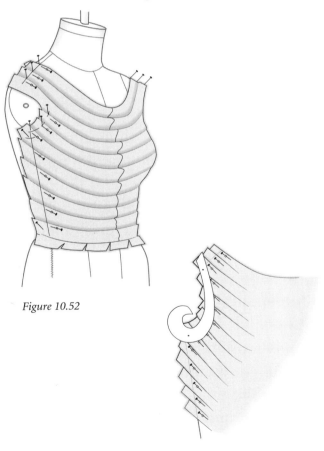

Figure 10.52

Figure 10.53

Figure 10.54

Unpin, true, and pencil the perforated lines.

Press the drape without steam.

Place the guideline center on the folded paper and pin to secure.

Use pushpins or tracing wheel to transfer pattern to paper.

Pencil in the shape of the patterns.

Removing Dart Excess

Mark the center of the pleat underlay that has the dart excess. Draw the legs of the dart intake.

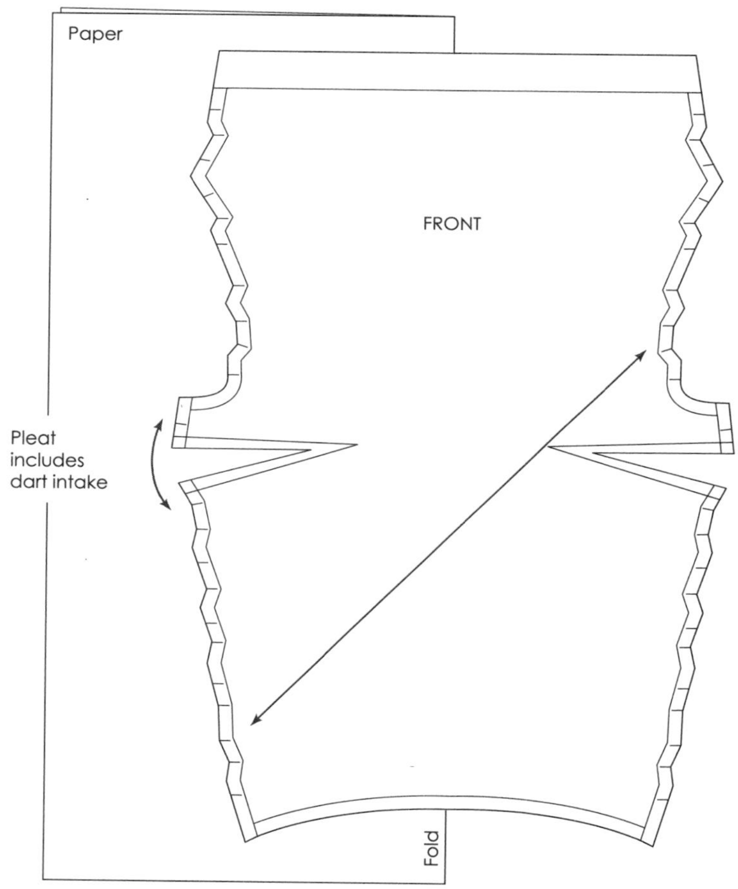

Do not include the pleat underlay. Add 1/2″ seam allowance, and trim the excess from the dart legs. The stitchline of the dart should lie at the turn of the pleat underlay, concealing the stitches. Add seams, and cut from paper.

Finished Back Pattern

Figure 10.55

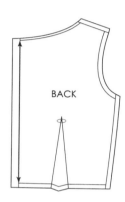

BACK

Figure 10.55

Paper

FRONT

Pleat
includes
dart intake

Fold

Figure 10.54

Undersupport

Figure 10.56

The undersupport is a base for tacking pleats and covering the raw seams of sleeveless garments.

Princess Styleline

For instructions on the Princess drape, see page 270. If available, trace the front princess pattern, allowing extra fabric at the top for a style change, if necessary.

Back

Use the copy of the back pattern to complete the drape.

Remove draped garment from the form and true.

Finished Pattern

Figure 10.57

Make two copies of the princess paper patterns.

Trace two copies of the back pattern. The second copies are for lining of the front and back garment.

The lining patterns are trimmed 1/8″ from the front and back armholes and neckline.

For facing instructions, see Chapter 11.

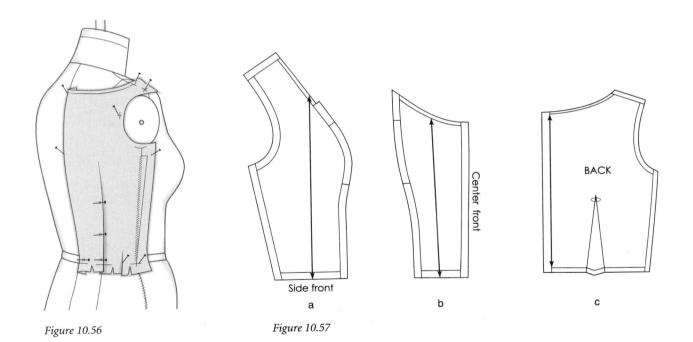

Figure 10.56   Figure 10.57

Draped Cowls from Stylelines

Figure 10.58

Cowls are very flexible and can be draped from any styleline for design variations (Figure 10.58).

Design Analysis

The built-up neckline curves around the neck and above the bust mound ending at the side seam at bust level. The shoulderline extends approximately 2″ beyond the shoulder-tip. Shoulder pads are an option and should be placed on the form when convenient to the drape. If pads are not desired and shoulderlines extend past the shoulder-tip, 1/2″ ease is draped into the front mid-armhole. Ease allows forward mobility of the arm and eliminates stress at the armhole of the garment. The cowl falls to about 1″ above bust level. A French dart takes up the remaining dart excess. The built-up neckline of the back garment is controlled by placing a shaped dart from the shoulder dart excess.

Preparing Form

Figure 10.59

Pin-mark or use style tape to establish the style-line.

Pin-mark 1″ above the bust level (A).

Pin-mark at intersection of princess and style-line (B).

Measure the cowl depth. Record (A-B).

Shoulder pad, if desired, is attached to the shoulder as shown in Figure 10.63. Ease at the front armhole allows room for the shoulder pad.

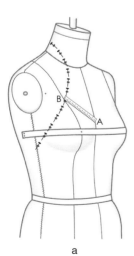

a

b

Figure 10.59

Preparing Fabric

Figure 10.60

Cowl Drape

Fold fabric so that the crossgrain is parallel with the straight grain. Mark foldline for guide.

Draw a square line at the point where the A-B measurement, plus 2″, touches the selvage. Mark (B) on the line.

Square a line 1 1/2″ parallel with the A-B line or a curved line for facing.

Square a line from the fold 18″ down from (A).

Drop Shoulder Yoke

Width: 12″

Length: 18″. Not cut on bias.

Back Bodice

Width and length on straight grain for the back plus 5″ (not illustrated).

Or

See page 31 for muslin preparation, and add 5″ to length.

Draping Steps

Figure 10.61

Drape the first cowl from the pin-mark at the princess line. Drape two more cowls. The guide-line must remain at the centerline through the drape. Pin bust points.

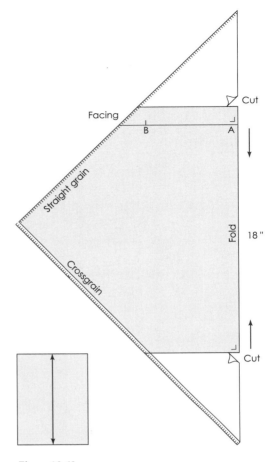

Figure 10.60

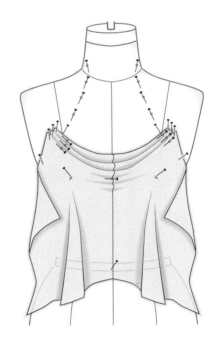

Figure 10.61

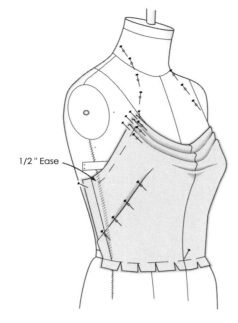

1/2 " Ease

Figure 10.62

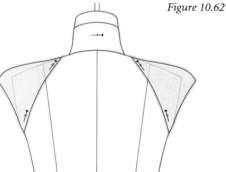

Figure 10.63

Figure 10.62

Complete the drape by pinning remaining excess as a French dart (on grain to bust, if possible).

Figure 10.63

Pin shoulder pads to shoulder.

Drop Shoulder Yoke

Figure 10.64

Place fabric on the form 2″ up from shoulder at neckline. Slash at the shoulder/neck, and pin.

Smooth fabric along the shoulder. Mark and pin.

Smooth fabric along the neck, smoothing fabric to the princess line.

Smooth fabric around the bust and armhole.

Pencil rub styline and side seam. Mark armhole depth 3″ below the plate. Remove from the form.

Back Drape

Figure 10.65

Place fabric 1 1/2″ up the center back neck.

Pin at the center back and smooth fabric across the shoulder. Pin.

Figure 10.64

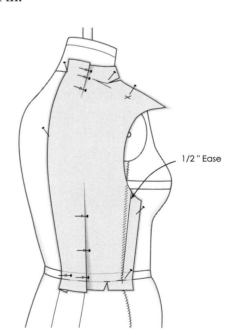

1/2 " Ease

Figure 10.65

Smooth fabric along the waist. Fold and pin waist dart with intake from 1″ to 1 1/2″.

Smooth fabric along the side seam. Pencil rub styleline.

Smooth fabric along shoulderline, moving excess to the neckline. Slash at the shoulder/neck.

Pin the dart excess to fit to the neck.

Mark waist, dart, side seam, and shoulder. Trim excess to within seam allowance.

Front and Back

Figure 10.66

Option: True the fabric patterns and duplicate before pinning the sections together.

Pin the front drape to the back at the shoulder and side, and along the styleline. Evaluate the fit.

Finished Pattern

Figure 10.67, Figure 10.68, and Figure 10.69

True and correct patterns, using instructions on page 232, Figure 10.15, and transfer to paper.

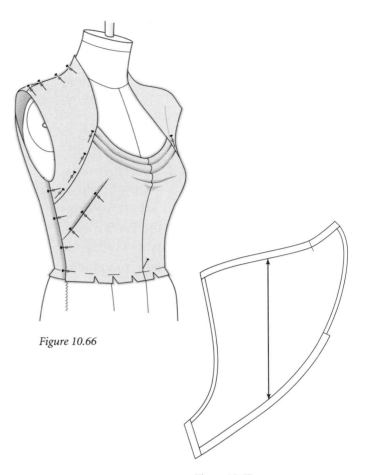

Figure 10.66

Figure 10.67

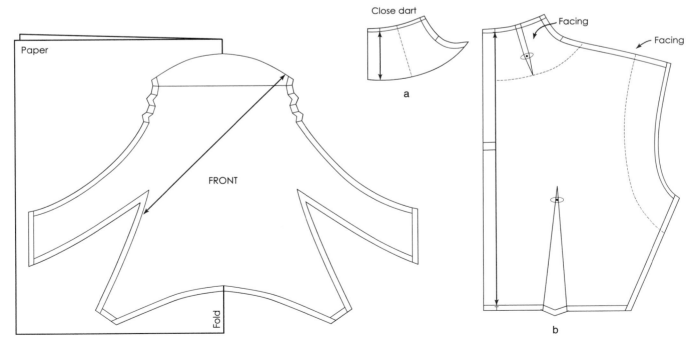

Figure 10.68

Figure 10.69

Armhole Cowls: Gathered

Fuller cowls can also be achieved with the use of gathers rather than pleats (see Figure 10.70).

Design Analysis

A series of cowls fall from gathers that start at the princess line and end 3/4″ in from the shoulder-tip. The guideline of the fold (true bias) aligns with the side seam of the form. Fabric preparation is similar to other cowls drapes. Gathers pass over the bust point and along the waistline of the front and back bodice. Elastic secures the distribution of the gathers for marking waistline. A banding covers the seamline of the gathers at the shoulder. The neckline is a V-cut in front and a curved cutout neckline in back.

Preparing Fabric

Figure 10.71

Measure full back length from shoulder/neck to center back.

Measure back waist and add 3″, or use #6 and #19 of the Form Measurement Chart.

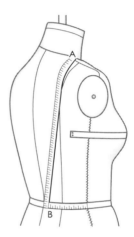

Figure 10.71

Figure 10.70

Figure 10.72

Fold fabric so that the crossgrain meets, or is parallel with, the selvage.

Mark the foldline as a guide for aligning bias grain with the side seam of the form or model.

Square a line from the selvage that is equal to twice the waist measurement (A).

(A) to (B) is equal to the back length measurement, plus 2″.

Square a line from (B) to equal (A), labeled D.

Square a line from fold (C) touching (D). (C) to (D) is the armhole part of the drape.

Draw a line 1 1/2″ for foldback facing.

Cut from the fabric.

Sew 6″ of gathering stitches from (D) on the front and back shoulders. Waistline can also be stitched for gathers.

Figure 10.73

Fold the facing and gather to a width of 2″. Pin the shoulders together to help control the drape when it is placed on the form.

Draping Steps: Front

Place drape on the form with the center of the gathers on the princess line at the shoulder, and pin. The guideline must align to the side seam. Adjust shoulders, if necessary.

Slash 1/2″ up the guideline from the waist at the side seam.

Smooth fabric from bust to center front. Pin.

Figure 10.74

Smooth fabric at the center back. Pin.

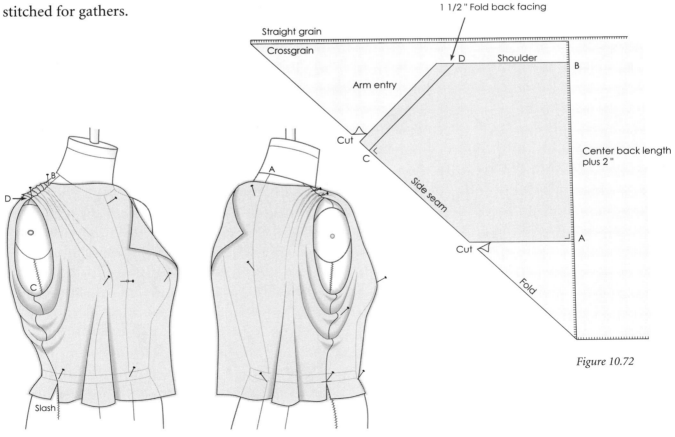

Figure 10.73   *Figure 10.74*

Figure 10.72

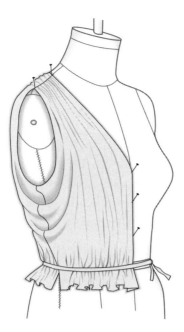

Figure 10.75

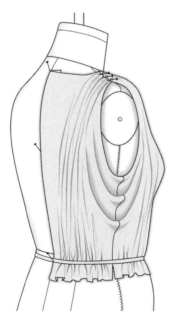

Figure 10.76

Draping Steps: Securing the Waistline

Figure 10.75

Place a 1/4″ elastic around the waist to hold the excess while the gathers are arranged along the waistline of the front and back bodice. Avoid diagonal pulls when distributing gathers. The center front and back should be on straight and crossgrain at the completion of the drape.

Mark the waistline over the gathers. The markings will be irregular, but will blend when the garment is trued.

Mark the V-neckline and center front. Trim excess.

Back

Figure 10.76

Follow the same instruction for the back, except that the neckline is curved.

Finished Pattern

Figure 10.77

Remove drape from the form. True the pattern, and transfer to paper. The front facing is indicated by broken lines.
Add seams and pattern information.

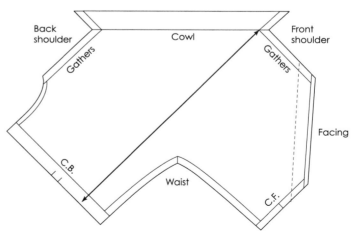

Figure 10.77

Back Cowls

The low cowl is the example to follow for the high and low cowl designs. The front can be of any design (Figure 10.78).

Design Analysis

The following instructions apply to all three cowl designs, which are measured for high, mid, and low depths (see Figure 10.79).

Measure from the shoulder of the cowl placement to the depths at the center back. Record A-B measurement for Designs 1, 2, and 3.

If draping in crepe or equivalent, see page 231, Figure 10.12 through Figure 10.14, for transferring the pattern to paper.

The crossgrain of the fabric is folded on line with, or parallel to, the straight grain.

A foldback facing is part of the fabric preparation. The foldback can be extended to include the armhole as a facing when the paper pattern is made (see page 237).

Both sides are draped, but one side is traced on folded paper.

The pattern is trued, and a paper pattern is made.

The garment is cut and stitched for a test fit. Remember that the fabric is bias and has stretched to fit the form. The recut is from the paper patterns and cut from fabric that has not yet been stretched to fit, so expect adjustments (see page 232, Figure 10.15) .

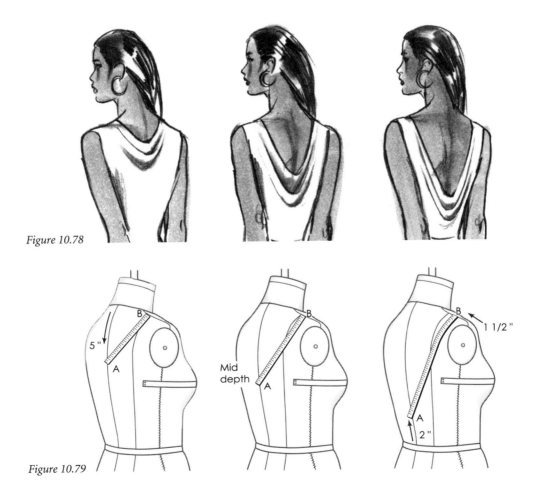

Figure 10.78

Figure 10.79

Low-Depth Cowl

Record the A-B measurement.

Figure 10.80 and Figure 10.81

Draw a square line at the point at which the A-B measurement meets the selvage. Mark (B) on the line.

Unfold and mark (B) on the other side.

Draping Steps

Figure 10.82

Pin points (B) at shoulder locations.

The guideline remains at the center back throughout the drape.

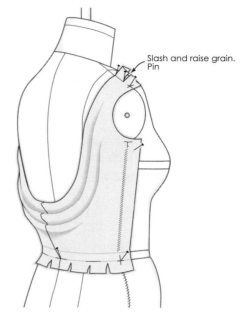

Figure 10.80

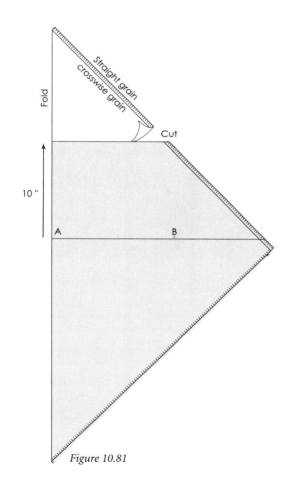

Figure 10.81

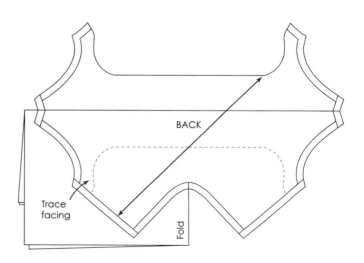

Figure 10.82

Mid-Depth Cowl

Preparing Fabric

Record A-B measurement.

Figure 10.83

Draw a square line at the point at which the A-B measurement, plus 2″, touches the selvage. Mark (B) on the line.

Unfold and mark (B) on the other side.

Draping Steps

Pin points (B) at shoulder locations.

Smooth fabric along the shoulder. Drape the waistline, side seam, and armhole.

Slash, mark, and trim excess to within 1/2″ of marked seamlines.

Remove the drape and true.

Make the paper pattern.

Finished Pattern

Figure 10.84

Facing is indicated by broken lines and is on the folded paper.

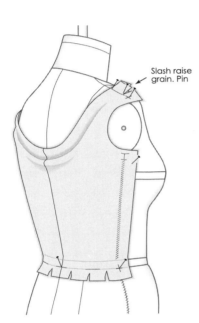

Figure 10.83

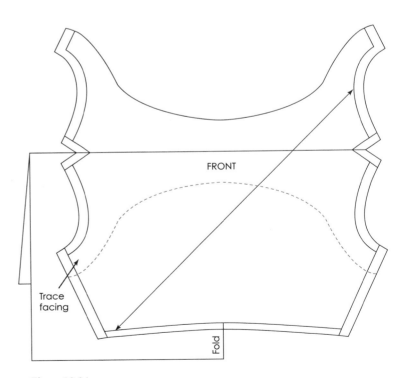

Figure 10.84

Facings

Facings are shaped pieces of fabric stitched to the raw edge of necklines and/or armholes providing support and giving a clean finish to the garment. The following instructions apply only to necklines and armholes. Foldback facings for hemlines and sleeves are part of the draped garment. Facings for shirts are a special category. The many variations will not be covered in this book.

Types of Facing

Separate facing: Individual facings for armhole and/or neckline.

Combined facing: All-in-one for armhole and neckline.

The general width of facings is from 1″ to 2″. The back neck facing often extends to a lower depth than the front neckline for hanger appeal. The facing pattern is created by tracing the facing from the completed pattern or the trued muslin.

Separate Facings

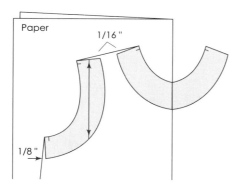

Figure 11.1

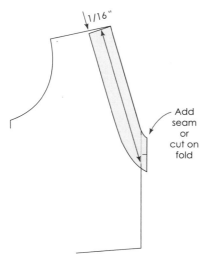

Figure 11.2

Draping Steps

Figure 11.1

Traced to follow the outline of the armhole and neckline.

The facing is trimmed at the shoulder area and armhole to offset stretching as noted.

V-Necklines

Figure 11.2

Facings for V-necklines are often cut on the straight grain to help prevent the bias from stretching.

The shoulder area is trimmed as noted.

All-in-One Facing

Front

Figure 11.3

The facing is trimmed 1/8″ at the armhole and neckline from the shoulder to zero midway.

Trim at the side seam.

Back

Figure 11.4

The facing is traced with the shoulder dart and trimmed at neck and armhole (see Figure 11.4a).

Cut from paper.

The dart is closed, and the shoulderline is straight from the shoulder-tip to the neckline (see Figure 11.4b).

Styleline Intercepting an Armhole or Neckline

Figure 11.5

Place the stitchlines on top of each other. Secure and trace the armhole and neckline area.

Trim 1/8″ at neckline and armhole from shoulder to zero at midway.

Trim 1/8″ at the side seam of the facing.

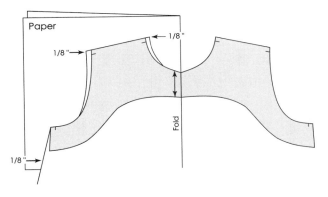

Figure 11.3

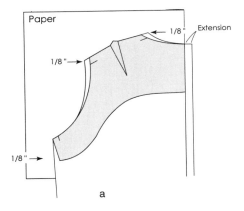

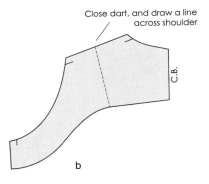

Figure 11.4

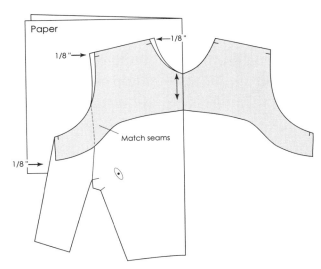

Figure 11.5

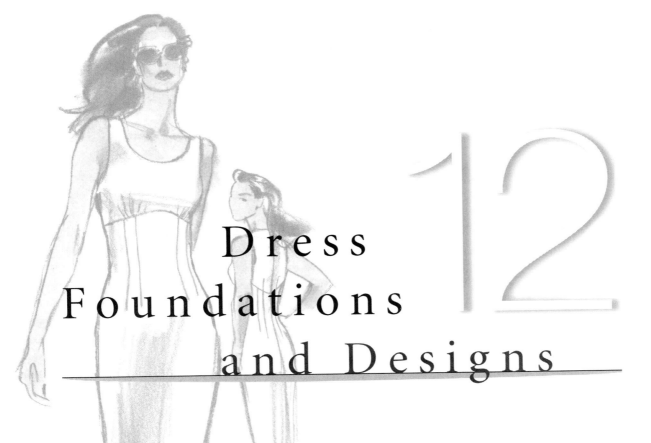

Dress
Foundations
and Designs

12

The Torso Foundation

Figure 12.1

The principle of the torso foundation is applied to garments that are designed with the bodice and skirt all-in-one, without the interruption of a waistline seam (Figure 12.1). To apply this principle, the crossgrain is held parallel with the floor at the hip level of the form and at the hemline of the garment. When the crossgrain is parallel to the floor, there will be excess above the waist at the side seam and looseness around the waist. The excess at the side seam is taken up with a side dart, but the excess can also be designed as a dart equivalent—stylized darts, gathers, tucks, pleats, or cowls—or as a styleline crossing over the bust. Looseness at the waistline is taken up by darts for a fitted dress; for a semi-fitted dress, half the excess is taken up by darts; and for a box silhouette, the looseness remains.

The principle of the torso foundation is illustrated in the drape of all-in-one dresses. The tent, Princess, and empire dresses are based on this foundation. Dresses that are based on the shirt, knit, and kimono foundations will be discussed in later chapters. The draping principles of the torso ends at the hip level (HBL). The length is added beyond the torso to complete the dresses.

Fashion magazines and other sources have many designs based on these foundations. The addition of collars, pockets, sleeves, tapering hems, or an A-line change the silhouettes and bring variety to these very basic foundations.

Fitted Basic Dress: Sheath

Design Analysis

The dress silhouette hangs straight from hip to hem. It is fitted, but not too closely, so that the crossgrain at the hip does not pull upward and unbalance the garment. Double-ended darts take up the excess at the waistline to control the fit:

Suggested Dart Intake

- Front: Two darts equal 1/2″ to 5/8″.
- Back: Two darts equal 1″ to 1 1/8″.

The hip guideline (crossgrain) must remain at the HBL of the form throughout the drape and when pinning dart intake.

Preparing Muslin

Figure 12.2

Measurements apply to front and back:

- Length: Measure from shoulder/neck to length of the dress. Add 3″.
- Width: Measure across bust. Add 3″.

Cut two lengths of muslin.

Figure 12.3

Fold 1″ on the straight grain.

Draw a temporary neckline following the measurement given.

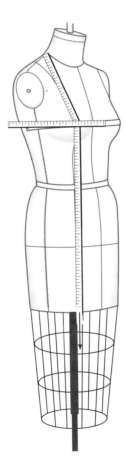

Figure 12.2

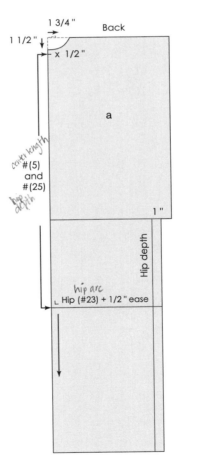
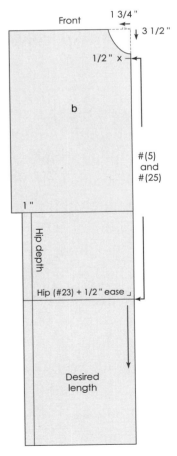

Figure 12.3

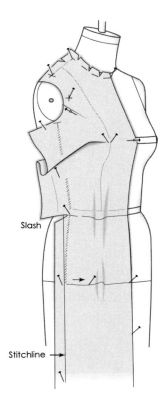

Slash

Stitchline →

Figure 12.4

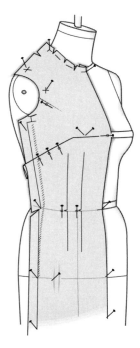

Figure 12.5

Mark center length (#5), and hip depth (#25) from the Form Measurement Chart. Square crossgrain lines across muslin.

Mark hip arc (#23). Add 1/2″ ease and square down and up from this mark (stitchline).

Trim from hem to waist.

Draping Steps: Front

Figure 12.4

Place fold of the straight grain on center with hip crossgrain guideline on the HBL of the form. Pin to secure.

Smooth across the hip, and pin stitchline at side seam of the HBL. Smooth ease away and pin on stitchline.

Smooth muslin upward along curve of the hip to the waist. The curve is now on bias, whereas the straight grain veers off. Pin and pencil rub.

Slash at waist to within 1/4″ of rub line.

Smooth muslin along 5″ of the side seam. Pin and pencil rub.

Drape upper part of the drape. Pin, slash, and mark key locations.

Figure 12.5

Fold the excess of the side dart downward. Pin.

Use two doubled-ended darts to take up looseness at the waist. The center fold of each dart is on the straight grain, and the darts are of equal intake. The darts can be corrected at the time of trueing.

Place the first dart at the Princess line. The second dart is spaced 1 1/4″ away.

Mark and pin dart excess outward. Slash at waist. The bust of some forms are small in shape and allow for one dart front. However, if the end of the dart indicates too much fullness, put in two darts.

Draping Steps: Back

Figure 12.6

Pin muslin to the form following the instructions given in Figure 12.14 of the lower torso.

Drape back bodice.

Mark dart excess at shoulder at the Princess line for dart legs.

Note: If the garment is designed for a sleeve, add 1/4″ out from pin-mark at the mid-armhole and 3/4″ for ease at the armhole depth mark.

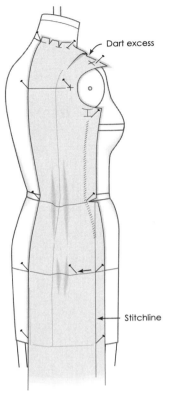

Figure 12.7

Pin fold of the shoulder dart toward center.

Looseness at waist is taken up by two double-ended darts.

Place first dart at the Princess line. The second dart is spaced 1 1/4″ away.

Mark pin dart excess outward. Slash at waist.

Figure 12.6

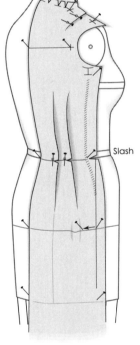

Figure 12.8

Unpin darts and fold under toward center. Re-pin.

Pin front shoulder over the back.

Pin front side seam over the back seam.

Check fit. Does the crossgrain of the hip align with the HBL line of the form? If not, release pins at the side seam and/or decrease dart intake. For filling armhole, see pages 33 to 35.

Check fit for strain or looseness at waist.

Remove the drape from the form and true. The center of each dart should be parallel with centerline on the straight grain. Adjust. Stitch muslin, or transfer to paper first for a test fit. To complete the pattern, see the instructions on pages 35 to 39.

Figure 12.7

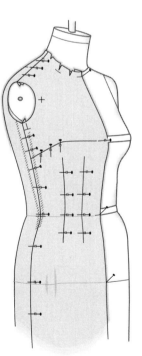

Figure 12.8

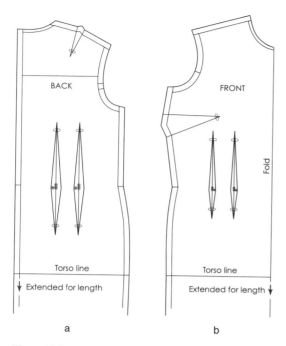

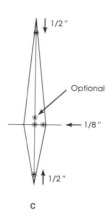

Finished Pattern

Figure 12.9

The punch/circles are placed in center of each dart intake at waist level and 1/8″ in from the stitchline. Mark 1/2″ down and up from the dart ends, shoulder, and side dart (see Figure 12.9c).

Figure 12.9

Semifitted Dress: Shift Silhouette

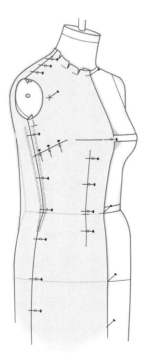

Draping Steps

Figure 12.10

Follow instructions for the fitted dress with the exceptions that half of the excess is taken in by dart front and back.

Figure 12.10

Finished Pattern

Figure 12.11

Make pattern with half of the excess taken in by dart front and back.

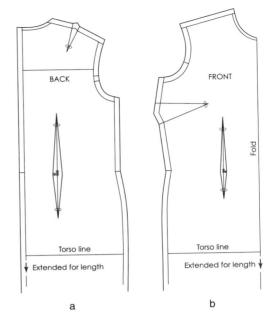

Figure 12.11

Loose Fitted Dress: Box Silhouette

Draping Steps

Figure 12.12

Follow instruction for the fitted dress with the exceptions that the looseness remains.

Allow additional ease at the side seam for a straight or slightly curved silhouette.

Finished Pattern

Figure 12.13

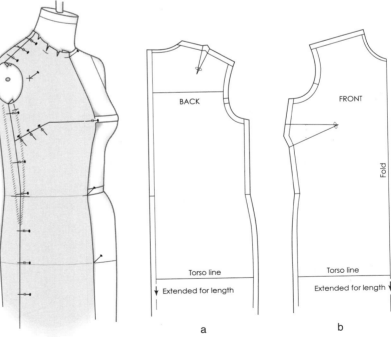

Figure 12.12   *Figure 12.13*

Princess Dress with Flare

Figure 12.14

The draping procedure for the upper part of the Princess dress is the same as for the Princess bodice. For the drape of designs based on the armhole Princess, see Chapter 6. To drape the bodice part of the design, follow the instructions below (Figure 12.14).

Design Analysis

The straight grain is centered on the two side panels of the muslin and pinned perpendicular to the crossgrain at the waist. The center panels are on the straight grain. Slash at the waistline of each panel, thereby releasing the muslin to smooth over the hip curve. To avoid lifting the crossgrain guideline at the side hip and/or stressing along the waistline, allow ease when pinning at the waist. The panels can be draped with flares that gradually float away from the waist or are fitted down from the waist, breaking away in a flare at any level. The panels can be draped as pleats or godet insets or designed as a straight-line dress. The designer/draper determines the dress length and the amount of flare at the hem.

Preparing Form

Figure 12.15

Measurements apply to front and back:

- Length: Measure from the shoulder/neck to the waist. Record and continue to dress length.
- Width across the shoulder: Use (#14) from the Form Measurement Chart. Add 2″.
- Width at the side panels: 14″.

Preparing Muslin

Figure 12.16

Cut two center panels for the front and back.

Cut two side panels for the front and back.

Prepare muslin using the illustrations below as a guide.

Draw a line through the center of the side panels indicating the straight grain.

Draw the crossgrain at waist level.

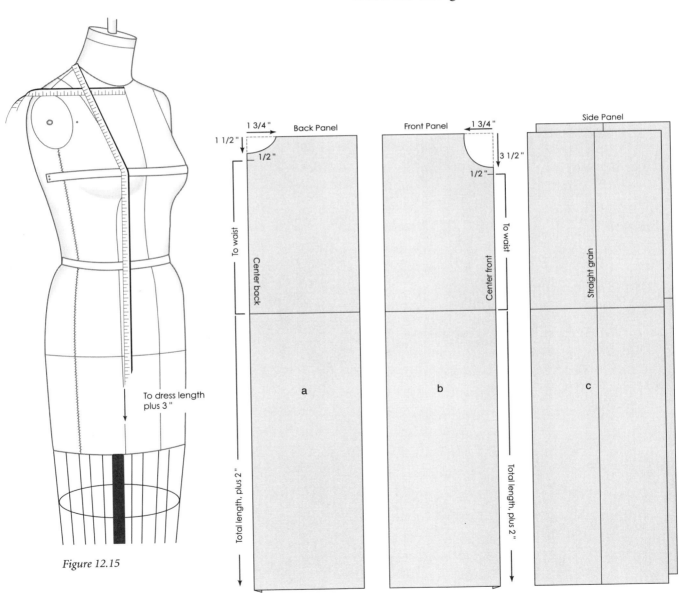

Figure 12.15

Figure 12.16

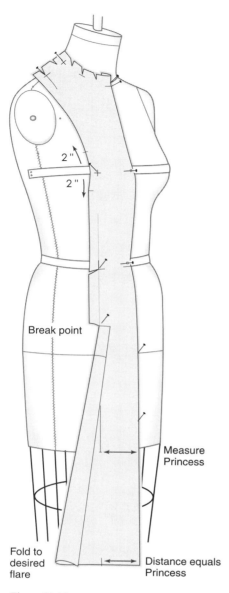

2"

2"

Break point

Measure
Princess

Fold to
desired
flare

Distance equals
Princess

Figure 12.17

Draping Steps

Figure 12.17

Place fold of the straight grain at the centerline. Pin at neck, bust bridge, waist, hip, and down the centerline. Drape the front panel to the waist, and slash. Pin and trim excess. Mark for ease control notches.

Smooth and mark muslin along Princess line to approximately 5″ below waist. Mark 1/8″ out from Princess for ease, and slash.

Mark the Princess line at the base of form, and mark equal width at the hem (guide for flare).

Flare: Measure from the Princess mark at the hem to the width of the flare desired. Crease a fold in the muslin from hem to break point. Trim to within 1″ of the fold.

Side Panel (Figure 12.18)

Pin straight grain at the center of the side Princess panel and crossgrain at waist.

Pin 1/4″ ease (1/8″ on the fold) at the waist.

Drape Princess bodice section. Slash to within 1/4″ of the marked waistline.

Smooth and mark Princess line and side seam at the base of the form.

Mark the hem to equal panel width.

Mark the break point for flare 5″ below waist to match front panel. Measure out 1/8″ for ease. Slash.

At the hem, measure the flare of equal width at the Princess and side panel as that of the front. Crease, and trim. Pin panel together.

Figure 12.19

Drape back panels using instructions for the front panel as a guide.

Pin back panels to the side panels.

Mark the hemline parallel to the floor.

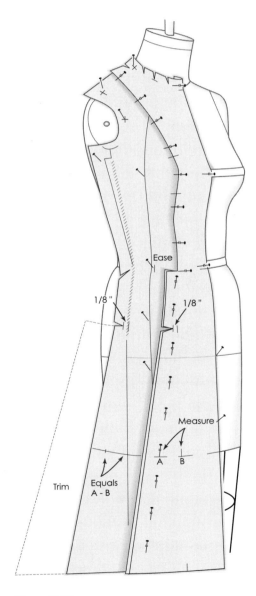

Figure 12.18

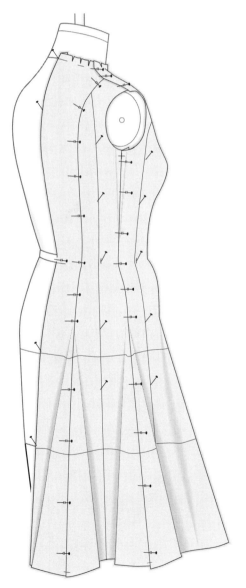

Figure 12.19

Fit Analysis

Repin the waist if looseness or stress appears along the waistline. Adjust flare if necessary.

Pin the hemline guide parallel to the floor. If fabric is soft, allow it to settle overnight before marking the hemline.

At the completion of the drape, remove and true. Stitch muslin or transfer to paper first for a test fit. To complete the pattern, see the instructions on pages 35 to 39.

Finished Pattern

Figure 12.20

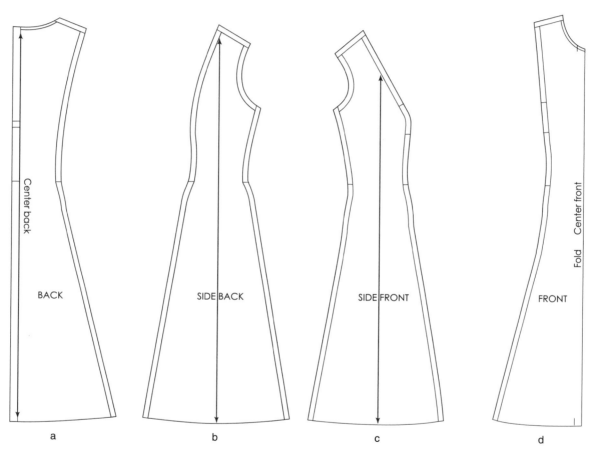

Figure 12.20

The Panel Dress

The basic panel style is a prototype for designs with similar features. Design variations follow the project (Figure 12.21).

Design Analysis

The panel styleline is placed at side of the bust at or just below mid-armhole to hemline. The styleline does not pass over the bust point. The excess is controlled by a French dart or gathers (dart equivalent) intersecting with the front panel styleline. The panel dress is generally semi-fitted. The side panel connects front and back panels and does not have a side seam. All panels are on the straight grain.

Figure 12.21

Preparing Form

Figure 12.22

Place style tape from the armhole of the front and back form (b), graduating to the waist and outward over the hip to the HBL line of the form (a). Place pinheads of equal width at the base of the form.

Preparing Muslin

Front and back form:

- Length: Add 3″
- Width: Add 3″

Panel:

- Length: Add 3″
- Width: Add 2″

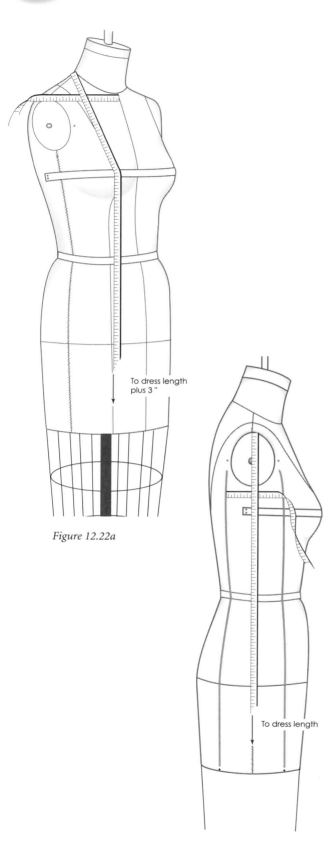

To dress length plus 3 "

Figure 12.22a

To dress length

Figure 12.22b

Figure 12.23

Cut panels, and use measurements given for front and back necklines.

Fold 1″ on the straight grain.

Draw the straight grain in the center of the side panel.

Square a line for hip HBL.

Draping Steps

Front

Figure 12.24

Place the fold of the straight grain at the center front. Pin.

Smooth, slash, mark, trim, and pin as muslin is draped from the center to the panel styleline. Drape the excess hanging from the bust mound to the side bust and fold into a French dart with excess toward the waistline.

Slash waist to within 1/4″ of the Princess line. Pin.

Pencil mark panel styleline.

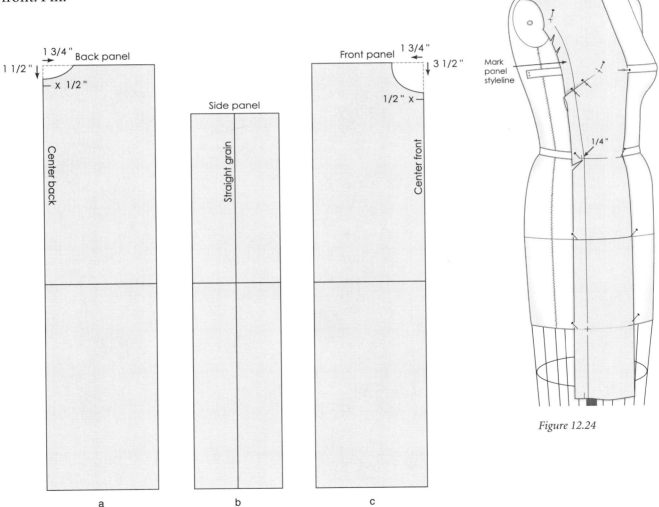

1 3/4 " Back panel

1 1/2 " ↓

⌐ x 1/2 "

Side panel

Center back

Straight grain

Front panel   1 3/4 "

3 1/2 "

1/2 " x ⌐

Center front

Mark panel styleline

1/4 "

a   b   c

Figure 12.23

Figure 12.24

Back

Figure 12.25

Pin the shoulder dart, or share its excess with neck, shoulder, and armhole as ease. (If a sleeve is desired, shift center cap 1/8″.)

Continue with the drape, as illustrated.

Side Panel

Figure 12.26

Place the straight grain on the side seam and crossgrain at hip. Pin along this line.

Mark armhole, side seam, armhole depth, and ease allowance.

Pin 1/4″ ease on each side of the grain at the waist.

Pencil mark panel styleline from waist to hip.

Figure 12.27

Mark hem to equal hip width.

Unpin upper part of the panel to just below the waist.

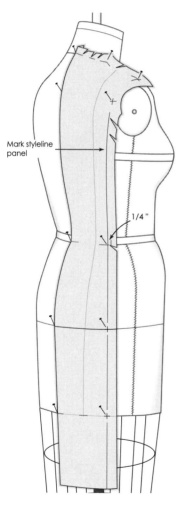

Figure 12.25

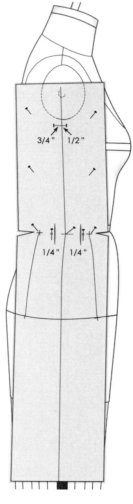

Figure 12.26

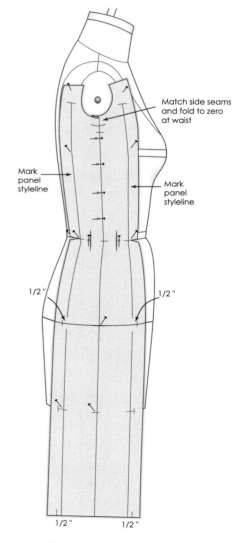

Figure 12.27

At armhole, pin ease allowance together (1/2″ for front ease, and 3/4″ for back ease) to zero at the waist.

Mark 1/2″ ease on each side of the hip depth and hemline.

Figure 12.28

Check that the hem is parallel to the floor. If not, adjust the drape of the panels.

Crease-fold seam allowance of the front and back seams and place over the seams of center panel. Pin.

At completion of the drape, remove, true. Stitch muslin, or transfer to paper first for a test fit. Panels should square from hip to hem on the straight grain. To complete the pattern, see the instructions on pages 35 to 39.

Finished Patterns

Figure 12.29

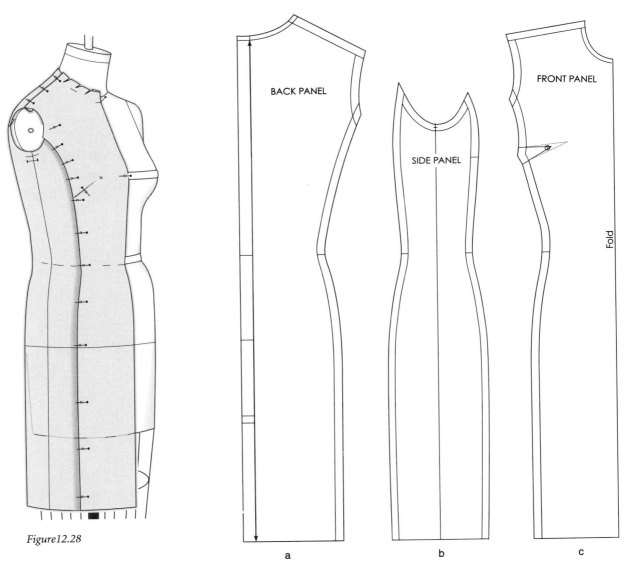

Figure 12.28

Figure 12.29

Empire Dress

Figure 12.30

Figure 12.31

The classic empire styleline crosses under the bust from the center line and gradually slopes to the center back. For design variations, the styleline can be directed anywhere, as long as it crosses under the bust. The empire styleline is generally associated with contour draping. However, the amount of fitting under the bust varies to adapt to current fashion trends. The lower part of the dress that joins to the empire styleline can be draped as fitted, flared, circular, or with panels. The draping procedure for the empire top is based on the empire bodice (Figure 12.30 and Figure 12.31).

Design Analysis

The design has a classic empire styleline. Gathers under the bust are spaced at 1 1/2″ (3/4″ out from each side of the Princess line). The depth of the neckline is as desired and ends at the Princess line of the shoulder. The fit of the dress is controlled by darts.

Preparing Form

Figure 12.32

Pin-mark the scoop neckline front and back.

Place style tape for empire styleline from center front crossing under the bust and sloping downward past side seam to approximately 4″ up from center back waist.

Preparing Muslin

Measurements apply to front and back:

- Length: Measure from shoulder/neck to length of dress. Record bust depth plus 4″.
- Width for bust arc: Use #17 from the Form Mesaurement Chart. Add 3″.

Cut two pieces of muslin equal to length and width.

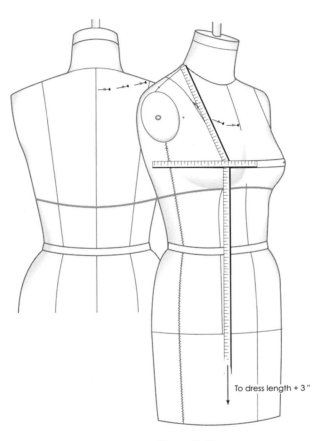

To dress length + 3 ″

Figure 12.32

Figure 12.33

Fold 1″ on the straight grain.

Draw and cut temporary front and back neck-lines following the measurements given.

Mark the bust depth plus 1″ down from X and square across muslin.

Mark 5″ below the bust depth and square across muslin.

Repeat this line on back muslin.

Cut along this line for front and back.

Mark hip depth using #25 from the Form Measurement Chart. Add 5″. Square across muslin.

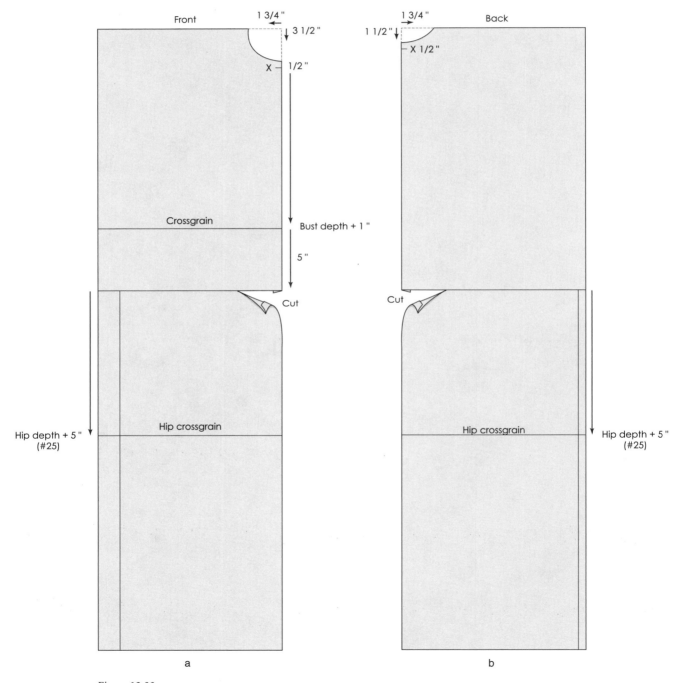

Figure 12.33

Mark hip arc using #23 from the Form Measurement Chart. Add 1/2″ ease on this line.

Draw lines up and down on the straight grain from each mark.

Draping Steps

Figure 12.34

Place the fold of the straight grain to the center front. Pin.

Smooth, mark, and slash muslin along the scoop neckline.

The crossgrain falls as the excess is draped to the Princess line under the bust.

Pin excess together at the Princess line and mark 1″ from each side of pinned dart (gather control notches).

Figure 12.35

Trim excess from the scoop neckline.

Spread dart excess between the two marks and hold with pins. Draw a line across the gathers. The markings are blended at the time the drape is trued.

Peel back or remove from the form.

Figure 12.36

Place the fold of the straight grain at center back. Pin.

Smooth, mark, and slash muslin along the scoop neckline and shoulder.

Pin 1/2″ dart at Princess line.

Smooth muslin at shoulder, armhole depth, and side seam. Pencil rub.

Mark empire styleline line. Trim excess.

Peel back or remove from form.

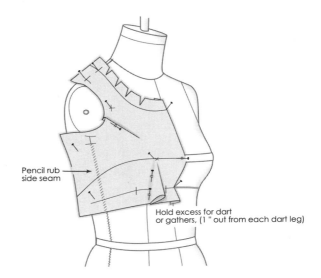

Pencil rub side seam

Hold excess for dart or gathers, (1 ″ out from each dart leg)

Figure 12.34

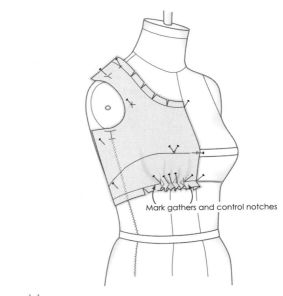

Mark gathers and control notches

Figure 12.35

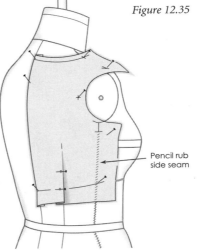

Pencil rub side seam

Figure 12.36

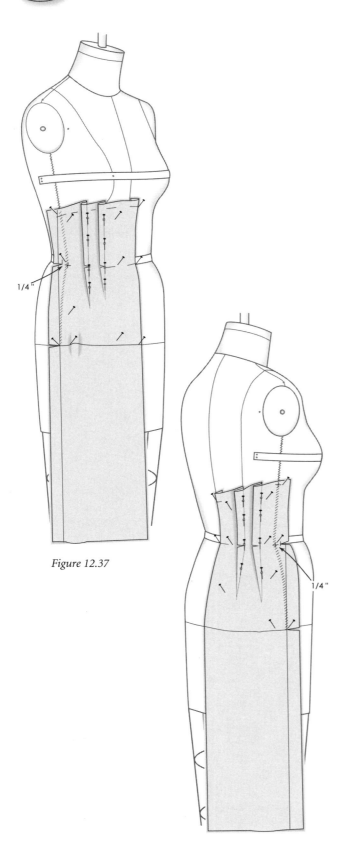

Figure 12.37

1/4"

Figure 12.38

1/4"

Lower Garment

Front

Figure 12.37

Place the fold of the straight grain at the centerline and hip guideline (crossgrain) on the HBL of the form.

Pin at empire style tape, waist, hip, and below.

Place hip guideline at the side seam matching the HBL. Pin at the stitchline and smooth ease allowance away from the side seam. Pin.

Smooth muslin along the curve of the hip to the waist. Pencil rub and slash at waist to within 1/4″ of rub mark.

Continue smoothing muslin upward to the style tape. Pin and pencil rub the side seam.

Darts

The looseness at the waist is taken up by two long darts with ease equally divided. The first dart is placed at the Princess line; the second dart is spaced 1 1/4″ at the waist. The dart length below the waist is approximately 3″. Mark the dart intake.

Pin excess outward. Slash at waist level.

Back

Figure 12.38

Drape the back according to the instructions for the front drape.

Each dart ends approximately 5 1/2″ below waist.

Slash at waistline.

Figure 12.39

Unpin each dart. Fold excess under and repin.

Pin the side seams together, but not so close as to cause stresslines at the waist or cause a guideline at the HBL to rise. This would unbalance the hang of the hemline.

Figure 12.40

Repin side seam. Join the upper front and back bodice drape with the lower drape.

Recheck for stress. Unpin and adjust if necessary.

At completion of the drape, remove and true. The centers of each dart should be parallel to the centerlines. Stitch muslin or transfer to paper first for a test fit. To complete the pattern, see the instructions on pages 35 to 39.

Finished Pattern

Figure 12.41

To mark long darts, see the instructions on page 268.

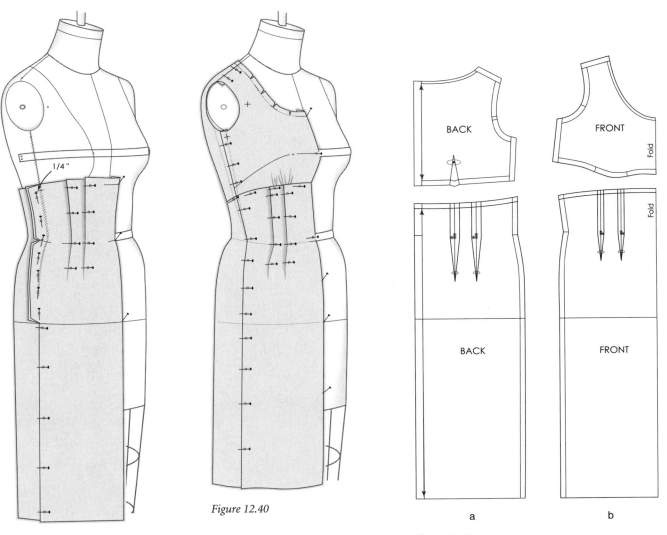

Figure 12.39

Figure 12.40

Figure 12.41

Basic Tent Foundation

The basic tent foundation has an A-silhouette and a sweeping hemline (Figure 12.42). The flare, hanging freely from the shoulder blade and bust, and the additional fabric at the sides create the silhouette and hemline. The sweep of the hemline can be increased by lowering the crossgrain at the curve of the armhole or decreased by raising the crossgrain at the side seam by taking up part of the original flare into a side dart.

Tent foundations 2 and 3 illustrate the principle of increasing or decreasing the flare at the hemline of the basic tent foundation. The tent foundations can be draped to any length and adapted to a variety of uses, including as a blouson, blouse, crop top, and beach cover-up.

Figure 12.42

Tent Foundation 1

Design Analysis

Figure 12.43

The tent foundation has a basic neckline and armhole. The flare hangs from the bust and shoulder blades, providing a sweeping hemline. The excess at the shoulder is draped around the armhole and hangs with the back flare. To create an A-silhouette, add fabric to the side seams half the width of front flare. At completion of the drape, the side seam may need to be adjusted for correct alignment.

Preparing Muslin

Figure 12.44

Length: Measure from shoulder/neck to dress length. Add 3″.

Width: 25″ for street length. Add 1/4″ for every additional inch of length.

Figure 12.43

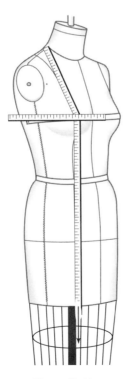

Figure 12.44

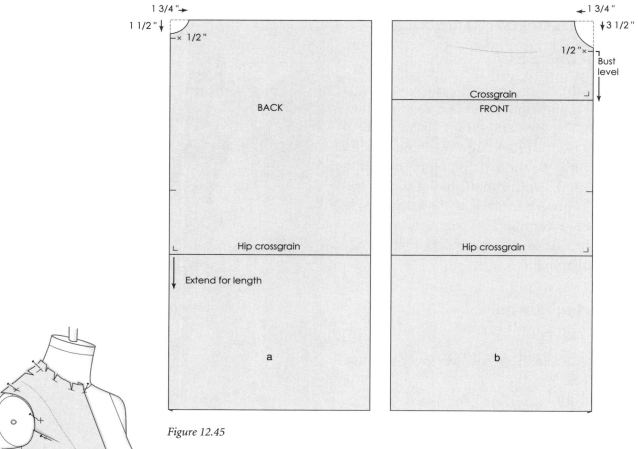

1 3/4 "→
1 1/2 "↓
×1/2 "

BACK

Hip crossgrain

↓ Extend for length

a

←1 3/4 "
↓3 1/2 "
1/2 "×

Bust level

Crossgrain

FRONT

Hip crossgrain

b

Figure 12.45

Equals
A - B

Measure

B   A

Figure 12.46

Figure 12.45

Fold 1″ on the straight grain. Follow illustration for front and back necklines.

Mark the bust level down from (X). Square a line.

Mark the waist depth.

Mark the hip depth down from waist. Square a line.

Draping Steps

Figure 12.46

Place the fold of the straight grain on the center of the form at the neck with the crossgrain guide on the HBL line of the form. Pin the neck, bust level, waist, hip, and down the center front.

Smooth, slash, and drape the neckline, shoulder, and armhole. Pin 1/8″ (1/4″ on the open) for ease. Mark armhole depth and 1/2″ ease. Trim excess.

Smooth muslin downward from the side bust to the base of the form, and pin. The crossgrain drops, as a flare hangs from the bust (the original dart excess).

Add to the Side Seam for A-silhouette

Pin the flare together at the Princess line. Measure width (A-B) at the hip guideline.

Mark the side seam, and dot mark the width (A-B) for the flare at the side of the drape.

Trim side excess to within 1 1/2″, and crease-fold on guide marks.

Peel drape back, and pin.

Figure 12.47
Place the fold of the straight grain to the center, and pin.

Smooth, and slash muslin around neckline, shoulder, and armhole. Pin.

Pin the flare together at the Princess of the hip guideline equal to the A-B measurement of the front flare. Mark an equal amount to the side seam.

Figure 12.48
Pin the front shoulder over the back shoulder. Crease-fold the side seam from the armhole to the hem, touching flare allowance marks. If the side seam does not align with that of the form, repin. Pencil mark the side seams.

After hanging overnight, mark the hemline parallel to the floor. Trim excess.

At completion of the drape, remove and true. Stitch muslin or transfer to paper first for the test fit. To complete the pattern, see the instructions on pages 35 to 39.

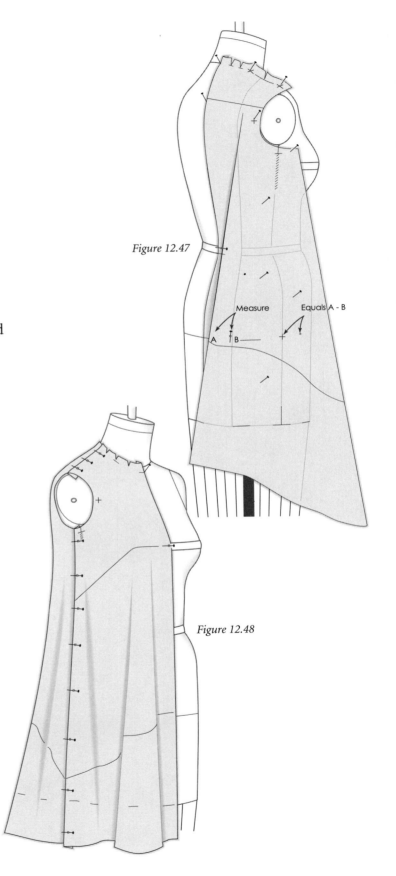

Figure 12.47

Figure 12.48

Finished Pattern

Figure 12.49

For facing instructions, see Chapter 11.

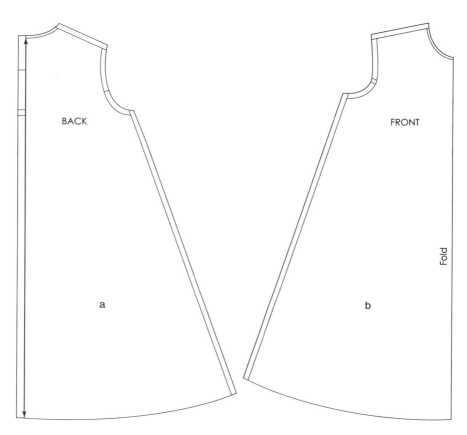

Figure 12.49

Tent with Added Flare: Tent Foundation 2

Design Analysis

Figure 12.50 and Figure 12.51

To increase the hemline sweep of the basic tent foundation, slash the muslin just below mid-armhole and allow the crossgrain to drop, thereby creating additional flare at hemline.

Preparing Muslin

For instructions on measuring and preparing the muslin, see page 287, Figure 12.44.

Figure 12.50

Figure 12.51

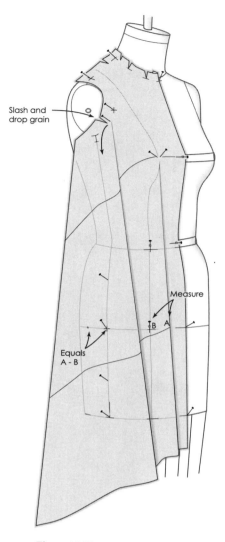

Slash and
drop grain

Measure

Equals
A - B

Figure 12.52

Draping Steps

Figure 12.52

Place the fold of the straight grain to the center, and pin.

Smooth, slash, mark, and pin the muslin around the neck, shoulder, and just below the mid-armhole.

Measure fold of flare A-B.

Slash at the mid-armhole and allow the grain to fall until the flare when folded equals no more (but may be less) than the A-B measurement.

Add equal amounts to side seam.

Repeat instructions for the back drape using the A-B measurement to control the amount of flare and addition to the side seam.

Strapless Dress Foundations and Designs: The Principle of Contour Draping

13

To reveal the contour shapes of the figure, fabric is draped to the hollow areas above, below, and in between the bust or buttocks rather than bridging them as does the basic garment. The bust having hollow areas under, above, and in between exemplifies this principle. Three strapless foundations were selected as prototypes for creating designs and constructing an undersupport for special garments (see Figure 13.1). The strapless foundations that introduce the principle of contour draping are:

- Princess torso (Figure 13.1b): Contoured under, between, and over the bust.
- Princess bodice (Figure 13.1c): Contoured under and over the bust (not between the bust).
- Bra-top empire torso (Figure 13.1a): Contoured under, between, and over the bust.

The strapless foundation can be draped to extend to any length.

Figure 13.1

Strapless Princess Torso

Figure 13.2

The Princess can be draped to the waist or torso (as illustrated) or to any length below (Figure 13.2). For design suggestions using the gore panels, see Skirts, Chapter 7. For instructions on constructing an undersupport, see page 313.

Princess Torso Foundation

Remove the bridge band. Drape to fit the hollows above, under, and in between the bust. The fit under the bust should not be snug (unless the panels are cut on bias), but should be close enough to give the appearance that it does. The style follows the Princess lines of the form. The centerlines have seams. The torso line can be of any distance below the waist, but 5″ is suggested. Outside draping may be preferred when draping the contour of the bust. The torso styleline can be created in a variety of styles, and the gore panels can be extended to desired lengths for other variations.

Preparing Form

Figure 13.3

Use pins or style tape for strapless and torso line.

Preparing Muslin

Front and back:

- Length and width: Add 3".
- Side length and width: Add 4".

Cut panels for front.

Add back measurements together and cut one panel.

Figure 13.4

Draw a crossgrain line 1" from hem.

Back

Mark the center back length and draw a line to the top at the other end. Cut along this line and cut the panel in half (a).

Fold 1" at the center back panel.

Draw a straight grainline through the center of the side back panel.

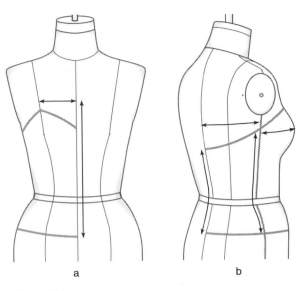

Figure 13.3

Front

Draw a straight grainline 1" from the fabric edge (c).

Draw a straight grainline in the center of the side front panel (bias grain is an option) (b).

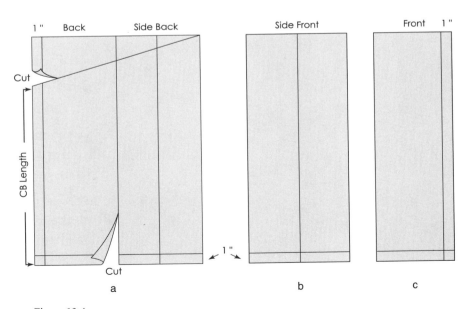

Figure 13.4

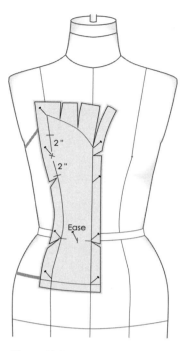

Figure 13.5

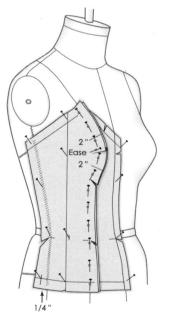

Figure 13.6

Draping Steps

Front Panel

Figure 13.5

Pin straight grainline at the center and 1″ below the torso style tape. Slash at the waist and bust level.

Pin 1/16″ for ease at waist (1/8″ on the open).

Smooth muslin upward from the center front at the bust level to the Princess line, draping to the shape of the bust.

Pin, slash, and mark strapless style tape.

Smooth across the torso line to the waist. Slash, mark, and pin.

Smooth muslin under the bust. Slash and drape closely to the bust shape along Princess line.

Mark the Princess line, and trim excess.

Mark 2″ up and down from the bust point for ease control notches.

Remove panel or peel back, and pin.

Side Front Panel

Figure 13.6

Pin a straight grainline at the center of the side panel and 1″ below the style tape.

Pin 1/8″ ease (1/4 on the open) at the waistline.

Smooth muslin draping to shape of the bust. Slash and pin under the bust mound.

A small amount of excess will appear as the muslin is draped over the bust point at the Princess line.

Pin remaining excess, and mark 2″ up and down from the bust point at the Princess line for ease control notches.

Smooth muslin up from the torso to the waistline. Slash and pin both sides.

Mark the Princess line and side seam.

Pin panels together along the Princess line.

Slash ease control marks.

Add 1/4″ at torso line for ease.

Remove panel or peel back, and pin.

Back Side Panel

Figure 13.7

A straight grainline is placed at the center of the side back panel and 1″ below style tape.

Drape both sides and slash at waist. Mark the torso and strapless line.

Back Panel

Pin a straight grainline at the center back of the form and 1″ below the torso style tape. Drape both sides. Slash, pin, and mark stylelines.

Pin the front to the back. Check the fit and balance of the drape. Remove the drape from the form.

Mark Inside Seams

Figure 13.8

Turn the drape over, and pencil rub each side of the inside pinned seams. Unpin and true all seamlines. Blend curved lines. Walk the pattern from the top down and bottom up to true ease control notches.

Stitch muslin or transfer the drape to paper first for a test fit. To complete the pattern, see the instructions on pages 35–39.

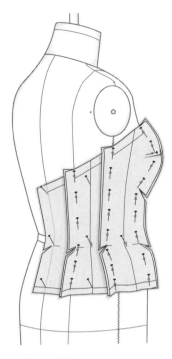

Figure 13.7

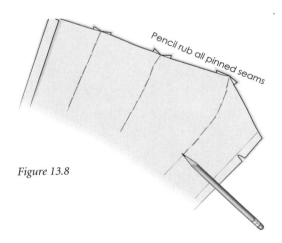

Pencil rub all pinned seams

Figure 13.8

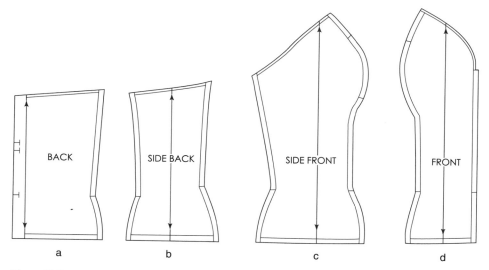

BACK

SIDE BACK

SIDE FRONT

FRONT

a

b

c

d

Figure 13.9

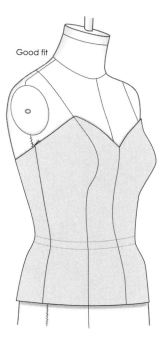

Good fit

Figure 13.10

Finished Pattern

Figure 13.9

Fit Analysis

Figure 13.10

Cut and stitch a full garment. Place on the form and evaluate the fit using the criteria given.

Good Fit

1. The bust cups fit the contour of the bust without stress and without the cups falling away at the centerline.

2. The garment has a smooth fit around the waist and torso.

3. There is sufficient ease at the torso and waist.

Poor Fit

Figure 13.11 and Figure 13.12

Problem: Stresslines appear above, at, or below the bust mound (see Figure 13.11a).

Cause: Insufficient room for the bust mound.

Solution: Release stitching from above to under the bust. The bust will push through. Measure the open space and correct the pattern (see Figure 13.12).

Poor Fit

Figure 13.13 and Figure 13.14

Problem: Bra cups fall away from the form.

Cause: Insufficient cup room for the larger bust size.

Solution: Release the stitches over the bust mound. Cut through the muslin from the bust point to the side seam and center front (see Figure 13.13). The mound of the bust will push through. Measure the open space and correct the pattern (see Figure 13.14).

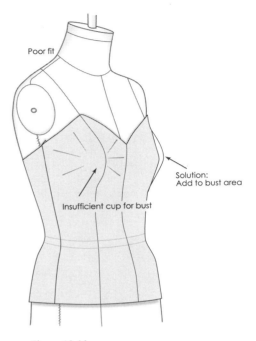

Figure 13.11

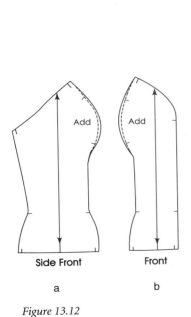

Figure 13.12

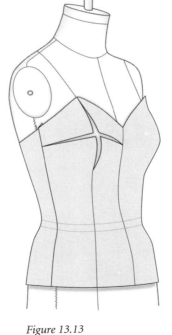

Figure 13.13

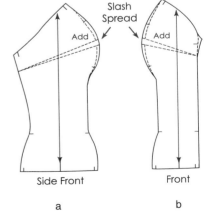

Figure 13.14

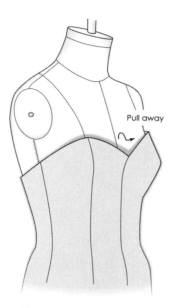

Figure 13.15

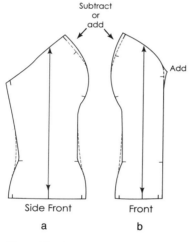

Figure 13.16

Poor Fit

Figure 13.15

Problem: Top falls away from the bust.

Cause: Insufficient bust cup room.

Solution: Same corrections given in Figure 13.12 and Figure 13.14 or trim, as illustrated in Figure 13.16.

Poor Fit

Figure 13.16

Problem: Too tight or too loose along the strapless line or the waist/hip.

Cause: Draped too tightly or too loosely.

Solution: If too tight, release the Princess seams the needed amount to release tension. If more room is needed at the strapless line, add to the center front. If loose, pin in closer. Correct the patterns by adding to the seams or trimming the excess.

Additional Information

To tighten the garment, collapse the shoulders and take in looseness at the center back or side seam. Correct the pattern. However, if the garment is to have a constructed undersupport, it is best to wait until the garment is complete before determining if the garment should fit closer.

Complete the design. For information on selecting the required type of innerconstruction, see page 313.

Princess with Gathered Overlays

The design is based on the Princess torso foundation (Figure 13.17). For instructions on the constructed undersupport, see page 313. The methods are prototypes for other designs with gathered overlays.

Design Analysis

The Princess panels are traced and trimmed to offset the bias stretch of the gathered overlay. The panels are sectioned, numbered, cut apart, and spread to equal the ratio of fullness desired (chiffon: 2 to 3 times the panel length). The front panel illustrates the process. Repeat for the remaining panels. The gathered panels are stitched to each panel and then joined together. The gathered panels lie over the constructed undergarment and are stitched across the strapless styleline.

Draping Steps: Preparing the Princess Panels

Figure 13.18 and Figure 13.19

Modify the front Princess panels, as illustrated. Two methods are illustrated for adding gathers to the Princess panels.

Trace two copies of the modified Princess panels. One set is for slash and spreading; the other set serves as the foundation for searching the gathered panels.

Figure 13.17

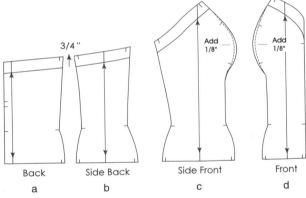

Figure 13.18

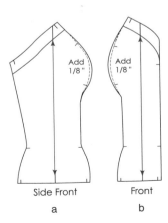

Figure 13.19

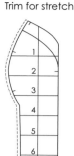

Trim for stretch

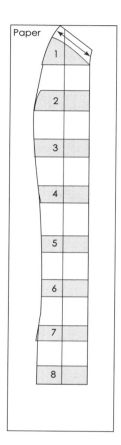

Figure 13.20

Figure 13.21

Method 1

Figure 13.20

One of the two sets will be marked into sections and numbered. The front panel is illustrated. Mark the sections to be spread for gathers.

Draw a guideline through the pattern parallel to the center front.

Figure 13.21

Draw a line through the paper.

Cut the numbered panel apart. Space and align with the line on paper. Secure to the paper. Trace and blend.

Cut the pattern from the paper.

Draw a grainline at the top of the pattern.

Cut in the fabric and place the grainline to the top of the panel. Pin and gather (gathers will be on an angle) and stitch to the panel (Figure 13.22). Trim excess.

Repeat the process for all the panels.

Figure 13.22

The gathered panels can be stitched to each panel of the undersupport, or joined to the panels and placed over the constructed under-support for a test fit.

Complete the design.

Method 2

The side front panel is illustrated. Repeat the process for the remaining panels.

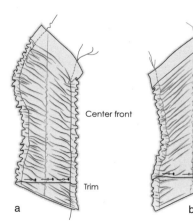

Center front

Trim

a   b

Center

c   d

Figure 13.22

Preparing Paper and Fabric

Width: Cut the fabric on the straight grain equal to the widest part of each Princess panel. Add 2″.

Length: Desired fullness (ratio: 2 to 1, 2 1/2 to 1, etc.). Add 3″ (crossgrain).

Cut paper to the same dimensions.

Draping Steps

Figure 13.23

Cut length and width for all panels.

Draw a guideline through centers of the fabric. Gather stitch through the centers and 1″ in from each side.

Start gathers 1″ from the top and finish so that the panel is 2″ longer than the pattern (Figure 13.24).

Figure 13.25

Place the top of the pattern to the top of the gathered fabric.

Angle the fabric to match the center guidelines (straight grain).

Hold the center with a pushpin.

Pin through the center and around the pattern outline.

Cut around the pattern. Unpin and remove pattern. Pull the gather threads from the fabric, and press.

True the ragged edges around each panel.

Place each panel on the paper, aligning the guidelines. Pin to secure, and trace.

Recut, gather, and stitch to the Princess panels.

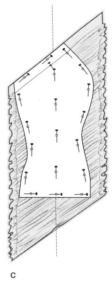

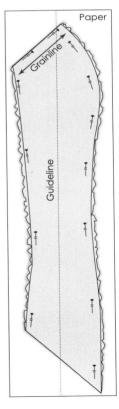

Figure 13.23

Figure 13.24

Figure 13.25

Layering Fabric over Princess Panels

The design for layering several plies of fabric over the Princess panels is a prototype for other foundations. Three methods are illustrated.

Design Analysis

Layers of lightweight fabric, usually chiffon, create different effects by changing the color of each layer. Layers can also add interest to the basic stylelines by laying cutout fabrics (eyelet) over other fabric(s) of a different color. Layering requires that the pattern be made slightly larger to prevent the overlay from buckling the frame to which it is stitched.

Preparing Paper and Fabric for the Princess Panels

Figure 13.19 (page 301)

Trace the Princess patterns.

Add 3/4″ to the top of each pattern.

Add 1/8″ at the bust points, and blend lines. The layers will be stitched to it.

Figure 13.26

Trace another copy and add 1/16″ to each seam.

Cut the layers from these patterns.

Figure 13.27

Examples of layers cut from the patterns.

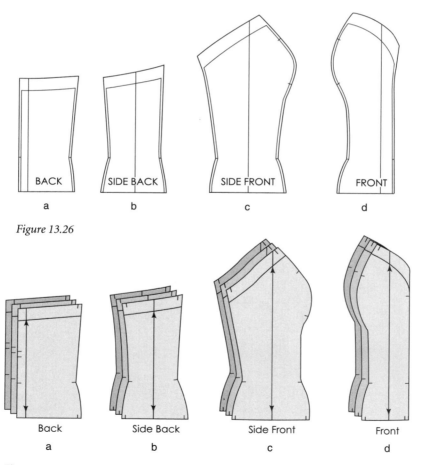

| BACK | SIDE BACK | SIDE FRONT | FRONT |
| a | b | c | d |

Figure 13.26

| Back | Side Back | Side Front | Front |
| a | b | c | d |

Figure 13.27

Strapless Princess Bodice

Design Analysis: Foundation

Figure 13.28 and Figure 13.29

Do not remove the bust tape. The front panel is draped over the bust tape, bridging the hollow between the bust mounds. The stylelines follows the Princess line of the form, contouring above and under the bust mound. The fit under the bust will not be snug (unless the panels are cut on the bias), but will be close enough to give the appearance that it is. The excess of the waist dart is removed at the Princess stylelines (dart equivalent). Outside draping may be preferred when draping the contour of the bust mound. The design can be draped as a torso or to different lengths for design variations. The designer/draper can create the skirt to complete the design or refer to Chapter 7 for suggestions.

Figure 13.28   *Figure 13.29*

Preparing Form

Figure 13.30

Use pins or style tape to establish the strapless line.

Preparing Muslin

Front and back panels:

- Width: Measure and add 4″.
- Length: Measure and add 3″.

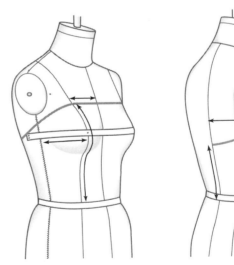

Figure 13.30

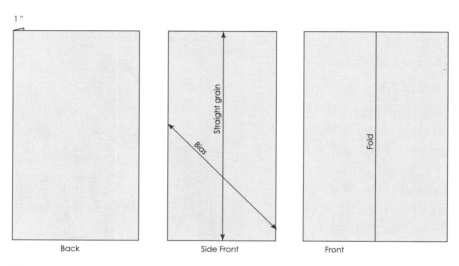

Back   Side Front   Front

Figure 13.31

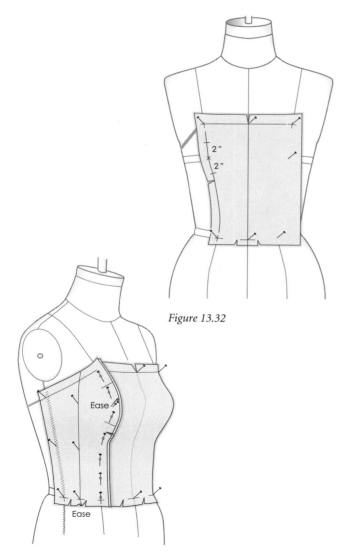

Figure 13.32

Figure 13.33

Figure 13.31

Draw straight grain in center of the front panel and center of the side front.

Fold 1″ at the center back.

Draping Steps

Front Panel

Figure 13.32

The straight grain is placed at the center front and pinned to secure the front (pin other side).

Smooth muslin along the waistline. Pin, and mark waistline and Princess line.

Smooth muslin under the bust at the Princess line. Slash and smooth to the shape of the bust fitting closely from the Princess line to the bust point.

Slash under the bust and mark Princess style-lines. Pin and trim excess.

Mark 2″ up and down from the bust point.

Peel back or remove drape from the form.

Front Side Panel

Figure 13.33

Pin the straight grain in the center of the side panel and side seam.

Pin 1/8″ ease (1/4″ on the open) at waist.

Smooth muslin to the Princess line, draping the shape above and below the bust. Slash under the bust.

Pin the remaining excess at the bust point and mark 2″ up and down on the Princess line for notches to control ease.

Smooth, slash, and mark waistline.

Mark the Princess and strapless stylelines. Pin.

Trim excess.

Back

Figure 13.34

Pin the fold of the straight grain to the center back.

Smooth muslin to the side seam. Pin. A waist dart is not needed.

Smooth, slash, and mark waistline.

Pin 1/8″ ease (1/4″ on open).

Mark side seam and strapless styleline.

Figure 13.35

Pin panels together. Check fit. Remove drape to mark seams.

Mark seams. Turn drape over and pencil mark both sides of all pinned seams (see page 297, Figure 13.8). Unpin and true seams, blending

the curved lines. To true notch placements, walk the pattern down from the top (adjust) and up from the bottom (adjust).

For instructions on transferring the drape to paper, see pages 35 to 39.

Cut in fabric and stitch. Recheck fit.

To solve fitting problems, see pages 299 and 300.

Finished Pattern

Figure 13.36

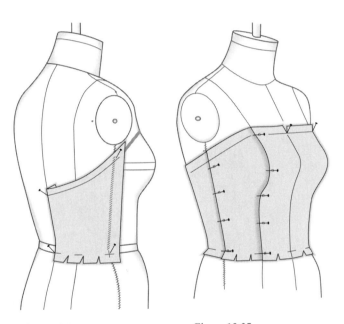

Figure 13.34   *Figure 13.35*

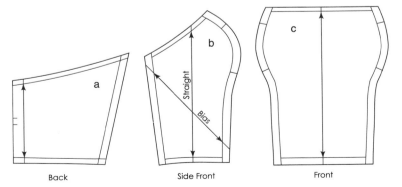

Figure 13.36

Strapless Empire Bra-Top Torso

Figure 13.37

The bra and torso part of the strapless empire can be designed in a variety of ways (Figure 13.37, the foundation, and Figure 13.38, the design). The styleline crossing bust points from center front to side seams (illustrated) and the Princess empire are among the most popular. The empire styleline crosses under the bust mound. From there, the styleline may be draped to any point along the side seam and center front. The empire styleline allows a contour fit that is closer to the hollows under the bust than that of the Princess styleline. The skirt part of the garment is the designer/draper's choice. For inspiration, see Chapter 7. To construct an inner support for the design, see page 313.

Empire Bra-Top Foundation

The bust tape is removed. The bra cup fits the hollows above, under, and in between the bust mound. Each bra panel is of equal width—approximately 1 1/2″ at the side seam and 1″ at the center front. The empire styleline follows along the bottom bra cup of the front. The torso line is 5″ below the waist at the center front, graduating to 3″ below the waist at the side seam to the back.

Figure 13.38

Preparing Form

Figure 13.39

Use pins or style tape for strapless, empire, and torso stylelines.

Preparing Muslin

Measure each side of the front and back as indicated by arrows:

Front
- Length: Add 6″.
- Width: Add 4″.

Back
- Length: Add 4″.
- Width: Add 4″.

Figure 13.40

Draw straight and crossgrains using measurements given.

Cut muslin to the measurements.

Divide the front and back in half. Cut apart and fold on the straight grain 1″ at the centerlines.

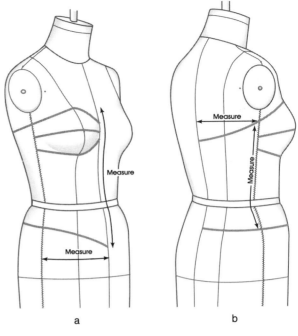

Figure 13.39

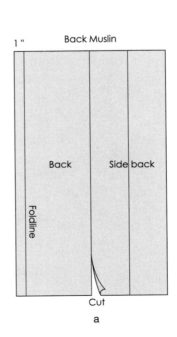

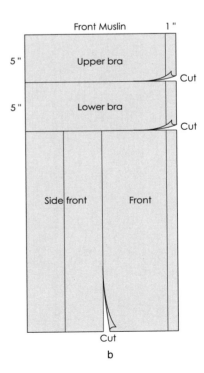

Figure 13.40

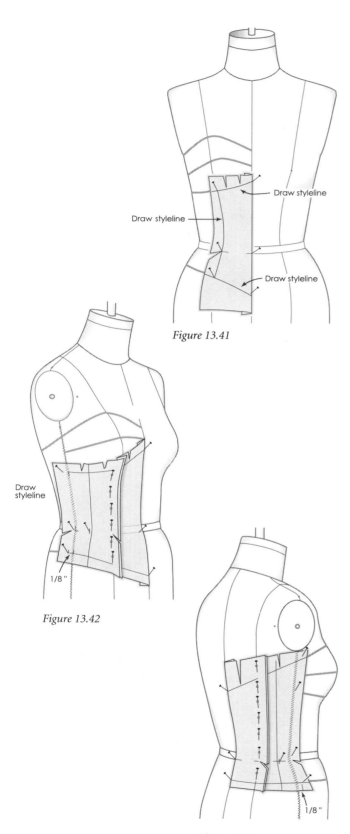

Figure 13.41

Figure 13.42

Figure 13.43

Draping Steps

Front Torso

Figure 13.41

Pin fold of straight grain at center and 1″ below torso style tape.

Smooth, slash, and mark muslin under the bust.

Slash at waist, and mark torso style tape.

Trim excess.

Side Panel

Figure 13.42

Pin straight grain guideline in the center of the side front panel and 1″ below torso style tape.

Pin 1/8″ ease (1/4″ on the open) at the waist.

Smooth muslin to the empire styleline, side seam, and Princess line. Slash, and pin.

Mark stylelines.

Back Panel

Figure 13.43

Pin fold of the straight grain at the center back and 1″ below torso style tape. Pin.

Smooth across waist. Slash and pin at the Princess line. Smooth muslin, and mark all stylelines.

Peel back or remove drape from form.

Side Back Panel

Pin straight grain in the center of the side panel and 1″ below torso style tape.

Pin 1/8″ ease (1/4″ on the open) at the waist.

Smooth muslin to the strapless styleline, side seam, and Princess line. Slash, and pin.

Mark stylelines.

Pin back panels together, and trim excess.

Upper Bust Cup

Figure 13.44

Pin straight grain of the muslin at the center front and 1″ above the strapless styleline. Pin.

Smooth muslin from the center front over the bust to the side seam, draping to the shape of the bust.

Slash, pin, and mark stylelines. Trim excess.

Peel the drape upward and pin or remove from the form.

Lower Bust Cup

Figure 13.45

Pin straight grain of the muslin at the center front and 1″ below the empire line.

Smooth muslin upward, draping to the shape of the bust. Slash, and pin.

Mark empire and bra styleline. Pin, and trim excess.

Remove drape from the form.

Mark Seams

Reverse the drape and pencil rub the pinned seams of the drape. For instructions, see page 297, Figure 13.8.

True and blend curved seams.

Repin (or stitch) and place on the form.

To analyze and correct the fit, see pages 298 and 299.

Front Drape Pinned Together

Figure 13.46

Pin (or stitch) front drape together.

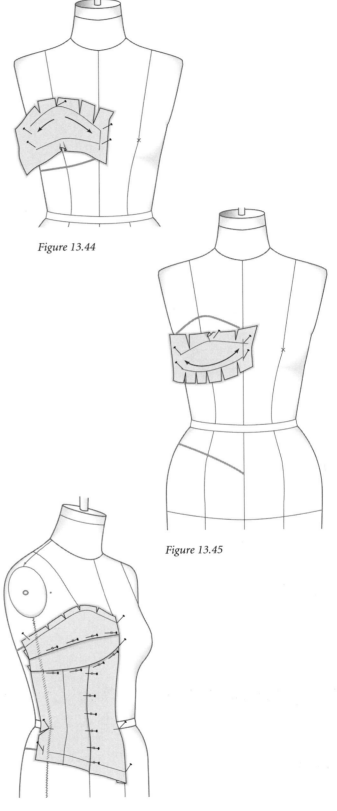

Figure 13.44

Figure 13.45

Figure 13.46

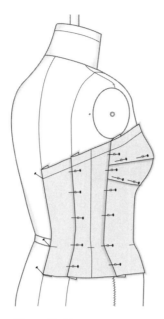

Figure 13.47

Front Pinned to Back

Figure 13.47

Pin side seams with the front folded over the back.

Remove ease pin at waist.

Check fit of the bust cups. If stressed, add to upper and under bust cup (see Figure 13.48).

Remove drape from the form and true, stitch muslin or make the paper pattern first for the test fit. For instructions on constructing the undersupport, see page 313.

Finished Pattern

Figure 13.49

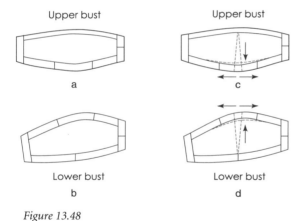

Upper bust

a

Lower bust

b

Upper bust

c

Lower bust

d

Figure 13.48

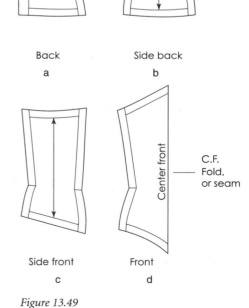

Center back

Back

a

Side back

b

Side front

c

Center front

Front

d

C.F.
Fold,
or seam

Figure 13.49

Support for Strapless Garments

Support for strapless garments ranges from minimal to extensive. Selection of the type of constructed undersupport depends on the characteristics of the design and the cost factor.

Types of Support

Minimal Support

Minimal support might include the use of shoulder straps and/or boning stitched over selected seams (for example, bust and side seams). The strapless design could also have facings or a lining. A fused or nonfusible interlining would add additional support, and should be lined.

Constructed Undersupport

An undersupport functions as a corset (a second garment) and is made of heavy fabric, boning, underlining—often with a lining. Extensive construction is required for designs that are heavily beaded or with overlays consisting of several plies of fabrics, multiple gatherings, or radiating drapery. After considering all factors, the designer/draper selects the appropriate support for the design. A lightweight construction of cotton netting, organza, or lightweight cotton may be appropriate for certain designs, particularly if the garment is featherweight and generally unlined. A heavily constructed undersupport provides the necessary security for design garments that overlay it.

Supplies: Lightweight Construction

Undersupport

- Fabrics: Cotton net, organdy, lightweight cottons for the base.

- Boning (optional) and twill tape.

A separate lining depends on which side of the support garment faces the underside of the design overlay.

Supplies: Heavyweight Construction

Undersupport

- Fabric: medium weight canvas, drill, poplin, a weighty satin or a sturdy (nonstretchy), preshrunk linen or a heavy satin Lycra.

If boning and raw seams of the constructed undergarment face the design overlay, a lining is not required, but an underlining is. If boning and seams do not face the design overlay, a lining is required to cover the raw seams.

Underlining

Underlining is the backing for the design overlay, which shields the garment from the boning and raw seams of the constructed undersupport that faces it.

- Fabrics: wool felt or a blend (not less than 50%), cotton flannel, or batiste.

Bust Padding

Bust padding is attached to the undersupport garment.

- Fabrics: thick fiber-filled batting, 2 to 3 ply of a stiff fabric (canvas or Belgian linen) or fuse several plies of interconstruction to the bust area.

Lining

- Fabrics: Rayon, China silk, silk crepe, or use the design fabric.

Other Items

Grosgrain ribbon or twill tape (1/4″) for holding ease at the top of the strapless garment.

Grosgrain or elastic (3/4″ to 1″ wide) for securing the garment to the waist. Closure of choice.

Preparing Patterns for the Undergarment

The Princess torso pattern is the prototype for the following instructions, but the information can be applied to other foundations. For the drape of the Princess torso, see page 295.

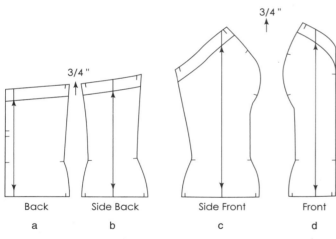

Figure 13.50

Lining and Underlining Patterns

Trace two copies of the Princess torso patterns and add 3/4″ to the top of each pattern to allow for adjustments.

First Copy

Figure 13.50

The first copy is for the lining, if required.

Second Copy

Figure 13.51

Add 1/8″ on each side of the bust mound to allow for boning and/or padding; to serve as an underlining for the design garment; and as a base for generating the design garment.

Cut in fabric of choice and stitch.

Press seams open.

If bra padding is not desired, go to Figure 15.36.

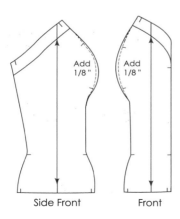

Figure 13.51

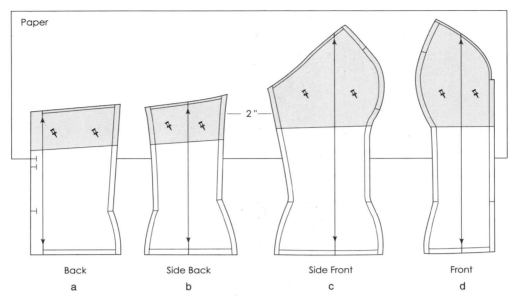

Figure 13.52

Padded Bra

Figure 13.52

Place the upper part of the basic Princess on paper.

Trace bust area and 2″ across the upper back patterns (indicated by shaded areas).

Bra Cup Seamless Pattern

Figure 13.53

Mark notches and cut from paper removing seam allowances.

Prepare Fabric

Figure 13.54

Choose fabric for padding (see page 313).

Cut fabric 9″ × 20″.

Top stitch 1/4″ rows vertically through the fabric.

Place bra patterns on the padding. Trace and cut.

Mark notches, but do not slash notch locations.

Join Bra Padding

Figure 13.55

Join raw edges by hand stitching or zigzagged by machine.

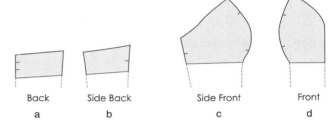

Figure 13.53

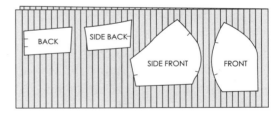

Figure 13.54

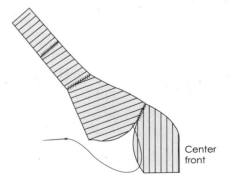

Figure 13.55

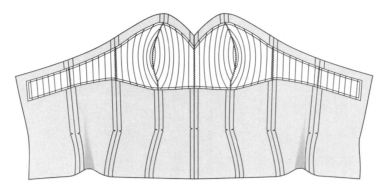

Figure 13.56

Figure 13.56

Fit padding snug to the garment 1″ from the top. Pin to hold.

Stitch around the outer edges to secure padding to undergarment.

Boning

Boning provides a lightweight skeletal frame that supports the garment. A variety of boning types are available through sourcing companies and fabric stores. They range from firm, ridged, or webbed plastic called Rigilene to a flexible wire boning with caps. Boning can be purchased with or without a casing. When needed, casings can be made. Placement of the boning depends on the type of support required. For example, boning may extend through the length of the torso (theatrical and show costumes) or end 1/2″ from the waistline. It can also be placed in between seams or can be stitched over a padded bust. Boning should not end at a point level with the ends of the seams or it may poke the figure. Boning generally finishes 1/2″ from each end of the selected seams.

Types of Boning

Rigilene

Figure 13.57

This type of boning is made of webbed plastic through which needles pass easily. It can be used with or without a casing. The cut ends are covered with twill.

Flexible Wire Boning

This type of boning is cut to length with a metal cutting device. The rounded caps are then attached with pliers. Wire boning requires a casing.

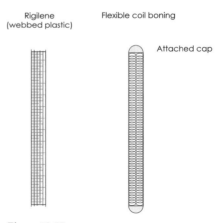

Rigilene
(webbed plastic)

Flexible coil boning

Attached cap

Figure 13.57

Casing for Boning

Figure 13.58

Cut strips of cotton to length of each seam and double the width of the boning. Add 1/2″ (a).

Fold and stitch, using 1/8″ seam (b).

Turn. Slip boning in. Fold 1/2″ at the ends (c).

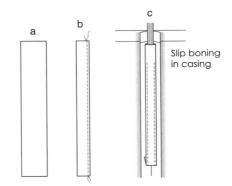

Figure 13.58

Encased Boning

Figure 13.59

Cut boning to the length of the selected seams (a).

Push casing down at each end. Trim 1/2″ from each end of the boning (b) or remove boning and trim 1″ put boning back (review Figure 13.56).

Fold 1/2″ and stitch to seam (c).

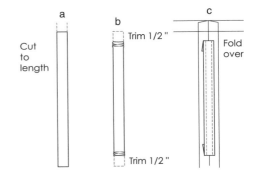

Figure 13.59

Attaching the Boning

Cased Boning

Figure 13.60

Casing of the boning is stitched at each side and through to the constructed support garment. (Boning over the bust is optional).

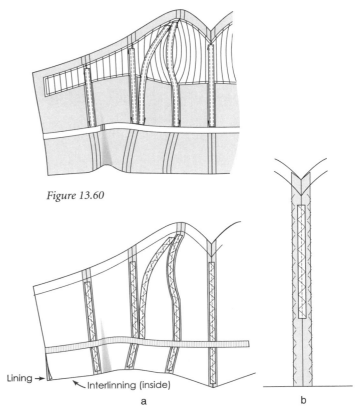

Figure 13.60

Uncased Boning (Rigilene)

Figure 13.61

Boning is stitched in the ditch of the seam. The constructed side of the support garment faces the underlining of the design garment. The raw seams are inside and do not require a separate lining, which may, however, be desired. An optional feature is to catch stitch the boning to the seams.

Figure 13.61

Attaching the Undergarment

The constructed undersupport is attached to the design garment in one of two ways—with or without a lining. If there is a lining, the design garment is placed in between the undersupport and the lining. All three are joined by stitching 1/8″ above the strapless line. If the design garment is beaded or has several plies of fabric, the stitchline may be more than 1/8″.

Lining Not Required

A lining is not required when the raw seams, boning, and padded bra face the underside of the design overlay. In these cases, the finished side of the undersupport serves as the lining. This type of construction requires that the design overlay be backed by an underlining. If a lightweight construction is chosen, an underlining is not required.

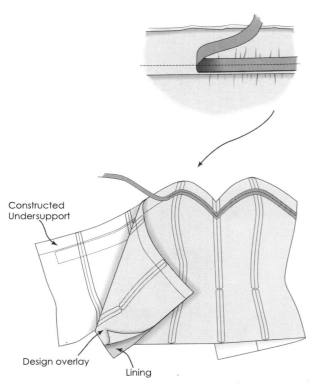

Constructed Undersupport

Design overlay

Lining

Figure 13.62

Lining Required

A lining is required when the finished side of the undersupport faces the underside of the design overlay. The lining covers the raw seams, boning, and padded bra to clean finish the garment.

Controlling Ease

Figure 13.62

Stitch twill or grosgrain 1/16″ above the stitchline of the strapless, starting at the center back to the side seam (Figure 13.62).

Hold 1/8″ ease from the side to the Princess line and 1/8″ to the center front. Repeat to other side to help secure the strapless top to the figure.

Trim the top to within a 1/4″ seam allowance.

Edge stitch when garment is turned.

A 3/4″ to 1/2″ grosgrain can be placed along the waistline and tacked at the center and sides and into the center back. It can be either caught in with the zipper or allow a 1″ opening in the fold of the lining at the center back. Pull though the grosgrain ribbon and secure with hook and eye across the inside of the zipper (see Figure 13.60 and Figure 13.61).

Fit Analysis

If the bust cup pulls away from the bust or does not fit into the cleavage (between the bust) comfortably, see pages 299 and 300.

Underskirt

An underskirt, or lining, stitched to the torso foundation may be required. It may be a straight, flared, or gathered skirt. Hoop or petticoat skirts can also be attached to give shape to the overskirt (Figure 16.63).

Figure 13.63

Gown with Radiating Drapery

Figure 13.64

Design Analysis

Figure 13.64

The constructed undersupport has an asymmetric style cut same as the gown. The undersupport is developed first. The side seams are basted—to be opened to include raw seams at completion of the drape. The skirt part of the design has a slit and can be draped to the undersupport before the overlay is draped. The back torso is draped to follow the shape of the undergarment. It extends 1″ below and allows for a 1″ turnback.

The left side of the strapless is draped over the bust with gathers directed to the center front. The gathers are pinned and tacked. The right side is draped over the bust and from side to side. Added fullness radiates from the right seam and held as pleats (gathers if preferred) on the left side. The pointed hemline of the overlay hangs freely (except at the side seams)and covers the joining seam of the skirt.

The pattern shapes of the back constructed undersupport are also cut in design fabric and stitched as the design overlay. Skirt can be draped before or after the Princess torso drape. For a guide to constructing the undersupport, see pages 314 to 318.

Preparing Form

Pin-mark or use style tape to mark strapless styleline (not illustrated).

Fabric Needed

Constructed Undersupport

To measure for the constructed undersupport and the back drape, see page 295, Figure 13.4.

Skirt

- Length: Cut to desired length. Add 2″.
- Width: For hip F/B arc, multiply #23 from the Model Form Measurement Chart by 2 and add 3″.

Radiating Draped Overlay

Cut bias 24″ × 28″.

Fall-out fabric can be used for bra drape.

Draping Steps

Construct the undersupport following the instruction starting on page 309. Use these patterns for the back drape overlay. Allow 2″ at the hemline.

Figure 13.65

Drape over the bust with the dart excess pinned as pleats (gathered later when tacked to the undersupport).

Slash and trim excess.

Figure 13.66

Place bias fabric over the right bust, allowing approximately 1″ to extend the left side of the form.

Smooth fabric over the right bust and under the left bust to the side seam. Fold fabric 1″ under, and pin to the left side seam.

Crosspin bust point.

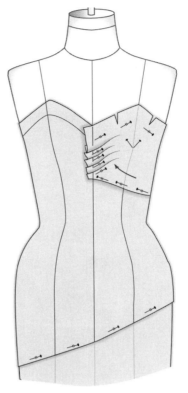

Figure 13.65

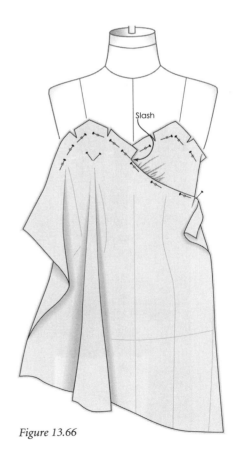

Figure 13.66

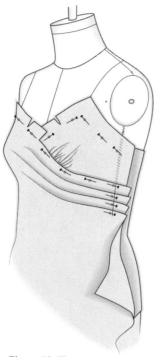

Figure 13.67

Figure 13.67 and Figure 13.68

Flare (dart excess) hanging below the bust is draped as pleats to the left side (see Figure 13.67).

Mark the side seam approximately 3″ down from the plate/side seam (see Figure 13.68).

Adding Fullness

Figure 13.69

Trim excess 3″ down.

On the right side, slash to the side seam. Pin and lift fabric as a pleat to side seam of the left side.

Repeat the process.

Mark the side seam. Trim excess.

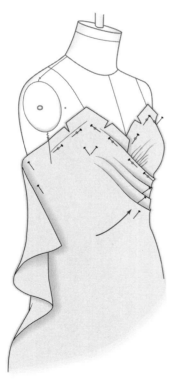

Figure 13.68

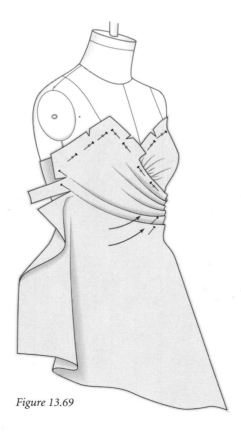

Figure 13.69

Figure 13.70

Pin pleats and mark the side seam.

Figure 13.71 and Figure 13.72

Continue to slash and lift the fabric for pleats pinned to the other side.

End the pleats 1″ above the finished seam of the undergarment.

Extend fabric beyond the seam of the undersupport. Allow for hem and turnback.

Mark the hemline to point over the Princess line (see Figure 13.71).

Complete pinning with the side seam marked (see Figure 13.72).

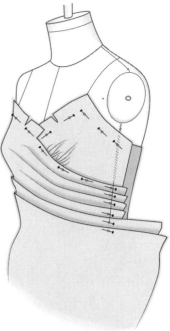

Figure 13.70

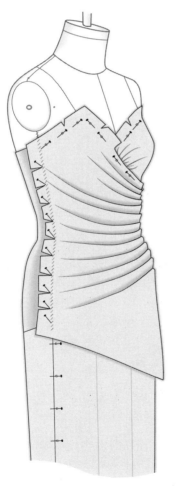

Figure 13.71

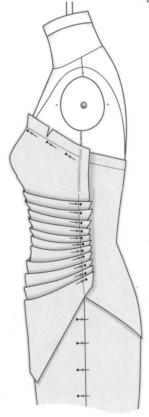

Figure 13.72

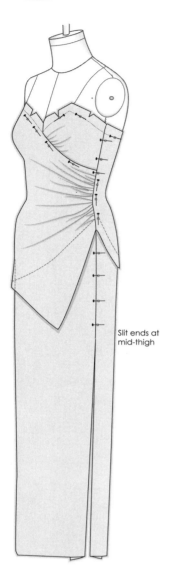

Slit ends at
mid-thigh

Figure 13.73

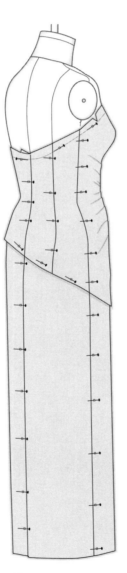

Figure 13.74

Check fit.

Make the patterns after removing and trueing the draped garment. The pleated side can be marked as pleats or the uneven marks can be blended for gathers.

Figure 13.73 and Figure 13.74

The garment is cut in the design fabric unless the original fabric has already been used in the drape. The garment is stitched for a final fit check.

Bias Cut Dresses

14

Before the advent of the bias cut dress, fashion garments used girdles to harness the body. Then, the late designer Madeleine Vionnet (1876–1975), called the "Euclid of Fashion," created the bias cut dress that clung to the natural curves of the figure. As the bias fell from the hip, it created flares at the hemline. The beauty of the bias dress was the graceful swing of its hemline as the body was in motion (see Figure 14.1 and Figure 14.2). Vionnet's designs revolutionized the way women wore clothes. Her bias dresses are timeless in style and have influenced the work of many other designers.

Figure 14.1

Figure 14.2

Madeleine Vionnet

Vionnet worked bias in very creative and ingenious ways, so that many of her bias cut dresses could be slipped over the head—they did not require zippers or any other closures. This was achieved through bias cuts, set-in gussets at strategic locations, low backs, halters, cowls, twists, and with the use of circles (Figure 14.3, Figure 14.4, and Figure 14.5). The bias stretched

around the narrow part of the dress as it was slipped over the shoulders or hip and then found its way back when the garment settled on the figure.

Another amazing characteristic was that the bias hemlines remained parallel to the floor even after having been on hangers for years. Although there is speculation as to her method for controlling bias, she never confided her technique to anyone. If her method were known, it might not have been adaptable to mass production of garments by the fashion industry.

Vionnet also designed other types of wearing apparel, including loosely fit garments and lounge pants, most often in bias, but not always. Vionnet experimented and created her designs on a half-size wooden mannequin with move-

able parts. Once satisfied with the design, she would then drape the garment to life size.

Vionnet experimented with many of her creations allowing the grain to fall as she worked the fabric, or toile (muslin). If she saw an interesting effect, she continued until a beautiful design emerged. You are encouraged to do the same as you venture into the following projects.

Figure 14.3

Figure 14.4

Figure 14.5

Nature of Bias Cut Fabrics

The straight grain and crossgrain run in opposite directions from the center of true bias as the draped garment is pinned to the form. The crossgrain, which is less firmly twisted than the straight grain, falls more easily on the bias. When the straight grain and crossgrain meet at a seamline, one hangs longer than the other and may skew the balance of the garment. To help solve this problem, see the one example of a pattern layout on page 357. It may be necessary for a pattern to have two sides that differ in shape.

All woven fabrics stretch on the bias. The amount of stretch depends on the weave and weight of the fabric. Garments cut in bias should be draped in lightweight muslin, or lightweight to medium-weight fabrics.

Although draping in design fabrics is desirable, it still can present problems. Lightweight fabrics cut on the bias stretch as they are being draped. The draped garment also stretches when removed from the form. The shape of the draped pattern parts becomes distorted and unruly, making it difficult to create the paper pattern. Special instructions are given to help eliminate the problem. These instructions are not required if the garment is draped in muslin or a medium-weight fabric, or if a pattern closely related to the design is traced before the drape begins (see page 334).

Light- and Medium-Weight Fabrics

- Crepe
- Flat crepe
- Crepe-de-chine
- Satin-back crepe
- Charmeuse
- Georgette
- Chiffon

Stretchy knits can also be used for the selections of designs that follow.

Slip Dress

The slip dress clings to and moves with the figure. To encourage freedom of movement, the skirt part of the dress is generally not lined. The bra top can be self-lined. Use a fabric that drapes well—lightweight crepe or its equivalent, a stretchy knit, or muslin suitable for draping in bias. Some fabrics stretch more readily than others and may require the use of the special instruction for establishing a pattern before the completion of the drape. The bias stretch of a fabric should be noted at the time of the drape. Read "Making A Paper Pattern: Special Instructions" page 334. If a pattern relating to the general shape of the skirt part of the design is available, trace and use it as a base for the drape. This will save one step in correcting the final pattern (Figure 14.1).

Design Analysis

The dress looks like and fits the figure as a slip (see Figure 14.6). It is somewhat loose through the waistline, slinking over the waist and hip before falling into a series of flares at the hemline. The dart excess of the slip top is darted under the bust; it can also be gathered. The bra top has spaghetti straps to hold the dress in place. An opening for entry should not be needed The dress can be of any length. Draping in lightweight crepe or its equivalent rather than in muslin or a medium-weight fabric requires the special instructions guide. Use the cut-away fabric to drape the bra top of the design.

Preparing Form

Figure 14.7

Remove bridge tape.

Use style tape for marking the empire styleline and bra-top design.

Preparing Fabric and Paper

Cut two 45″ squares of fabric for a full length skirt.

Cut two 45″ squares of paper for the paper patterns.

Figure 14.6

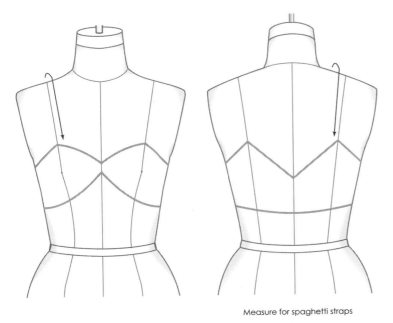

Measure for spaghetti straps

a

b

Figure 14.7

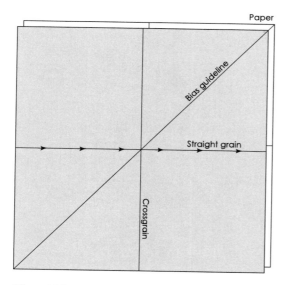

Figure 14.8a

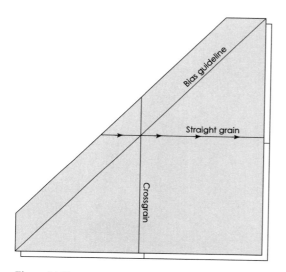

Figure 14.8b

Figure 14.9a

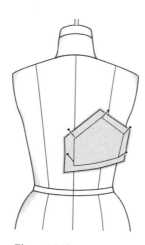

Figure 14.9b

Preparing the Front Drape

Figure 14.8a

Draw and mark guidelines for straight and cross-grains. Draw a line from point to point marking the true bias on fabric and paper. Use tailor's chalk or handstitch guidelines in different color threads. The designer/draper may choose which grain to run upward at the time of draping the garment.

Preparing the Back Drape

Figure 14.8b

Draw one line through the center of the true bias, and another line 4″ out from the bias line.

Cut and separate.

Use the excess fabric for the bra-top drape.

Draping Steps: Bra-Top Drape

Figure 14.9a

The bra top can be draped on the straight grain parallel to the centerline or placed on the V-cut of the bra top.

Options: The bra top can be draped with a dart or gathered. If gathered, the lining should have a dart to eliminate thickness under the bust.

Mark empire and bra-top stylelines.

Figure 14.9b

Drape the back bra top.

Mark empire and bra-top stylelines.

Peel back the drape or remove it from the form, and true.

Figure 14.10

Place corner of bias at the center and raise until sides of the square are at least 1″ above the empire line at the side seam.

Pin bias guideline to the center of the form.

Smooth fullness away from centerline of the form directing excess to the side seam. The fabric should slightly bridge the waistline, and not fit to it. Pin.

Smooth fabric upward beyond the empire styleline. Slash and pin.

Smooth fabric across the hipline. Pin.

Raise the form to allow room at the end of fabric for flare(s).

Pin on both sides of each flare for control.

The other side of center can be draped or left undraped. It will not be the side that is traced in making the pattern.

Mark the empire styleline and side seam to the base of the form.

Mark waist, hip (HBL), and base of the form at side seam.

If draping in crepe or equivalent remove the drape from the form. Drape the back (page 332, Figure 14.12). For instructions on transferring the drape to a paper pattern, see page 334.

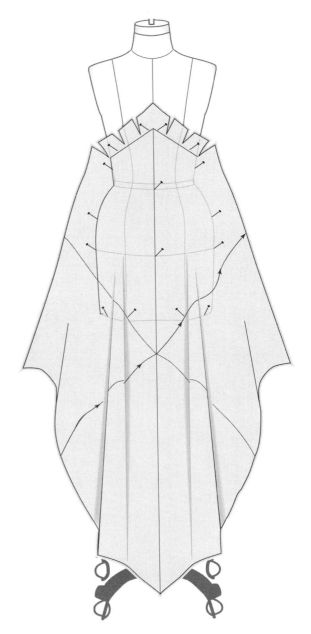

Figure 14.10

Figure 14.11

Trim excess to within 1″ of the empire styleline and side seam to the waist.

Add 4″ out from the base of the form.

Extra fabric is needed for the A-silhouette because the bias has a tendency to shift forward after hanging overnight.

Trim gradually to the waist, graduating outward to the end of fabric (see Figure 14.11).

Slash to within 1/8″ of the waist and hip. Pin.

Trim overhang for a temporary hemline.

Peel back the drape or remove it from the form. Pin and true.

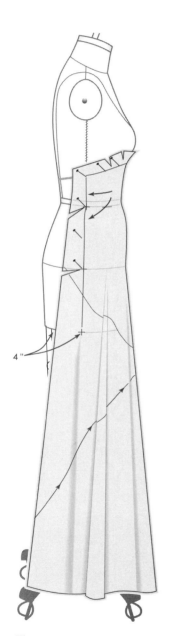

Figure 14.11

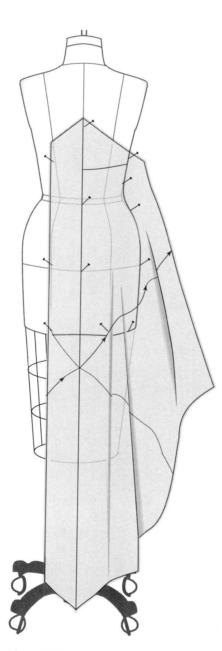

Figure 14.12

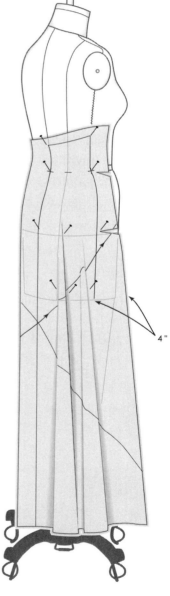

Figure 14.13

Figure 14.12

Apply the same instruction for the back drape as for the front drape (see Figure 14.10).

Figure 14.13

Apply same instruction as for the front drape (see Figure 14.11).

Peel back the drape or remove it from the form. Pin and true.

Figure 14.14

Pin side seams together from the empire line to the hip (HBL). The remaining seam is left un-pinned to allow the bias to fall freely or with the help of drapery weights (single or chained) placed around the hemline.

Figure 14.15

After hanging, pin bra top to the garment and check the drape for fit.

Adjust the side seam adding flare to an amount that balances the silhouette of front and back skirt. Mark and pin.

Pin-mark hemline up from the floor and parallel to it.

Remove drape and true. Stitch muslin or trans-fer to paper first for the test fit. To cut for a test fit, see Figure 14.19 and Figure 14.20. If the pa-per pattern is already made, correct as needed and cut for a test fit.

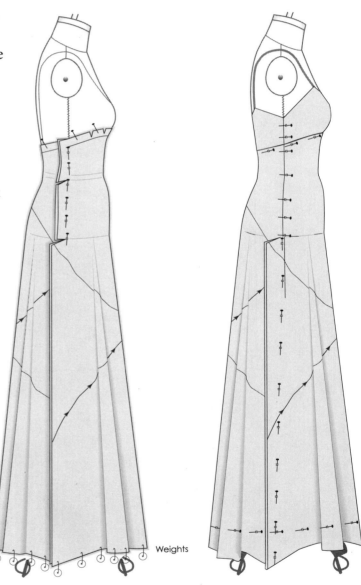

Weights

Figure 14.14   *Figure 14.15*

Making a Paper Pattern: Special Instructions

This procedure is used when draping in lightweight crepe or its equivalent. It is advisable to have a pattern of the bias drape before trimming the excess from around the garment. To trim first causes the shape of the bias garment to become distorted after removal from the form, making it difficult to establish the original shape when tracing for a paper pattern. By aligning the straight and crosswise markings of the fabric with the markings of the paper underneath, the shape of the draped garment is more easily controlled. The stretch that took place on the form may cause the centerline of the drape to pass the centerlines of the paper. Let it. The cut garment from these patterns will stretch to fit when draped on the form. Further corrections are made to the paper patterns (see page 232, Figure 10.15).

Preparing the Patterns

Front

Figure 14.16

Place fabric on paper and pin edges together matching the grainline markings.

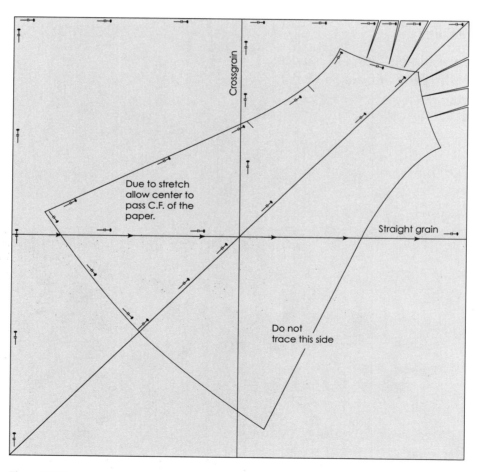

Figure 14.16

Smooth fabric across the paper. Some rippling may occur from the bias stretch.

Pin along the grainline markings

Allow centerline of the drape to pass the centerline parallel with the paper underneath.

Pin the outline of the drape.

Trace through with a tracing wheel. Do not trace the centerline.

Remove paper underneath. Fold on center and pencil in shape of the pattern.

Back

Figure 14.17

Apply the procedures given for the front drape. See Figure 14.18 for adding seams to the traced patterns.

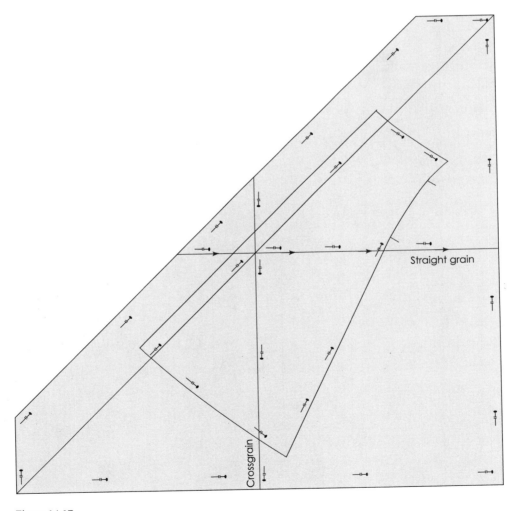

Straight grain

Crossgrain

Figure 14.17

Add Seams

Figure 14.18

1/2″ at the top.

3/4″ at the sides to the hip (HBL).

4″ out from the base mark of the pattern.

From the hip seam, draw a line passing through the 4″ mark, ending at the hem.

Cut from fabric (see Figure 14.19 and Figure 14.20).

Return to Figure 14.14 to complete the drape and for fit analysis.

Preparing to Cut the Patterns

To help control the fabric when cutting the patterns, place tissue down first, the fabric next, and the marker of the traced pattern pieces on top. Two layout methods are given. (The author would like feedback describing the results achieved using each of the layout configurations with different fabrics.) Only the skirt part of the dress is illustrated; other design patterns are drawn on the open spaces.

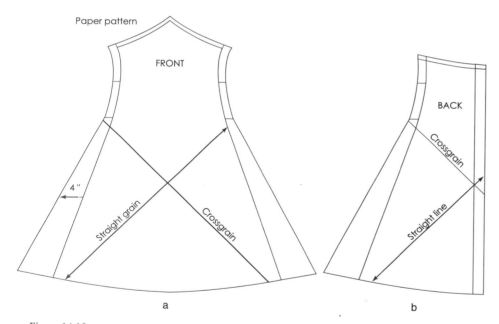
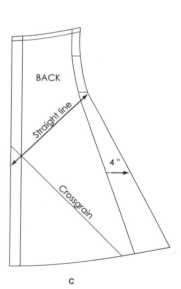

Figure 14.18

Layout 1

Figure 14.19

The tops of each pattern are marked to lie in the same direction. The grain falls downward equally on each of the joining seams.

Layout 2

Figure 14.20

The top of the back patterns lie in opposite directions. One of the back patterns will be turned around to join the side of the one-piece front having an opposing grain. Each front and back seam on that side of the garment will hang differently. The difference will be noticed after the garment has hung overnight. The two seams, when corrected, may not true, but will hang to correct length when stitched. A two-piece front would also be placed in the opposite direction, with the same results.

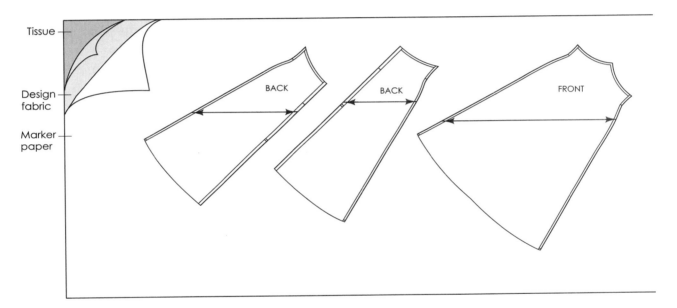

Figure 14.19

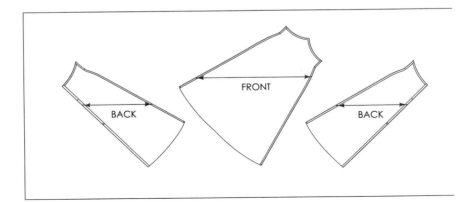

Figure 14.20

Bias Dress with a Twist Top

Figure 14.21

The twist top dress is an interpretation of a Madeleine Vionnet creation (Figure 14.21). The part of the dress that twisted was of chiffon. However, crepe, stretchy knits, and other fabrics can be used. The cowl design is another Vionnet favorite for the designs of dresses. (See Chapter 10 to develop this design.)

Design Analysis

The twist top creates a V neck and an empire styleline. The dart excess is absorbed in the twisting of the fabric. The right side is draped, and the fullness at center is folded in a series of pleats. The pleats are held as the fabric is twisted and brought to the left side. Tack stitch through the pleats for control, if necessary. To drape the lower part of the slip top dress, see pages 330 through 333 as a guide. The front is modified to show flesh below the empire by draping from Princess to Princess under the bust to a V at the center back.

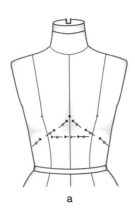
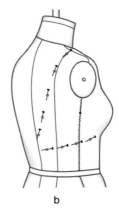
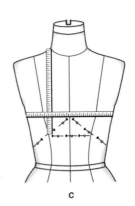

a   b   c

Figure 14.22

Preparing Form

Figure 14.22

Pin-mark form for the stylelines.

Length: Measure from shoulder/neck to under the bust. Add 3″.

Width: Measure from side to side over the bust. Add 2″.

Figure 14.23

Cut a bias strip of fabric for the twist top front and one half the amount cut on the straight grain for the back drape.

Prepare fabric and paper, as shown on pages 329 to 330. To drape the lower garment, see pages 331 to 333.

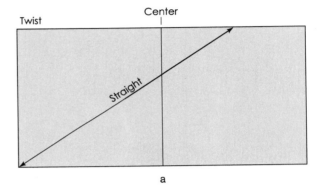

a

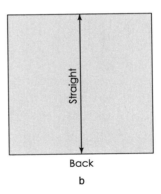

b

Figure 14.23

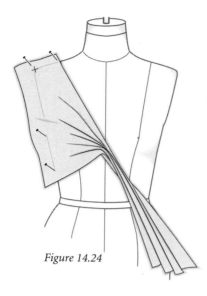

Figure 14.24

Figure 14.25

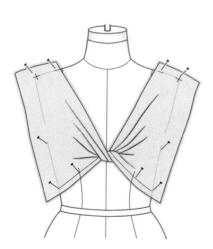

Figure 14.26

Draping Steps

Right Side

Figure 14.24

Place fabric on the form, with the fabric 1″ below the empire styleline.

Drape from the shoulder, armhole, and side seam. Pin.

Bring fullness together at the center. Fold into narrow pleats and hold to prepare for twisting.

Twist

Figure 14.25

Twist under and bring right side of the fabric up to the left shoulder. Pin.

Left Side

Figure 14.26

Smooth and mark fabric from empire styleline to side seam and upward around the armhole to the shoulder. Trim excess.

Back

Figure 14.27

Place fabric on the form with the straight grain placed on the V neck styleline of the back.

Drape, mark, trim, and pin to the front.

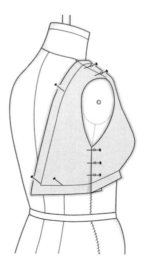

Figure 14.27

Figure 14.28

Drape the bias skirt and pin to the twist. Check fit. Remove and true. Stitch the drape or transfer to paper for the test fit.

Figure 14.29

Complete the pattern.

Finished Pattern

Figure 14.30

Stitching suggestions for the raw edges: merrow edged, top-stitched, or zigzagged.

Figure 14.28

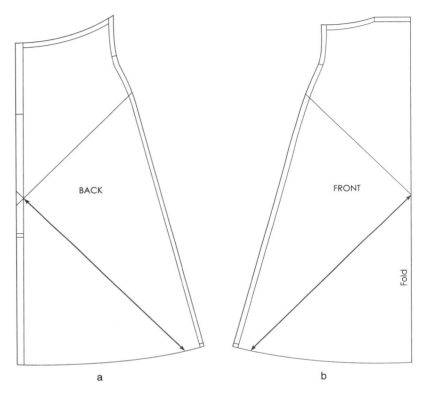

Figure 14.29

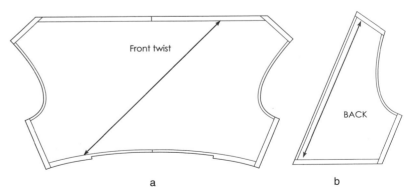

Figure 14.30

Bias Dress with Center Seams

The bias dress is draped to any length and uninterrupted by stylelines, except for design above the bust. The seams of the center front and back allow for additional flare to the skirt part of the design. The dart excess shown above the bust level can be used in a number of creative ways. The designer/draper should explore other creative possibilities using the dart excess. If the fabric is not wide enough to cover the full length of the dress, additional fabric will be needed to compensate.

Design Analysis

The bias dress clings to the figure, slinking over the hipline or below the hip, where the flares start (Figure 14.30). They end at the hemline (of any length). Extra flares are draped at the centerlines of the front and back seams. The fabric should not be draped too closely to the contour of the figure, but should slightly bridge the hollow areas under the bust and around the waist. The drape is the same for all three designs, with the exception of the design above the bust. The dress should be draped in lightweight fabrics, such as crepe or its equivalent, muslin, or stretchy knits. For transferring the drape to paper, see pages 334 to 335. This process is optional if the pattern is draped in muslin or a fabric of a firmer weave. Add a basic or leg-of-mutton sleeve to complete this design.

Preparing Fabric

Use a 45″ to 60″ square (depending on fabric width). Cut the paper and fabric to the same width and length.

Draw straight and crossgrain on the fabric and paper (see pages 329–330).

Fold so that the crossgrain is parallel to the selvage.

Mark a guideline on the fold with chalk or hand-stitch with a color thread. Repeat 4″ from the centerfold on both sides. Cut through the centerfold of the bias. One side is for front drape; the other is for back drape.

Figure 14.30

Draping Steps

Figure 14.31

Place center bias guideline to the center of the form raising the fabric approximately 2″ past the shoulder/neck. Pin. Crosspin the bust point.

Smooth fabric across the hip (HBL) and upward, moving the dart excess along the side seams around the armhole and across the shoulder. Pin. The dart excess is moved past the centerline. Pin.

Mark armhole and side seams to the base of the form.

Smooth fabric outward from the center at the waist.

Pin and mark new centerline.

If draping in crepe or its equivalent, remove drape from the form. Drape the back (see Figure 14.12). For instructions on transferring the drape to paper, see pages 334 to 335.

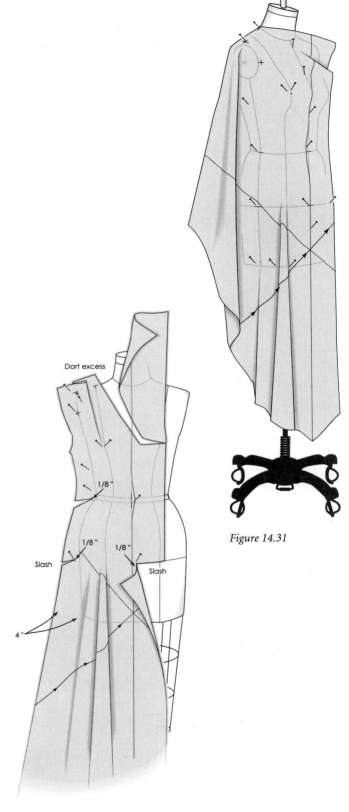

Figure 14.31

Figure 14.32

Trim excess around the armhole and side seam to the hip (HBL).

Allow 4″ at the base of the side seam.

Slash to within 1/8″ of waist, hip, and centerline.

Trim excess below the hip, graduating to the hemline.

Raise form so that the flares have room to hang freely.

Trim excess 1″ out from centerline starting from bust level.

Fold excess as a temporary dart and trim excess from the shoulder.

Figure 14.32

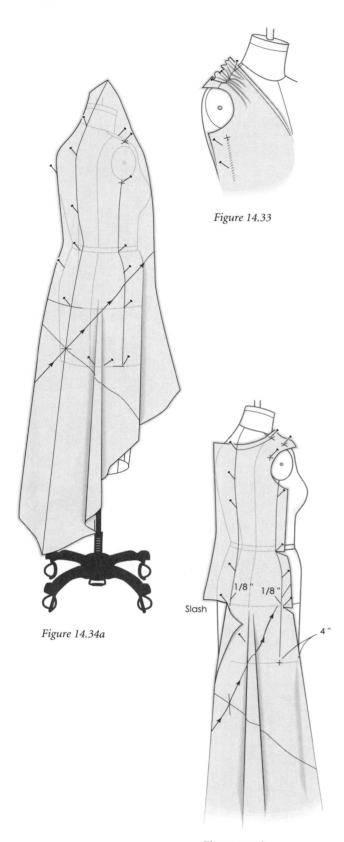

Figure 14.33

Figure 14.34a

Figure 14.34b

Slash

1/8 " 1/8 "

4 "

Gathers

Figure 14.33

Place gathers when back is pinned or stitched to the back (see Figure 14.33).

Peel back the drape or remove it from the form.

Back Drape

Figure 14.34a

Drape the back following the instructions for the front drape, except that the shoulder dart excess is draped with some excess at the armhole, neckline, and shoulder (tape shoulder to control ease and gathers).

Pencil back neck shape.

Mark shoulder, armhole, and side seam to form base.

Figure 14.34b

Trim excess, allowing 4″ at base of the side seam.

Slash to within 1/8″ at the center back and hip (HBL).

Remove drape from the form to true. Stitch drape (full) or transfer to paper first for the test fit (unless pattern has already been made).

Finished Patterns

Figure 14.35 through Figure 14.38

The patterns are given for the short skirt along with an example of a long dress with added sections to complete the length of the garment.

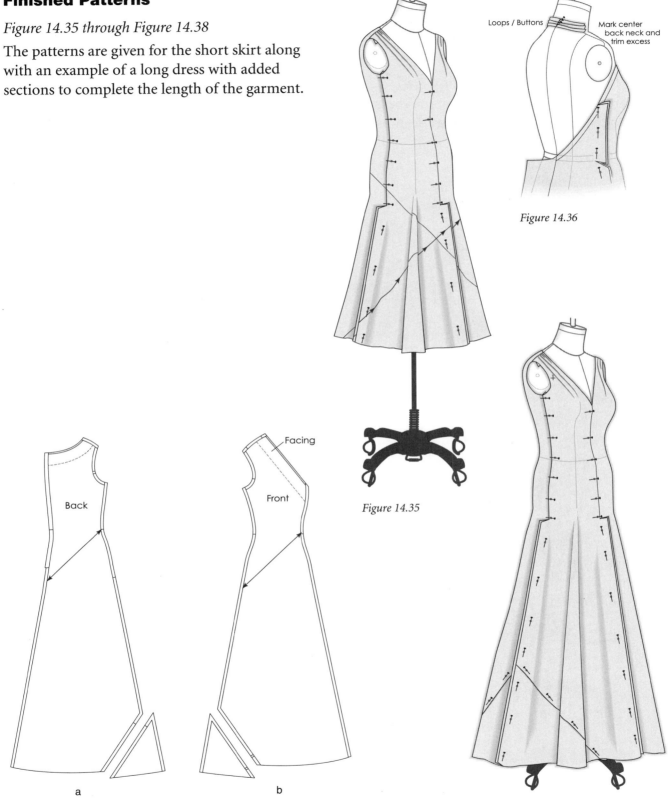

Figure 14.36

Figure 14.35

Figure 14.37

Figure 14.38

Knot-Tie Bias Dress

Design Analysis

Figure 14.39, Figure 14.40, and Figure 14.41
The dart excess is used as gathers above the bust and knotted for control. The tie may be directed to the shoulder/neck and may tie at the back neck or be directed over the shoulder, continuing down the back to meet at the center back of the low cut back. Follow the instructions for the bias dress on pages 342 to 344.

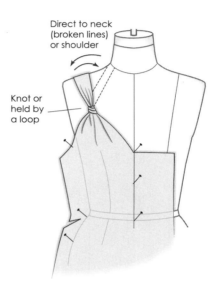

Figure 14.40

Figure 14.39

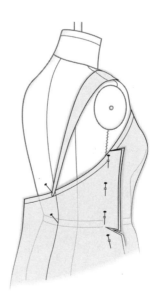

Figure 14.41

Crisscross Bias Dress

Design Analysis

Figure 14.42, Figure 14.43, and Figure 14.44
The dart excess is used as gathers above the bust and passes the center to the center back neck of the other side of the garment. Loops and buttons are added for the closure. Follow the instructions for the bias dress on pages 342 to 344.

Figure 14.42

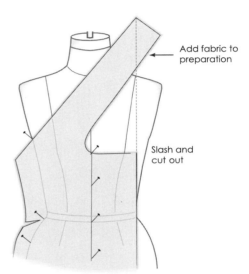

Add fabric to preparation

Slash and cut out

Figure 14.43

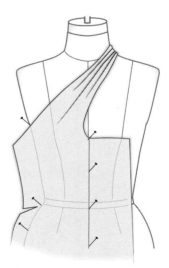

Figure 14.44

Kimono, Raglan, and Drop Shoulder

15

The kimono, raglan, and drop shoulders are the foundations and prototypes on which other popular designs are based (Figure 15.1). Their common characteristic is the combining of the bodice and sleeve in special ways to complete the design. The kimono, for example, is draped in one with the length of the sleeve. The armhole of the bodice and sleeve are not visible in the design. In comparison, the raglan and drop shoulder designs are draped so that part of the curve of the bodice armhole and the lower curve of the sleeve form part of the drape. Many other stylelines can be created from the point of the drape where the armhole and sleeve converge.

The kimono, raglan, and drop shoulder foundations are usually designed for casual wear. They are appropriate for many types of garments including bodices, tops, shirts, blouses, activewear, jackets, and coats. The basic armhole depth is lowered and extra ease is added to the side seams for comfort in a casual garment. The sleeve is modified to adjust to the changes made to the drape.

Figure 15.1

Kimono Foundation

Figure 15.2

The kimono sleeve is in-one with the bodice and draped to follow the slope of the shoulder. The sleeve part of the kimono has an overarm sleeve with the underseams joining the front and back at varying distances below the armhole. The sleeve part of the foundation can be draped to any length and can be designed as a flared sleeve, a gathered sleeve, or as a lowered shoulder. The kimono is draped as a bodice, but by adding length, it can be draped as a batwing dress or be adapted to a caftan (Figure 15.2).

Basic Kimono

Design Analysis

The basic principle of a kimono is that the sleeve and bodice are combined as one to complete the garment. The underarm depth of the kimono can vary, as can the length of the sleeve. Pin a shoulder pad to the form, if desired. Included in the project is the batwing dress, which illustrates that by lowering the underarm seam, the silhouette changes the look of a garment. By adding length to the floor, a caftan is created (Figure 15.3).

Preparing Form

Figure 15.4

Place straight arm to the form and adjust to the desired angle. Tape to secure.

Figure 15.3

Figure 15.4

Preparing Muslin

Figure 15.5

Front and back:

- Length: As desired.
- Width: 30″

Mark front and back neckline and trim.

To drape a kimono dress, cut the muslin to the desired length. Drape fabric with full width, as for the batwing dress (see Figure 15.10).

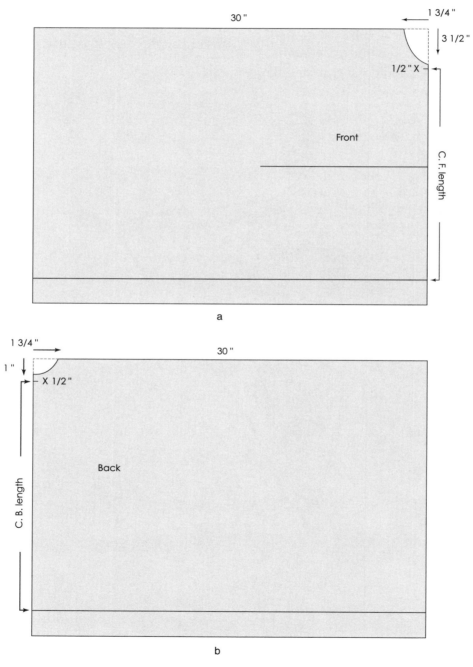

Figure 15.5

Draping Steps

Figure 15.6

Place straight grain to the center of the form and crossgrain at the front waist. Pin. Drape the excess over the extended arm, raising the crossgrain to be level with the floor. Crosspin at bust point. Pin at extended arm temporarily.

Smooth, mark, and slash the muslin at the neckline and along the shoulder to the Princess line at the waist. Pin.

Slash muslin about 12″ out from center front.

Figure 15.7

Remove the temporary pin on the arm to allow the fabric to fall as the muslin is smoothed over the bust to side seam. Pin. The muslin is smoothed downward along the side seam.

Pencil rub 4″ to 5″, and slash 1″ from mark.

Smooth, mark, and slash along the waist. Pin 1/4″ ease, with remaining dart excess pinned at the Princess line.

Mark overarm seam.

Trim to within 2″ of marked seams at the side and over the arm. Peel back or remove for back drape.

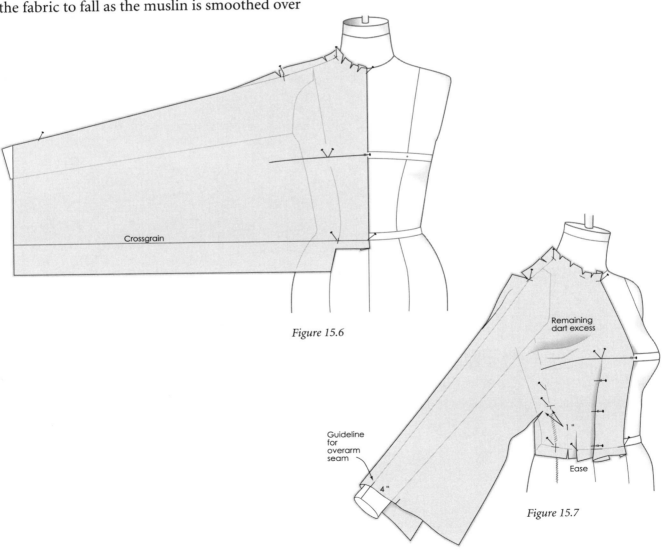

Figure 15.6

Figure 15.7

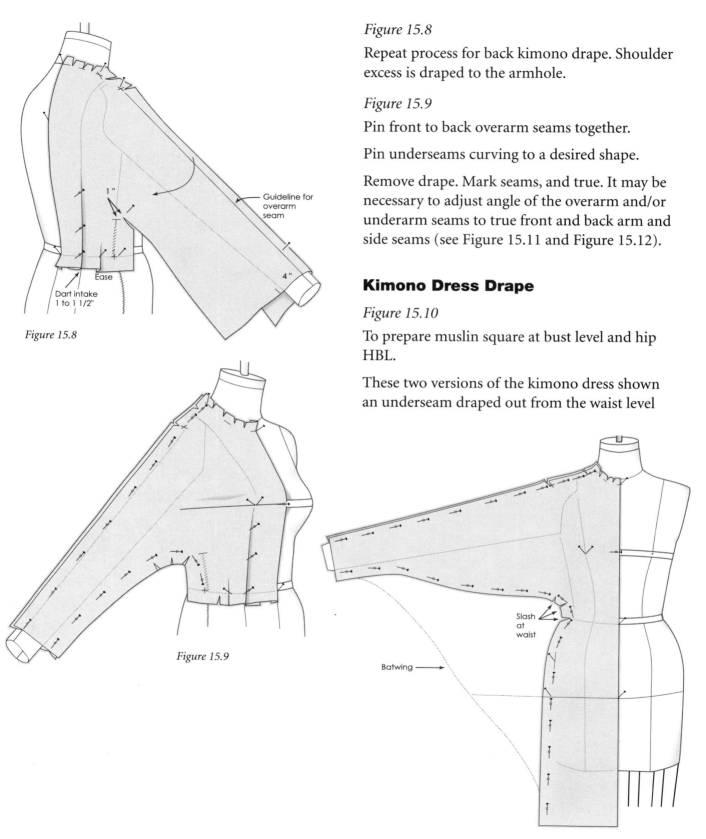

Figure 15.8

Repeat process for back kimono drape. Shoulder excess is draped to the armhole.

Figure 15.9

Pin front to back overarm seams together.

Pin underseams curving to a desired shape.

Remove drape. Mark seams, and true. It may be necessary to adjust angle of the overarm and/or underarm seams to true front and back arm and side seams (see Figure 15.11 and Figure 15.12).

Kimono Dress Drape

Figure 15.10

To prepare muslin square at bust level and hip HBL.

These two versions of the kimono dress shown an underseam draped out from the waist level

Figure 15.8

Figure 15.9

Figure 15.10

and a batwing dress (broken lines). The sleeve can be draped for gathers or flare and to any length down from the shoulder.

Pin the fold of the straight grain to the center-line of the form.

Pin the crossgrain guideline to the HBL guideline of the form at the side seam for a waist-fitted kimono dress, or pin away from the side waist, gradually pinning to the hem, for a loosely fitted dress.

Adjusting Patterns

Figure 15.11

Place pushpin at the front and back side waists.

Swing front muslin so that the front and back shoulder-tips align. Shoulder-tips can be equalized if the heights vary.

True the lengths of the overarm and underarm sleeve by equalizing the differences or correcting the sleeve angles by following the instructions given with Figure 15.12.

Figure 15.12

To correct the angles of the front and back sleeves, slash the front and/or back from the underseams to the stitchline of the shoulder-tips. Overlap or spread until the arms are at the same angle. Tape and mend or make new patterns. The curves of the underseam curves should be notched in three places to release tension.

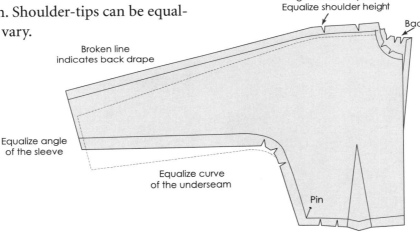

Figure 15.11

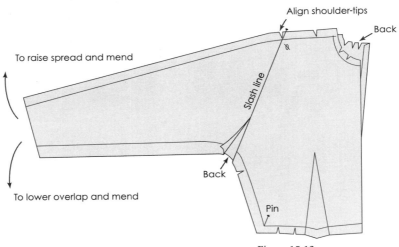

Figure 15.12

Basic Raglan Sleeve

Figure 15.13

Figure 15.14

The basic raglan is a prototype for designs relating to it. The raglan can be adapted to many variations, deeper armhole, to any type of garment bodice, blouse, shirt, jacket, and coats. The sleeve can be tapered, flared, gathered, and to any lengths (Figure 15.13 and Figure 15.14).

The underarm seams of the raglan sleeve is extended to increase lift when the armhole of the garment is lowered beyond its basic depth. The modification creates folds under the armhole when the arm is relaxed. As a general rule, the amount that an armhole is lowered from the armhole plate is the same for the adjustment of the sleeve and for the sleeve lift. After draping the basic raglan, drape a raglan with an armhole depth of 3″ or more. Add 2″ outside ease. Modify the sleeve.

Design Analysis

The basic raglan is draped to wrist length with a basic neckline. The bodice is draped with a waist and a side dart. Apply the principle of the raglan for increasing the underarm seam of the raglan sleeve.

Preparing Form

Figure 15.15

Front and back: Pin-mark or use tape 1″ down from the shoulder/neck to the mid-armhole pinhead, which will be referred to as X. This line is a convex curve.

Use the pinhead to mark the armhole depth 1 1/2″ below the plate, ending at the mid-arm.

Sleeve Modification

Figure 15.16

The basic sleeve is modified to correspond to the changes in the depth of the armhole and to the additional ease added to the side seam of the drape. For example, if the armhole depth is lowered an additional 3/4″ (total 1 1/2″ from the plate), the biceps of the basic sleeve is lowered an additional 3/4″. The additional ease that is added to the side seam of the garment is the same amount added to the underseam of the sleeve. The sleeve is further modified in Figure 15.20.

Preparing Muslin

Front and back bodice: See pages 26 and 27.

Sleeve:

- Length: Sleeve length, plus 7″
- Width: biceps, plus 12″

Draping Instructions

Figure 15.17 and Figure 15.18

Drape the front and back bodice following instruction for the basic waist-side dart bodice. Pin 1/2″ ease at mid-armhole. The back shoulder dart excess is draped to the back armhole.

Draw or pencil rub the raglan styleline on the muslin. Mark X for reference.

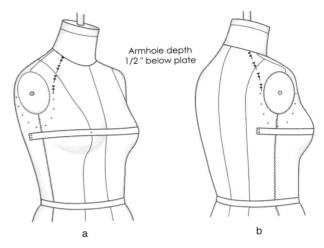

Figure 15.15

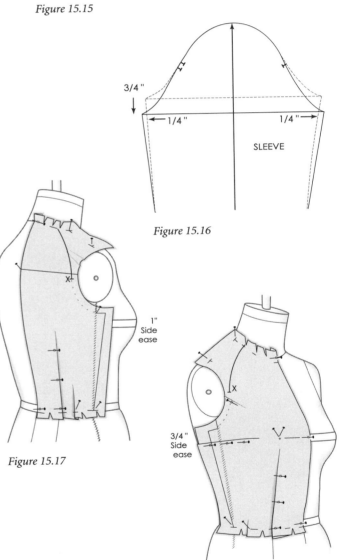

Figure 15.16

Figure 15.17

Figure 15.18

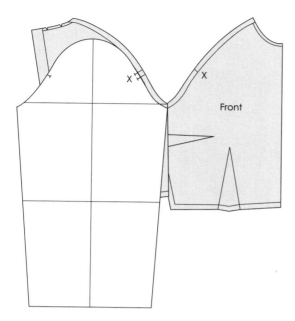

Figure 15.19

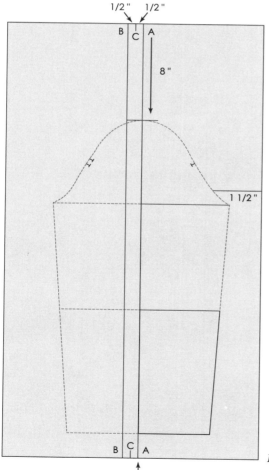

Figure 15.20

Figure 15.19

Remove drape from the form and true (use a French curve to draw the under armholes). Mark X and trim to the seam allowance.

Pin or baste side seams.

Sleeve Marking

Walk the seamless sleeve from the side seam to X. Mark sleeve X.

Repeat for the front sleeve.

Preparing Muslin

Figure 15.20

Mark the center of the muslin C on the top and bottom.

Draw a straight grain 1/2″ out from each side of C to allow ease around the biceps.

Draw a line 8″ down from the top.

Drafting Steps: Placing the Sleeve

Place sleeve grain on guideline A, with sleeve cap touching the line.

Trace the wrist to the elbow.

Draw a guideline 1″ up from biceps line of the sleeve (lift line).

Figure 15.21

Place a pushpin 1″ from the center cap and pivot sleeve up to meet the lift guideline.

Draw sleeve from the underseam to X mark. The broken lines indicate the position of the sleeve when pivoted and is not traced.

Shift the grainline of the sleeve to the B guideline and repeat the process.

Figure 15.22

Add seam allowance and cut sleeve preparation from muslin to X mark. Slash at X.

Pin, stitch, or baste the underseam and join to the curve of the bodice armhole meeting at the X marks.

Return drape to the form.

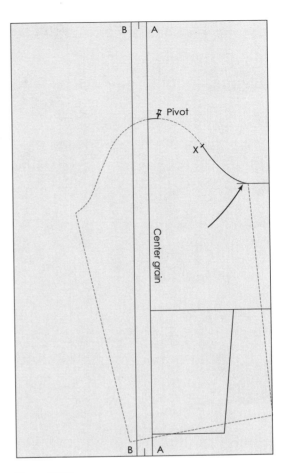

Figure 15.21

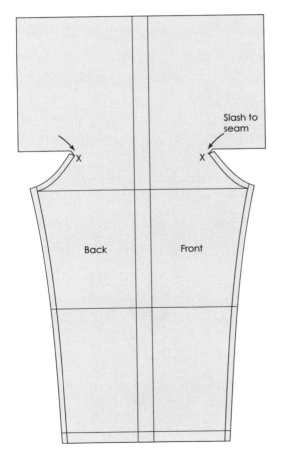

Figure 15.22

Figure 15.23

Lace the sleeve cap mark 1/4″ out from the shoulder-tip of the form.

Smooth the muslin along the shoulder with the fabric lying smooth. Mark raglan styleline.

Repeat for the back drape.

Figure 15.24

Pin muslin together following the shoulderline, and pin 1/4″ above the shoulder-tip curving several inches over the shoulder. Blend the pinning out to the center of the guidelines. Ease may occur along the shoulderline. This can be remedied by smoothing the excess to the neckline. From there, smooth the muslin to the unpinned raglan line. Redraw the raglan line.

Remove the finished drape. True the raglan sleeve. Stitch the muslin or make the pattern first for the test fit.

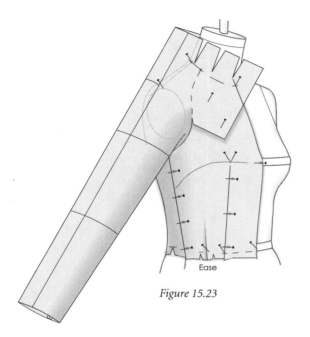

Figure 15.23

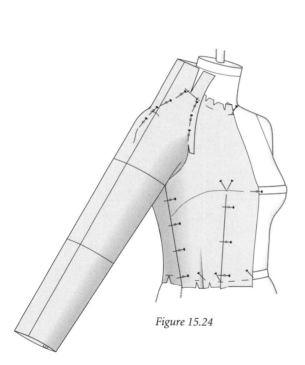

Figure 15.24

Finished Pattern

Figure 15.25
The one-piece sleeve.

Figure 15.26
The bodice and divided sleeve. Mark desired grain.

Figure 15.25

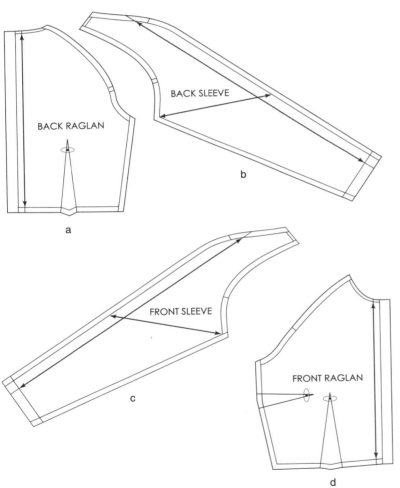

Figure 15.26

Drop Shoulder Sleeve

The drop shoulder foundation can be draped with or without a sleeve. It is also very versatile. It is the prototype for designs illustrated on page 365. Figure 15.27b is draped as an off-the-shoulder bodice, with the drop shoulder trimmed to expose part of the upper arm. It can also be draped as a strapless bodice with only the lower sleeve attached (Figure 15.27a), or with the upper part of the sleeve attached or a puff sleeve (Figure 15.27b). These are but a few design variations based on the drop shoulder foundation. You may want to design other variations.

The drape of the drop shoulder foundation is different from that of the raglan. The similarity is that the styleline converges at the mid-armhole (X).

Figure 15.27

Design Analysis

Figure 15.28

The cap part of the sleeve is draped with the bodice to create the drop shoulder effect. The lower sleeve is seamed to it. The armhole depth is 1 1/2″ below the plate, but may be draped lower or higher. The sleeve must be modified when the armhole depth is lower than 3/4″. Follow the instructions given for the raglan on pages 359 and 360 for marking the armhole depth and for the sleeve modification.

The drop shoulder styleline starts at mid-armhole (X) and continues around the sleeve. The styleline of the drop shoulder is basic, but can be designed in many other ways. Pin shoulder pads to the form, if desired.

Preparing Muslin

For muslin preparation, see page 357.

Draping Steps: Preparing the Sleeve (Method 1)

Figure 15.29

Follow the instructions on page 358, Figure 15.20 and Figure 15.21.

After the sleeve modification has been completed, draw a line down 2″ from the cap and cut across to trim.

Pin underseams of the sleeve.

Figure 15.28

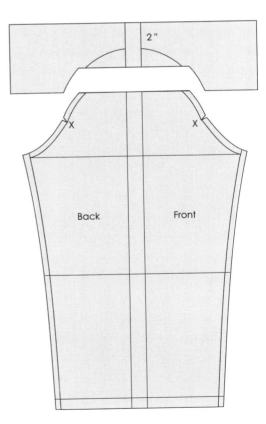

Figure 15.29

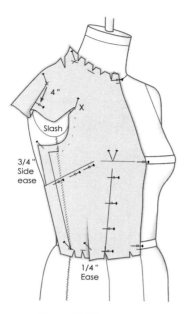

Figure 15.30a

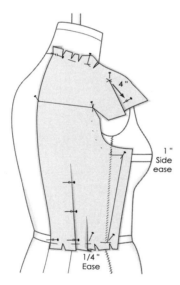

Figure 15.30b

Drop Shoulder Bodice

Figure 15.30a

Place the muslin on the form. Drape the neckline, waist, and side seam. Mark 3/4″ ease at the side seam.

Pin waist and side dart.

Pencil rub pins from the armhole depth to mid-armhole (X).

Drape the shoulder and trim excess, allowing 5″ of muslin to extend past the shoulder-tip.

Mark 4″ down from the shoulder-tip.

Slash to mid-armhole (X).

Remove the drape to true.

Figure 15.30b

Drape the basic back following the instructions given for the front drape, except add 1″ ease.

Figure 15.31

Remove the drape from the form and true.

Draw front and back drop shoulder styleline as shown.

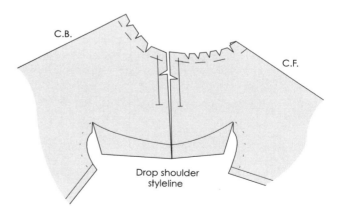

Figure 15.31

Figure 15.32

Pin front and back drapes together and pin the underseam of the sleeve to the armhole of the garment.

Place the garment on the form.

Fold and pin the drop shoulder styleline to the lower sleeve.

If the sleeve hangs too far from the form, release the pins, lower the sleeve, and repin. The styleline should be smooth and even around the sleeve.

Finished Pattern

Figure 15.33

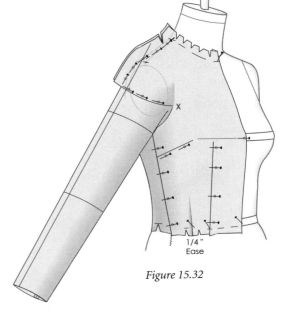

Figure 15.32

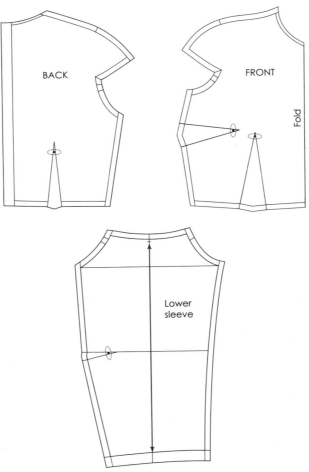

Figure 15.33

Yoke In-One with the Sleeve

The yoke is based on the principle of the basic raglan. The difference is the location of the styleline from point X (the intersecting point of the sleeve and bodice).

Design Analysis

The yoke styleline is one of many stylelines based on the raglan principle. The styleline is squared from the centerline to point X. The sleeve is based on the same preparation. The sleeve can be draped, tapered, full, or exaggerated. Shoulder pads may be pinned to the shoulder, if desired.

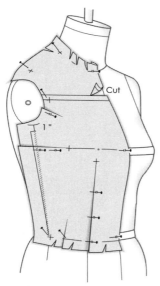

Figure 15.34

Preparing Form

Pin-mark a point at the centerline that squares to point X.

Preparing Muslin

For muslin preparation, see page 352.

Prepare the sleeve following the drape procedure for the basic raglan, except that the yoke styleline will be pinned instead of the raglan styleline (see pages 357–359).

Note: If the design is a flare sleeve, the sleeve lift is not required.

Draping Steps

Figure 15.34 and Figure 15.35

Drape the front and back as for the basic waist and side dart bodice.

Mark the yoke stylelines. Square from the center.

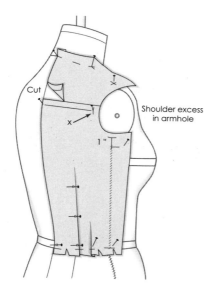

Figure 15.35

Completing the Drape

Figure 15.36

Pin the sleeve underarm to the armhole of the bodice.

Place drape on the form. Smooth muslin and pin to yokeline, keeping straight grain at the center. Drape the neckline. Pin shoulders and overarm seam.

Remove the drape from the form and true. Stitch the muslin or make the pattern first for the test fit.

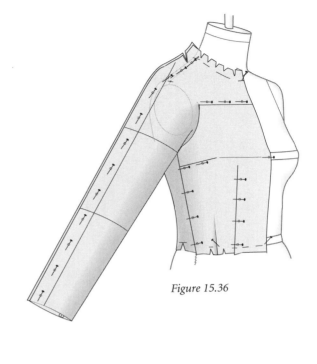

Figure 15.36

Finished Pattern

Figure 15.37 and Figure 15.38

The broken lines are the basic sleeve. The basic sleeve can be modified for a flared sleeve or a tapered sleeve and can be designed to any length.

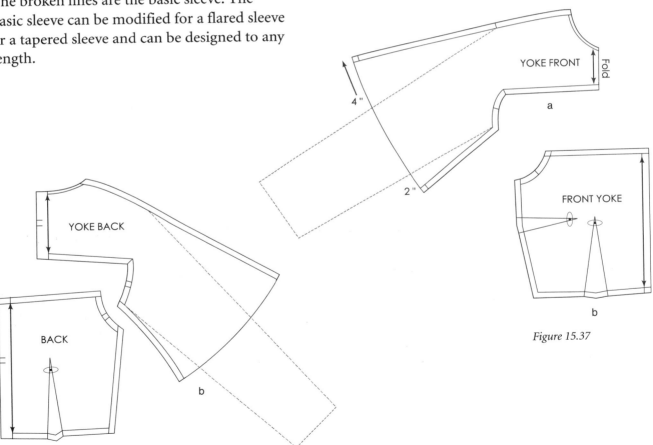

Figure 15.37

Figure 15.38

Princess In-One with the Sleeve

Figure 15.39

The Princess styleline curves into the armhole at X. The drape is prepared differently from the raglan. The similarity is that the styleline converges at the mid-armhole (X). The styleline can be designed on dresses, blouses, shirts, jackets, coats, and capes (Figure 15.39).

Design Analysis

The Princess raglan is draped as a bodice. The sleeve pattern can be developed with or without an overarm seam. The sleeve can be tapered, loose, or gathered, and designed to any length. The drape is based on the armhole Princess. To modify sleeve, see page 357, Figure 15.16.

Preparing Form

For guidance in placing straight arm to form, see page 351.

Preparing Muslin

For muslin preparation, see page 352.

Figure 15.40

Follow instructions for the measurements given in preparing muslin. Disregard crossgrain at bust level.

Cut 2 panels 15″ × 20″.

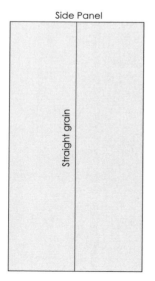
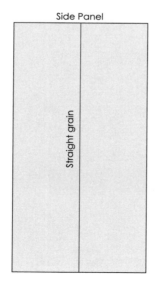

Figure 15.40

Draping Steps

Figure 15.41 and Figure 15.42

Drape side Princess panels for front and back. Princess ends at the mid-armhole (X) or slightly lower, if preferred.

Figure 15.43

Remove panels. With a French curve, draw the under armhole curve.

Walk the underseams of the modified sleeve to X points. Mark locations on the front and back sleeve (see page 358, Figure 15.19).

Figure 15.44

Place muslin on the form and drape the Princess styleline to the mid-armhole (X). Mark neck and shoulder, and draw Princess line. Remove drape from the form and true.

Repeat the process for the back Princess.

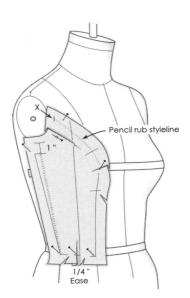

Figure 15.41

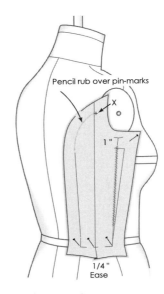

Figure 15.42

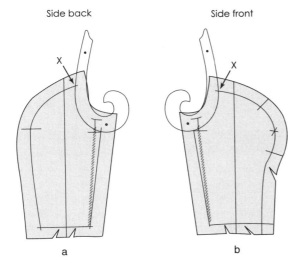

Figure 15.43

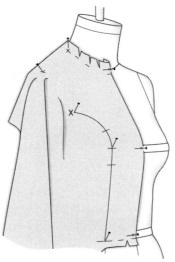

Figure 15.44

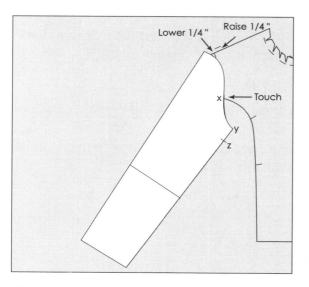

Figure 15.45

Front

Figure 15.45

Mark guidelines 1/4″ up and out from the shoulder-tip of the drape.

Touch (X) points of sleeve (half sleeve is shown for clarity), Princess, and sleeve cap 1/4″ from the shoulder-tip mark. Pin.

Trace the curve of the sleeve from X to Y. Mark a line 1″ down from Y, lableled Z to provide lift.

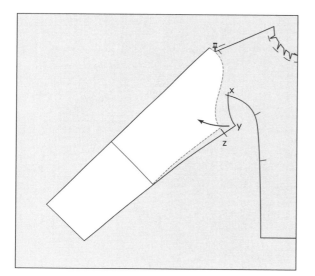

Figure 15.46

Figure 15.46

With a pushpin at the guideline of the shoulder, pivot the sleeve until the corner of the sleeve is at level or touches the Z mark.

Trace from the underseam of the elbow to the wrist and the center grainline.

Remove the sleeve and draw a slight inward curved line from Y to the elbow to complete the underseam.

Repeat the process for back sleeve.

Figure 15.47

Add seams around the tracing. Allow 1″ to 1 1/2″ of seam allowance at the overarm for design variations.

Draw a curved line over shoulder.

Repeat the process for back drape.

Figure 15.48

Pin, or stitch all seams except the overarm seam.

Pin front and back at the center.

Pin front and back overarm muslin from the shoulder/neck to the 1/4″ mark at shoulder-tip.

Pin up from the sleeve hem 1/2″ out from the sleeve grainline (for ease). Continue pinning, gradually curving a rounded shape to the shoulder-tip.

Figure 15.49

If the excess at the joining of the pins is more than 1/4″, mark 1″ up on the shoulder and 2″ down below the shoulder for ease. Pin the excess flat to the muslin. Remove the drape from the form, true, and make paper patterns.

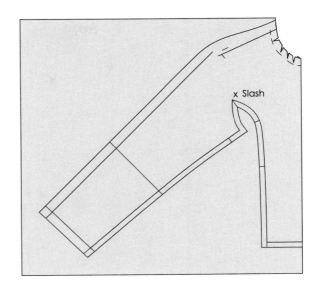

Figure 15.47

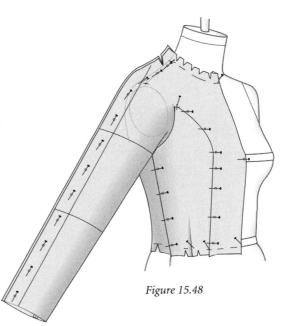

Figure 15.48

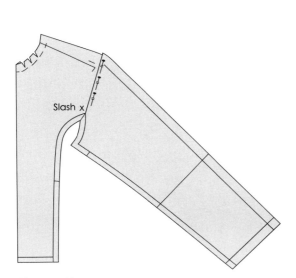

Figure 15.49

Shirts and Blouses 16

Shirts and blouses, although different by design, are both worn with skirts and pants (Figure 16.1). Shirts have a tailored mannish look and blouses have a feminine touch, but there are similarities. The armhole of shirts and blouses are placed at varying depths below the armhole plate and made larger by draping the excess to the armhole. The larger armhole requires changes to the dartless sleeve to accommodate the new armhole.

Shirt and blouse designs are based on draping principles of the torso foundation. Stylelines, yokes, tucks, added fullness, collars, pockets, cutout necklines, and a variety of sleeve designs (especially those for blouses) give variety to the foundation. Separate blouse designs are not included in this chapter. Shirts and blouses become dresses by extending the length when preparing the muslin.

Figure 16.1

Three Shirt Foundations

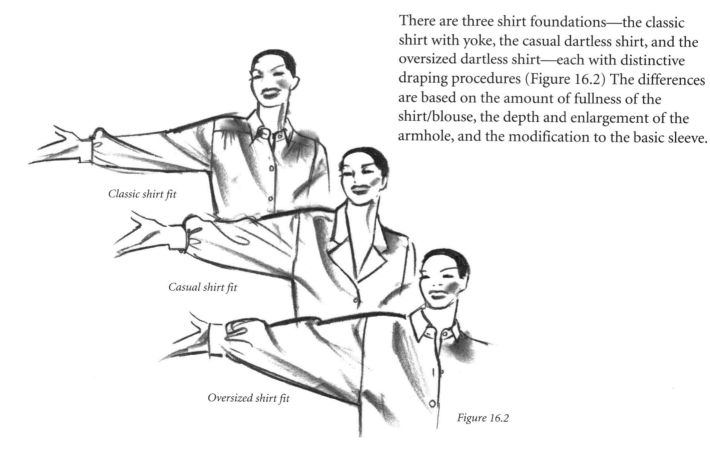

Classic shirt fit

Casual shirt fit

Oversized shirt fit

Figure 16.2

There are three shirt foundations—the classic shirt with yoke, the casual dartless shirt, and the oversized dartless shirt—each with distinctive draping procedures (Figure 16.2) The differences are based on the amount of fullness of the shirt/blouse, the depth and enlargement of the armhole, and the modification to the basic sleeve.

Dartless Sleeve Pattern

Design Analysis

The dartless sleeve is derived from the basic sleeve. It simplifies the development of shirt sleeves that do not require an elbow dart. It is a useful pattern for drafting other sleeve designs given in patternmaking books.

Draping Steps

Figure 16.3

Trace the basic sleeve pattern. Include all markings.

Square a line from the center grain to the corner of the front wrist. Measure the length and continue a line across the back sleeve equal to the measurement.

Draw the underseam from the biceps to the wrist marks (see Figure 16.3a).

Cut the pattern from paper (see Figure 16.3b).

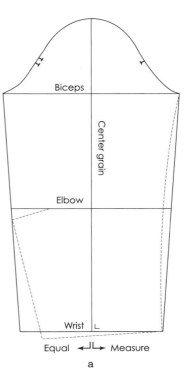

a

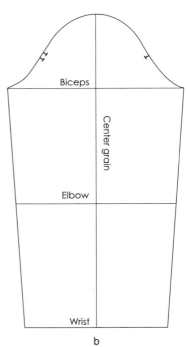

b

Figure 16.3

Classic Shirt with Yoke

Figure 16.4

Figure 16.5

The classic shirt fits closer to the figure than does a casual or oversized shirt. However, the slightly enlarged armhole requires an adjustment to the basic sleeve. The back and/or front yoke and lower part of the back shirt can be designed in a number of creative ways (Figure 16.4 and Figure 16.5).

Design Analysis

The shoulder excess is transferred to the back armhole as the yoke extends 1/2″ beyond the shoulder-tip and ends 1″ over the shoulder to the front shirt. To balance the armholes, 1/2″ ease is added to the front armhole. The remaining excess of the front drape is gathered into the yoke (dart equivalent). In the illustrations, the shirt is based on the draping torso principle, and the sleeve is based on the dartless sleeve. To drape the basic collar, see page 196. Three styles for the back shirt are illustrated.

Yoke with Back Design Variations

Although Figure 16.1 illustrates the straight yoke (a), any design can be created (b and c are two examples). Draping instructions of several designs are given for the lower back shirt. Preparation of the muslin should include the added measurements needed for each design (Figure 16.6).

Preparing Form

Figure 16.7
Pin-mark front and back yokes stylelines.

Preparing Muslin

Yoke

Length: Measure from the longest point of the back yoke design to the front yoke. Add 3″.

Width: Measure from the center back to the shoulder-tip. Add 3″.

Lower Shirt: Front and Back

Length: Measure from the highest point of the back yoke to the waist. Add 8″.

Width: Measure from the center front to the side seam at the bust level. Add 3″. If gathers or an action pleat is chosen, add 6″ to the width.

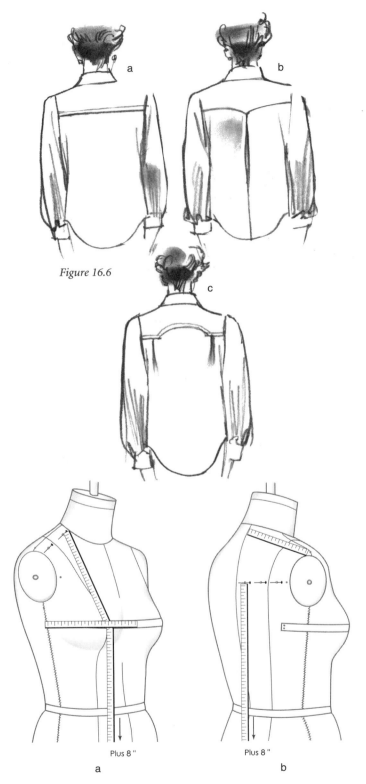

Figure 16.6

Figure 16.7

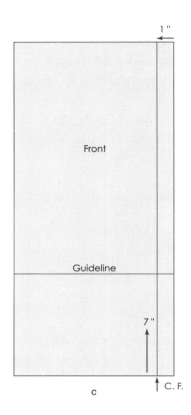

Figure 16.8

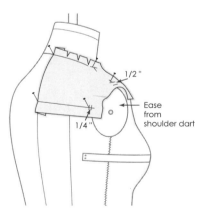

Figure 16.9

Yoke

Figure 16.8a

Mark 2 1/2″ down and 1 1/2″ out from the muslin edge. Square out and up from marks.

Draw tentative neckline, and trim.

Lower Shirt

Figure 16.8b and 16.8c

Square a crossgrain line 7″ up from the muslin edge.

Draping Steps

Back Yoke

Figure 16.9

Place fold 1/2″ above the back neck. Pin.

Smooth crossgrain to mid-armhole. Pin and mark 1/4″ beyond this point.

Drape neckline to the shoulder/neck. Pin.

Smooth muslin over the shoulder.

Mark shoulder-tip and 1/2″ beyond. Pin (shoulder excess has been transferred to the armhole).

Front Yoke

Figure 16.10

Mark yokeline on muslin.

Mark gathers and control notches.

Remove yoke from the form and true.

Front Shirt

Figure 16.11

Pin the straight grain at the center front, and the crossgrain at the waistline. Pin.

Raise the crossgrain until the hemline is parallel with the hip HBL guideline. Pin and smooth to armplate. Pin.

Mark armhole plate and pencil rub the side seam. Armhole depth will be marked when trueing.

Pin 1/2″ ease at the armhole.

Drape the remaining excess to the yokeline, and pin a pleat to hold.

Mark the mid-armhole and 1/4″ beyond. Pin.

Figure 16.12

Pin the yoke to the front shirt, dispensing the excess as gathers between the notch marks.

Draw a line over the gathered area as a guide for blending.

Remove drape from form.

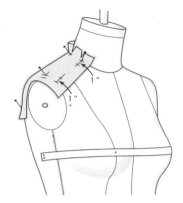

Figure 16.10

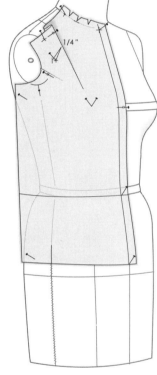

Figure 16.11

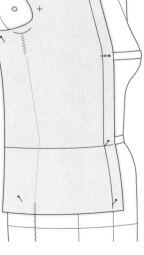

Figure 16.12

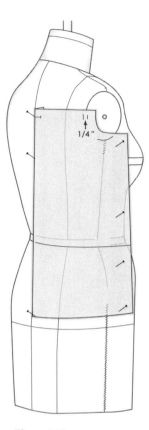

Figure 6.13

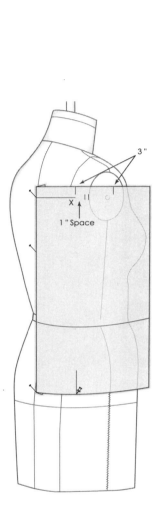

Figure 6.14

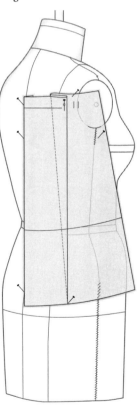

Figure 6.15

Basic Back Shirt

Figure 16.13

See the section of three design variations (Figure 16.14, Figure 16.15, action pleat, and Figure 16.16, gather with box pleat). The draper may choose one of them for the back. To drape a basic back, use the following instructions.

Pin the straight grain at the center back, and the crossgrain at the waistline. Pin.

Raise the crossgrain until the hemline is parallel with the hip HBL guideline. Pin and smooth to the armplate. Pin.

Mark armhole plate and pencil rub side seam where shown.

Smooth muslin to mid-armhole. Mark 1/4″ beyond this point. Pin.

Smooth muslin past the side seam. Pin. To continue the drape of the front shirt, see Figure 16.11.

Action Pleat

Figure 16.14 and Figure 16.15

Repeat the instructions given in Figure 16.13 with the following changes (see Figure 16.14):

- Mark 1″ in from the mid-armhole (X) and out 3″ from this mark.
- Pin at hem in line with X.

Fold a pleat that vanishes at the hemline (see Figure 16.15). To continue the shirt drape, see Figure 16.17.

Center Back Pleat with Gathers

Figure 16.16

Add 4″ to the muslin preparation shown in Figure 16.14.

Fold 1″ for a box pleat at the center back. Gather remaining excess. To continue the shirt drape, see Figure 16.17.

Trueing Patterns

Figure 16.17

Front Shirt

Unpin the front yoke.

Draw a seamline blending over uneven pencil marks of the gathered area.

Mark the armhole depth 1 1/4″ below the armhole plate.

Mark 1″ ease at the side seam and draw a light line to hem.

Mark 1/2″ in from the waistline.

Draw a side seam from the armhole to the waist mark to the hemline. Add 1/2″ seam.

Draw hemline straight or curved. Trim excess.

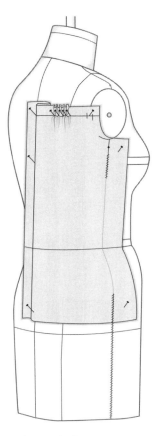

Figure 16.16

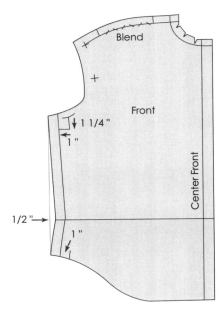

Figure 16.17

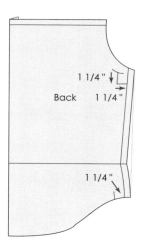

Figure 16.18

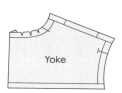

Figure 16.19

Back Shirt

Figure 16.18

To complete side seam and hemline curve, follow the instructions for completing the front, except that the ease is 1/4″.

Yoke: Drawing Armhole

Figure 16.19 and Figure 16.20

True the neckline and shoulder. The armhole will be drawn later.

Pin the front part of the yoke to the stitchline just past the gather notch.

Lay the shirt flat. The curve rule touches the extended marks at the shoulder and mid-armhole and blends with the armhole depth line.

Measure the front armhole, and record.

Yoke: Back

Figure 16.21

Unpin the yoke and pin to the back shirt.

Repeat the instructions. If curve rule does not reach the shoulder, use vary curve.

Measure back armhole, and record.

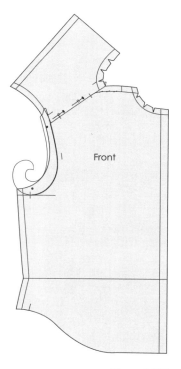

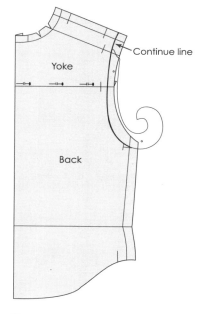

Figure 16.20   Figure 16.21

Sleeve Modification

Figure 16.22

Trace the dartless sleeve lightly on paper. Include the biceps, elbow, and center grain.

Draw a parallel line 1/2″ up from the biceps.

Pivot the back cap upward to meet this line and draw the sleeve cap. (Broken lines indicate the original sleeve.)

Repeat for the right side.

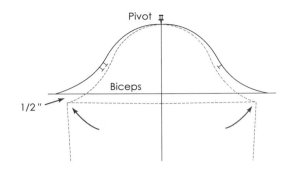

Figure 16.22

Figure 16.23

Square a line 1/2″ below the cap height, and re-draw the cap blending with the notches. Measure the capline. It should measure 1/2″ more than the front and back armhole. If not, add to or subtract from the biceps line equally. Draw the underarm seam.

Shorten length 2″ (cuff width).

Mark a point between the underarm seam and the center. Square down 3/4″. From this point, continue a line up 2 1/4″ for the slit opening.

Cut from paper.

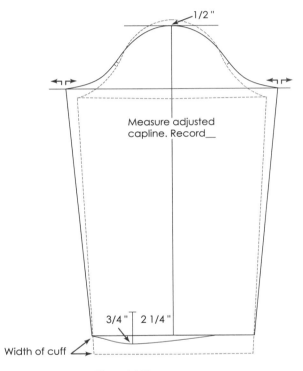

Figure 16.23

Cuff

Figure 16.24

Fold the paper and draw the cuff to the measurements given. For example, 9″ plus 1″ extension. Cuff width 2″.

Attaching Cuff to Sleeve

Figure 16.25

Add 1/4″ seams at each end and 1/2″ to attach to the sleeve. The sleeve can be pleated, gathered, or tapered.

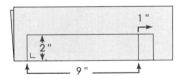

Figure 16.24

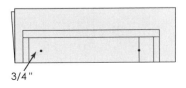

Figure 16.25

Casual Shirt

A casual shirt is characterized by the depth and enlargement of its armhole. Casual shirts can be designed with yokes, pockets, tucks, or stylelines (Figure 16.26).

Design Analysis

The casual shirt is based on the draping principle of the torso foundation. The front armhole is made larger by draping the excess to it. To bal-ance the back armhole so that it equals the front, the back shoulder is draped forward and additional ease is added to the back side seam. The armhole depth is 1 1/2″ or more below the armhole plate. The shoulderline overhangs the shoulder-tip by 1/2″. The dartless sleeve is modified to fit the larger armhole. For the basic collar, see page 196.

Preparing Form

Place a pinhead 1/2″ forward of the shoulder-tip toward the front.

Measure the form from side neck to HBL, plus 4″.

Repeat for back.

Preparing Muslin

Figure 16.27

Cut muslin from measurements taken.

Trim neckline and square a line at waist.

Figure 16.26

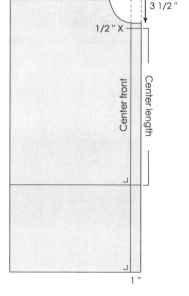

Figure 16.27

Draping Steps

Figure 16.28

Pin the straight grain at the center front, and the crossgrain at the hemline HBL. Pin.

Smooth, slash, and mark the neckline and shoulder to the pinhead. Extend the shoulder 1/2″.

Drape to the mid-armhole. Mark and extend 1/2″. Pin.

Smooth the crossgrain upward along side seam. Pin and smooth excess past the armhole plate. Pin.

Drape the remaining excess at the mid-armhole and pin as a pleat to secure.

Mark the armhole plate, pencil-rub the side seam, and mark the armhole depth below the plate. Add side seam ease.

Figure 16.29

Repeat the instructions given in Figure 16.28. The remaining excess from the shoulder area is draped to the back armhole.

Remove the drape from the form and true.

Figure 16.30

Draw the front and back armholes.

Draw a straight line at the side seam.

Indent 1/2″ at the waist and redraw side seam.

Hemline can be straight or curved and of any length.

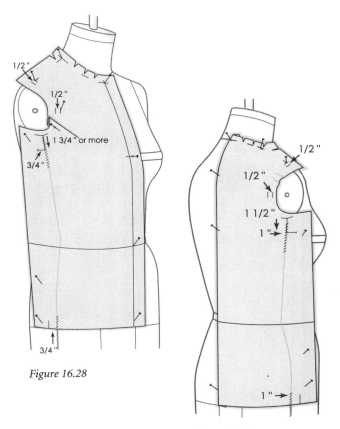

Figure 16.28

Figure 16.29

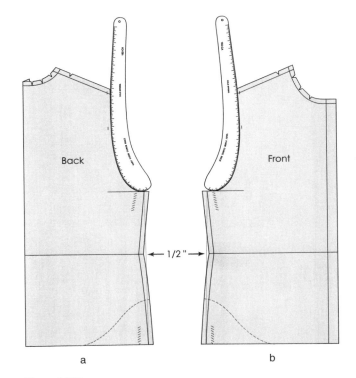

Figure 16.30

Figure 16.31

Measure armholes. Add measurements, divide in half, and add 1/4″.

Record X-Y measurement.

Figure 16.32

Trace the dartless sleeve and include all markings.

Draw a parallel line 1 1/2″ above the biceps.

Lower the cap 1/2″ (X).

Mark 2″ up from the wrist for the cuff.

Figure 16.33

Draw a line from X to Y equal to the recorded armhole measurement. Mark the midpoint.

Draw cap curve, using the measurements given.

Repeat to other side.

Finish the hemline of the sleeve with pleats or gathers.

To complete the cuff, see page 383, Figure 16.24 and Figure 16.25.

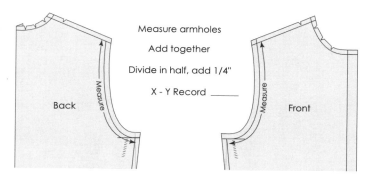

Measure armholes

Add together

Divide in half, add 1/4"

X - Y Record _____

Back

Front

Figure 16.31

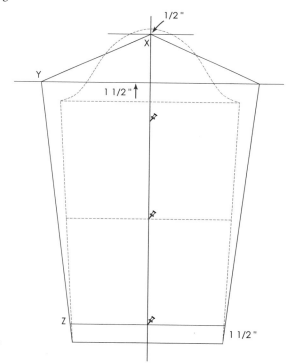

Figure 16.32

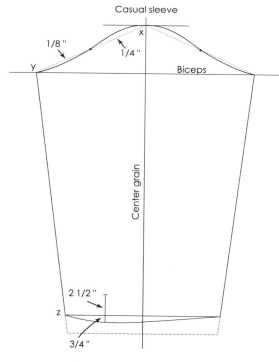

Figure 16.33

Oversized Shirt

An oversized shirt is roomy and hangs over the shoulder-tip by varying amounts. The armhole depth is very low and enlarged by draping the excess to it (Figure 16.34 and Figure 16.35).

Design Analysis

Follow the draping instructions given for the casual shirt. The difference is the extra muslin needed for oversizing. The extra fullness is held as a temporary pleat and is released at the completion of the drape. The armhole depth is 3″ or more below the armhole plate. The oversized sleeve is based on the dartless sleeve.

Preparing Form

Figure 16.36

Add 2″ or more to the width measurement for oversizing.

Fold a 1″ pleat (2″ on the open) 4″ in from the center front and back.

Figure 16.35

Figure 16.34

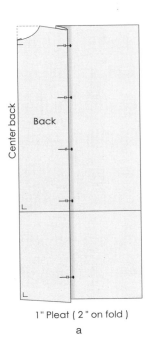

1″ Pleat (2 ″ on fold)

a

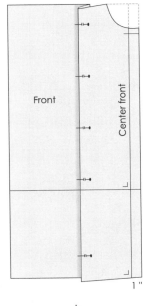

1 ″

b

Figure 16.36

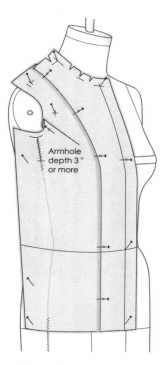

Figure 16.37

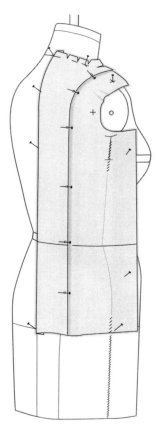

Figure 16.38

Draping Steps

Figure 16.37

Pin the straight grain to centerline, and the crossgrain at the waistline.

Drape the front shirt with the side excess pinned at the mid-armhole.

Mark armhole depth 3″ or more down from the armhole plate. No side ease is required.

Figure 16.38

Repeat the process for the back shirt. Remove the drape from the form and true.

Figure 16.39 and Figure 16.40

Unfold pleat and true the drape.

Draw a straight line from the shoulder/neck to the end of the shoulder.

Draw the front and back armholes.

The hem can be straight or curved.

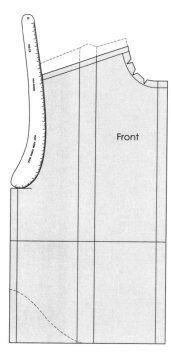

Figure 16.39

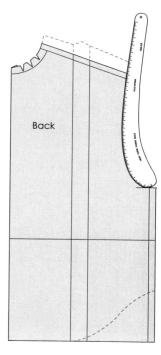

Figure 16.40

Figure 16.41

Measure armholes. Add measurements, divide in half, and add 1/4″. Record X-Y measurement.

Sleeve Modification

Figure 16.42

Trace the dartless sleeve and include all markings.

Extend the biceps line.

Sleeve Length Options

Cut 2″ from the sleeve length for the cuff or attach the cuff to the original sleeve length for a longer sleeve.

Lower sleeve cap 2″ (X).

From X, draw a line that intersects with biceps line equal to the X-Y measurement.

From X, draw a line to Z.

Finished Pattern

Figure 16.43

To complete sleeve, follow instructions for the cuff on page 386, Figure 16.32 and Figure 16.33.

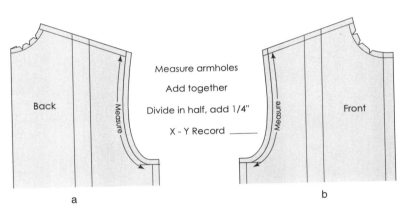

Figure 16.41

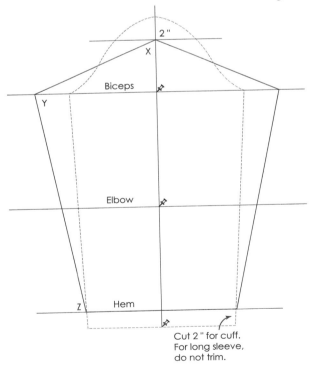

Figure 16.42

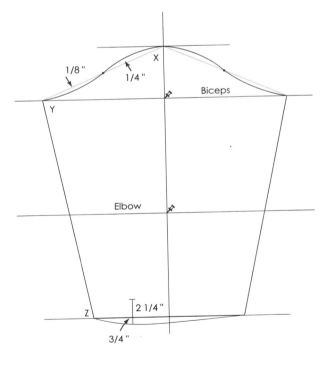

Figure 16.43

Jackets and Coats

Jackets serve many fashion purposes. They are parts of suits when designed to go with a specific skirt, but a separate item when worn with skirts, pants, dresses, and over other garments. Jackets can be designed with a tailored, feminine, or sporty touch. The sleeve choices also vary, from a basic one-piece sleeve, a two-piece sleeve to a raglan, drop shoulder, or kimono sleeve. Additional design considerations are the extended cap and the leg-of-mutton, which can be found in patternmaking texts. The notched collar is basic to a jacket with the low notch and portrait collars as options. The shawl, other collars, and necklines give variety to the jacket. Stylelines ranging from the Princess, armhole Princess, panel, and empire are appropriate choices for jackets and coats. Interconstruction can be minimal or extensive, as is illustrated at the end of this chapter. Jackets and coats are worn over other garments, and they are draped larger than the size of the form.

Figure 17.1

The draping of coats is not illustrated, but instructions are given for that purpose.

Terms

Figure 17.1

Breakpoint End of the lapel roll at the extension.

Center front depth Designated point at which the lapels cross each other.

Collar stand Height at which the back collar folds over.

Lapel Fold over of the front of the jacket/coat.

Notch Space between the collar and the lapel that creates a wedge (gorge).

Rever (revers) Part of a lapel (not including the collar) showing the reverse side (facing).

Roll line Foldline of the lapel and collar.

Shawl Extended lapel that includes the collar part.

Jacket Foundation

Jacket and coats are worn over other garments, therefore they are draped to a larger size than the form. In enlarging a jacket or coat, ease is added at the neckline and armhole areas. This allows room for interconstruction, lining, and shoulder pads. The shoulderline is extended past the shoulder-tip, and greater ease is added to the side seams. It is best to drape the garment on a form that is one size larger than the actual size of the model. Thus, for a size 10 model, drape the garment on a size 12 form (requires less modification). A basic jacket sleeve and two-piece tailored sleeve are illustrated.

Draping a Basic Jacket Foundation

The basic jacket foundation is based on the torso principle. Practicing the drape of the foundation helps to establish a base for understanding fit and balance when creating jacket designs. The jacket will not include a lapel or collar unless the draper/designer makes that decision and follows instructions given for the classic notch or other lapels that follow. To drape the classic notch lapel, see page 400, at the completion of the drape.

Preparing Form

Neckline

Figure 17.2a and 17.2b

Place the pinhead 1/8″ away from the back neckline to shoulder, and gradually drop to 1/2″ below center front neck.

Move the bust point 1/4″ toward the side seam. Pin-mark.

Pin-mark the location where the lapel overlaps the chest at the center front.

Shoulder Pad

Figure 17.2b

Center the pad over the shoulderline and extend 1/2″ past shoulder-tip. Pin to secure.

Mark shoulderline (Figure 17.2c).

Hold string in line with shoulderline and mark.

Armhole Depth

Figure 17.2c

Mark 1 1/4″ below the armhole plate.

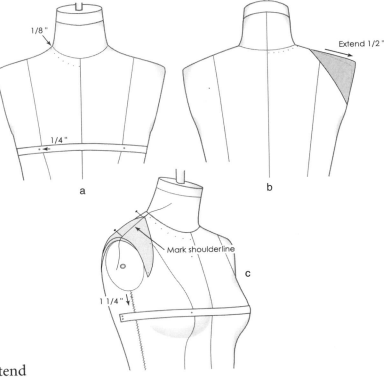

1/8″

1/4″

a

Extend 1/2″

b

Mark shoulderline

1 1/4″

c

Figure 17.2

Preparing Form: Coat

Place pinhead 1/4″ from the back neckline and gradually drop to 3/4″ at the center front.

Move the bust point 1/2″ toward the side seam. Pin-mark.

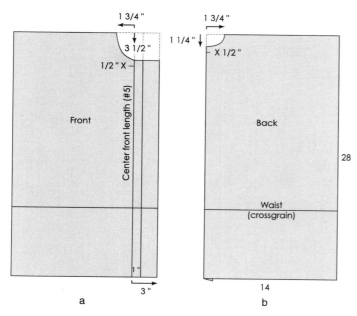

Figure 17.3

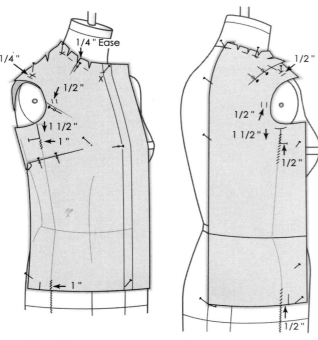

Figure 17.4   *Figure 17.5*

Pin-mark location where the lapel overlaps the chest at the center front.

Center the pad over the shoulderline and extend 1/2″ past the shoulder-tip. Pin to secure.

Armhole depth should be at least 1 1/2″ below the armhole plate.

Preparing Muslin

Drape in a heavy weight muslin or fabric of its equivalent.

Figure 17.3

- Length: desired length, plus 3″.
- Width: across bust, plus 5″.
- Examples: 28″ (straight grain) × 14 (crossgrain).

Cut and prepare muslin, as illustrated.

Draping Steps

Front

Figure 17.4

Place the centerline to the form, and *hem parallel with the hip HBL guide.* Pin.

Follow illustration as the muslin is draped.

Drape and slash the neckline, slash at center neck (X).

Drape shoulder, and extend 1/4″ to 1/2″. Drape armhole pinning 1/2″ ease.

Mark armhole depth 1 1/2″, and add 1″ ease at the side seam.

Back

Figure 17.5

Place the centerline to the form, and *hem parallel with the hip HBL guide.* Pin.

Complete the drape foundation, as illustrated.

Pin front over back drape.

Remove from the form, and true.

Draw front and back armhole.

Basic Jacket Sleeve

Armhole Measurements

Figure 17.6

Measure the front and back armholes.

Add together, and record.

Sleeve Modification

Figure 17.7

Trace the basic sleeve. Lower the underarm 1/2″.

Add 1/2″ to the underseams, graduating to 1/4″ at hem.

Raise the sleeve cap to the desired thickness of a shoulder pad (example, 1/4″) and blend the capline.

Measure the adjusted capline and subtract from the armhole measurement. The difference is the amount of cap ease.

Cap ease should be between 1 1/4″ and 1 1/2″.

Double all measurements for coat sleeves.

Stitch sleeve to armhole for the test fit.

Fitting

The jacket will tend to hang loosely until inter-construction is added.

The jacket should hang straight from the shoulderline; if not, adjust the shoulder. Do not over-fit at this time.

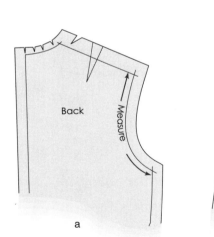

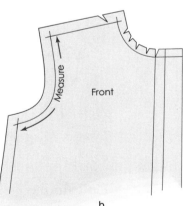

Figure 17.6

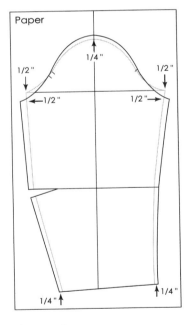

Figure 17.7

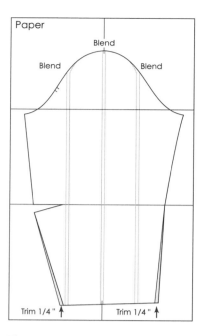

Figure 17.8

Increasing Cap Ease: Slash/Spread Method

Figure 17.8

Place the sleeve on paper and draw the center, biceps, and elbow lines. Remove and connect lines.

Divide biceps of the sleeve into four equal parts.

Square up and down from each mark, and cut on the lines.

Place sleeve sections on the prepared paper.

Align cut sections with the center, biceps, and elbow lines.

Spread each section equally to increase cap ease as required.

Trace and cut from paper.

Grading the Jacket Sleeve

Grading Method and Terminology

The terms are in relation to the position of the grader and to the guidelines placed on the paper.

- *Out.* Away from the grader (↑).
- *In.* Toward the grader (↓).
- *Up.* To the right of the grader (→).
- *Down.* To the left of the grader (←).

The top pattern is to the right of the grader.

Figure 17.9

Draw a 25″ guideline.

Square a line across 7″ down from top.

Place the biceps and grainline of the sleeve on the guidelines.

Draw the hemline extending 1/4″ out from each corner.

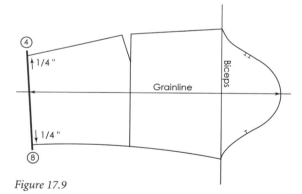

Figure 17.9

Figure 17.10

Move the sleeve pattern in direction indicated by the arrows. Follow the numerical order and the amounts given. Sections of the cap are drawn with each set of moves.

Back Sleeve Grade

The grainline and biceps *must* be parallel with the guidelines as the pattern moves from grade to grade. The back grade ends at number 3. Return the pattern to the guideline aligning biceps and grainline.

Measurements apply to the jacket sleeve. The following method can be simplified with the use of the Hinged Ruler. Cap ease should total 1 1/2″ to 2″. The measurements are doubled for a coat sleeve.

Front Sleeve Grade

Figure 17.11

The grainline and biceps *must* be parallel with the guidelines as the pattern moves from grade to grade. Start grade with number 5 and end with number 7.

Back Underseam

Figure 17.12

Place the back underseam at points 4 and 3 and draw the underseam.

Front Underseam

Place the back underseam at points 8 and 7 and draw the underseam.

Cap Line

Use the grading sleeve to help shape and blend the capline and this completes the sleeve grade.

Measure the cap and subtract from the front and back armholes. To increase, or decrease cap ease, see page 51 to modify the sleeve.

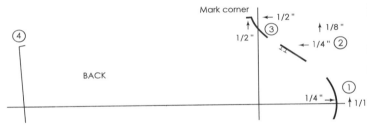

Figure 17.10

Figure 17.11

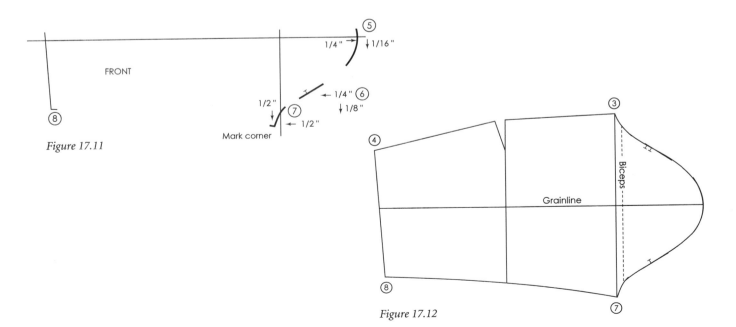

Figure 17.12

Two-Piece Sleeve

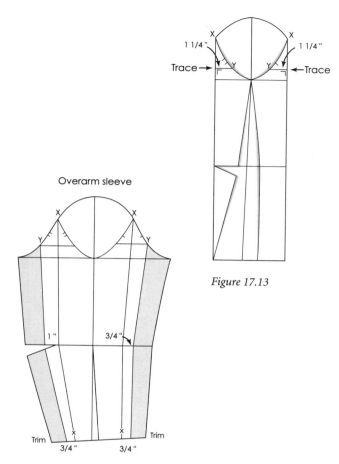

Overarm sleeve

Figure 17.13

Figure 17.14

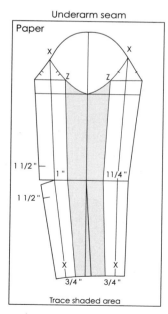

Figure 17.15

Drafting Steps

Figure 17.13

Trace and cut the jacket sleeve.

Fold on biceps line touching at centerline.

Fold at cap is labeled X.

Trace the front and back underarm curved lines.

Square a line from the fold where the measurement equals 1 1/4" to the curved line.

Trace across on this line. Label Y.

Overarm Sleeve

Figure 17.14

Unfold and draw the traced lines.

Divide the distance between the elbow and wrist in half from the centerline. Mark.

Draw connecting lines from the wrist mark to the elbow mark to X at the cap.

Mark out from X line using measurements given for the elbow and wrist.

Draw connecting lines from the wrist mark to the elbow mark to Y at the cap. The lines should curve slightly outward on the back sleeve and slightly inward on the front sleeve.

Cut unneeded sections (gray areas).

Undersleeve

Figure 17.15

Mark ease control notches 1 1/2" up and down from the dart legs. Blend.

Mark in from X line using measurements given for the elbow and wrist.

Draw connecting lines from the wrist mark to the elbow mark to Z at the cap.

Place paper underneath, and trace a copy of the undersleeve.

Remove paper and draw the outline of the undersleeve. The lines should curve slightly outward on the back sleeve and slightly inward on the front sleeve.

Cut from paper.

Mark ease control notches on the undersleeve by measuring down from the seamline and up from the wrist.

Blend the front seam at hemline.

Finished Pattern

Figure 17.16

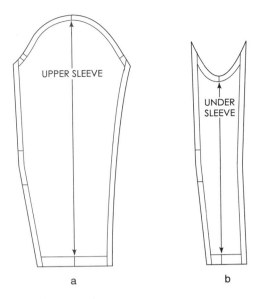

Figure 17.16

Lapel Designs

Figure 17.17, Figure 17.18, and Figure 17.19
Lapel designs for the jacket projects in this chapter are conventional, but can be more freely adapted as illustrated in Figure 7.17 to Figure 7.19.

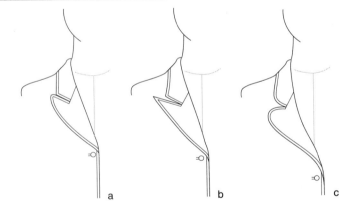

Figure 7.17

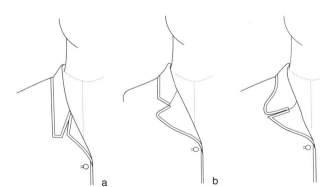

Figure 7.18

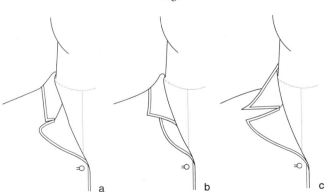

Figure 7.19

Classic Notched Lapel Jacket

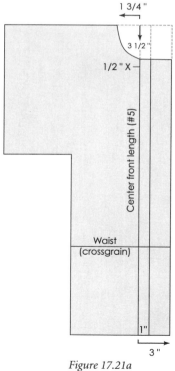

Figure 17.20

Design Analysis

A classic lapel is notched at level with the neckline and is the focus of the drape. The jacket can be draped as a foundation, see page 394; or as the example illustrates a Princess styleline armhole with a front curved hemline. (See Figure 17.20).

Preparing Muslin

Figure 17.21a

For muslin preparation, see the instructions for the armhole Princess panel on page 96, Figure 6.17.

Collar

Figure 17.21b

Cut muslin 12″ × 5″, and mark as shown.

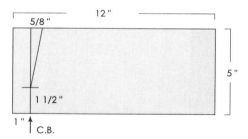

Figure 17.21b

Figure 17.21a

Draping Steps

Front Panel

Figure 17.22

Place the centerline to the form, and pin.

Mark neckline, slash, pin 1/4″, and mark at the center front neck (X).

Complete the panel drape, and trim the neckline to the seam allowance.

Lapel Shape

Figure 17.23

At 2″ down from shoulder/neck, fold muslin and cross over the chest at a desired depth.

Thumbnail the crease on the roll line.

Cut on the extension line to the crease-fold and cut away excess (breakpoint of the lapel).

Draw a curved line starting at the neck area of the fold and ending at the slash indicated as the center front X.

Draw lapel out from X to a desired shape ending at the breakpoint of the extension.

Figure 17.24

Cut lapel from breakpoint to X.

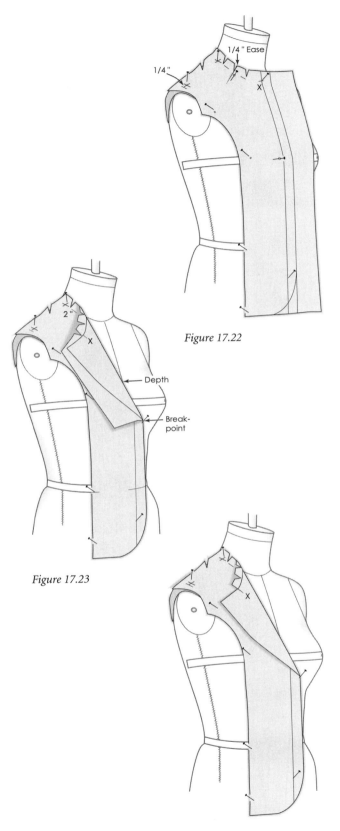

Figure 17.22

Figure 17.23

Figure 17.24

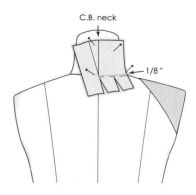

Figure 7.25

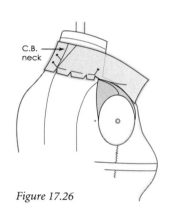

Figure 17.26

Collar Drape

Figure 17.25

Pin the collar so that the angle line is at the center back, and crossmark at the pinhead location.

Slash and drape collar to the shoulder/neck at the pinheads. Trim excess (see Figure 17.25a).

Figure 17.26

Move the center back collar to the straight line and pin 1″ up at the center back of the form.

Figure 17.27a

Pin the front panel drape.

Smooth, slash, and mark muslin around the front neckline.

Figure 17.27b

Pin the collar to the front panel.

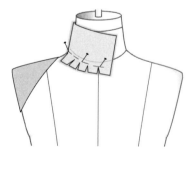

a

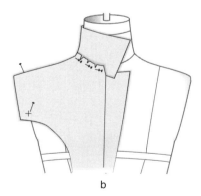

b

Figure 17.27

Figure 17.28

Fold the collar over and slash to allow the collar to fall approximately 1/4″ below the pinheads.

Figure 17.29

Draw the collar to the desired shape, blending to the shoulder.

Complete the armhole Princess drape and true. Stitch muslin or make patterns first for the test fit.

The jacket sleeve (page 395) or two-piece sleeve (page 398) completes the drape.

For instructions for facings, lining, and interconstruction, see Chapter 11.

Finished Patterns

Figure 17.30

Pattern shapes of draped part of the design.

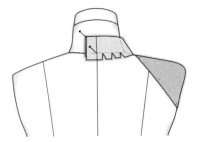

Figure 17.28

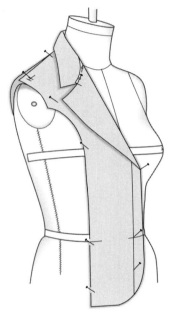

Figure 17.29

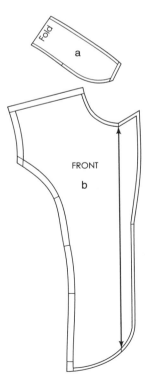

Figure 17.30

Low Notch Collar Jacket

Figure 17.31

Design Analysis

Figure 17.31

The notch location of the lapel is placed at a lower level than for the classic lapel. The location, however, varies, as a lapel can be draped to cross the chest at any depth below the center front neck. The drape of the lapel is emphasized. The jacket can be draped as a foundation, see page 394, or as the Princess styleline as illustrated. For a review of the Princess draping instructions, see Chapter 6.

Preparing Muslin

Figure 17.32

For muslin preparation, see the instructions for the armhole Princess panel on page 271, Figure 12.16.

Collar

Figure 17.33

Cut muslin 15″ × 5″, and mark as shown.

Figure 17.32

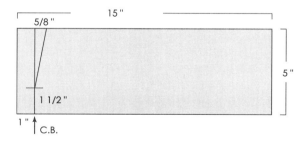

Figure 17.33

Draping Steps

Front Panel

Figure 17.34

Place the centerline to the form, and pin.

Drape the neckline, and pin 1/4″ ease.

Mark along pinheads of the neckline.

Complete the panel drape.

Lapel Shape

Figure 17.35

At 2″ down from shoulder/neck, fold muslin and cross over the chest at a desired depth.

Thumbnail the crease on the roll line.

Cut on the extension line to the crease-fold and cut excess away (breakpoint of the lapel).

Approximately one third of the way down from the roll line, draw a curved line of 1 1/4″ (X) for neckline.

From X draw the desired shape of the lapel to the breakpoint.

Figure 17.36

Cut the lapel from the breakpoint to X.

Trim to within 1/4″ of the curved neckline.

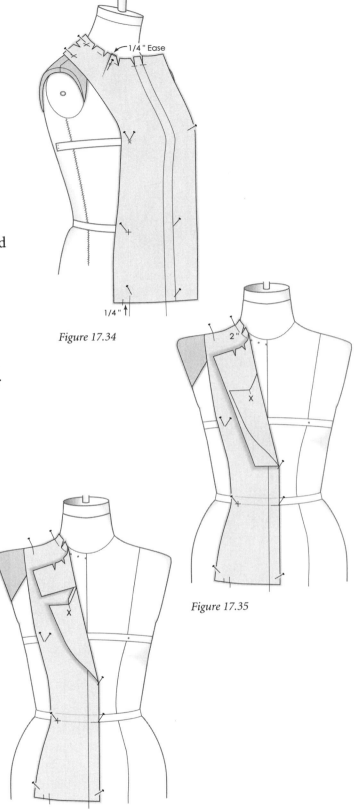

Figure 17.34

Figure 17.35

Figure 17.36

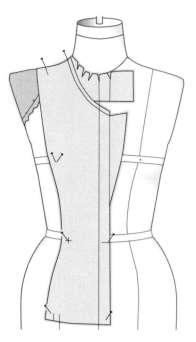

Figure 17.37

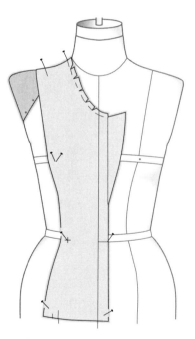

Figure 17.38

Neckline

Figure 17.37

Unfold and draw the neckline to the pin-mark at the shoulder.

Add 1/4″ seams.

Figure 17.38

Trim excess from neckline.

Slash to the seamline.

Collar

Figure 17.39

Pin the collar so that the angle line is at the center back, and the crossmark is at the pinhead.

Slash, smooth, and mark the collar at pinhead locations of the neckline.

Trim excess to within 1/4″.

Remove holding pin at the center back.

Figure 17.40

Move the straight line on the muslin to the center back of the form, and pin 1″ up.

Fold over and slash to allow the collar to fall approximately 1/4″ below the pinheads.

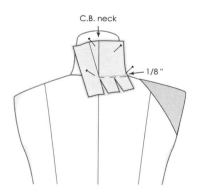

Figure 17.39

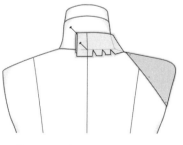

Figure 17.40

Figure 17.41

Smooth muslin flat to the form and pin to the neckline of the front jacket.

Pencil mark along the pin section of the collar.

Finishing the Lapel Drape

Figure 17.42

Make adjustments to the collar and lapel, if required.

Complete the Princess drape, remove and true. Stitch muslin or complete patterns first for the test fit.

For the sleeve, use the basic sleeve (page 395) or the two-piece sleeve draft (page 398).

For instructions for facings lining, and interconstruction, see Chapter 11.

Finished Pattern

Figure 17.43

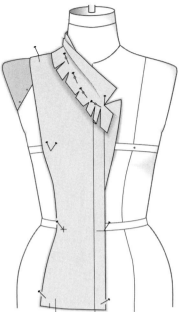

Figure 17.41

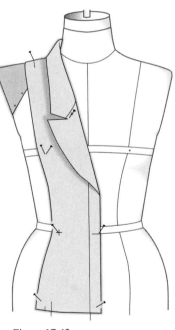

Figure 17.42

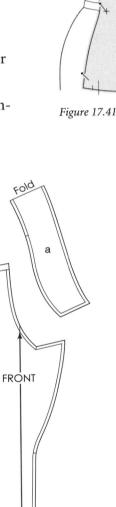

Fold

a

b

FRONT

Figure 17.43

Portrait Collar

Figure 17.44

Design Analysis

Figure 17.44

The portrait collar begins at the mid-shoulder. The lapel crosses the centerline 1″ above the bust level, but both locations can vary. The drape of the lapel is emphasized. The jacket can be draped as a foundation (see page 394, or as a panel styleline as illustrated). For a review of the panel draping instructions, see page 107.

Preparing Form

Figure 17.45

Pinhead 1″ above the bust level.

Pinhead mark the back neckline.

Measure the back neck, and record.

Preparing Muslin

For muslin preparation, see the instructions for panels on page 275.

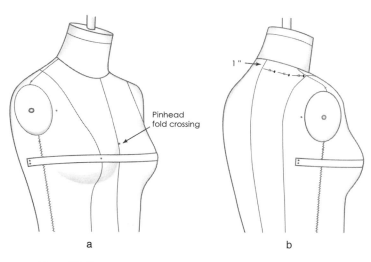

Pinhead
fold crossing

1 ″

a

b

Figure 17.45

Collar

Figure 17.46 and Figure 16.47

Cut muslin on true bias, 14″ × 9″ (lines indicate the direction of the straight grainline).

Draw the collar using the measurement given (see Figure 17.46).

Cut from muslin, and slash at the neckline (see Figure 17.47).

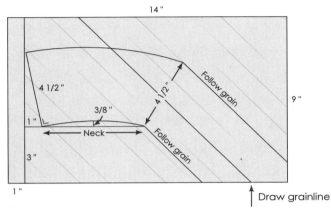

Figure 17.46

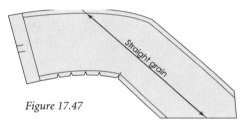

Figure 17.47

Draping Steps

Front Panel

Figure 17.48

Place the centerline to the form, and pin.

Drape the neckline, and pin 1/4″ ease.

Complete the front panel drape.

Lapel

Figure 17.49

At the mid-shoulder, fold the front muslin over the chest, crossing the center at the pinhead.

Thumbnail the crease on the roll line.

Cut the extension line to the crease-fold and cut away the excess (breakpoint of the lapel).

Mark a point on the foldline that is 4″ down from the mid-shoulder.

From the mark, draw a curved line 1 1/4″ from the fold, X.

Draw the shape of the lapel from X to the breakpoint.

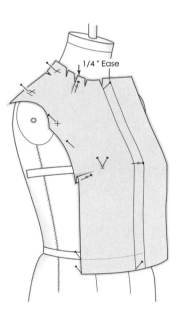

Figure 17.48

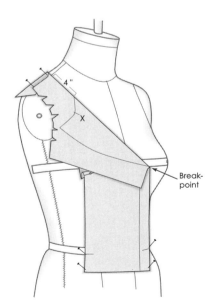

Figure 17.49

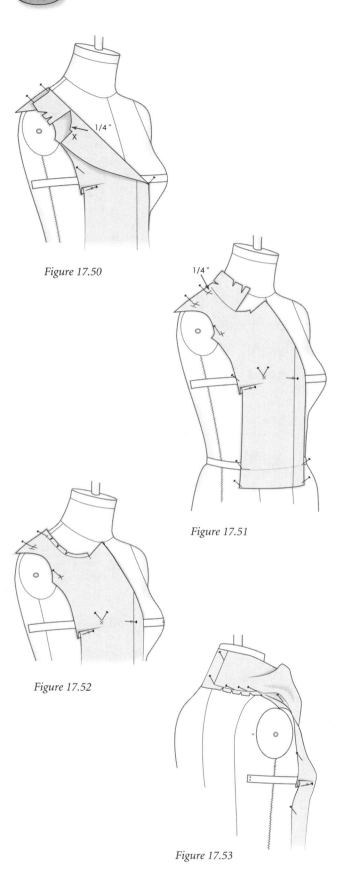

Figure 17.50

Figure 17.52

Figure 17.51

Figure 17.53

Figure 17.50

Cut the lapel from the breakpoint to X.

Draw a 1/4″ seam up from X and cut away excess.

Neckline

Figure 17.51

Unfold and draw the neckline to the shoulder, allowing 1/4″ for seam.

Figure 17.52

Trim excess from the neckline.

Slash to the seamline.

Collar

Figure 17.53

Place the collar at the center back with the guideline on the pinhead mark. Pin.

Place a pin 1/2″ up at the center back for the location of the collar foldover.

Smooth, slash, and mark muslin along the pinheads to the shoulder. Pin.

Figure 17.54

Smooth the collar to the front.

Slash 1/4″ past the collar guideline to form a curved line when pinning the collar to the jacket.

Fold the collar over, and pin at the center back.

Trim the collar to the desired shape.

Figure 17.55

Smooth the collar under the foldline, and pin the collar to the lapel.

Figure 17.56

Draw the shape of the collar.

Trim excess from the collar.

Complete the panel drape and true. Stitch muslin or make the patterns first for the test fit.

For the sleeve, use the basic sleeve (page 395) or the two-piece sleeve draft (page 398).

For instructions for facings, lining, and inter-construction, see Chapter 11.

Finished Pattern

Figure 17.57

Pattern shapes of the draped part of the design.

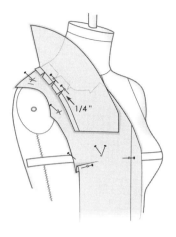
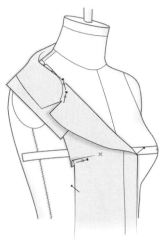

Figure 17.54

Figure 17.55

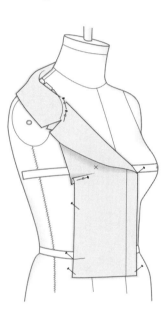

Figure 17.56

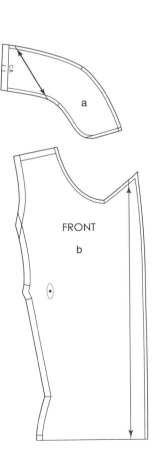

a

FRONT

b

Figure 17.57

Double-Breasted Jacket

Figure 17.58

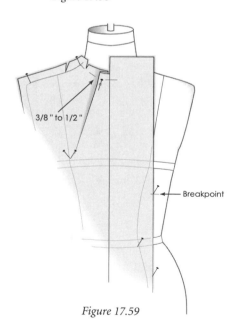

Figure 17.59

A double-breasted jacket has a wide extension to accommodate two rows of buttons. The lapel of a double-breasted jacket can be of any design—basic notch, low notch, or portrait. The jacket can be without a collar or have a built-up neckline.

Design Analysis

The double-breasted jacket is draped with a basic notch collar. The jacket lapel overlaps high on the chest. For a more relaxed lapel, an excess of approximately 3/8″ to 1/2″ is draped into the front lapel area. The width of the extension accommodates two rows of buttons. Buttons are placed equally from each other and equally out from the centerline. Mark location of the breakpoint—4″ up from the waist on the edge of the extension. The drape of the lapel is emphasized, but the jacket can be of any style.

Preparing Muslin

For muslin preparation, see page 394.

Draping Steps

Figure 17.59

Place prepared muslin to the form, aligning the centerlines. Pin.

Mark the neckline along the pinhead and pin 3/8″ to 1/2″ excess at the neckline.

Mark the breakpoint, and pin.

Figure 17.60

Unpin excess of the neckline.

Fold the roll line for the lapel to the break-point.

Draw lapel and trim excess.

Follow instructions for the basic notch collar.

Complete the drape and true. Stitch muslin or make the patterns first for the test fit.

For the sleeve, use the basic sleeve (page 395) or the two-piece sleeve draft (page 398). For instructions for facings, lining, and interconstruction, see Chapter 11.

Finished Pattern

Figure 17.61

Mark buttonhole placements. Buttons are placed equidistant from each other and equidistant from the centerline. (Back not shown.)

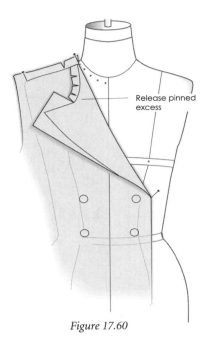

Release pinned excess

Figure 17.60

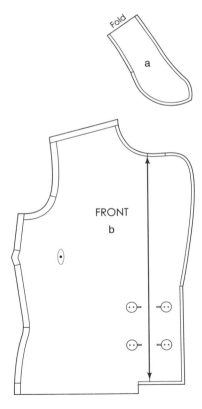

Fold

a

FRONT
b

Figure 17.61

Design Variations

Figure 17.62

Figure 17.63

Basic Shawl Collar

A shawl is an all-in-one collar with the lapel. Design 1 is an example of a basic shawl. The collar stand may be draped as a full roll (1″ stand), partial roll (1/2″), or a flat roll (1/8″ stand). The shawl can also be draped without a foldover collar at back, leaving the stand with a design collar in front, Design 2. Shawl collars are designed for dresses, shirts, blouses, jackets, and coats (Figure 17.62 and Figure 17.63).

Basic Shawl Drape

Design Analysis

Figure 17.64 and Figure 17.65

The collar stand is 1″ and overlaps the center front at a depth 2″ above bust level. The lapel part of the collar rounds to the breakpoint (end of the extension). The shoulder shifts 1/4″ downward at shoulder/neck. The drape of the shawl is illustrated. The jacket can be of any style.

Figure 17.64

Figure 17.65

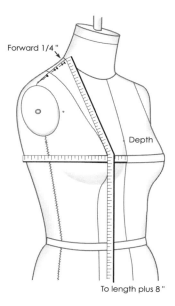

Figure 17.66

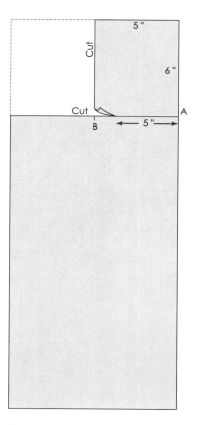

Figure 17.67

Preparing Form

Figure 17.66

Pin-mark from shoulder-tip to 1/4″ forward at neck.

Place a pinhead approximately 2″ above the bust level at the center front (where the lapel crosses the center front).

- Length: Measure from the shoulder/neck over the bust to the length of the garment. Add 8″.
- Width: Measure across the bust, and add 4″.

Preparing Muslin

Figure 17.67

Mark 6″ down (A) and square a line across muslin. Mark center of the muslin at top, square down to the line. Cut away.

Mark 5″ out from A, and label B.

Cut to B.

Draping Steps

Figure 17.68

Place muslin to form with slit at the forward shoulder pin-mark. Pin and pivot muslin until the front edge is parallel with the center front at the bust level and with the bottom edge. Pin. Stress folds will appear from the shoulder/neck area.

Pin centerline, bustline, and below the waist.

Figure 17.69

Determine width of extension from centerline.

Mark and cut parallel with edge of the muslin, ending 2″ from the depth mark.

Fish-eye Dart

Figure 17.70

The fold appearing from the pin at the shoulder is ignored if the shawl collar is designed for a blouse, dress, or shirt. It is stitched for jackets, as illustrated.

Smooth and pin muslin along the upper part of the neck.

Pin the excess as a double-ended dart ending approximately 1 1/2″ from the center front to zero at the shoulder. The intake is from 1/4″ to 3/8″.

Drape the front jacket design or drape a straight jacket.

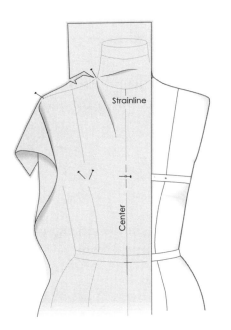

Figure 17.68

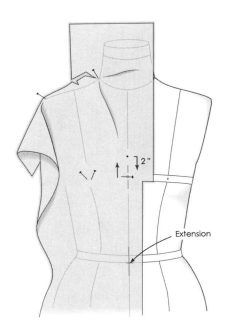

Figure 17.69

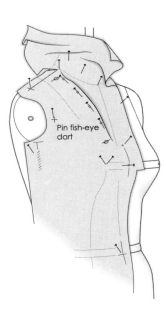

Figure 17.70

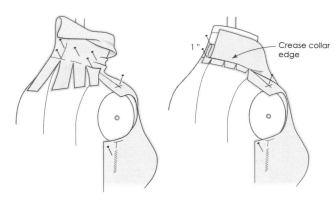

Figure 17.71

Figure 17.72

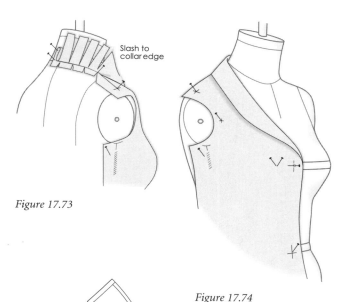

Figure 17.73

Figure 17.74

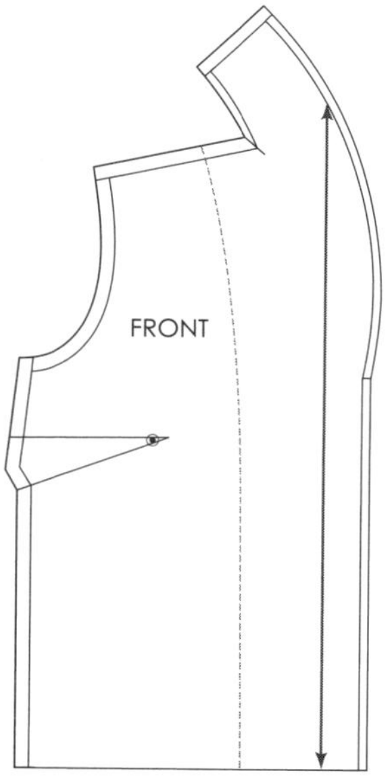

FRONT

Figure 17.75

Figure 17.71

Smooth slash, and pin muslin collar to the center back.

Pin center back and 1″ above for fold of the collar.

Figure 17.72

Fold muslin over from pin-mark at the center back. Allow excess muslin to flip upward from just below the neckline. Run fingers in between the fold to assure that the muslin is smooth along the back neck.

Figure 17.73

Slash downward to the fold (collar edge).

Trim to collar edge.

Figure 17.74

Trim front lapel to the desired shape. The fish-eye dart should not be seen when the collar folds back on the jacket.

Complete the drape design. Remove from the form, and true. Stitch the muslin or complete the patterns first for the test fit.

Finished Pattern

Figure 17.75

The fish-eye dart is stitched on the jacket, not on the facing. The excess is trimmed from the lining pattern instead.

For the sleeve, use the basic sleeve (page 395) or the two-piece sleeve draft (page 398).

For facings, lining, and interconstruction guides, see Chapter 11. (Back not shown.)

Variation: Portrait Shawl Collar

Figure 17.76

The portrait shawl can be draped at varying distances from the shoulder/neck. It crosses the center front at varying depths below the center neck. The collar is wide and can be shaped to any design. The portrait shawl gives a feminine touch to all types of garments: blouse, day or evening dress, jacket, coat, and cape.

Design Analysis

The design is draped 1 1/2″ in from the shoulder-tip and crosses to a depth of 1″ above the bust level. The collar is as wide as desired, but usually 5″ to 6″. To help simplify the drape of the portrait shawl, trace the neckline, and shoulder, the armhole and side seam from the basic front and back pattern.

Preparing Form

Figure 17.77

Pin-mark neck 2″ down from the center back neck. Pins curve upward, ending 1 1/2″ from the shoulder-tip.

Fabric Needed

See page 416, Figure 17.67. Add 2″ to the length.

Figure 17.76

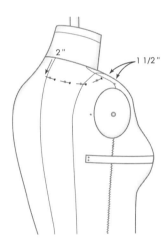

Figure 17.77

Preparing Muslin

Figure 17.78

Draw a line through the straight grain 1″ from the muslin edge. Square a short guideline 8″ down from top of the muslin.

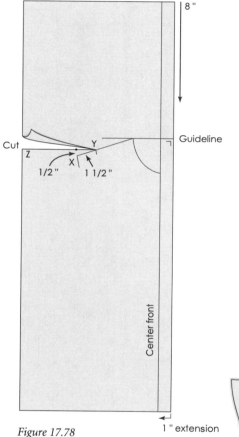

Figure 17.78

Place the center front of the pattern to the straight grainline with the shoulder/neck touching the guideline. Trace the neckline, shoulder, and remaining pattern required by the design.

Mark shoulder 1 1/2″ in from the shoulder tip (X). Draw a line across muslin on grain from Y. Cut on line to Y.

Draping Steps

Figure 17.79

Place straight grain of the muslin at the center of the form.

Pin center and align with the shoulder. Pin at Y. Smooth muslin over shoulder. Pin at shoulder-tip.

Pin the bust point and bridge at the centerline.

Figure 17.80

Fold muslin at Y and across the chest, passing at the depth of the center front. Crease-fold.

Pin-mark the shape of the front collar and trim along pin-marks, ending at the shoulder level.

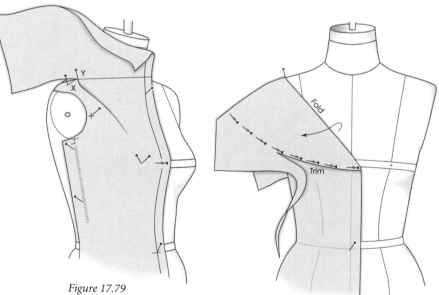

Figure 17.79

Figure 17.80

Figure 17.81

Flip front collar upward.

Pin a fish-eye dart (intake from 1/2″ to 1″ at the center), ending at least 1″ from the center front and zero at Y. Slash at the center fold.

Figure 17.82

Lift collar and place the muslin 1/2″ below the pin guide at the center back.

Pin collar following the pin guides to zero at the shoulder Y.

Figure 17.83

Fold over collar and pin-mark collar shape. Cut collar edge parallel to the center back. Pin-mark the shape of the collar, and trim.

Figure 17.84

The collar roll should be approximately 1″ up from the shoulder (Y) for a smooth transition to the back collar.

Increase the intake of the fish-eye dart if necessary to prevent the front collar from lying flat to the chest.

Remove the drape and true. Stitch muslin, or make the patterns first for a test fit.

Finished Pattern

Figure 17.85

The broken lines indicate facing placement.

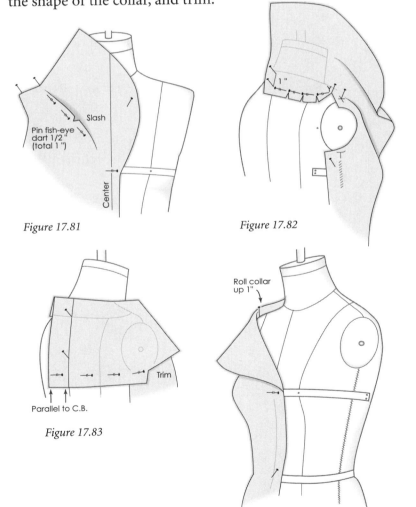

Figure 17.81

Figure 17.82

Figure 17.83

Figure 17.84

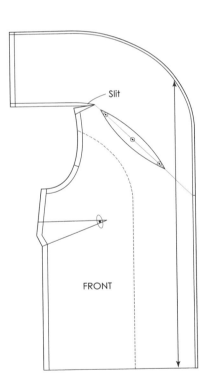

Figure 17.85

Interconstruction, Lining, and Facing

Interconstruction Guide

The Princess line jacket is the prototype for all designs illustrated. Fabric and cost determines type and amount of interconstruction considered for the jacket or coat. The illustrations, which are by Facemate® and the Frudenberg Corporation-Vilene®, are to be used as a guide.

Use jacket patterns to develop fusible and woven interconstruction parts. Seam allowances may or may not be removed from fusible parts. A woven part may be trimmed to within 1/8″ of the seam. A bridle strip placed along the fold of the lapel holds 1/4″ ease and helps the roll line stay in place. The chest piece can be a single ply or layered, with a mix of fusible and woven parts. The chest piece, which helps to bridge the hollow from the shoulder-tip to the bust, extends 1″ past the shoulder for a smooth transition over the seams.

Trace Patterns of the Design Jacket

Figure 17.86

Patterns are with seam allowance. Use as the basis for developing lining and interconstruction parts of the garment.

Variation: Facing for Curved Hemline

Figure 17.87

Add 1/8″ to the lapel to zero at the breakpoint and to the notch at the point where the collar starts (see Figure 17.87a).

Place a notch 1/2″ up from the stitchline at the hem. This marks the location of the lining fold (see Figure 17.87b).

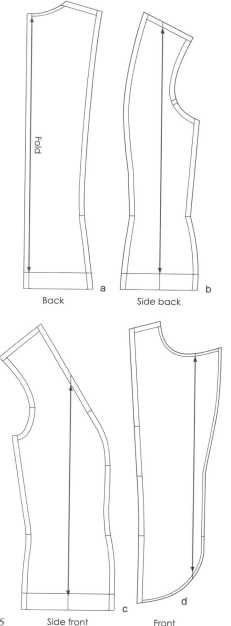

Figure 17.86   Side front   Front

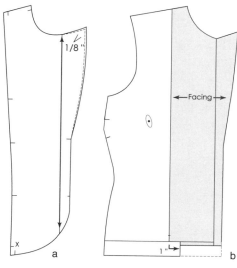

Figure 17.87

Variation: Facing for a Squared Hemline

A squared hemline is trimmed to 1″ in from the width of the facing to secure the raw edge (see Figure 17.87b).

Mark notch 1/2″ up from the stitchline. This marks the foldline of the lining.

Back Facing

Figure 17.88

Place the folded paper at the center back and trace the back facing. Mark 1/2″ seam allowance (see Figure 17.88a).

Cut the facing section from the back pattern mark (see Figure 17.88b).

Lining Patterns: Side Front, Side Back, and Back

Extend the shoulders 1/2″, raise the armholes 1/2″, and add 1/4″ to the side seams.

Blend the adjusted armhole.

Lining hem is 1″ less than the jacket hem.

Add 1 1/4″ to the center back for the knife pleat (to the hem or to end at the waist).

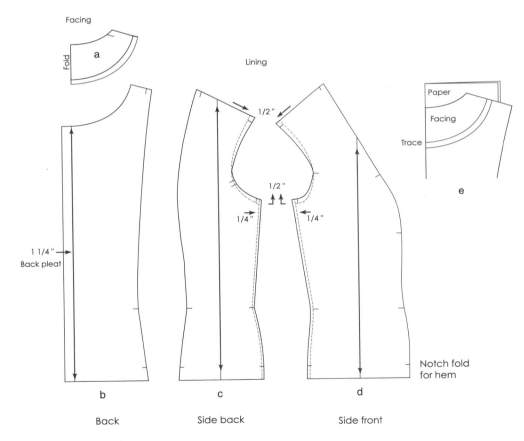

Figure 17.88

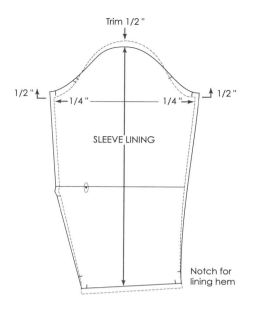

Trim 1/2"

1/2" ↑   ↑ 1/2"
← 1/4 "   1/4 " →

SLEEVE LINING

Notch for
lining hem

Figure 17.89

Sleeve Lining

Figure 17.89

Trace the sleeve.

Lower the cap 1/2″, raise the armhole 1/2″, and add 1/4″ to the underarm seam. Hem allowance: 1″ less than the sleeve hem. Notch for the hem allowance.

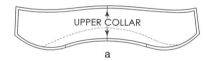

UPPER COLLAR

a

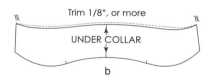

Trim 1/8", or more

UNDER COLLAR

b

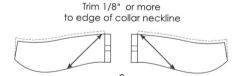

Trim 1/8" or more
to edge of collar neckline

c

Figure 17.90

Collars

Figure 17.90

Trace upper collar, and modify (see Figure 17.89a).

Trim 1/8″ (more for thickly woven fabric) at the center back to zero at the collar tip (or to the end of the collar).

- One-piece under collar (see Figure 17.89b).
- Two-piece under collar (see Figure 17.89c).

Cut on bias for a smooth roll line.

Pants

Pants are designed for all occasions from sporting events to formal dinners (see Figure 18.1). The styles and silhouettes of pants abound, allowing the consumer to select those that flatter her figure. Pants are fashion items. This places a demand on the draper/designer to know how to develop them.

Pants are draped on a pant form, preferably one with a removable leg. Draping pants can be difficult because the shaping of the crotch takes place between the legs of the form or model. To help simplify the pant drape, muslin preparation will be based on a formula developed by the author. If a leg form is unavailable, the pant should be drafted unless draped for a private clientele.

Four pant foundations are discussed and illustrated. They are given the following names to identify the fit rather than the style: trouser, slack, jean, and culotte. Each pant foundation differs in looseness at the crotch level. The amount of

Figure 18.1

looseness is based on a percentage of the front and back hip measurements. The measurement affects the length of the crotch extension, and the crotch extension affects the looseness of the pant. Differences in the length of the crotch ex-

tension establishes the pant foundations. Once the formula for each foundation is understood and applied to the muslin preparation, the draper/designer is free to create any pant design with balance and fit.

Four Pant Foundations

Principle

Figure 18.2

The length of the crotch extension controls each pant foundation to be draped. The longer the crotch extension, the looser the fit at the crotch level. The shorter the crotch extension, the closer the fit at the crotch level. The extensions are based on a percentage of the back and front hip arc measurements.

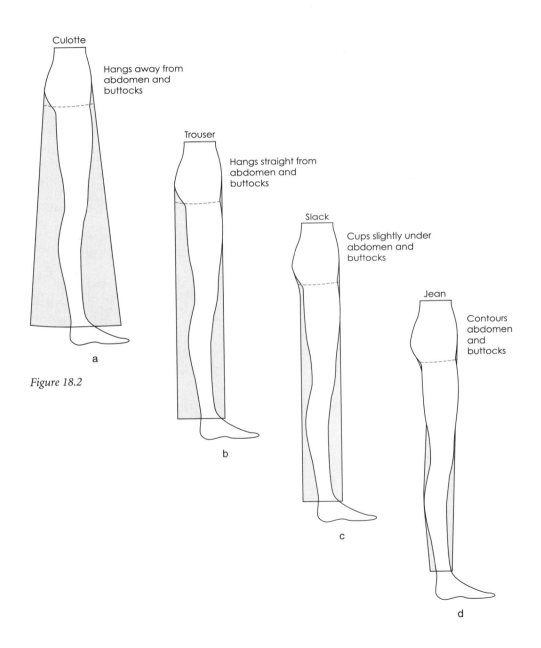

Culotte — Hangs away from abdomen and buttocks

Trouser — Hangs straight from abdomen and buttocks

Slack — Cups slightly under abdomen and buttocks

Jean — Contours abdomen and buttocks

a

b

c

d

Figure 18.2

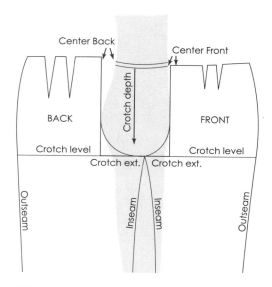

Figure 18.3

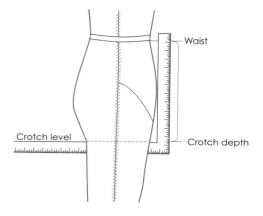

Figure 18.4

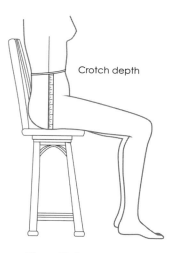

Figure 18.5

Pants Terminology

Figure 18.3

The following terms relate to the pant drape and the form.

Crotch Base between the legs of the torso.

Crotch depth Length down from the waist to the base of the torso.

Crotch extension Added fabric extending out from the center at the crotch depth to allow coverage of the inside leg. The amount of extension determines the pant foundation.

Crotch level The length from the back crotch extension to the front crotch extension.

Hip Depth Length down from the waist at level with the widest part of the hip.

Inseam Seam joining the pant between the legs.

Outseam Side seam of the pant.

Measurements Needed

All measurements (form or personal) are taken from the bottom of the waist tape. Record all measurements on the Measurement Chart in space provided.

Crotch Depth

Figure 18.4 and Figure 18.5

- Form: Measure as illustrated (see Figure 18.4).
- Model: Measure from the waist to the base of the chair (see Figure 18.5).

Record measurements #24.

Horizontal Balance Line

Figure 18.6 and Figure 18.7

Pin-mark 8″ below the waist at the center front.

Measure up from the floor to the center front pin-mark. Using this measurement, measure up from the floor to the side seam and center back. Pin-mark each location.

Hip Arc

Measure from center front pin-mark to the side seam. Record #23.

Measure from center back pin-mark to the side seam. Record #23.

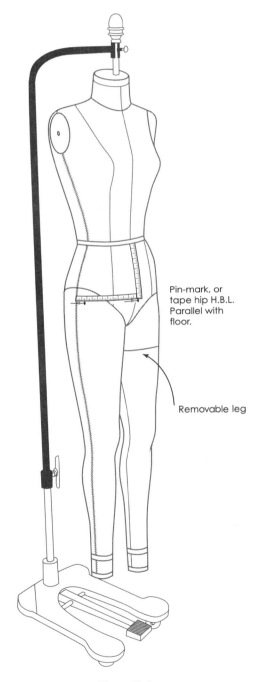

Pin-mark, or tape hip H.B.L. Parallel with floor.

Removable leg

Figure 18.6

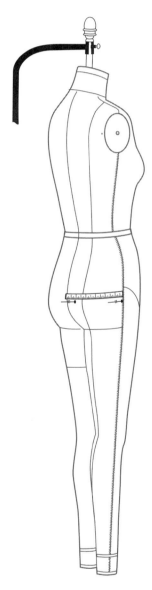

Figure 18.7

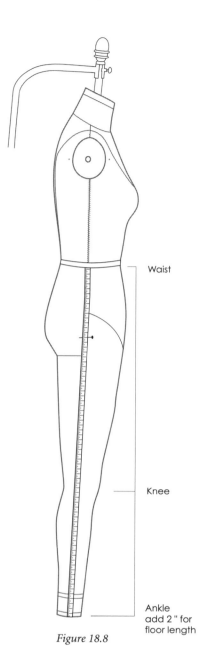

Figure 18.8

Pant Length

Figure 18.8

Measure side length to ankle. Add 2″ for floor length. Record #27.

Measure side waist to knee. Record #27.

Trouser Foundation

The trouser foundation is a base for the traditional pleated pant and the prototype for a gathered or flared pant (illustrated later) (Figure 18.9).

Figure 18.9

Basic Trouser

Design Analysis

The traditional trouser pant has a two-pleat front and two-dart back. The waist dart excess with additional fabric forms the pleats. A fabric support is placed under the front to hold the pleats in place. The support is stitched to the side pockets. The fly front can be placed on either side of the center front. Front and back creaselines are on the straight grain. The foot entrance can be of any measurement. An example is given. Always cut, stitch, and test fit the pant for balance, fit, and comfort.

Preparing Muslin

Figure 18.10

Back

Cut muslin to length, plus 3″.

Tear in half on straight grain.

Mark 7″ from corner and square down to equal:

- Crotch depth, plus 3″ (X).
- Hip depth, 8″, plus 2″. Mark.
- Crossmark 2″ up from hip mark.

Square out from X for hip arc Y.

X to Z = one half of back hip measurement.

Mark center between Z and Y and square through length of the muslin (creaseline).

Draw crotch curve from Z to crossmark.

Mark hemline to be adjusted to desired width at the time of draping.

Repeat instructions for front muslin.

X to Z = one fourth of front of hip arc.

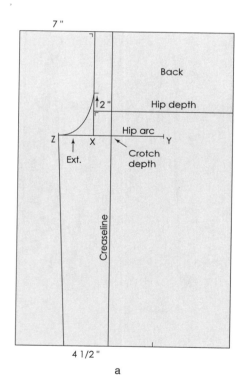

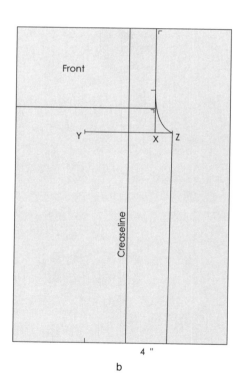

Figure 18.10

Draping Steps

Figure 18.11

Extend lines down from Z (inseam location).

Mark foot entry using the suggested measurements.

Trim excess allowing 1/2″ along the crotch curve and 1″ at the inseam.

Pin inseams together.

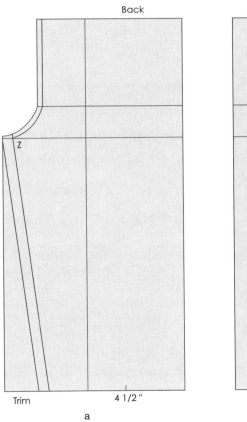
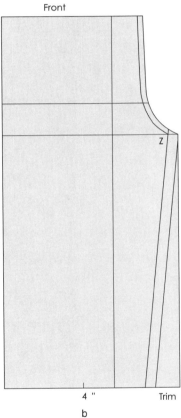

Figure 18.11

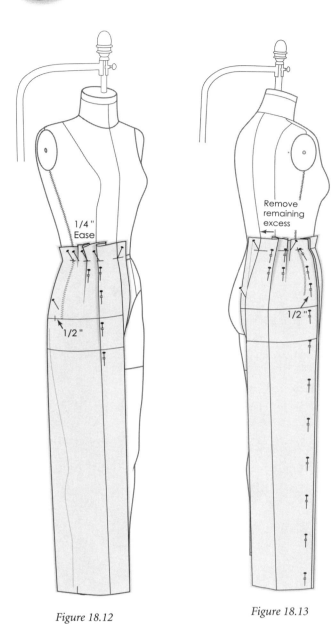

Figure 18.12

Figure 18.13

Second pleat is at least 1 1/4″. Pleat terminates approximately 7″ below the waist. Pin the pleat flat.

Pin 1/4″ ease at the waist.

Mark waistline and each side of the pleat fold.

Pencil rub from the side seam to the hip.

Mark 1/4″ to 1/2″ for hip ease.

Trim excess, allowing 1″ at the side seams.

Back

Figure 18.13

Pin two darts, with an intake of 1″ each.

Pin 1/4″ ease.

Remaining excess is smoothed out at center back.

Draw center back to blend with crossmark.

Mark the waistline and fold of the darts.

Pencil rub the side seam.

Mark 1/4″ to 1/2″ for hip ease.

Pin the outseams from the waist to the hip, and pin the straight seam to the guide marks at the hem.

Trim excess to within 1/2″ of the seam.

Draping Steps

Figure 18.12

Slip the pant up the leg, aligning center lines and HBL guidelines. Pin.

Front Two Pleats

First pleat is at least 2 1/2″. Place at the Princess line. Pleat decreases as it reaches the pant hem. Pin the pleat flat.

Fit Analysis

Check silhouette and adjust legline, if necessary.

Determine length and mark hemline.

Remove the drape with pleats pinned in place. With a curved rule, draw the waistline. Mark 1/2″ for the seams and trim.

True and blend the legs (see finished patterns for guide).

Pleat Support: Pocket

Figure 18.14 and Figure 18.15

With pleats pinned in place, draw an outline of the pocket/support pattern on the muslin drape.

Place paper behind the front drape (Figure 18.14).

Trace the outline of the pocket/support and pleat locations (Figure 18.15).

Pocket Backing

Figure 18.16

Trace and cut one pattern of the copy along A, B, C, and D labels.

Pocket Facing

Trace and cut another pattern along A, E, C, and F labels.

Sewing Guide

Cut pocket lining, facing, and backing in fabric.

Pocket backing is stitched on top of the lining labeled A, B, C, and D (see Figure 18.15).

Pocket facing is stitched to the right side of the the front pant and turned over to the underside. It is stitched to the lining from E to F (see Figure 18.15).

The lining is stitched to the side seam, waist, and centerline.

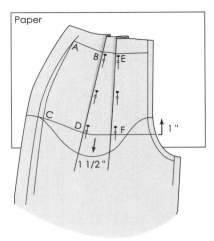

Figure 18.14

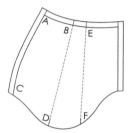

Figure 18.15

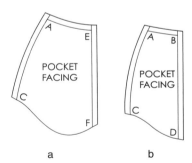

a   b

Figure 18.16

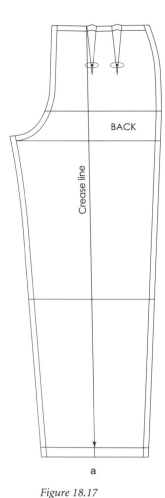

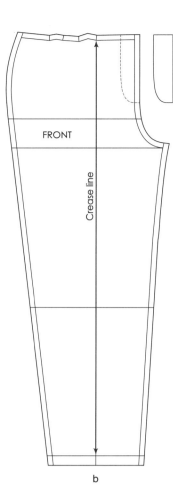

a   b

Figure 18.17

Finished Pattern

Figure 18.17

Add a fly front to either side.

Baggy Pant

The baggy pant is an extension of the design possibilities of the trouser pant, as are the other designs shown. It is suitable for activewear or evening wear (Figure 18.18).

Design Analysis

The baggy pant is based on the trouser foundation. A baggy pant design with gathers at the waist may require all of the fabric width. For less fullness, pin closer to the side seam and trim the excess. A pull-cord at the waistline is part of the design, with a band at the hemline to hold the gathers.

Design Variations

Design 1: Elastic insert at waist and leg hem can replace the cord and band.

Design 2: A waistband holds gathers, and the legline is unconfined.

Design 3: Legline can be of any length.

Preparing Muslin

For muslin preparation, see the trouser formula on pages 432 and 433, Figure 18.10 and Figure 18.11.

Mark page and return.

Design 2

Design 1

Design 3

Figure 18.18

Draping Steps

Figure 18.19

Pin a 1/2″ seam down the inseam to the hem for extra fullness.

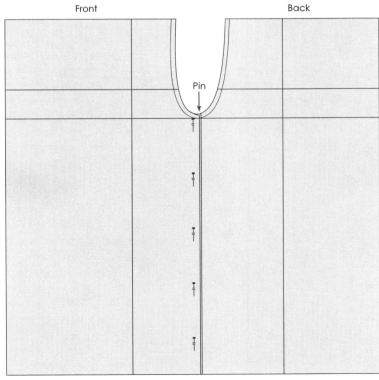

Front   Back

Pin

Figure 8.19

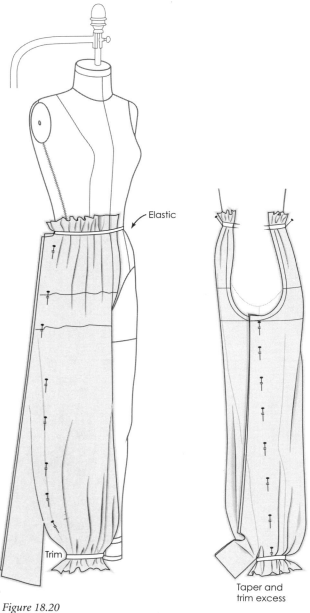

Figure 18.20

Figure 18.21

Taper and
trim excess

Figure 18.20 and Figure 18.21

Place elastic around the waist and ankle.

Pull muslin under the elastic until the crossgrain guideline aligns with the hip guide.

Align the front and back centerlines.

Arrange fullness evenly at the waist and ankle.

Taper to the hem to control the amount of fullness.

Mark the waist and ankle.

Remove pant. True and blend.

Finishing the Pattern

Figure 18.22

Allow 2 1/4″ above the waistline for foldover (insertion for elastic).

If a pocket is desired, draw its shape (broken line). Place paper underneath and trace the pocket shape (see Figure 18.23).

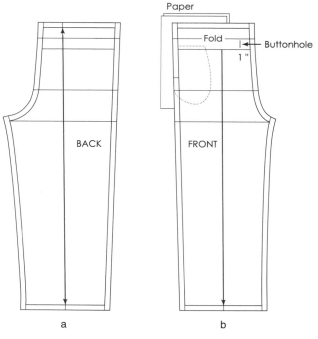

Figure 18.22

Pocket

Figure 18.23a

Cut two copies for lining and backing.

Hem Band

Figure 18.23b

Follow the illustration.

Buttonholes and Cording

Figure 18.23c

Stitch vertical buttonholes 1″ from each side of the center front up from the waist level before folding.

Fold 1 1/4″ over at the waist, and stitch.

Pull cording through buttonholes.

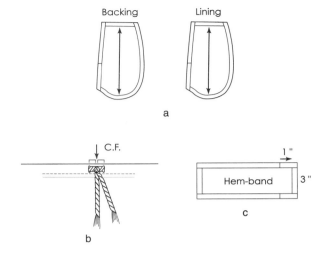

Figure 18.23

Slack Foundation: Basic Slack

The slack foundation does not fit as loosely as the trouser or as closely as the jean pant. It is a popular pant for most figures. It is a prototype for many pant lengths and designs (Figure 18.24).

Design Analysis

The basic slack pant has one dart in front and one in back. There will be a slight cupping under the buttocks and abdomen because of the closer crotch extensions. The creaseline is on the straight grain.

Figure 18.24

Preparing Muslin

Back

Cut muslin to length, plus 3″.

Tear in half on straight grain.

Mark 7″ from corner and square down to equal:

- Crotch depth, plus 3″ (X).
- Hip depth, 8″ plus 2 1/2″. Mark.
- Crossmark 2″ up from hip.

Square out from X for hip arc Y.

X to Z = one third of back hip measurement.

Mark center between Z and Y and square through length of the muslin (creaseline).

Draw crotch curve from Z to crossmark.

Mark suggested hemlines to be adjusted to desired width at the time of draping.

Repeat instructions for front muslin.

X to Z = one fourth of front of hip arc.

Figure 18.25

Draw a temporary guideline for an inseam and trim excess allowing 1″ for adjustments if required.

Trim excess to within 1/2″ of seams at the crotch and remove 2″ from the muslin.

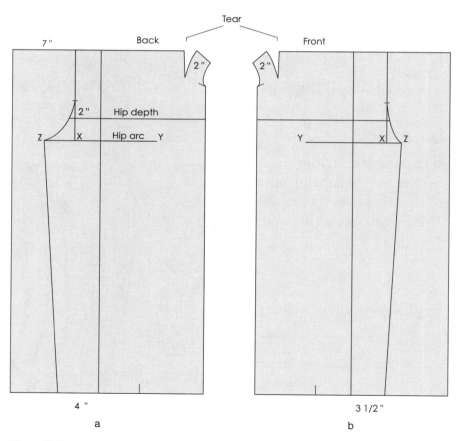

Figure 18.25

Draping Steps

Figure 18.26

Pin the inseams and slip up the leg of the form aligning centerlines and HBL guidelines (crossgrain). Pin.

Front

Move seam 1/2″ from center front. Pin. Pin a 1/2″ dart at the Princess of the front pant and 1/4″ ease (see Figure 18.26).

Back

Figure 18.27

Pin 1″ dart at the back of the Princess.

Smooth out remaining excess at center back and draw centerline blending with cross mark.

Mark waistline and dart legs.

Pinning the Legline

The pant width at the knee is approximately 1/2″ wider on each side of creaseline than at the hem.

To balance the pant leg, pin equally out from each side of the creaseline to crotch level.

The pant may have a fly front or a zipper back. Pin.

Remove the drape. True and blend.

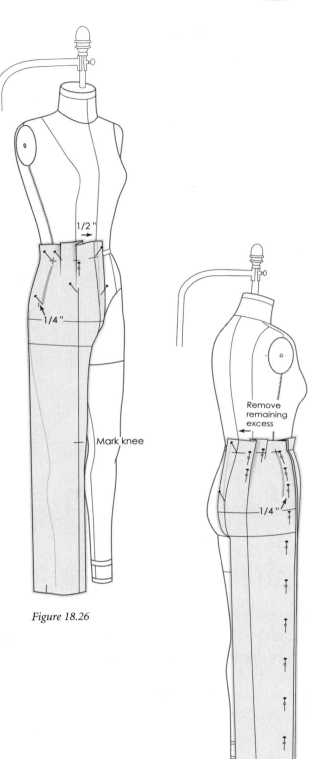

Figure 18.26

Figure 18.27

Finished Pattern

Figure 18.28

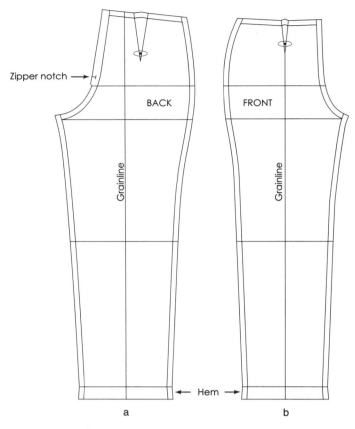

Figure 18.28

Jean Foundation

The jean foundation fits close to the contour of the abdomen, buttocks, and legs. The pant leg can be draped straight or flared, as bell-bottoms (illustrated later). The pant leg and the waistline can be raised or lowered. The jean can be draped without darts, as illustrated (Figure 18.29).

Design Analysis

The traditional jean has a back yoke, cutout pockets in front, and the front waist lowered at the center. To make this type of jean, draw the stylelines on muslin and cut apart after draping the pant.

Design Variations

The jean drape is designed with a straight leg with one dart in front and one in back. A dartless version is also illustrated. The crotch depth is without ease. The pant leg is draped as close as comfort allows. The creaseline is on the straight grain and center of the finished pant legs.

For a jean with a flared hemline see page 446.

Figure 18.29

Basic Pant Jean

Preparing Muslin

Back

Cut muslin to length, plus 3″.

Tear in half on straight grain.

Mark 7″ from corner and square down to equal:

- Crotch depth, plus 3″ (X).
- Hip depth 8″, plus 3″. Mark.
- Crossmark 2″ up from hip.

Square out from X for hip arc Y.

X to Z = one fourth of back hip measurement, plus 1/2″.

Mark center between Z and Y and square through length of the muslin (creaseline).

Draw crotch curve from Z to crossmark.

Mark suggested hemlines to be adjusted to desired width at the time of draping.

Repeat instructions for front muslin.

X to Z = 2″.

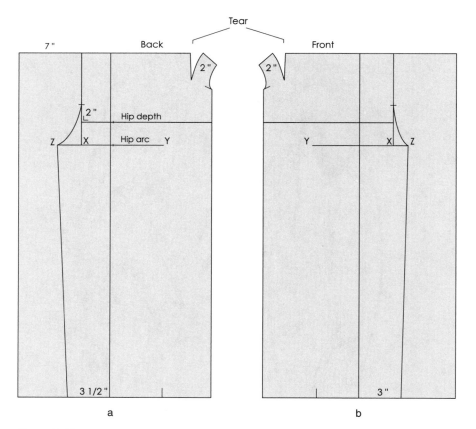

Figure 18.30

Figure 18.30

Trim excess to within 1″ at inseam and 1/2″ of the seams at the crotch. Remove 2″ from the muslin.

Draping Steps: Darted Waistline

Figure 18.31 and Figure 18.32

Slip pant up the leg of the form aligning the centers and crossgrain with the hip guide. Pin.

Move centerline 1/2″ from center front.

Pin a 1/2″ dart at the Princess line in front, and a 1″ dart in back.

Pin 1/4″ ease at front and back waist.

Smooth out remaining excess at center back and draw line blending to crossmark.

Mark waist, and pencil rub the side seam.

Pinning the Legline

Pin the pant legs together to the desired fit. The pant widths at the crotch, knee level, and hem must measure equally out from each side of the creaseline to balance the hang of the pant.

Remove and pencil mark along the pins of the leglines. True and make the patterns. Refer to the finished pattern shapes as a guide for shaping the leglines.

Draping Steps: Dartless Waistline

Figure 18.33 and Figure 18.34

Smooth out excess to the center and side seams.

Mark waist, and pencil rub the side seams.

To drape the legline of the pant, refer to Figure 18.31 and Figure 18.32.

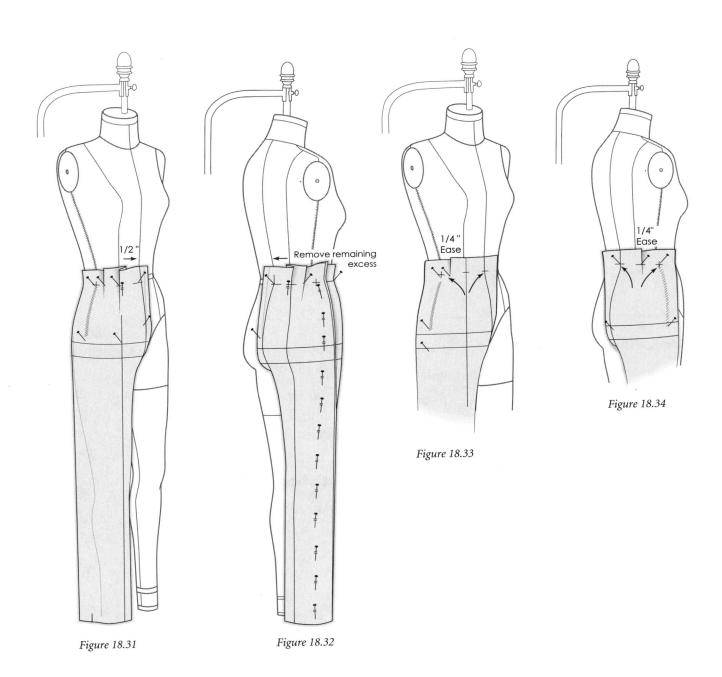

Figure 18.31

Figure 18.32

Figure 18.33

Figure 18.34

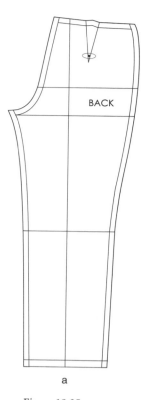

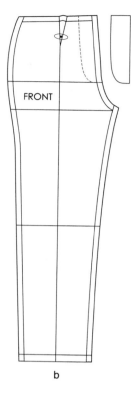

BACK

FRONT

a

b

Figure 18.35

Finished Pattern

Figure 18.35 and Figure 18.36

With waist darts, see Figure 18.35.

Without darts, see Figure 18.36.

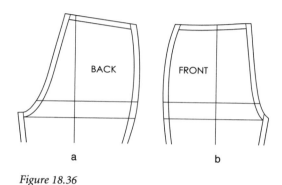

BACK   FRONT

a   b

Figure 18.36

Flared Pant Jean

Preparing Muslin

For muslin preparation, using jean foundation instructions.

Figure 18.37

Square down from the crotch level to the hemline to establish the hem width. From the marks, flare may pinned to any width.

Draping Steps: Pinning the Pant Leg

Figure 18.38 and Figure 18.39

Alternate the pinning between the inseams and outseams from the crotch to the hemline. Taper the pins to a point where the flare begins.

Inseams and outseams are pinned equally out from the creaseline.

Remove pant and pencil mark along the pins. True and blend. Make the patterns. Cut, stitch, and test the fit.

Finished Pattern

Figure 18.40

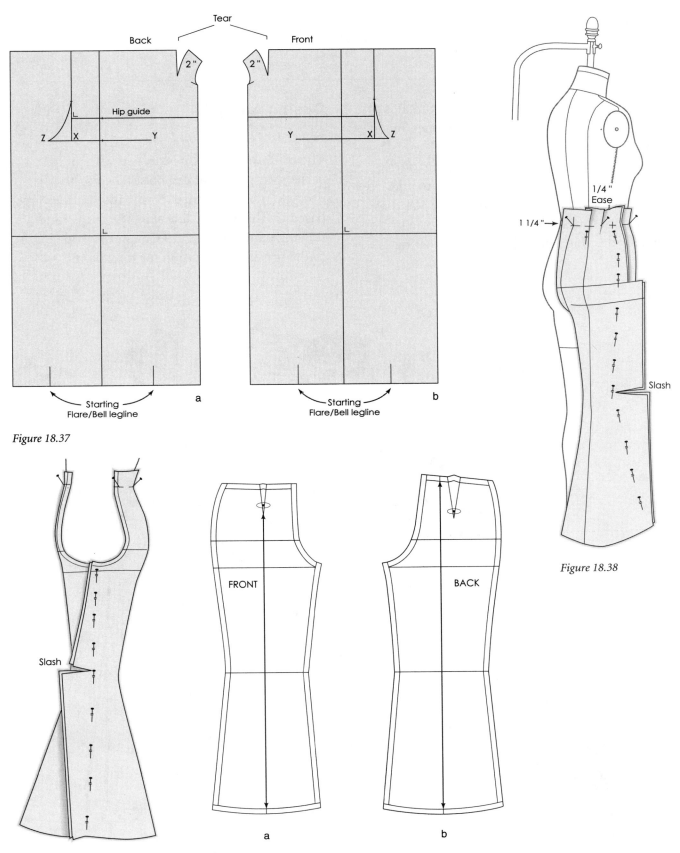

Tear

Back | Front

2"   2"

Hip guide

L

Z X Y | Y X Z

L | L

L | L

Starting
Flare/Bell legline   a

Starting
Flare/Bell legline   b

Figure 18.37

1/4"
Ease

1 1/4"

Slash

Figure 18.38

Slash

Figure 18.39

FRONT | BACK

a | b

Figure 18.40

Culottes Foundation: Traditional Culottes Drape

A culotte appears to be a skirt, but bifurcates when the model is walking and becomes a pant. Any skirt (flared, gathered, pleated, or yoked) can be converted to culottes by adding crotch extensions to the centerline of the front and back skirt. The extensions can also be based on the trouser foundation. Culottes can be a prototype for draping long full pants for evening wear.

Design Analysis

Figure 18.41 and Figure 18.42

The traditional culotte is draped with an inverted box pleat that can be stitched 5″ to 7″ down, or left unstitched. Drape instructions are based on the basic A-line skirt. To drape long flowing pant legs, refer to Chapter 7. Add length to the muslin preparation for long pants.

Figure 18.41

Figure 18.42

Preparing Muslin

Length: as desired, plus 7″.

Width:

- Front = 30″.
- Back = 25″.

Front

Figure 18.43

Mark 7″ in from muslin edge and square down equal to:

- Crotch depth, plus 6″ (X).
  X-Y = Hip arc. Square a line.

- Crotch extension.
  X-Z = one-half of the front hip arc, less 3/4″. Square down.
- Hip depth, plus 5″.
  Mark and square across the muslin.

Mark 5″ down and square out 5″ for pleat allowance.

Mark and continue the line for 2″.

Draw the crotch curve with the French curve.

Trim excess allowing 1/2″ seam.

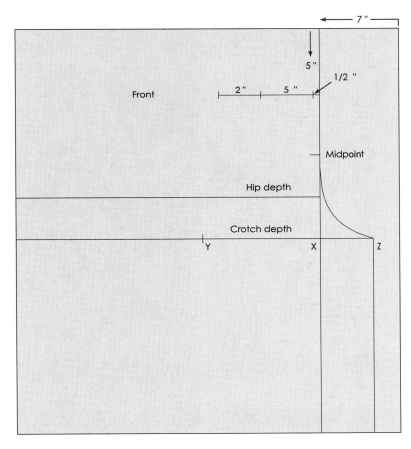

Figure 18.43

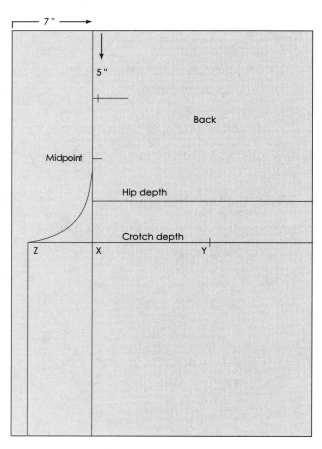

Figure 18.44

Back

Figure 18.44

Repeat the instructions for the back muslin, minus the pleat allowance. X-Z equals one half of the back hip arc, plus 3/4″. Square down.

Draping Steps

Figure 18.45

Fold pleat to the seam allowance line.

Pin to hold the pleat throughout the drape. Mark.

Pin the front and back inseams together.

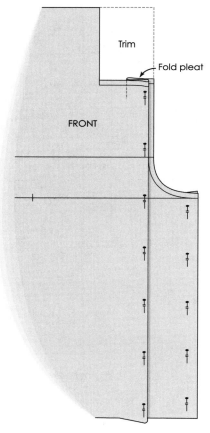

Figure 18.45

Figure 18.46

Slip muslin up the leg. Align the centerlines and crossgrain with the hip guide. Pin.

Smooth across abdomen and downward along side seam. Pencil rub side seam, add side flare. Mark waistline.

Figure 18.47

Drape the back skirt following the front drape instruction.

Remove the drape from the form. True and make the patterns.

Finished Pattern

Figure 18.48

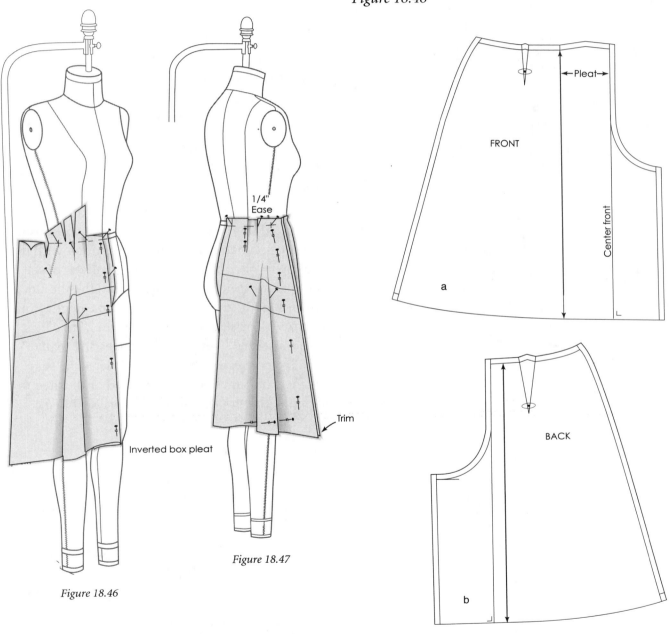

Figure 18.46

Figure 18.47

Figure 18.48

Jumpsuit

Figure 18.49

The drape of the pant part of the jumpsuit can be based on the crotch extensions of the trouser, slack, or culottes pant formulas (Figure 18.49). The jumpsuit has three drape possibilities:

1. The top and pant are draped without a waistline seam. This example is illustrated.

2. A one-piece front, with the back draped with a waistline seam.

3. The top and pant of the front and back are joined together by a waistline seam (any top can be stitched to any of the pant foundations to create a jumpsuit). (See page 45).

Design Analysis

The looseness of the jumpsuit is as desired. The following measurements are suggested for the oversized jumpsuit. The top part of the jumpsuit is based on one of the shirt foundations, with the pant part based on the crotch extensions of the culottes or trouser formula. Extend the shoulders from 1″ to 2″, and mark the armhole depth from 2″ to 3″. The side seam ease is from 2″ to 4″. See the casual sleeve draft on pages 384 to 386. A large pocket and buttons completes the garment. The pant hem can be rolled or finished to length. The trouser foundation is illustrated.

Preparing Muslin

For measurement, see pages 428 to 430.

Length is from the shoulder/neck to the floor, plus 5″.

Measure across the bust from the center front to the side seam. Add 10″.

The measurements apply to the front and back.

Cut the length and width for the front and back drape.

Figure 18.50

Mark the pant length up from the hem. Add 2″ and square across the muslin for the waist level.

Mark 7″ in from the top of muslin edge and square down to the waist. Continue the line to equal the crotch depth, plus 1 1/2″ (X). Square a

line for the hip arc Y. X-Z equals one half of the back hip arc and one fourth of the front hip arc.

Mark the hip depth, and square across the muslin.

Draw crotch curves.

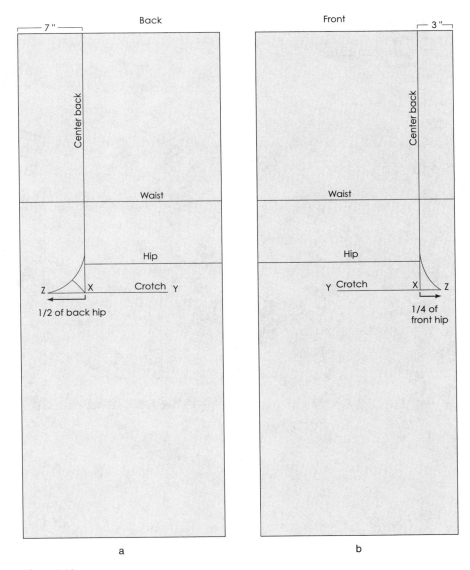

a   b

Figure 8.50

Figure 18.51

Draw a line 1″ from the center front extending 7″ down from the waist.

Cut 2″ into the muslin, 1 1/2″ down the the back and 3″ down the front.

Draw lines from the crotch point to the hem.

Trim excess to within 1/2″.

Figure 18.52

Pin the inseam from the crotch point, ending 2″ in from the inseam at the hemline.

Slip up the legline. Align centerline and hip guideline with the form. Pin.

Drape the bodice part of the jumpsuit.

The excess from the side seam is draped to the mid-armhole, enlarging the front armhole.

Mark the mid-armhole and extend to the amount allowed past the shoulder-tip.

Pencil rub the side seam and hip curve.

Mark the armhole depth 2″ below the armhole plate.

Allow 2″ ease along the side seam.

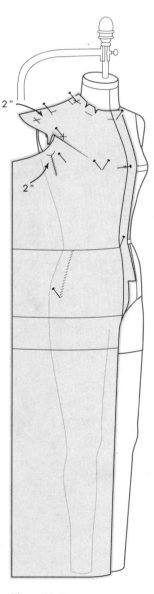

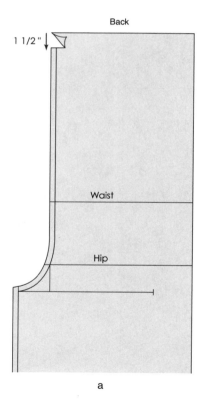

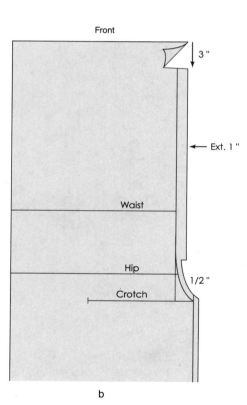

Figure 18.51

Figure 18.52

Figure 18.53

Drape the bodice back and smooth the shoulder excess to the armhole. Mark the shoulder-tip and 1″ to 2″ beyond.

Mark the mid-armhole, and 1″ past.

Pin the inseam and outseams to the desired width.

Remove the drape. True, and make the patterns.

Measure the front and back armhole and draft oversize sleeve (see pages 387 to 389).

Finished Pattern

Figure 18.54 and Figure 18.55

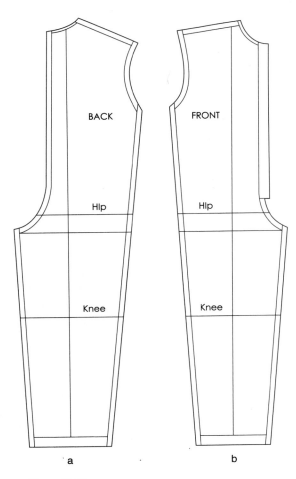

Figure 18.54

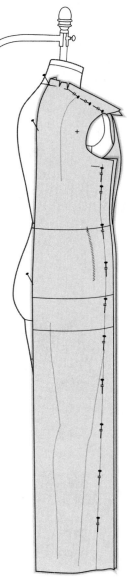

Figure 18.53

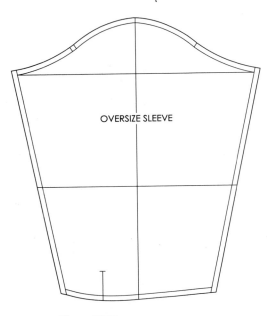

Figure 18.55

Knit
Characteristics

19

Knits are one of the most versatile fabrics. They are a popular choice with designers and consumers because of their unique qualities:

- Structure: Knit fabrics are made of natural and synthetic fibers:

- Versatility: Knits are suitable for evening wear, daytime wear, and activewear.

- Stretchiness: Knits have the ability to stretch in length and/or width and on the bias.

Characteristics of Knit Fabrics

Stretch and Recovery Factors

Memory: The ability of a knit to return to its original length after being stretched.

Recovery factor: The degree to which a stretched knit returns to its original measurement.

Stretch factor: The amount of stretch per inch on the lengthwise (wale) and crosswise (courses) when stretched to its maximum length and width. Stretch ranges from 18% to 100%, or more.

The degree of stretch varies among knits, as does the degree of stretch between the length and crosswise of each specific knit. Knits that stretch in both directions have two-way stretch. Some knits, such as Milliskin, stretch in all directions. It is important to know the characteristics of the different types of knits when making a selection. Keep in mind what the garment is expected to do.

Classification of Knit Fabrics

Knits may be composed of many fibers: including cotton, and nylon. Fibers combined with Lycra®/spandex or Lycra®/latex will vary in weight, texture, direction, and degree of stretch and shrinkage.

Single- and double-knit

They are generally classified as follows:

Single knits (called plain knits or jersey): The smooth right side has vertical ribs. The wrong side, horizontal ones.

Double knits: Two sets of yarns locked together. A firm knit with minimal stretch.

Stable (firm) knits: 18% stretch from 5″ to 5 7/8″. Stretch only on the crossgrain.

- Example: double-knit of any fiber similar to woven fabrics and must have a bust dart.

Moderate-stretch knits: 25% stretch from 5″ to 6 1/4″. Stretches only on the crosswise.

- Example: Nylon tricot, which combines characteristics of stable and stretchy knits. Used in sportswear.

Stretch knits: 50% stretch on the crosswise also 18% to 50% on the straightwise. 5″ stretches to 7 1/2″. It is lightweight. It stretches and drapes well for garments that contour the figure. Excellent for bodysuit, leotard, and swimwear.

- Example: cotton/spandex, nylon/spandex, and any fabric containing the correct amount of spandex or latex.

Superstretch knits: 100% or more stretch in the lengthwise and crosswise. 5″ stretches to 10″ or more. Excellent for activewear, dance wear, and swimwear.

- Example: any fabric containing correct amount of spandex or latex.

Rib knit: 100% stretch (1″ x 1″ ribs will stretch less than 2″ x 2″). Rib knits are designed for tops and banding.

- Example: "knit two, purl two" are used for the traditional wrist and neck bands. Ribbing should be stretched when stitched to the neckline and hem of sleeves.

Direction of Stretch

Knits are also classified by direction of their stretch:

Wales: Stretch yarns run lengthwise.

Courses: Stretch yarns run crosswise.

Two-way stretch: Stretch in both direction.

Four-way stretch: Stretch yarns run in all directions equally.

The maximum stretch is placed in the direction going around the figure for swimwear, dresses, jackets, and tops. The maximum stretch is placed in the direction of the length of active-wear (bodysuits, leotards, and jumpsuits) to allow greater flexibility.

Stretch and Recovery Guage

Figure 19.1

The gauge (Figure 19.2) is used to find the degree of stretch and memory of the lengthwise and crosswise of a knit. The findings help to determine the appropriateness of a knit for a specific design.

Caution: Do not overstretch a knit (appearance of folds). If folds do appear, relax stretching until they disappear. Record the distance beyond the 5″ point of the ruler. The example illustrates a knit marked for 5″, which has stretched 50%, or 2 1/2″, crosswise. The knit is also stretched on the straight to complete the test. Place swatch samples in box provided for each type of knit noted.

Stable (firm) Knit: 18% Stretch
Moderate Stretch Knit: 25% Stretch
Stretch Knit: 50% Cross, 50% Straight
Super-Stretch Knit: 100%, or more, Stretch
Rib Knit: 100%, or more, Stretch

Stable (firm) Knit: 18% Stretch

Moderate Stretch Knit: 25% Stretch

Stretch Knit: 50% Cross, 50% Straight

Super-Stretch Knit: 100%, or more

Rib Knit: 100% Stretch

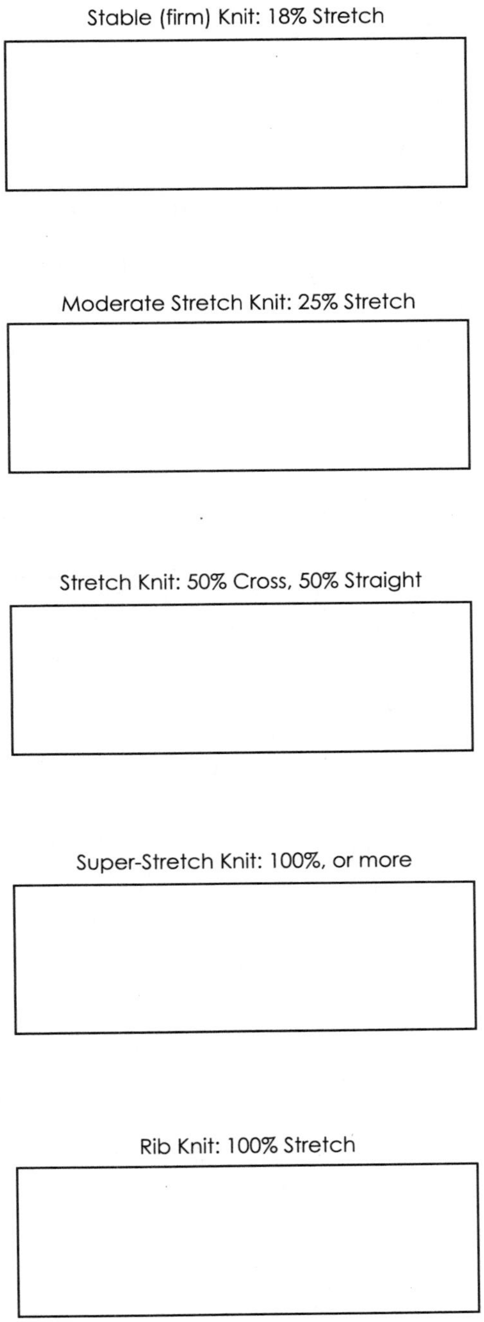

Figure 19.1

Crosswise Stretch

Figure 19.2

Fold on the crossgrain and place a pin several inches in from the edge of the selvage.

Place another pin 5″ from first pin.

Put the fold and pin at the 1″ mark on the ruler. Place a second pin at the 5″ mark.

Hold the fold down with palm of one hand and smooth firmly across fold with other hand. The fabric will stretch to the percentage noted above the ruler. Record the percentage of stretch and the distance extended.

Straightwise Stretch

Repeat process folding on the straight grain.

Record the percentage of stretch and the distance extended.

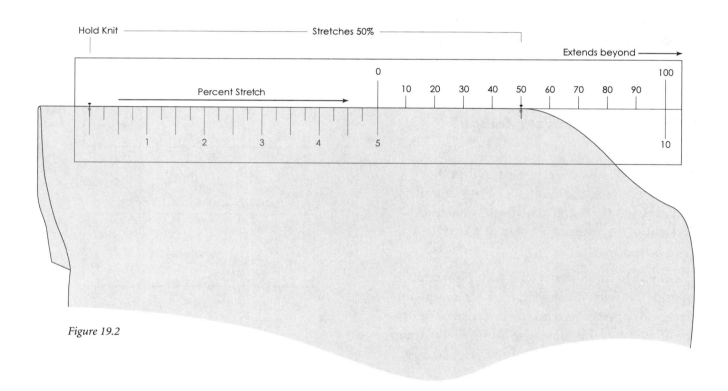

Figure 19.2

Knit Torso Foundation

The knit torso foundation (draped in a one-, or two-way stretch). It is a prototype for knit tops, dresses, bodysuits, leotards, and maillots. It is a simple foundation that fits close to the contour of the figure without need of dart control. The foundation should be draped in a moderate one-way stretch knit having approximately a 25% stretch (around the form) for tops and a two- or four-way stretch of 50% or more for activewear, with the greater stretch placed vertically on the form. The torso foundation as a base for knit garments may require adjustments if the characteristics of the knit changes. However, their usage saves time and simplifies the patternmaking process.

For other knit foundations, refer to the dartless foundation of the casual shirt (page 384) to develop tops and dresses in a firm knit. To drape an oversized knit top, refer to the over-size shirt foundation (page 387). Knit information can also be applied to the dress designs in Chapters 12 and 14.

Figure 19.3

Notch Guide

Two types: Notch to a depth of 1/8″ or cut a pyramid 1/4″ wide and 1/8″ high.

Design Analysis

Figure 19.3

The torso foundation is draped to fit as close as possible to the waist without stresslines. Allow extra width to pin on the opposite side of the form. This will help stabilize the knit while draping. Add additional length for draping a dress.

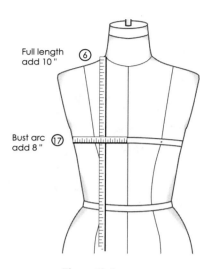

Full length
add 10 " ⑥

Bust arc ⑰
add 8 "

Figure 19.4

Preparing Form

Figure 19.4

Measure form for length. Add 10″.

Measure width. Add 8″.

Preparing Knit

Figure 19.5

Test knit on a stretch gauge to determine the stretch (see page 460).

The greater stretch is placed on width of the knit.

Draw a line on the length 5″ from fabric edge.

Square from this line 3″ up from the bottom (applies to front and back).

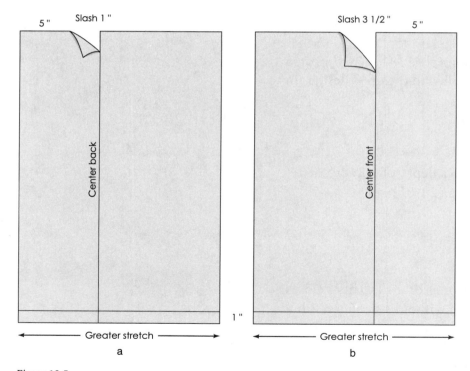

5 "   Slash 1 "

Center back

Greater stretch

a

Slash 3 1/2 "   5 "

Center front

1 "

Greater stretch

b

Figure 19.5

Draping Steps

Front Drape

Figure 19.6

Pin knit to the form with a straightline on the center and horizontal line on the hip guideline.

Pin to hold knit fabric on both sides.

Smooth, but do not stretch the knit when draping the neckline to the shoulder-tip.

Smooth fullness from the centerline to the side seam (some excess remains at the waistline).

Pin at and past the side seamline.

Lay knit over the armhole plate, smoothing all excess from the armhole ridge. Pin.

Check to see that the knit lies smoothly along the side seam, armhole shoulder, and neck.

Mark the following:

- Neckline
- Shoulder/neck
- Side seam (crossmark side waist)
- Front and back waist
- Armhole plate
- Mid-armhole
- Shoulder-tip
- Neckline

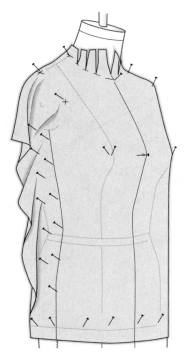

Figure 19.6

Back Drape

Figure 19.7

Repeat draping instructions given for the front. Remove the drape from the form.

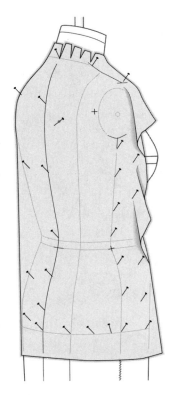

Figure 19.7

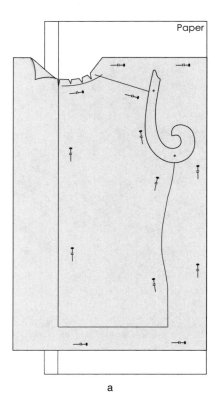

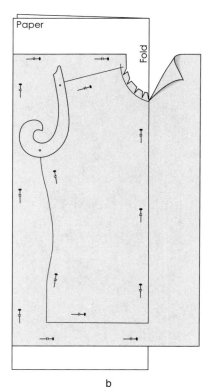

Figure 19.8

True the Front and Back Drapes

Figure 19.8

Place drape on paper (front on fold).

Pin to secure to paper.

True side seams and shoulderlines.

If lengths differ, equalize at the armhole/side seams and shoulder-tips.

Blend side seams.

Use a French curve to draw the armholes and necklines. Armhole may be lowered 1/2″.

Trace pattern.

Remove and draw outline.

Finishing the Pattern

Figure 19.9

Add 3/8″ for seam and hem allowances, as desired.

Measure front and back armholes. Add together and record for the knit sleeve.

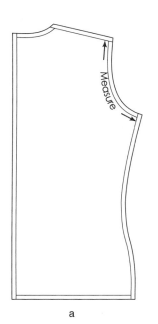

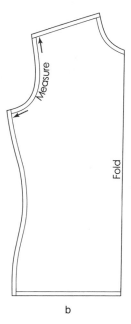

Figure 19.9

Knit Sleeve Draft

Figure 19.10

Measurement needed: individual elbow and wrist, or the standard for company.

Fold paper.

Place grainline of the front sleeve on the paper fold.

Trace the sleeve cap and biceps. Mark elbow and hem.

Square a line from the fold at each mark.

Figure 19.11

Mark 1/2″ above biceps and square a line from the fold.

Mark 1/2″ in from the corner of the sleeve.

Draw the curve of the sleeve blending with the cap.

Mark the wrist (example: 4″ wide; it can vary).

Mark the elbow (example: 5″; it can vary).

Draw a curved line to the new biceps (underseam).

Adjust the elbow and wrist when testing the fit.

Measuring the Sleeve Cap (Figure 19.12)

The sleeve cap should measure 1/2″ more than the front and back armhole measurement.

Adjust by adding to or subtracting from the biceps line.

Blend the capline if adjustments are made.

Figure 19.13

Add 3/8″ seams and cut from paper.

Notch in 1/8″ or cut a pyramid.

Figure 19.10

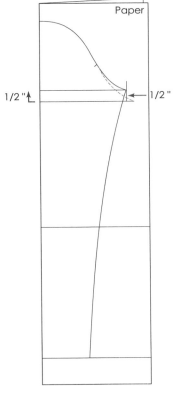

Figure 19.11

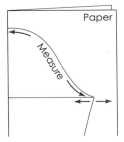

Figure 19.12

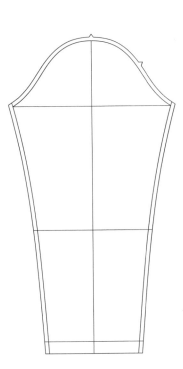

Figure 19.13

Oversized Top with Short Sleeve

Figure 19.14

Design Analysis

Figure 19.14

Follow the draping instructions given for the oversized shirt. The placket inset is 1 1/2″ wide. It is twice the length of the cutout. The collar is of rib knit, which can be ordered, or is cut in a self-knit. Fabric suggestion: use a cotton knit.

Finishing the Pattern

Figure 19.15

Placket Inset

Draw 3/4″ from each side of the center and to a length desired. Label A and B.

Draw 3/8″ seams. Cut out the inset.

Draw inset band 1 1/2″ wide and the length of the A-B line. Cut two plackets.

Rib Collar

Length of neck measurement, less stretch.

Sleeve

Trace casual sleeve and shorten, allowing for the hem.

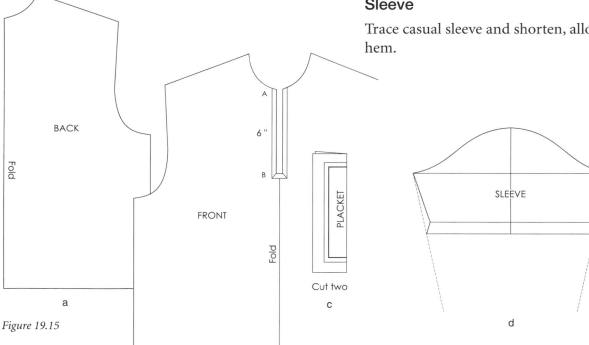

Figure 19.15

Fitted Crop-Top with Muscle Sleeve

Design Analysis

Figure 19.16

The crop-top ends a few inches under the bust and the scoop neck ends just above the bust. The back neck is less scooped. The crop-top can be made from an existing torso foundation by tracing a copy and marking the stylelines on it (see Figure 19.18) or it can be draped. The example shows a knit foundation on the form, with the neckline marked and cut to the desired length.

Draping Steps

Figure 19.17

Draw desired neckline.

Pin side seams for closer fit, if required.

Remove drape.

Figures 19.18

Transfer to a traced copy of the torso knit foundation or make a copy of the draped top.

Figure 19.16

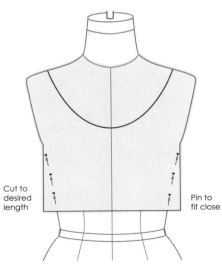

Cut to desired length

Pin to fit close

Figure 19.17

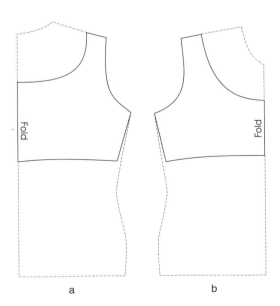

Fold

Fold

a

b

Figure 19.18

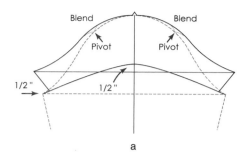

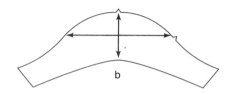

Figure 19.19

Short Muscle Sleeve

Figure 19.19

Trace knit sleeve.

Draw a line 2″ up from the biceps.

At 3″ down from cap, pivot the sleeve up to the new biceps line. Trace capline.

Repeat on other side of the sleeve.

Blend the cap.

Draw underseams 1/2″ in from original biceps.

Draw hemline curve 1/2″ above the biceps (see Figure 19.19a).

Cap should measure 1/2″ more than the armhole. If not, adjust the biceps (see page 465, Figure 19.12). Mark with notch or pyramid shape.

Bodysuit
and
Swimsuit
Foundations

20

The bodysuit is a flexible garment that fits the contour of the figure. It is as popular for exercising and dancewear, as it is for street and evening wear. It can be designed with or without sleeves. The bodysuit foundation can be separated above the waist to develop tights or the foundation can be separated into a top and bottom set.

Lycra®/spandex is a desirable fabric because of its excellent recovery after being stretched. The bodysuit can be based on the torso knit foundation or can be draped on the form directly from the fabric. It is more convenient to use the knit torso foundation because of the difficulties in draping between legs of the form.

Remember that the bodysuit is cut with the greater stretch going through the length of the garment. Save the test fit garment for use later. Place stylelines on it as a guide in making design patterns. The foundation is a base for all knits; however, changes in the fit may be required if the stretch and recovery factors change.

Bodysuit Foundation

Figure 20.1

Design Analysis

Figure 20.1 and Figure 20.2

The bodysuit fits the contour of the figure. It is based on the knit torso foundation. The front and back pattern draft are developed together and separated when finished. Seam allowances are included with measurements given. Suggested fabric: use a two- or four-way stretch knit. Use the torso knit foundation if available (see pages 461–465).

Figure 20.2

Preparing Fabric

To take and record measurements, see pages 428 and 430. Measurements below are from the Model Form Measurement Chart. Personal measurements may also be used.

- Waist (#19) and hip (#18).
- Crotch depth (#24).
- Length from waist to ankle (#27).
- Knee (#30).
- Ankle (#32).
- Length: Center back neck to ankle.

Paper Preparation

Figure 20.3

Trace the front pattern. Mark the waist and bust point.

Place the back pattern on top of the front, aligning the centerline and hip (HBL).

Shoulder/neck of the back may not match with the front, but blend to it when drawing the neckline.

Draw a line parallel with the centerline, starting from the shoulder/neck through the length of the paper.

Mark the waist, less 1/2″, and hip, less 1/2″. Draw a new side seam to zero at the armhole for a sleeved garment. For a sleeveless garment, draw the side seam to end 1/2″ in at the armhole.

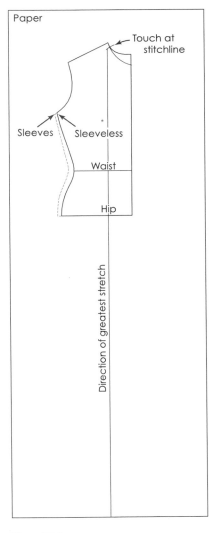

Figure 20.3

Figure 20.4

Pant length, less 2″, measured down from waist (X).

Mark ankle (Y).

Mark the crotch depth, less 1 1/4″ down from the waist and square from the centerline.

Mark the knee location half the length between the crotch depth and ankle. Square from the guideline following these measurements:

- Knee width: one fourth, less 1/4″ each side of the line.

- Ankle width: one fourth, less 1/4″ each side of the line.

Draw lines from the ankle touching the knee marks and beyond.

Figure 20.5

Extend the line for crotch to one fourth of the hip, and mark. Add another 3/4″ for the back crotch (broken lines). Draw the crotch curve.

Outseam: Draw an outward curved line from the hip and an inward curve connecting with the knee line.

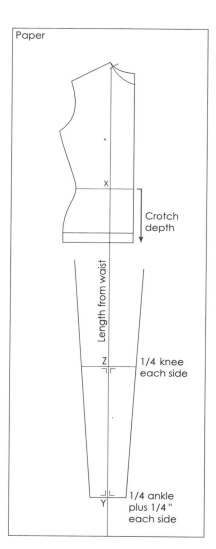

Figure 20.4

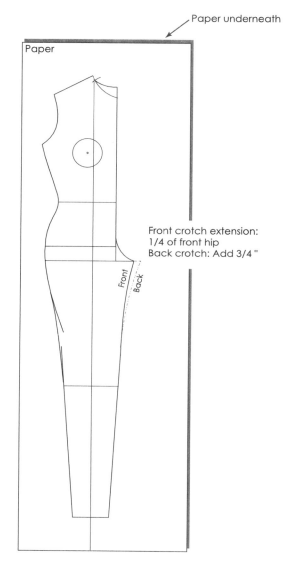

Figure 20.5

Inseam: Draw inward curve from the crotch extensions blending with legline for the front (solid line) and back (uneven broken line).

Place paper underneath. Secure with pins.

Cut from the paper following the back pattern.

Finishing the Pattern

Back Pattern

Figure 20.6

The center back waist can fit closer by draping to the curves of the back. Use only when needed.

Front Pattern

Figure 20.7

Trim the front neckline.

Trim the back crotch extension.

Mark the bust point and bust radius at the test fitting.

Analyze Fit

If too loose around the figure, pin the excess along the side seam and re-mark the armhole. Correct the pattern.

If too loose in the length, pin the excess along the waistline. Cut pattern across the waist, and overlap.

Always make a traced copy when corrections are required and save the original foundation pattern.

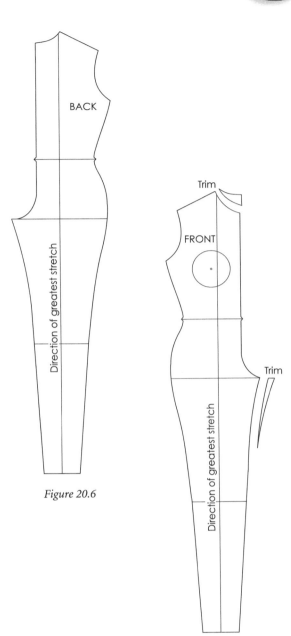

Figure 20.6

Figure 20.7

Bodysuit with Cutout Design

Figure 20.8

This is an example to follow in creating other designs. Suggestion: Stylelines are drawn directly on a traced copy of the bodysuit pattern or put the test fit garment on the form. Draw stylelines with washable pen or pin-mark. Remove and transfer stylelines to the pattern (do not cut the garment apart) (Figure 20.8).

Marking Stylelines

Figure 20.9

To attach the elastic, see the instructions on pages 487 to 488.

Finished Pattern

Figure 20.10

Stylelines are transferred to the traced patterns.

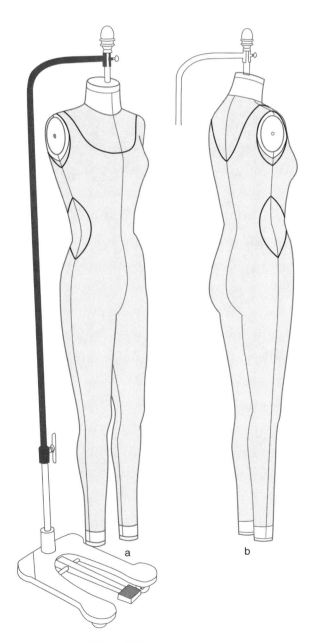

Figure 20.9

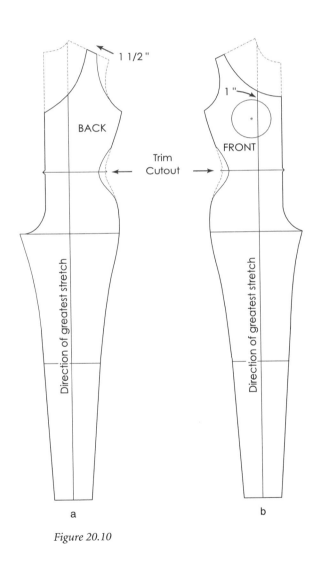

Figure 20.10

Tights

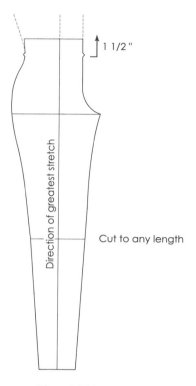

1 1/2 "

Direction of greatest stretch

Cut to any length

Figure 20.11

Draping Steps

Figure 20.11 and Figure 20.12

Trace from 1 1/2 to 2″ up from the waist to the desired pant length.

Elastic width, as desired and measuring 1″ less than the waistline is inserted in the foldover of the waistline.

length variations

Figure 20.12

Leotard Foundation

The leotard has a cutout legline of varying heights and can be designed with or without sleeves (consider the raglan, drop shoulder, or kimono sleeve). It is a versatile garment that can be worn for exercising, as dancewear, and for street wear under skirts and pants (Figure 20.13, Figure 20.14, and Figure 20.15).

Lycra®/spandex is a desirable fabric because of its excellent recovery after being stretched.

The leotard can be based on the torso knit foundation or can be draped directly from the fabric. It is more convent to use the knit torso foundation because of the difficulties in draping between legs of the form.

Remember the leotard is cut with the greater stretch going through the length of the garment. Save the test fit garment for use later. Place stylelines on it as a guide in making design patterns.

Figure 20.13

Figure 20.14

Figure 20.15

The leotard foundation is a base for all knits, but changes in the fit may be required if the stretch and recovery factors change.

Design Analysis

If the knit torso foundation is not available, see pages 461 to 465. The crotch is drafted to the torso foundation. The front and back draft leotard patterns are developed together. After com-pletion, the front and back patterns are sepa-rated. The leotard foundation is the base for all leotard designs.

Preparing Torso

Refer to the instructions for the bodysuit, but exclude the length line. Record crotch length by measuring from center front waist, under crotch, to center back.

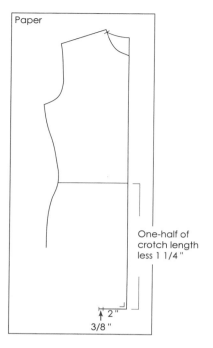

Figure 20.16

Draping Steps

Figure 20.16

Subtract 1 1/4″ from crotch length and extend the line down from the center front waist.

Square a 2″ crotch line. Crossmark 3/8″ from this mark.

Figure 20.17

Square a line.

Measure down from the waist and mark half of the crotch length. Square to the side seam.

Draw a legline following the illustration and crossmark 3/8″.

Back Leg Cut

Figure 20.18

Draw a straight line through the 3/8″ marks. Square out 1″ at the midpoint. Draw the legline following the illustration.

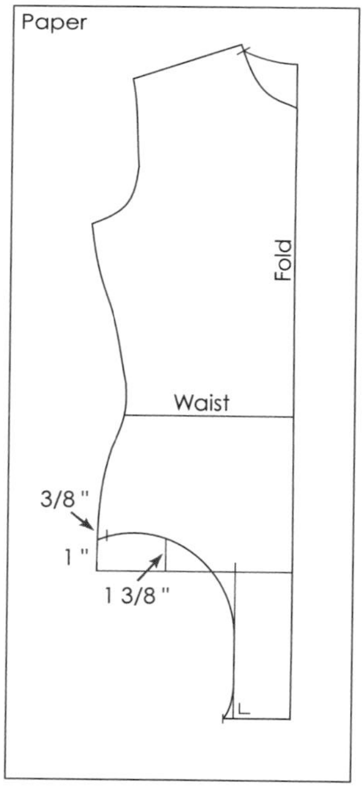

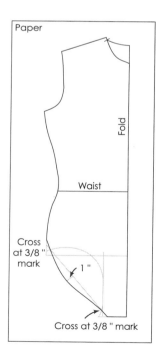

Figure 20.17

Figure 20.18

Finishing the Pattern

Figure 20.19

Back

Place paper under the pattern. Pin to secure and cut from the paper. The undercopy is the back pattern. For a tighter fit, draw a curved line as shown at waist.

Front

Trim front neckline for front pattern (see Figure 20.19b).

Higher Cut Legline

Figure 20.20

Draw the legline higher, using the illustration as a guide.

Analyze Fit

Place on form and check fit, adjusting as needed. Remember that the fit applies to the fabric of the drape. Knits having different stretch factors will require another fitting. Always remember to make a traced copy when corrections are required.

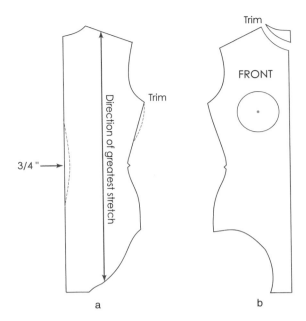

Figure 20.19

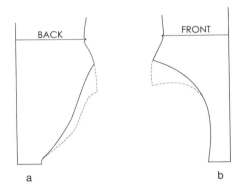

Figure 20.20

Leotard with Short Cap Sleeve

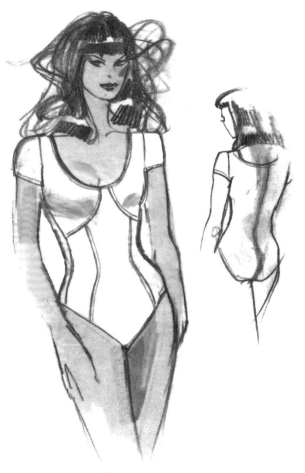

Figure 20.21

Design Analysis

Figure 20.21

Cut the garment from a traced copy of the leotard foundation. For accuracy in marking designs with many stylelines, place the stylelines on the garment while stretched on the form. Crossmark to identify joining sections. Remove and cut stylelines. Make the pattern from the separated sections. Use the muscle sleeve (page 468) to complete the design.

Marking Stylelines

Figure 20.22

Mark stylelines (color blocking) and notches.

Remove and cut each section apart.

Finished Pattern

Figure 20.23

- Upper styleline (a and b).
- Front panel (e).
- Side front panel (c and d).
- Back (g).
- Sleeve (f).

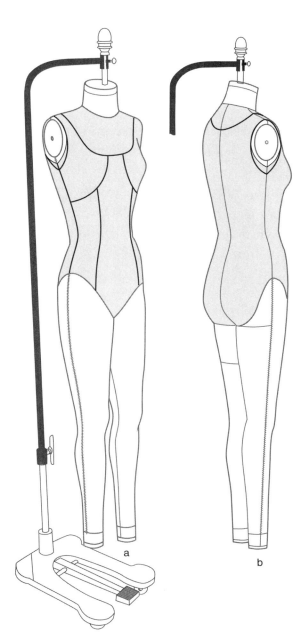

Figure 20.22

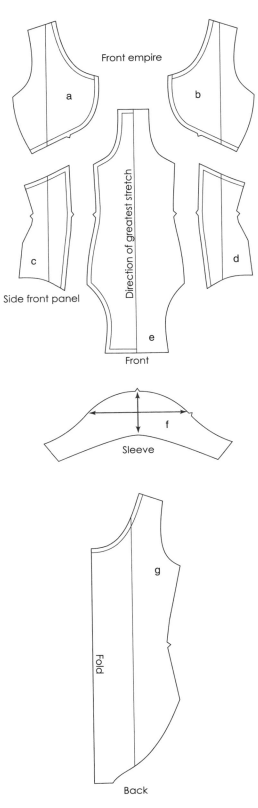

Figure 20.23

Swimsuit Foundation

Two swimwear foundations are discussed in this chapter—the maillot and bikini. The swimsuit can be based on the leotard foundation or draped in the fabric of choice. For multiple stylelines, follow the instructions given for the leotard.

Maillot: One-piece swimsuit with cutout legs at varying heights at the side. The swimsuit is cut in stretchy knit. It is based on the drape instructions of the leotard with the exception that the greater stretch goes around the figure instead of the length.

Bikini: Two-piece swimsuit—bra top and bottom pant legcut at varying heights at the side. The swimsuit can be cut in stretchy knits or woven cottons and other fabrics.

Maillot Foundation

Figure 20.24

Figure 20.25

Figure 20.26

Design Analysis

Figure 20.24, Figure 20.25, and Figure 20.26

The tank top is a popular design for the maillot and is developed from the leotard foundation. It is cut in a stretch knit, with the greater stretch going around the figure. Stitch and place on the form. If loose, pin side seams for a closer fit. Adjust the traced pattern. Mark stylelines (any design) on the foundation while on the form. Remove from the form, cut stylelines apart, and make the pattern.

Marking Stylelines

Figure 20.27

The back strap of low cut swimwear is marked further in from the shoulder-tip than the front strap when transferred to paper. The strap will upright itself when worn and will help to secure the strap on the shoulder

Finishing the Pattern

Figure 20.28

Trace the leotard pattern and pin the knit drape on form. Mark stylelines and allow 3/8″ seams.

Front pattern (Figure 20.28).

Mark the back shoulder strap 1″ from the shoulder/neck (Figure 20.28).

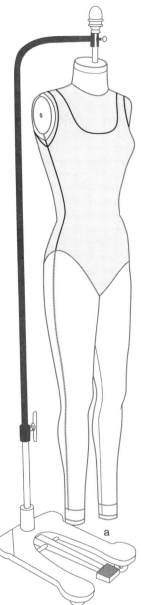
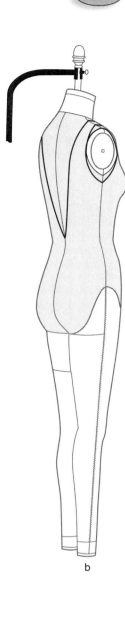

a

b

Figure 20.27

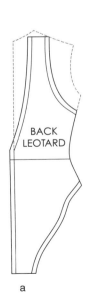

BACK LEOTARD

FRONT LEOTARD

Fold

a

b

Figure 20.28

Bikini: Bottom and Top

Design Analysis

Figure 20.29 through Figure 20.32

The bottom part of the maillot can be cut for the bikini pant. The style of the bikini cut is as desired. The bra-top design is a horizontal style-line that crosses the bust point to the side or can be draped as a Princess. The bra can have a bust cup added to it. Other styles are also shown.

Figure 20.29

Figure 20.30

Figure 20.31

Figure 20.32

Draping Steps

Figure 20.33

Cut bikini bottom to a desired cut.

Bra top

The bra top should be draped in muslin, as it should not be stretched to fit. The bra can be cut in almost any fabric.

Figure 20.34

Drape the upper bra (Figure 20.34). Mark above and across the bust mound to the side seam. Remove.

Drape the lower bra (Figure 20.35). Mark below the bust mound and across the bust to the side seam

Figure 20.36 and Figure 20.37

Pin bra together and drape the back strap.

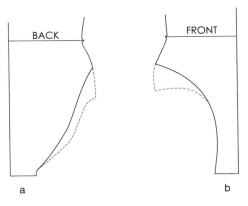

Figure 20.33

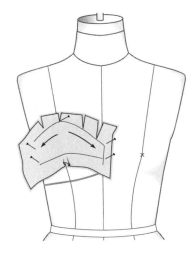

Figure 20.34

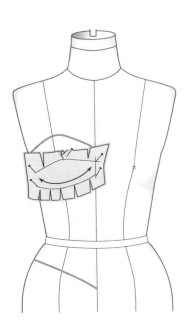

Figure 20.35

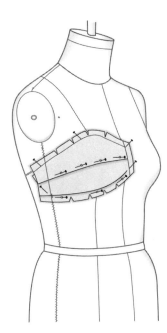

Figure 20.36

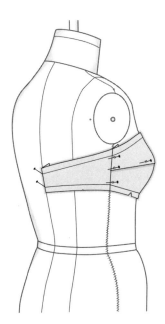

Figure 20.37

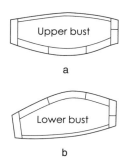

a

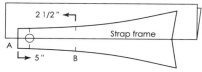

b

Figure 20.38

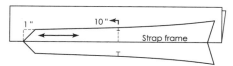

Figure 20.39

Figure 20.40

Figure 20.41

Bra Pattern

Figure 20.38

Bra patterns can be self-lined or lined with tricot.

Draping Steps: Strap Variations

Tie Strap

Figure 20.39

Cut strap on the fold, add 10″, and shape the end of the tie.

Add 1/4″ seams.

Button Control with Elastic

Figure 20.40

Trace strap on fold.

Extend 2 1/2″ and mark 1″ in label A.

Mark button/buttonhole placement.

Mark B 4″ from A.

Cut elastic strips 3/4″ wide and 4″ long. The elastic is attached at A and stretched to point B between the folds.

Elastic and Hook Strap

Figure 20.41

Note The closure requires a bra design with 1/2″ wide side seams.

Cut two strips 1 1/2″ × 12″.

Cut two elastic strips 1/2″ × 6″. (Stretch elastic as it is inserted between the folds.) Fold strap to make loop and stitch. The hook is inserted into the loop to secure garment.

Elastic, Tapes, and Bra Cups

The following information is a general guide in completing actionwear garments.

Supplies Needed

Needles: Use ballpoint, sizes 9 to 11, and 10 to 12 stitches per inch.

Thread: Core spun (nylon or polyester) or cotton.

Bra cups: Purchase at fabric stores, notions counter, or supply houses.

Power Knit or nylon tricot: for bra cup frames and crotch and/or swimsuit lining.

Elastic: 1/4″ for necklines and 3/8″ for the leg cutout.

Elastic

Whether cut in rigid or knit fabrics, elastic is stitched to all raw edges of the garment. The elastic has two purposes:

1. Cut shorter than the raw seam, it is stretched to hold excess under the bust, between the bust, and under the buttocks (hollow areas).

2. Cut to the length of a raw seam. Do not stretch.

The elastic prevents a raw seam from being pulled out of shape.

Elastic is attached to a bikini waistline and cut-out areas.

Elastic Guidelines

The sample illustrates how elastic is attached and the length needed at different areas of the garment.

1:1 Ratio: Elastic is cut to the length of the seam and is not stretched.

Elastic is attached to the garment with a zigzag, overlock, or straight stitch.

Elastic is placed on the wrong side of the garment (shaded area, Figure 20.42). It is top stitched when folded over. Stretch the elastic evenly, as it is being stitched. Pin midway to control stretching (back legline).

Length of Elastic for Specific Areas

Figure 20.42

Necklines:

- Front: 1″ less than measurement.
- Back: 1:1 ratio (no stretch).

Cutout armhole: 1/2″.

Legline: 2″ (allows 1/2″ overlap to connect the ends).

Front: 1:1 ratio (no stretch).

Remaining elastic is stretched across the back legline. Pin at the middle of the legline to help evenly distribute the excess.

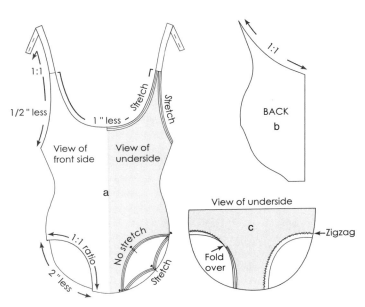

Figure 20.42

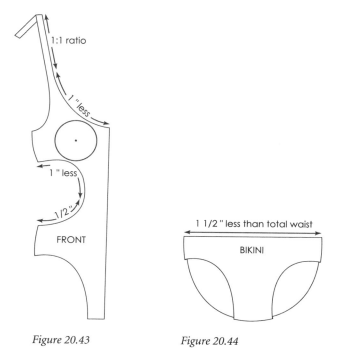

Figure 20.43

Figure 20.44

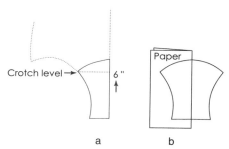

Figure 20.45

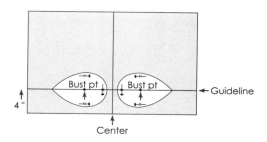

Figure 20.46

Figure 20.47

Cutouts

Figure 20.43

Elastic should be 1″ less. Stretch 1/2″ under the bust and 1/2″ stretch for the rest of the styleline.

Bikini

Figure 20.44

Cut elastic 1 1/2″ less than the total.

Crotch lining

Figure 20.45

Crotch lining is traced from the pattern (see Figure 20.45a).

Pattern on fold. Lining is faced on the garment and attached with the elastic (see Figure 20.45b).

Shoulder Tape

Figure 20.46

Shoulder tape prevents the shoulder from stretching.

Bra Cups Attachment

The maillot and bikini tops may or may not be designed with bra cups. There are several ways a bra is attached to the swim garment. One method is illustrated.

Measurements Needed

Bust span (#10).

Fabric Needed

Tricot or power knit.

Draping Steps

Figure 20.47

Cut fabric equal to the length and width of the top of the maillot pattern (see Figure 20.49).

Draw a chalkline through the center and a horizontal line 4″ up.

Crossmark the bust span (bust point) out from the center.

Place bust cups on the fabric, aligning bust points on fabric with the cup.

Pin on fabric and trace.

Repeat on the other side of center.

Figure 20.48

Allow 1/2″ for seams and cut out the centers for each cup.

Place on the form and adjust the bust cup. Re-mark, if necessary.

Pin the cup to the fabric. Remove from form and stitch the cup to the fabric.

Figure 20.49

Stitch 1/4″ wide elastic lace around the cups on the underside.

Pin or stitch lining to the wrong side of the garment. Trim around garment.

Stitch a 1/2″ wide elastic (felt-back) that is 1/2″ less than the width of the lining across the bottom.

The lining, elastic, and garment are stitched together. The elastic is folded over and zigzagged or straight stitched.

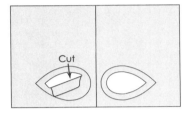

Figure 20.48

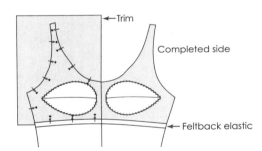

Figure 20.49

Index